Asset Accounting Configuration in SAP ERP

A Step-by-Step Guide

Andrew Okungbowa

Apress®

Asset Accounting Configuration in SAP ERP: A Step-by-Step Guide

Copyright © 2016 by Andrew Okungbowa

ISBN-13 (pbk): 978-1-4842-1366-7

ISBN-13 (electronic): 978-1-4842-1365-0

Trademarked names, logos, and images may appear in this book. Rather than use a trademark symbol with every occurrence of a trademarked name, logo, or image we use the names, logos, and images only in an editorial fashion and to the benefit of the trademark owner, with no intention of infringement of the trademark.

The use in this publication of trade names, trademarks, service marks, and similar terms, even if they are not identified as such, is not to be taken as an expression of opinion as to whether or not they are subject to proprietary rights.

While the advice and information in this book are believed to be true and accurate at the date of publication, neither the authors nor the editors nor the publisher can accept any legal responsibility for any errors or omissions that may be made. The publisher makes no warranty, express or implied, with respect to the material contained herein.

Managing Director: Welmoed Spahr
Acquisitions Editor: Susan McDermott
Developmental Editor: Chris Nelson
Technical Reviewers: Rehan Zaidi, Naveen D'Souza
Editorial Board: Steve Anglin, Pramilla Balan, Louise Corrigan, James DeWolf, Jonathan Gennick, Robert Hutchinson, Celestin Suresh John, Michelle Lowman, James Markham, Susan McDermott, Matthew Moodie, Jeffrey Pepper, Douglas Pundick, Ben Renow-Clarke, Gwenan Spearing
Coordinating Editor: Rita Fernando
Copy Editor: Kezia Endsley, Laura Lawrie
Compositor: SPi Global
Indexer: SPi Global

Distributed to the book trade worldwide by Springer Science+Business Media New York, 233 Spring Street, 6th Floor, New York, NY 10013. Phone 1-800-SPRINGER, fax (201) 348-4505, e-mail orders-ny@springer-sbm.com, or visit www.springer.com. Apress Media, LLC is a California LLC and the sole member (owner) is Springer Science + Business Media Finance Inc (SSBM Finance Inc). SSBM Finance Inc is a Delaware corporation.

For information on translations, please e-mail rights@apress.com, or visit www.apress.com.

Apress and friends of ED books may be purchased in bulk for academic, corporate, or promotional use. eBook versions and licenses are also available for most titles. For more information, reference our Special Bulk Sales–eBook Licensing web page at www.apress.com/bulk-sales.

Any source code or other supplementary materials referenced by the author in this text is available to readers at www.apress.com. For detailed information about how to locate your book's source code, go to www.apress.com/source-code/.

This book is dedicated to the creator of heaven and earth, God Almighty,
who kept me alive to see the completion of this book.

Contents at a Glance

Contents

About the Author

Andrew Okungbowa is an accountant and a certified SAP FI professional with many years of experience in SAP FICO. Because of his depth of expertise in SAP, many who know him often refer him to as a SAP-FI guru. He is an ardent professional writer and the author of *SAP ERP Financial Accounting and Controlling Configuration and Use Management*. He is the CEO of Wonderful Consulting, a company offering SAP ERP, business analysis, training, risk management, and project management to large and medium corporations worldwide. He holds a master's degree in investment and finance.

About the Technical Reviewers

Naveen D'Souza is an SAP MM Certified Consultant with overall experience of 17 years and over 7 years of SAP consulting experience. He has handled end-to-end full-cycle implementations, rollouts, support, and up-gradation projects. He has worked on site Go-Live (Hyper Care) Support and Offshore Production Support. He has also provided SAP consulting to diverse business environments, including retail, tobacco manufacturing, oil and gas, trading and dealership, and chemical manufacturing. He has international experience and has worked with clients around the globe, including in Oman, the United Arab Emirates, Singapore, and Jordan.

Rehan Zaidi is a consultant for several international SAP clients (both on-site and remotely) on a wide range of SAP technical and functional requirements. He also provides writing and documentation services for SAP- and ABAP-related products. He started working with SAP in 1999 and writing about his experiences in 2001. Rehan has written several articles for *SAP Professional Journal* and *HR Expert*, and also has a number of popular SAP- and ABAP-related books to his credit.

Acknowledgments

First, I want to acknowledge Susan McDermott, the acquisition editor, who initiated the idea of writing a second book with Apress Publishing and for reviewing the first draft of the book. Your suggestions and contributions were immensely appreciated. I also want to thank the Apress editorial team, who contributed to the success of this book.

Secondly, I want to thank Rita Fernando, the coordinating editor, for working with me on a second book. Rita, I appreciate the way you professionally coordinated this book project. I also want to thank Chris Nelson, the developmental editor, for his professional editing skills and for painstakingly editing this book line-by-line, page-by-page, and chapter-by-chapter to get it in the finest state. Chris, without you, I don't think this book would have been completed professionally. My thanks also go to Rehan Zaidi and Naveen D'Souza, the technical reviewers of this book, and SPi Global, for converting the manuscript into this book.

Finally, I want to thank all those who have contributed in one way or another to the success of this book but whose names are not mentioned. I will not forget to say a big God bless to my beautiful daughter Zoe-Chelsea and to my lovely wife Hephzibah for the moral support while I was working on this book.

Introduction

This introduction explains what asset accounting is, discusses the integration of asset accounting into other SAP modules, explains who should use this book, and includes a quick overview of the book's content.

Asset Accounting (FI-AA)

Asset accounting is a subsidiary ledger to the general ledger in SAP R/3 and it provides an enterprise-detailed way to relate to all the transactions that took place in the system related to fixed assets. Asset accounting serves as a component in SAP R/3 for managing and monitoring fixed assets. The SAP system comes with various fixed asset country-specific standard settings, which cut across industries. The country-specific features make the asset accounting component adaptable and easy to customize. To minimize the spookiness that can be involved in customizing, SAP provides standard country-specific settings for most countries where necessary.

Integration of Asset Accounting to Other SAP Modules

Due to the robust nature of integration modules in SAP R/3, transactions posted in other modules can be transferred to asset accounting (FI-AA). For example, assets purchased or produced in-house can be posted directly from MM (Material Management) to FI-AA, and depreciation and APC (acquisition and production cost) values can be posted from FI (Financial Accounting) to FI-AA.

Easy Access

The Easy Access menu is a user-specific point of entry into the SAP system. It is the first screen that comes up when you log on to SAP. It is designed as a tree structure containing a list of several key items, which allow you to navigate the system and perform tasks and business processes. For example, you can perform transactions, generate reports, and access web addresses (where you can access documents from a remote Internet server).

IMG

The implementation guide (IMG) is a generic tool you can use to customize asset accounting requirements to meet specific needs of a company. SAP contains three implementation variants:

- **SAP Reference IMG**. A standard structured hierarchical tool in the R/3 system (real-time three-tier architecture) that contains the procedure for customizing various country settings and application modules.

- **Project IMG**. The configuration process can be very daunting. To help manage the complexity involved in customizing when using the reference IMG, you can create each implementation project based on specific functions needed for business processes and the project requirements. For example, you can reduce the project scope to specific objects such as countries.

- **Project View IMG**. You choose certain properties by specific criteria in order to generate views to organize your project activities. For example, a project view could hold each activity required in a project IMG.

Matchcodes

Matchcodes are user-friendly search functions designed specifically to help you look up or retrieve data records stored in the system. They provide an efficient way of looking for records stored in the system when you do not remember the key.

Real-Time Three-Tier Architecture (R/3)

SAP supports a real-time three-tier architecture made up of these three layers:

- **Presentation Layer**: This is the first layer in a typical three-tier architecture and it serves as the input device that is used to control a SAP system. It is a user-friendly Graphical User Interface (GUI) used by the end users to input data into the system. It also serves as a data output device. The presentation layer communicates with the application layer.

- **Application Layer**: This is the middleman in the SAP system, where all the processing takes place. The application layer could be referred to as the central processing unit (CPU). It collects data from the database, processes it, and passes it to the presentation layer.

- **Database Layer**: It allows data to be stored, called up, and modified.

The real-time three-tier architecture allows separate business processes to function under a single, integrated business management information system.

Who Should Read this Book

This book is specifically written for SAP FI, MM, and SD functional consultants, application consultants, business analysts, accountants, SAP support teams, and project management teams in charge of asset accounting.

A Quick Overview of the Book's Contents

Each chapter follows a step-by-step sequence to customize asset accounting (FI-AA) in SAP from start to finish. The sequence has been arranged in a systematic manner to give you the opportunity to gain adequate hands-on experience in configuring SAP FI-AA. Each chapter includes all the configuration concepts or activities necessary for customizing, or draws on a previous chapter.

Chapter 1 sets the scene by explaining what the organizational structure is. It defines charts of depreciation with emphasis on the legal requirements for calculating depreciation and asset valuation management for country-specific disclosure requirements. It also explores asset classes and screen layout rules.

Chapter 2 explains and defines the system settings required for integrating asset accounting. It also provides specifications for layout control parameters for G/L accounts, how to set input tax indicators for transactions that are not subject to taxes, how to specify financial statement versions for asset accounting, and how to specify document types for periodic posting of asset balance sheet values.

Chapter 3 explores the chart of depreciation in-depth and explains the importance of the chart of depreciation in asset accounting. Other aspects that this chapter explores include parallel valuations, low value assets, and fiscal year variants.

Chapter 4 explains and defines system settings for ordinary depreciation, unplanned depreciation, and various valuation methods. It also defines the cutoff value key and the maximum base value.

Chapter 5 explores the purpose of special valuation in asset accounting. It explains and defines reserves for special depreciation by specifying gross or net procedures for special depreciation. This chapter also examines how to determine the general ledger accounts for the write-off or allocation of special reserves, and explains how to define investment support measures, the revaluation of fixed assets, and index replacement values in special valuation of fixed assets.

Chapter 6 looks at asset master data, the purpose of screen layouts, how to define screen layouts for asset master data, how to define screen layouts for asset depreciation areas, how to define asset master records, including group assets and subnumbers, and how to display asset master records.

Chapter 7 looks at accounting treatment of asset retirement and explains how to post transactions in asset accounting for asset acquisitions. It defines transaction types for acquisitions, asset retirements, and asset transfers, the determination of gain/loss posting variants, and the specification of posting variants for retirement transfers. It also explains how to define the account assignment category for asset purchase orders and intercompany asset transfers. It covers how to define cross-system depreciation areas and the capitalization of assets under construction. You learn how to allow transfer types for asset classes and how to post asset transactions with external acquisition, credit memos, and in-house production.

Chapter 8 looks at validation and substitution in asset accounting, and the customizing steps involved.

Chapter 9 looks at system settings for report selection in the asset accounting information system and introduces how to generate various asset reports.

Chapter 10 looks at the appropriate asset data transfer by performing the following settings in the system: setting the company code status, specifying the sequence of depreciation areas, specifying parameters for data transfer, and defining transaction types for transferring open items.

Chapter 11 explores the preparation for production start-up in asset accounting and looks at other configuration steps involved in production settings.

Chapter 12 looks at processing periodic programs in asset accounting, which includes depreciation runs, display logs, and year month/year end closings.

Appendix A covers most of the appropriate G/L accounts needed for your configuration.

Appendix B provides some useful transaction codes that allow you to access tasks easily rather than going through the menu path, which may be time-consuming.

CHAPTER 1

■ ■ ■

Customizing Organizational Structures in SAP Asset Accounting (FI-AA)

This chapter introduces you to the basic aspects of Asset Accounting (FI-AA) and explains how they are configured in SAP ERP. You will learn how to:

- Create settings for country-specific disclosure requirements
- Copy reference chart of depreciation/depreciation area
- Copy reference chart of depreciation
- Assign chart of deprecation to company code
- Specify number assignment across company codes
- Define asset classes

Organizational Structures

Organizational structures are the minimum basic settings in Asset Accounting (FI-AA) needed to meet various business functions. They also determine how assets accounts are managed. They depict how business processes are broken into manageable units that allow the classifications and assignments of FI-AA components to other organizational units at a given point in time in the SAP system (e.g., cost centers, plants, etc.). The classification of assets plays a significant role, because it allows you to organize assets accounting based on defined accounting criteria (e.g., according to asset classes, depreciation methods, etc.).

Asset Accounting (FI-AA) is a component in SAP R/3 that serves as a subsidiary ledger to the Financial Accounting (FI) general ledger containing information that relates to fixed asset transactions posted in the system.

Specifying the Setting for Country-Specific Disclosure Requirements

Asset accounting disclosure requirements vary from country to country based on the accounting standards prevalent in a particular country. For example, the amount allowed for Low Value Assets (LVA) differs from country to country.

SAP comes with settings for most countries. Hence, you don't need to do anything here, but it's smart to check the existing settings to make sure that they meet your requirements.

You check your country-specific settings from the Change View "Asset Accounting: Country information": Overview screen (see Figure 1-1). To access this screen, use the menu path: IMG ➤ Financial Accounting (New) ➤ Asset Accounting ➤ Organizational Structures ➤ Check Country-Specific Settings. The screen shown in Figure 1-1 appears.

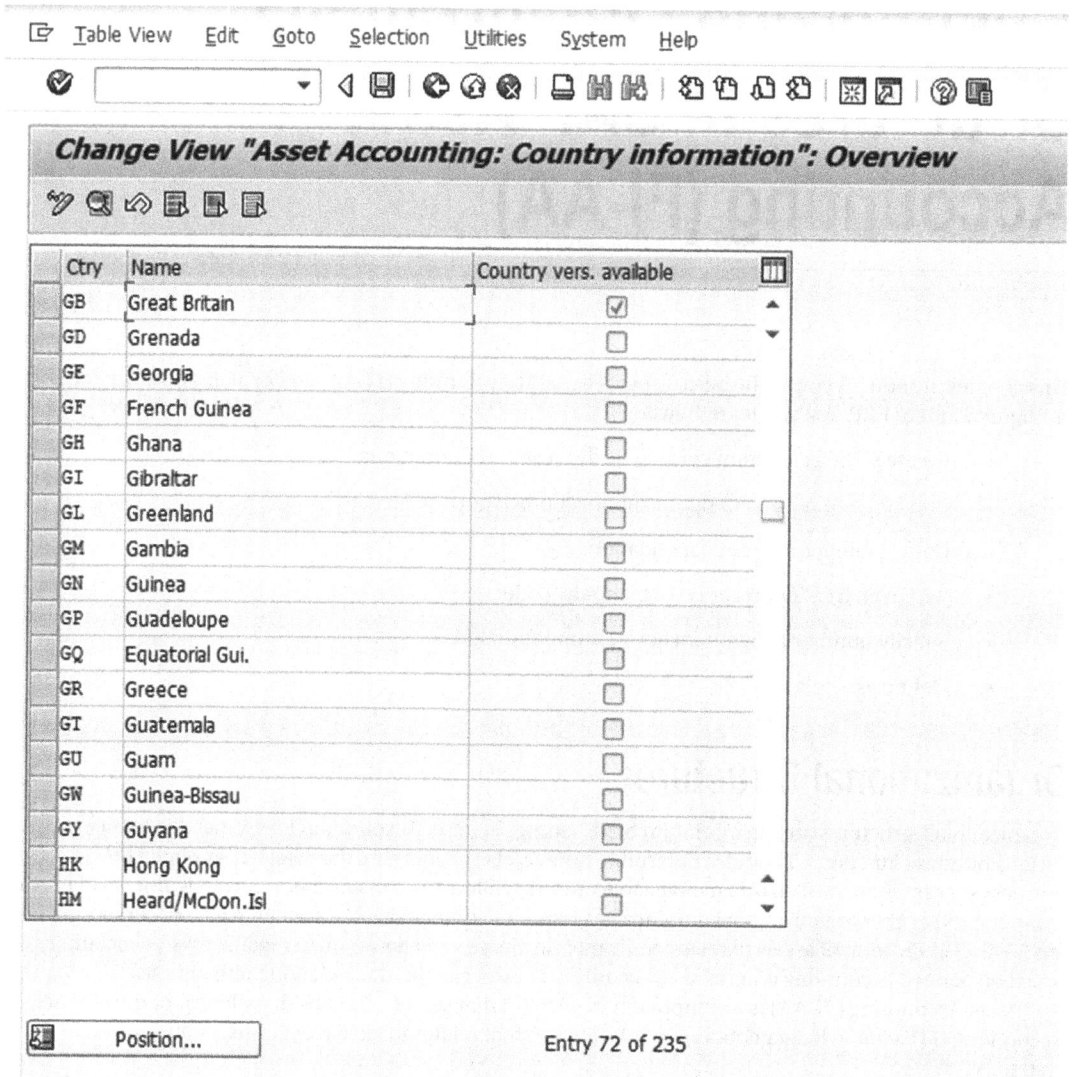

Figure 1-1. *List of country-specific settings supplied by SAP in the system for Asset Accounting*

Defining Chart of Depreciation and Depreciation Areas

It is important to note that in SAP R/3 system all GL accounts are defined in the chart of accounts and Asset Accounting works with the chart of accounts assigned to the company code in FI. A chart of accounts dictates the structure of general ledger accounts and contains the list of G/L accounts used by a company code(s) for business processes and for posting daily financial transactions from which financial statements and balance sheet are drawn at any given time. A detailed discussion of the charts of accounts is outside the scope of this book. However, the chart of accounts is covered in the book entitled *SAP ERP Financial Accounting and Controlling: Configuration and Use Management* (Apress 2015), which can serve as a very good reference.

Chart of Depreciation

A chart of depreciation is a list of country-specific depreciation areas supplied by SAP to meet legal and business disclosure requirements for your company code. Depreciation areas are predefined settings for calculating different values in parallel for individual fixed assets to meet certain disclosure requirements.

SAP comes with a predefined sample chart of depreciation for most countries that you can use. The system also allows you to create your own chart of depreciation by copying existing chart of depreciation in the system and modifying them to meet your requirement. This will be discussed in detail in the "Copying Reference Chart of Depreciation/Depreciation Areas" section later in this chapter. The chart of deprecation is country specific. It means that chart of depreciation varies from country to country. Hence it is important to use the chart of depreciation that is applicable to your country. Like chart of accounts, each company code is only entitled to use one chart of deprecation. Just as it is possible for several company codes to use the same chart of accounts, more than one company code can use the same chart of depreciation simultaneously.

Depreciation Area

The depreciation area is defined in the chart of depreciation with two numeric digits. SAP ERP comes with predefined depreciation areas, which specifically meet each country's accounting treatment and disclosure requirements. It is also possible for you to define your own depreciation area. Whether you want to use the chart of depreciation supplied by SAP or define your own chart of depreciation is a matter of choice. Once the depreciation key is defined and assigned to the asset master record, it is then possible to post values and depreciation to the assigned accounts.

The chart of depreciation contains different depreciation areas with depreciation keys such as 01- Book depreciation, 15-Tax Balance sheet, 20-Cost-accounting depreciation, 41-Investment support deducted from asset, etc. Depreciation key 01 is usually the leading depreciation area in SAP ERP. SAP ERP has the flexibility that allows you to display different depreciation areas with the same value and depreciation terms in different currencies. The system also allows different assets valuation to be carried out to meet different needs. For example, to produce financial statements to meet local requirements, for internal management reporting, financial statements according to IAS, US GAAP, etc.

Copying Reference Chart of Depreciation/Depreciation Areas

This is where you actually commence the customizing of your chart of depreciation. The chart of depreciation is nothing other than a list of depreciation areas that hold the appropriate parameters that enable you to conform to certain countries legal requirements on asset valuation. You can only define chart of depreciation by copying the country-specific reference charts of depreciation provided by SAP. When you copy the required predefined chart of deprecation for your company code country, the system copies all the depreciation areas in the reference chart of deprecation. Go through the depreciation area carefully and delete the unwanted depreciation areas.

The chart of depreciation you will define in this section will be assigned to your company code later in the "Assigning the Chart of Depreciation to a Company Code" section.

1. To get to the screen where you define a chart of depreciation, use this menu path: IMG: Financial Accounting (New) ➤ Asset Accounting ➤ Organizational Structures ➤ Copy Reference Chart of Depreciation/Deprecation Areas. The Choose Activity screen containing a list of options you can choose from is displayed in Figure 1-2.

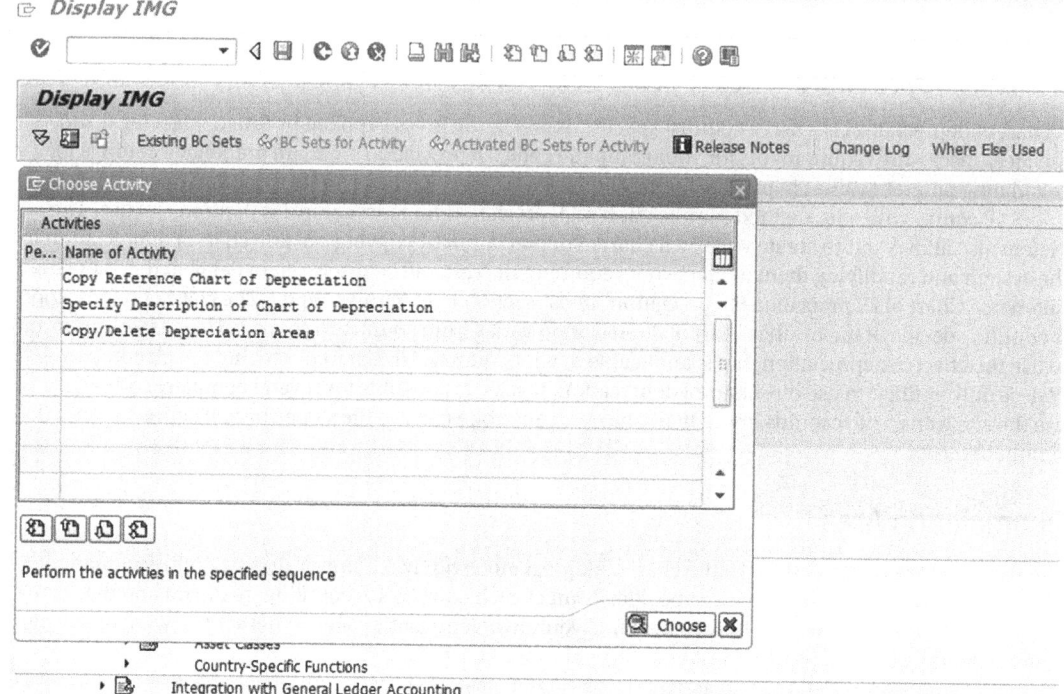

Figure 1-2. *The initial screen where you commence defining the chart of depreciation*

2. The screen gives you the sequence of activities you can perform. Select Copy Reference Chart of Depreciation from the list of activities options displayed on the screen (by clicking on it) and then click the `Choose` button at the bottom right of the screen. The Organizational Object Chart of depreciation screen appears. This is the screen where you can display, copy, check or transport the organizational object.

3. Choose the Copy button at the top-left side of the screen in order to copy a chart of account reference object that is specific to your company code.

4. The Copy screen pops up. This screen has two input fields: From Chart of dep and To Chart of dep. Enter the reference chart of the depreciation code you are copying, **1GB**, in the From Chart of Dep field. Then enter your proposed chart of depreciation code, **B10**, in the To Chart of dep field (the target chart of depreciation code). Click the Enter ✅ button at the bottom right of the screen to confirm your specifications.

▪ **Note** SAP comes with standard country-specific settings you can choose from. This activity uses the UK specific settings. 1GB is the UK country-specific chart of depreciation. B10 is the code we are using as the chart of depreciation code. You can use any code of your choice.

You can access the list of standard chart of depreciation codes provided by SAP using the matchcode by the From Chart of Dep. field. The Information screen is displayed with the message "Chart of depreciation 1GB copied to B10". Click the Enter ✅ button at the bottom-left side of the screen. The Organizational Object Chart of Depreciation screen appears, displaying the action you carried out. In this case, that's "Chart of dep. 1GB copied to B10."

5. The next step is to name your chart of depreciation by specifying the description for your chart of deprecation B10. To return to the previous screen (Choose Activity in Figure 1-2), click the Back ↩ button at the top-left side of the screen. Select the Specify Description of Chart of Depreciation from the displayed list of activities by clicking on it and clicking the 🔍 Choose button at the bottom-right side of the screen. The Change View "Chart of depreciation: Specify Name": Overview screen contains a list of existing chart of depreciations, as shown in Figure 1-3.

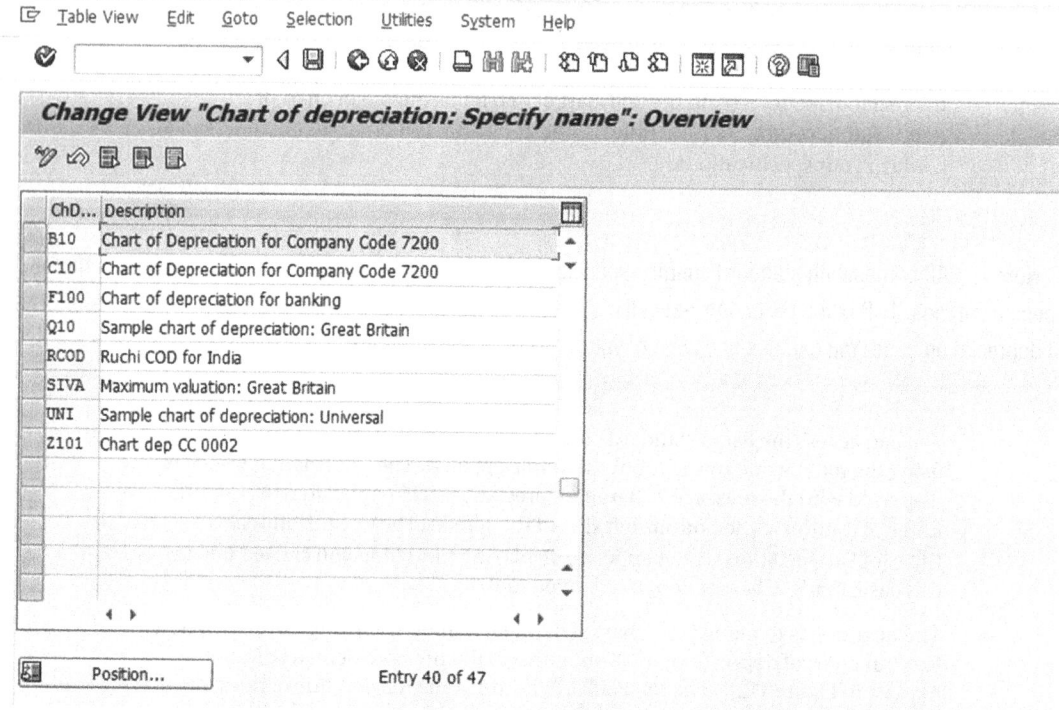

Figure 1-3. *The screen where you change the description name for your chart of depreciation*

6. Search for your company code using the ![Position...] button at the bottom of the screen. Change the inherited description name to your proposed description. For example, use Chart of Depreciation for Company code 7200. Save 💾 your chart of depreciation. The system will indicate in the status bar at the bottom of the screen that "Data was saved."

7. The final step in this activity is to delete any unwanted depreciation areas in the chart of account you defined. Click the Back 🔙 button at the top-left side of the screen to return to the Choose Activity screen (Figure 1-2). Select Copy/Delete Depreciation Areas from the displayed list of activities on the screen and click the ![Choose] button at the bottom-right side of the screen. The Determine Work Area: Entry screen pops up. Enter your chart of deprecation code B10 in the Work Area field on the screen and click Enter ✅ at the bottom of the screen. The Change View "Define Depreciation Areas": Overview screen contains the list of the depreciation areas copied from the reference depreciation 1GB, as shown in Figure 1-4.

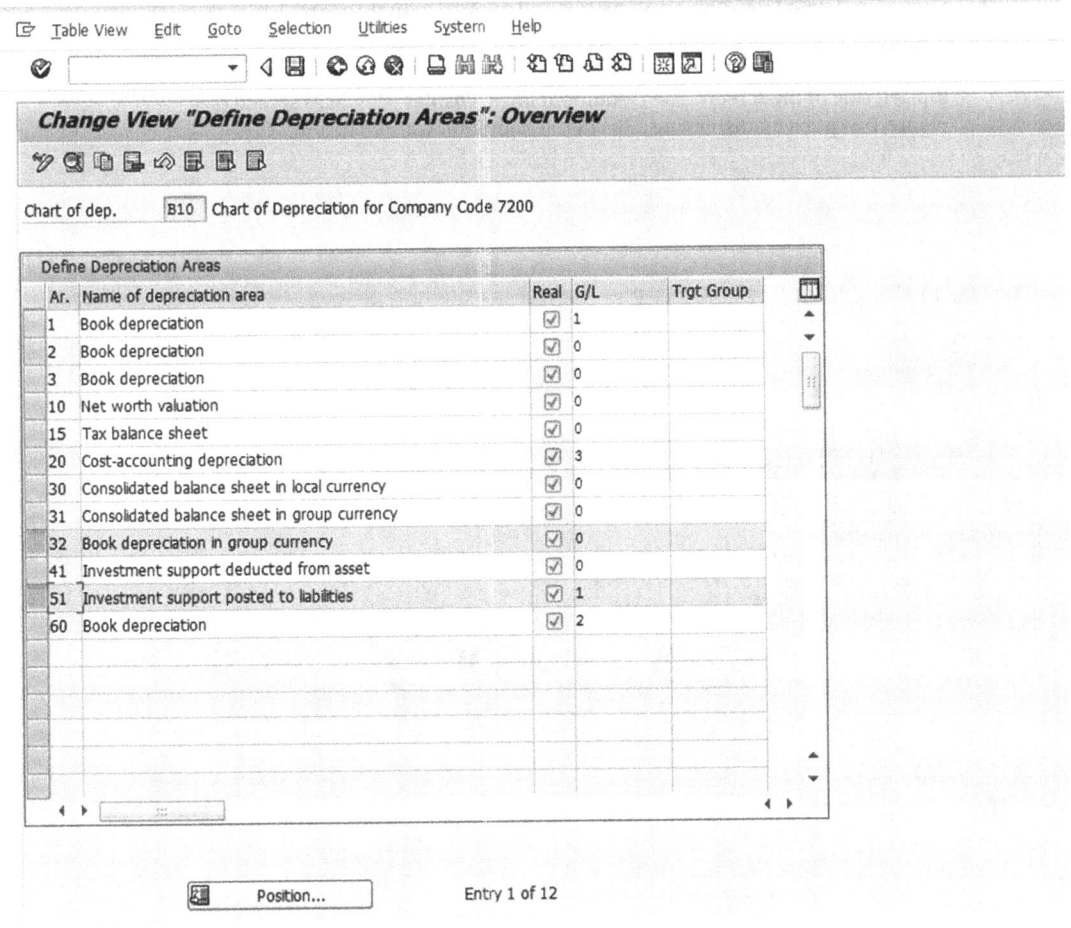

Figure 1-4. *The screen for displaying and adjusting depreciation areas*

8. Select the items you do not want from the list of the displayed items and delete them by clicking the Delete ![icon] button at the top-left side of the screen. In this activity, we deleted the following depreciation areas we did not want:

    - 32-Book depreciation in group currency

    - 51-Investment support posted to liabilities

■ **Note**   You select the item you want to delete by clicking it. Notice that the items you select turn yellow.

---

9. Since you deleted two items, the system will notify you in the status bar at the bottom of the screen that two entries were deleted ("Number of deleted entries: 2"). Then save your depreciation areas by clicking the Save 🖫 button at the top-left side of the screen. The Document lines: Display Messages screen (see Figure 1-5) pops up displaying a list of the items you want to delete.

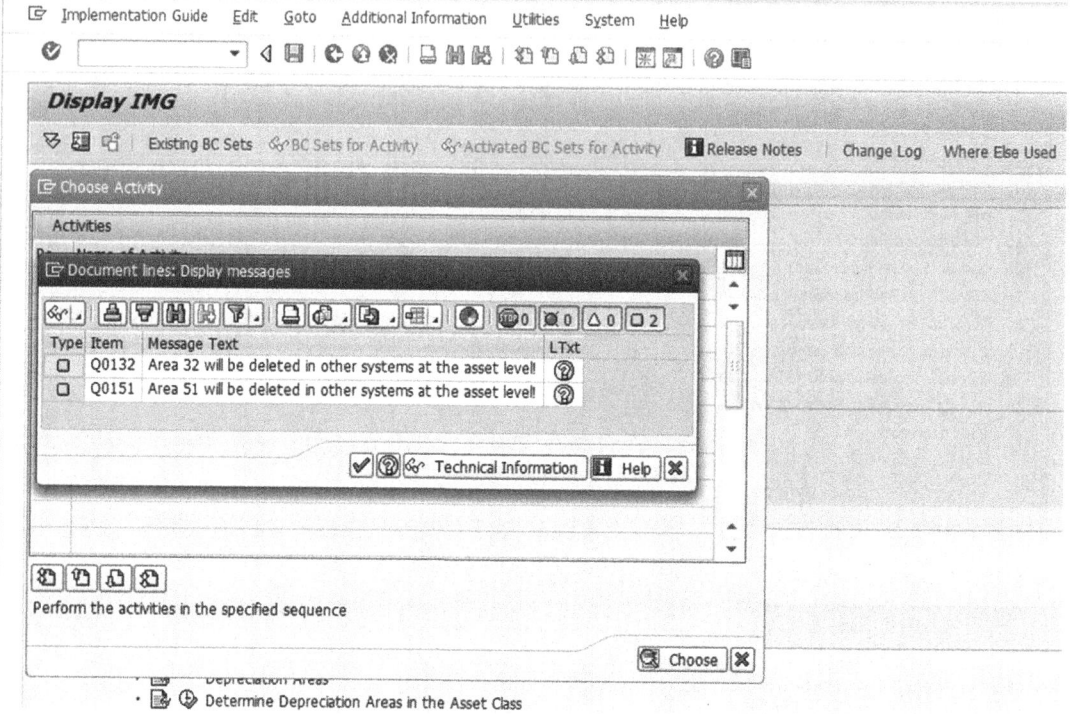

Figure 1-5. *The screen dislaying line items marked for delection*

10. If you are satisfied with the items you deleting, click the Continue ☑ button at the bottom of the Document lines: Display Messages screen to confirm your deletions. The system will then display the message that "Data was saved" in the status bar at the bottom of the screen.

11. You can view and make changes to each depreciation area setting. To do this, select the 1-Book depreciation area from the the displayed list of depreciation areas in Figure 1-4 and click the Details 🔍 button at the top-left side of the screen. The Change Vew: "Define Depreciation Areas": Details screen comes up (Figure 1-6). Check the settings provided by SAP and see if they meet your requirements. You can change them using the drop-down arrow next to each field.

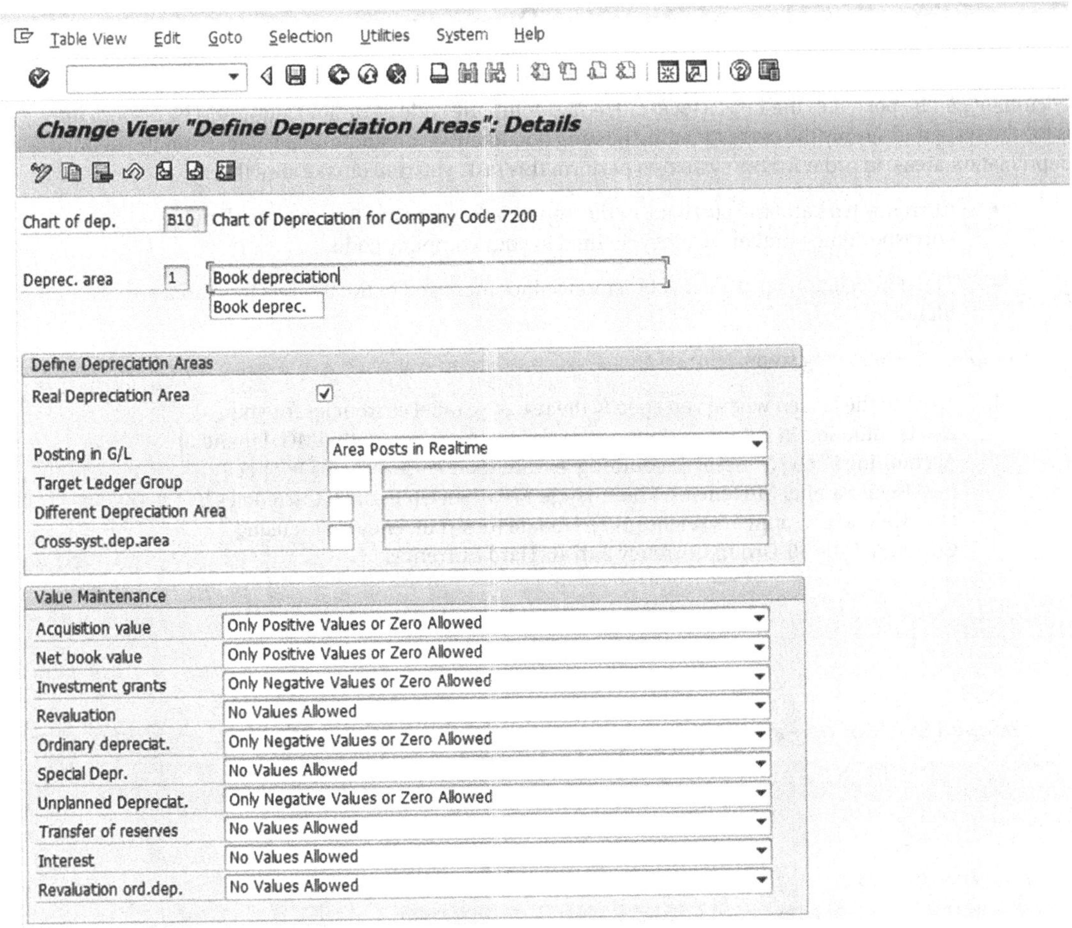

Figure 1-6. *The screen where further specifications to the business areas can be performed*

12. Click Save 🖫.

■ **Note** The next step in this activity is to assign a chart of depreciation to your company code. Before you do this, we recommend that you specify the use of parallel currencies first. Otherwise, you may experience problems when assigning company codes to the chart of depreciation.

Specifying the Use of Parallel Currencies

Values posted in asset accounting can be updated in various currencies, and at the same time, a parallel FI document can be posted in the FI as a local currency (company code currency) amount. The bottom line is for the system to supply the corresponding posting documents with additional values from the defined depreciation areas. In order for the system to perform this task, you must make sure that:

- Currency type and the currency in the depreciation area are the same, with the corresponding parallel currency defined in your company code.

- The depreciation terms and acquisition values managed in the depreciation area are identical.

Complete the following steps:

1. To go to the screen where you specify the use of parallel currencies for your assets valuation in the depreciation area, follow this menu path: IMG: Financial Accounting (New) ➤ Asset Accounting ➤ Valuation ➤ Currencies ➤ Specify the Use of Parallel Currencies. The Change View "Set Up Parallel Currencies": Overview screen appears (Figure 1-7). Update these currency types: using Currency Type 30-Group Currency and 40-Hard Currency.

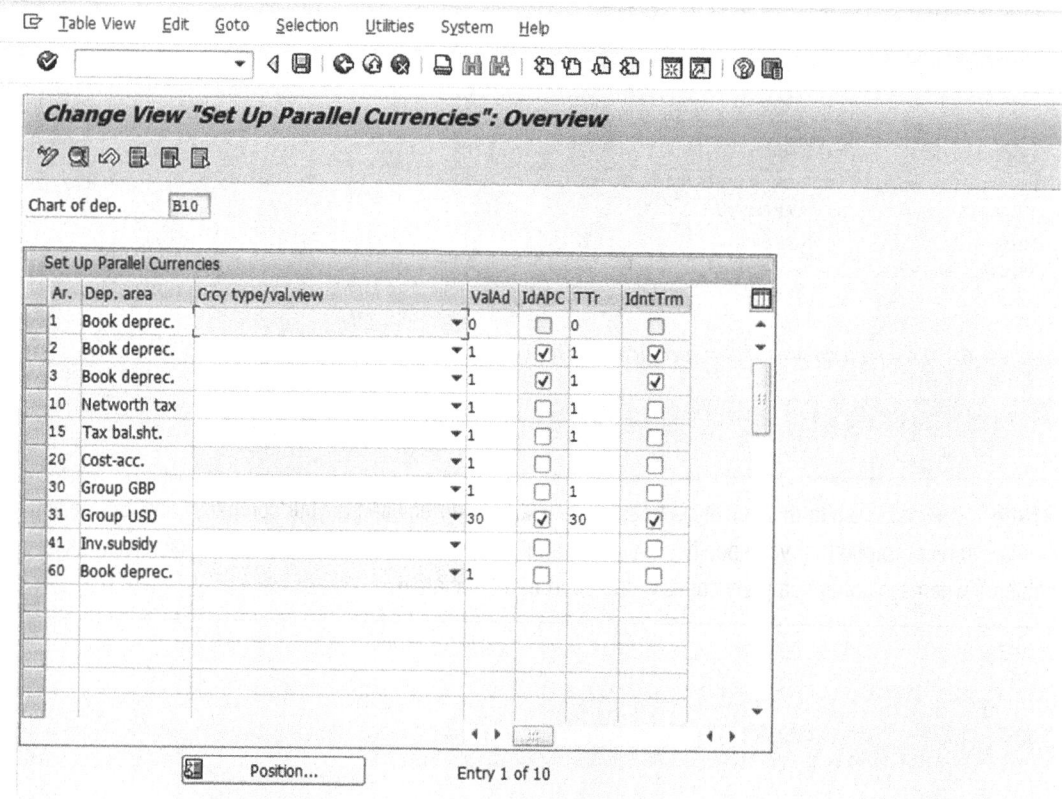

Figure 1-7. *The screen where you set up parallel currencies for depreciation areas*

■ **Note** Make sure that the currency type and the currency in the depreciation area are the same with the corresponding parallel currency defined in your company code. This is not covered in this book, so for more details on how to define parallel currencies in FI, refer to our previously mentioned Apress book called *SAP ERP Financial Accounting and Controlling: Configuration and Use Management*.

---

2. Using the drop-down arrow by each field, specify the 30-Group currency for 2-Book depreciation and 40-Hard currency for 3-Book depreciation. These specifications will allow to maintain legal consolidation for your fixed in group and hard currencies, respectively. Save 💾 your specifications.

Assigning the Chart of Depreciation to a Company Code

In this activity, you assign the chart of depreciation you defined to your company code.

1. To go to the screen where you assign a chart of depreciation, follow the menu path: IMG: Financial Accounting (New) ➤ Asset Accounting ➤ Organizational Structures ➤ Assign Chart of Depreciation to Company Code. The Change View "Maintain Company Code in Asset Accounting": Overview screen is displayed (Figure 1-8).

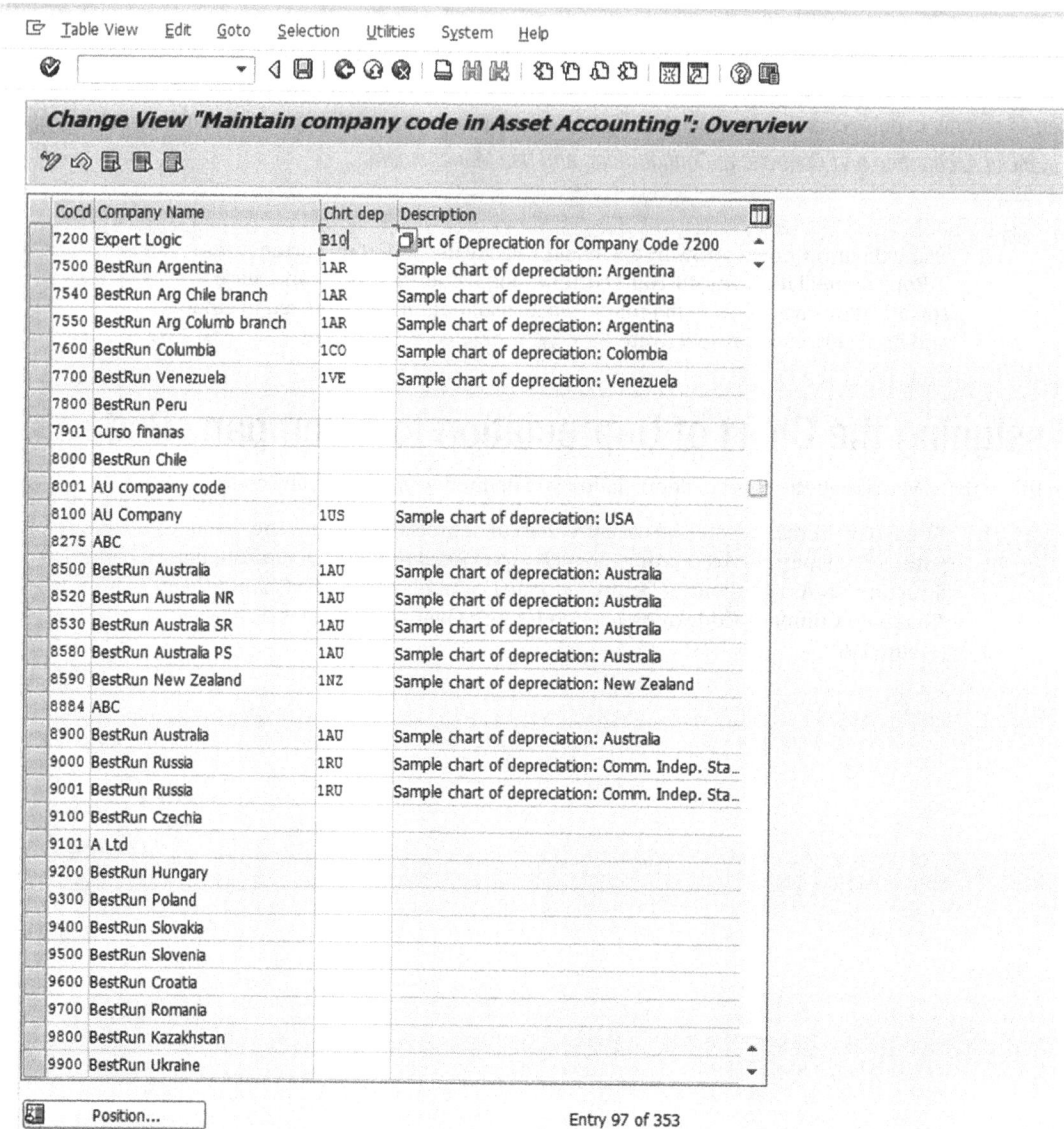

Figure 1-8. The screen where you assign the chart of depreciation you defined to your company code

2. Search for your Company Code 7200 using the [⊞ Position...] button at the bottom of the screen and assign the Chart of Depreciation – B10 you created previously.

3. Save 💾 your work.

■ **Note** You may not be able to assign the chart of depreciation you have defined to your company code unless key important settings are already defined in Financial Accounting for your company code (7200) such as currency, chart of accounts, fiscal year variant, and input tax indicator for non-taxable transactions. So you have to first complete these entries. (We cover these entries in *SAP ERP Financial Accounting and Controlling: Configuration and Use Management*). Otherwise, if you try to save your settings, an information screen comes up with the message "Company code entries for 7200 (your company code) are incomplete – See long test".

Asset Classes

Assets are structured systematically into groups often referred to as asset classes. For example, assets with similar characteristics are classified in the same asset class such as machinery, furniture and fittings, motor vehicles, land and buildings, etc. You can define several asset classes in the system. Like charts of depreciation, asset classes are created at the client level. This makes asset classes available to all company codes. Each asset class usually has master data and depreciation area sections. Master data is data about the asset class held in the system database that remains relatively unchanged over a period of time. It contains information that needs to be used over and over, over a period of time, the same way.

In asset class customizing, we will be looking at the following control parameters:

- Account determination
- Screen layout rules
- Number ranges

Specifying Account Determination

Account determination for asset accounting is defined in the asset class and it serves as the primary connection between asset accounting and the G/L accounts in FI. Posting all related assets values in the system to the general ledger is determined by the company code chart of accounts, the depreciation area, and the account determination key. Based on the specification of account determination in your customizing, the system will automatically calculate all the changes in the asset values arising from depreciation, asset revaluation, and other form of reduction in value and update the asset values. Depending on your configuration, the system will perform online updates for the master data depreciation area, while all other depreciation areas are posted directly or during periodic processing.

When defining account determination for your asset classes, you should take the number of G/L accounts on your asset balance sheet into consideration. In other words, you should make sure that the account determination you are creating in this activity is the same number of G/L accounts defined for your assets. Interestingly, you may not need to create account determinations in practice, because the standard account determinations supplied by SAP will be sufficient. However, we have decided to define our own account determination in this activity in order to take you through the steps involved just in case you need to create an account determination.

1. To get to the screen where you specify account determination for your asset class, use this menu path: IMG: Financial Accounting (New) ➤ Asset Accounting ➤ Organizational Structures ➤ Asset Classes ➤ Specify Account Determination. The Change View "FI-AA: Account Determination": Overview appears.

■ **Note**   You can create several asset classes based on your requirements.

---

2. Click the New Entries button at the top-left side of the screen to go to the screen where you create the account determinations for your asset classes.

3. Using the data in Figure 1-9, update the following fields:

    - **Acct. Determ.:** You can enter up to eight digits as your account determination identifier, which you will assign to your asset classes later.

    - **Name for Account Determination:** Enter a name that best describes your account determinations.

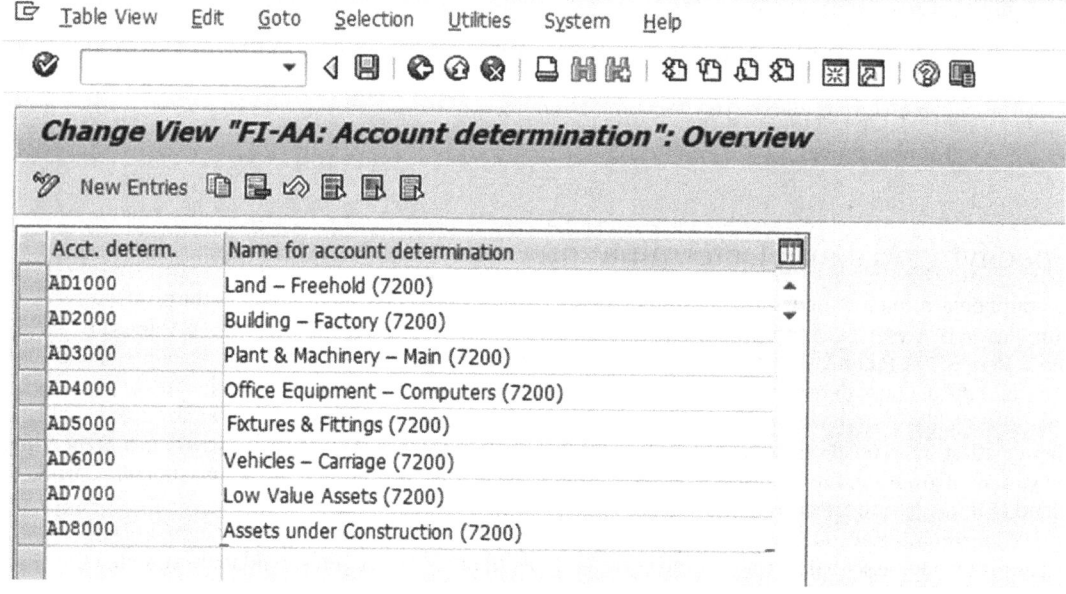

Figure 1-9. *Creating Account determinations for Asset Classes*

■ **Note** There is no hard rule on how to define account determination. It is possible to define your account determination using numbers (i.e., 1000, 2000, etc.) or you can use alphabetic or alphanumeric characters. It is purely a matter of choice or based on your company's requirements. You will also notice that the company code is added to the name of the account determinations in Figure 1-9. This allows you to identify your account determination with ease, especially in an environment where you have other people using the same platform with you.

4. Click Enter ☺ at the top-left side of the screen and save 💾 your account determinations.

■ **Note** The system will not allow you to use account determination numbers that are already used by the system. So if you are creating a new account determination, use a new identification number as your account determination key.

Creating Screen Layout Rules

The screen layout controls the field status in the asset master record. For example, the screen layout determines whether a field is required, optional or suppressed.

In this activity, you will create the appropriate keys for your screen layout rules and descriptions. Normally, the field group rules for screen layouts are defined in the asset master data. You create the screen layout rules by copying the standard screen layout rules supplied by SAP and adjust them to meet your requirements. It is possible to use the predefined screen layout instead of creating your own screen layout rules.

1. You can create screen layout rules using the menu path: IMG: Financial Accounting (New) ➤ Asset Accounting ➤ Organizational Structures ➤ Asset Classes ➤ Create Screen Layout Rules. The Change View "Asset Accounting: Screen Layout for Master Record": Overview screen is displayed, as shown in Figure 1-10. Although you will be creating your own screen layout rules for asset accounting in this activity, we recommend that you stick to the standard screen layout rules supplied by SAP.

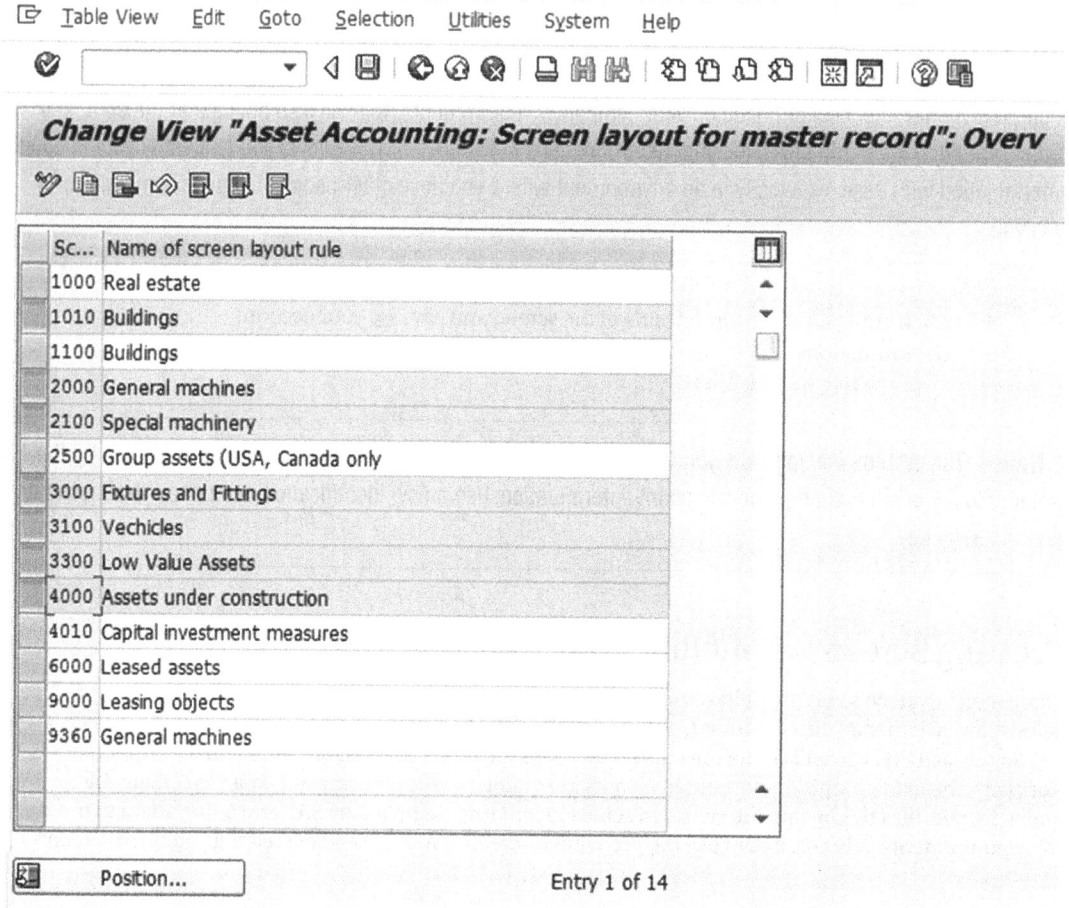

Figure 1-10. *The screen where you copy the standard screen layout rules supplied by SAP, which you can then adjust to meet your requirements*

2. You can only copy the existing screen layout rules provided by SAP and modify them to meet your requirement. The system does not enable you to create your own screen layout rules. So you can only copy existing screen layout rules and then modify them to meet your requirements. To copy items from the displayed screen, click on the items you want to copy to select them. You will notice that the items you select turn yellow. To copy the selected screen layout rules, click the Copy 🗎 button at the top-left side of the screen.

3. Change the copied items using the data in Figure 1-11.

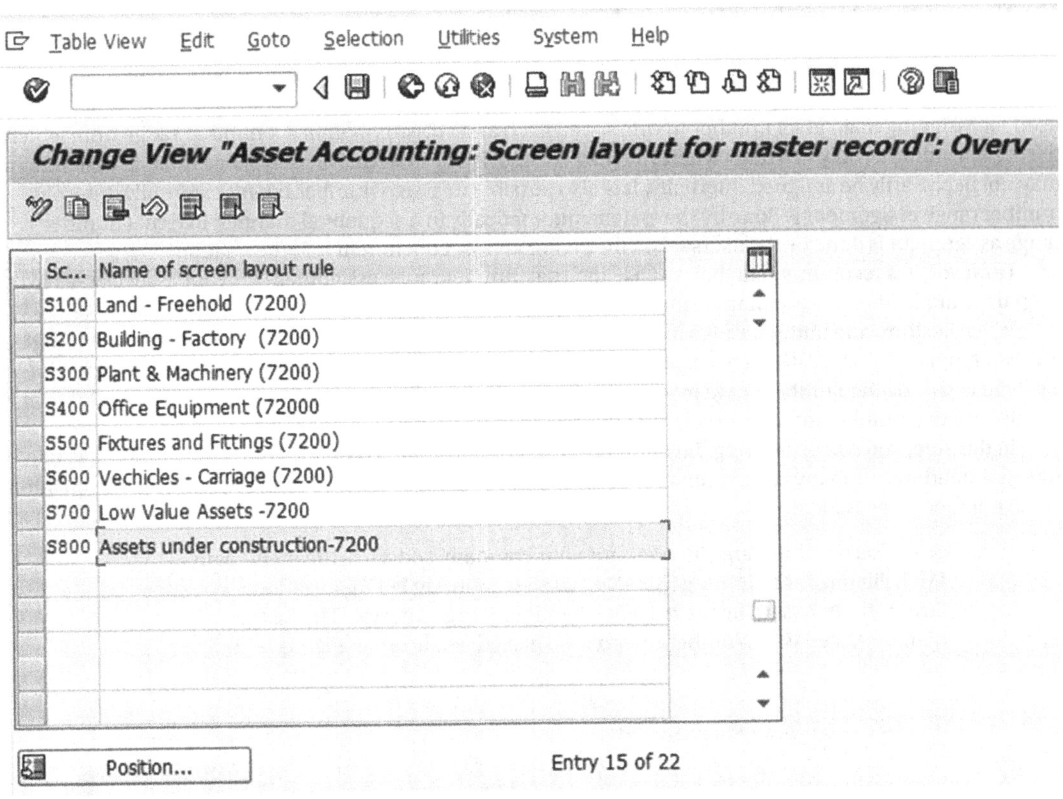

Figure 1-11. *The modified screen layout roles specifications to meet your requirements*

■ **Note** When defining the screen layout rules for your asset classes, you should take the number of G/L accounts for your asset balance sheet into consideration as you did when defining account determinations.

---

4. Click the Enter 📀 button at the top-left side of the screen to confirm your changes and then 💾 save your screen layout rules.

■ **Note** When creating your screen layout rules, make sure that the identification key you are using for the screen layout. Otherwise, you'll encounter problems when trying to save your work as the system will not allow you to use the existing screen layout key already. We advise that you use keys that are not already used by the system.

Defining the Number Range Interval

It is important to classify asset portfolio on the basis of structured number ranges for better asset management. It is customary to define number ranges for asset classes for your company code, which is used for assigning main asset number to your asset. Each asset class is assigned a number range from which the system automatically can draw when you post an asset in the system. Number range interval assignment may not necessarily be assigned internally; it is also possible to assign number ranges externally. Internal number range assignment is done by the system automatically in a sequential manner. External number range assignment is done by the users when they enter an asset document into the system.

However, it is recommended that you use internal number range assignment for your asset classes to keep the complexities of asset management to a minimum.

When customizing number range intervals, we recommend that you copy the standard number range interval supplied by SAP. Although it is possible to create your number range intervals afresh, but it is a lot easier to copy existing number range intervals and adjust them to meet your requirements. Better still, you can use existing number range intervals already created in the system.

In this step, you will be copying the number range intervals from company code 1000. Company code 1000 is a standard company code supplied by SAP. Using company code 1000 as the template in the creation of the number range is ideal.

1. To define number range intervals for your company code, use the menu path: IMG: Financial Accounting (New) ➤ Asset Accounting ➤ Organizational Structures ➤ Asset Classes ➤ Define Number Range Interval. The Range Maintenance: Asset Number screen is displayed, as shown in Figure 1-12.

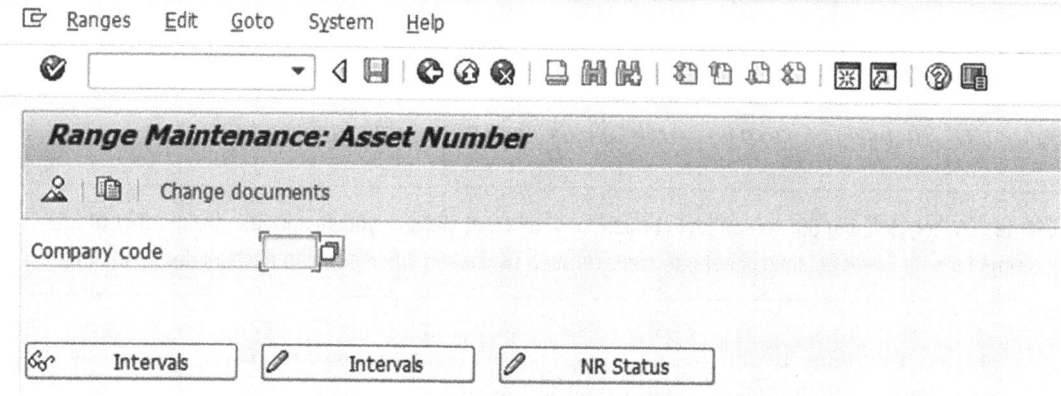

Figure 1-12. *The initial screen where number range intervals are created or copied*

2. Since you are copying number range intervals in this activity, enter the company code 1000 in the Company code field and click the Copy 🗐 button at the top-left side of the screen. The Copy Company Code dialog screen pops up. Update the following fields:

   - **From:** The Company code 1000 you are copying is the system default. You can overwrite it if you chose to.

   - **To:** Enter the target company code 7200 in this field. This is the company code you are transporting the company code 1000 number range intervals to.

3. Click the Copy ☑ button at the bottom of the Copy Company Code screen to copy the number range intervals for company code 1000 to your company code 7200. The Transport Number Range Intervals screen is displayed with a message, as shown in Figure 1-13.

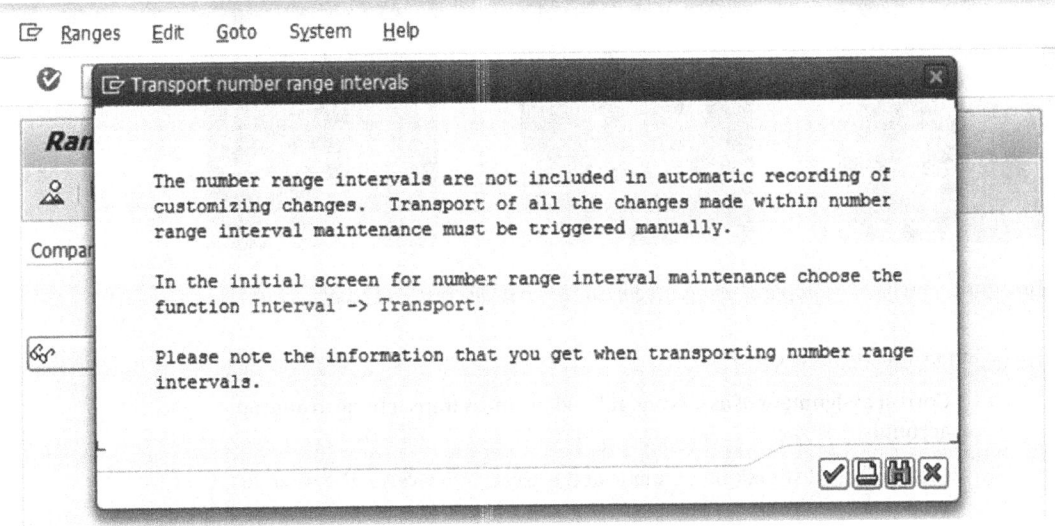

Figure 1-13. The system message explaining the transport number range intervals you have copied

4. Click the Continue ☑ button at the bottom-right side of the screen. The system will notify you at the bottom of the Range Maintenance: Asset Number screen that "the company code 1000 was copied to 7200".

Defining the Asset Classes

Assets are structured into classes in Asset Accounting (FI-AA) for efficient asset portfolio management and for asset reporting purposes. You assign assets to the appropriate asset class. Therefore, asset classes are a vital aspect of asset accounting.

Asset classes are an important aspect of Asset Accounting in FI-AA. It allows assets to be structured in a systematic manner by assigning assets to the appropriate asset classes. The benefit of asset classes is that they allow efficient management of your asset portfolio and asset reporting purposes. You can assign multiple assets to an asset class, as depicted in Figure 1-14. On the other hand, it is not possible to assign an asset to more than one asset class.

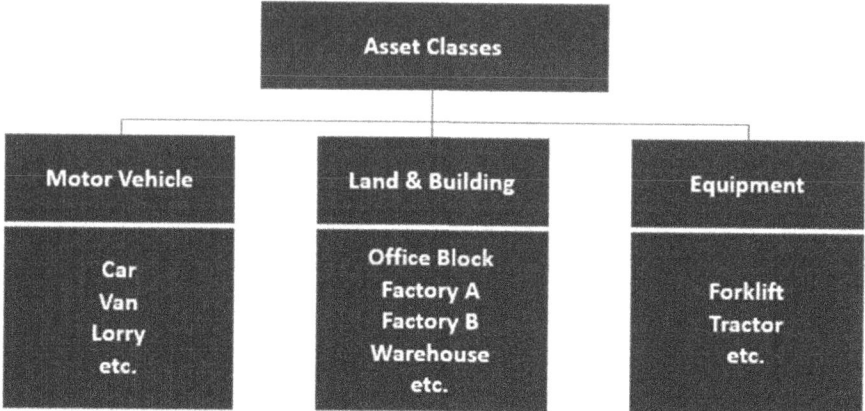

Figure 1-14. *A typical example of asset categorization in asset classes in asset accounting*

The importance of asset classes:

- Correct assignment of assets and related business transactions to appropriate GL accounts.

- Clearer asset distinctions are made at the asset class levels rather than in GL accounts.

- It allows default values to be assigned when creating assets.

- It allows adequate asset grouping for reporting purposes.

In this activity, you will define the following asset classes:

- Land—Freehold

- Building—Factory

- Plant & Machinery

- Office Equipment

- Fixtures & Fittings

- Vehicle—Carriage

- Low Value Assets

- Assets under Construction

Complete the following steps:

1. To define the asset classes for your asset accounting, use the menu path: IMG: Financial Accounting (New) ➤ Asset Accounting ➤ Organizational Structures ➤ Asset Classes ➤ Define Asset classes. The Change View "Asset classes": Overview screen is displayed.

2. Click the New Entries button on the top-left side of the screen to go to the screen where the specifications of your asset classes will be carried out (Figure 1-15).

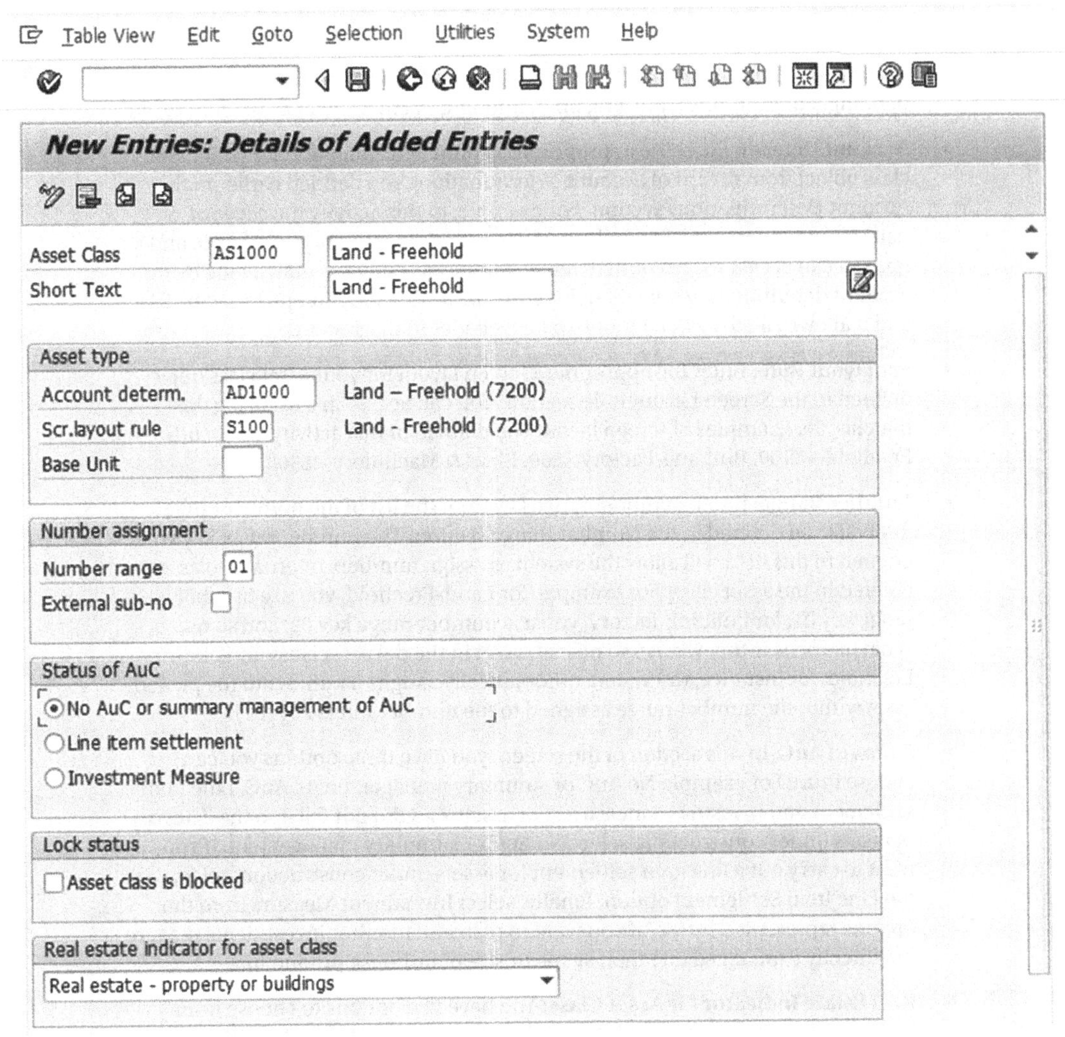

Figure 1-15. The screen where you define asset class for your asset accounting

3. Update the following fields:

    -   **Asset Class:** Enter your proposed asset class key for the object you are defining the asset class for (AS1000 Lan—Freehold) in this field. Make sure you use a meaningful asset class as your asset key. For example, AS1000, AS2000, AS3000, etc.

    -   **Short Text:** Enter a short description that best describes the asset class you are defining. For example, Land-Freehold, Building-Factory, Plant & Machinery, etc.

    -   **Account Determ:** Enter the appropriate account determination for your asset class object from the list of account determinations you defined earlier in the Account Determinations section. For example, in this activity the account determination for Land-Freehold is AD1000, Building-Factory is AD2000, and so on. You can access the account determinations list using the matchcode by the account determination field. Matchcode is the search function provided by SAP and it allows you to search or lookup items codes in the system.

    -   **Scr.layout Rule:** Enter the appropriate screen layout for your asset class object defined in the Screen Layout Rule section. You can access this list using the matchcode. Examples of screen layout you defined in this activity are: Land-Freehold – S100, Building-Factory S200, Plant & Machinery – S300, etc.

    -   **Number Range:** Enter a number range key from the list of the number range intervals you defined in the Number Range section. The number range key you entered in this field will allow the system to assign numbers internally to assets entered in the asset class. For example, for Land-Freehold, you use number range key 01, for building-factory, you use number range key 02, and so on. What happens is that when you post an asset in the the asset class for Land-Freehold, for instance, the system automatically assigns a number to the posted asset within the number range assigned to the number range key (01).

    -   **Status of AuC:** In this section of the screen, you have three options you can choose from. For example No AuC or summary management of AuC, Line item settlement and Investment measure. For assets that did not fall into the category of assets under construction, select No AuC or summary management. If you want to carry out a line item settlement for assets under construction, select the Line Item Settlement option. Finally, select Investment Measure from the options represented by SAP if you want to plan and monitor investments that are not directly capitalized due their scope or size of in-house production.

    -   **Real Estate Indicator for Asset Class:** You have two options to choose from in this section. For assets that are not real estate, specify "Other Asset Without Real Estate Management" and for assets that are real estate, specify "Real Estate Property or Building".

4. Click the Enter 🗸 button at the top-left side of the screen and save 🖫 your asset class.

5. To create the remaining asset classes, repeat steps 2-4 with the appropriate settings for each asset class in Step 3.

Summary

In this chapter, you looked at how to customize organizational structure in asset accounting. You checked country-specific settings provided by SAP in the system to see if it meets your country disclosure requirements. You learned what the chart of accounts and chart of depreciation are. You learned how to copy the reference chart of depreciation and depreciation areas. You customized this activity to take you through the steps involved in parallel currencies specifications and assign chart of depreciations to your company code.

Finally, you looked at the various customizing steps in asset classes. In this step, you defined account determinations, created screen layout rules, and defined number range intervals for your asset classes.

In the next chapter, you will be looking at how to integrate asset accounting with G/L account in FI, specify posting keys for asset posting, define field status variants for asset accounting, assign input tax indicator for non-taxable acquisitions, specify financial statement version for asset reports, and then specify document types for posting depreciation and posting rules.

CHAPTER 2

Integrating Asset Accounting with the General Ledger (FI-GL)

This chapter looks at the steps involved in the integration of asset accounting with the general ledger and also explains the various steps involved in the integration of asset accounting with the general ledger. You will learn how to:

- Define how depreciation areas post to the general ledger
- Assign G/L accounts
- Specify posting key for asset posting
- Change the field status variant of the asset G/L accounts
- Assign the input tax indicator for non-taxable acquisitions
- Specify financial statement versions for asset reports
- Post depreciations to the general ledger
- Specify document type for periodic posting of asset balance sheet values

Defining How Depreciation Areas Post to the General Ledger in FI

Technically, the setting you carry out in this step will allow you to determine how depreciation areas are posted in the general ledger. A list of standard options regarding depreciation areas are posted in general ledger are supplied by SAP in Post to G/L accounts. For example:

0- Area does not post

1- Area posts in real time

2- Area posts APC and depreciation on specific basis

3- Area posts depreciation only

4- Area posts APC directly and depreciation

5- Area posts APC only

6- Area posts only APC directly

Again, APC in asset accounting is acquisition and production cost. This applies when an asset is purchased from an outside vendor (externally) or produced in-house (internally). The definition of how depreciation areas post to G/L accounts will determine whether APC transactions and/ or depreciation areas in asset accounting should be directly transferred to FI.

In this activity, you will specify the APC transactions and/or deprecation areas you defined in Chapter 1 in "Copying Reference Chart of Deprecation/Depreciation Areas" section.

1. To get to the screen where you perform these specifications, use this menu path: IMG: Financial Accounting (New) ➤ Asset Accounting ➤ Integration with the General Ledger ➤ Define How Depreciation Areas Post to General Ledger. The Determine Work Area Entry screen pops up, as shown in Figure 2-1. This screen will allow you to enter your chart of depreciation in the Chart of Depreciation field in order to call up your depreciation area.

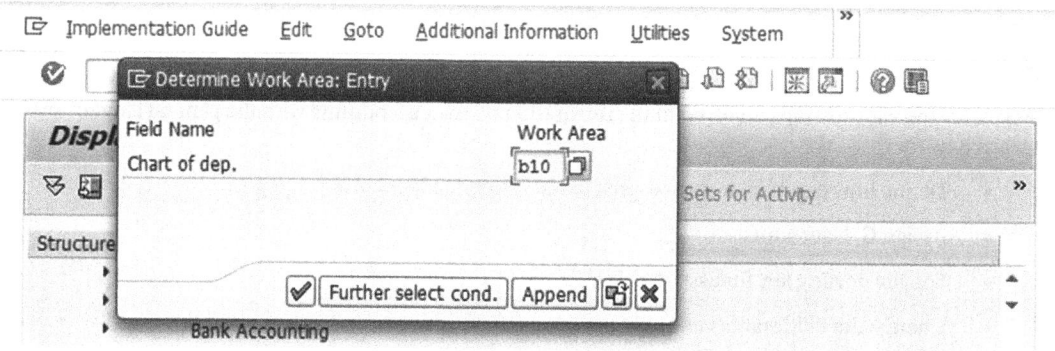

Figure 2-1. *The specification of the depreciation area to call up your depreciation area*

2. Enter your Chart of Depreciation (**B10**) in the Chart of Dep. Field and click the Enter ☑ button at the bottom of the screen. The Change View "Define Depreciation Areas": Overview screen (Figure 2-2) appears, displaying the list of depreciation areas you have defined.

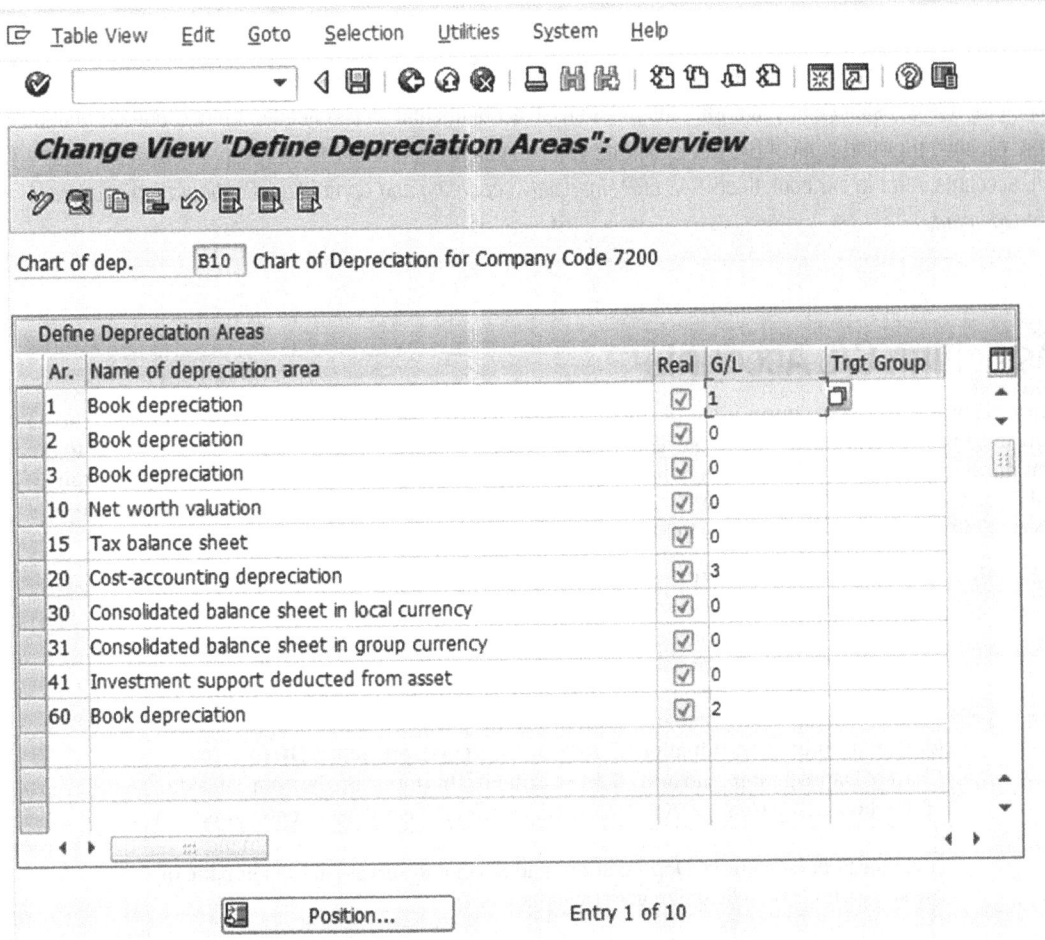

Figure 2-2. The list of depreciation areas you defined

▓ **Note**   The system automatically defaults to how depreciation areas are posted to GL accounts. You can manually change the defaulted settings to meet your requirements.

---

3. When you have specified how you want your deprecation areas to post to G/L accounts, save 🖫 your specification.

■ **Note**   The system normally comes with predefined G/L posting specifications. You can either use the predefined specifications or specify your own. Before proceeding to the next step in this activity, assigning G/L accounts, it is advisable that you create the required GL accounts that will be needed for account assignment first. We have provided a list of G/L accounts that you can use in Appendix A. For a recap on how to create G/L accounts, refer to our book titled *SAP ERP Financial Accounting and Controlling: Configuration and Use Management.*

Assigning G/L Accounts

The assignment of G/L accounts is simply integrating general ledger accounts to asset accounting. The customizing you carry out in this step will allow asset accounting transactions to post automatically to the general ledger accounts based on your specifications. As part of your configuration you can specify the balance sheet accounts, the depreciation accounts, and the special reverse accounts that you want asset accounting transactions to be posted in FI.

1. To get to the screen where you carry out account assignments, use this menu path: IMG: Financial Accounting (New) ➤ Asset Accounting ➤ Integration with the General Ledger ➤ Assign G/L Accounts. The Determine Work Area Entry screen that you saw previously in Figure 2-1 opens. This screen will allow you to enter your chart of depreciation in the Chart of Dep. field in order to call up your depreciation area. This screen will allow you to specify the chart of depreciation for your account determination. Enter your chart of depreciation (**B10**) in the Chart of Depreciation field and click the Enter ☑ button at the bottom-left side of the screen. The Change View "Chart of Accounts": Overview screen appears in Figure 2-3, displaying the chart of accounts objects in account determination (Balance Sheet Accounts, Depreciation, and Special Reserves) in the left pane of the screen that you will assign general ledger accounts.

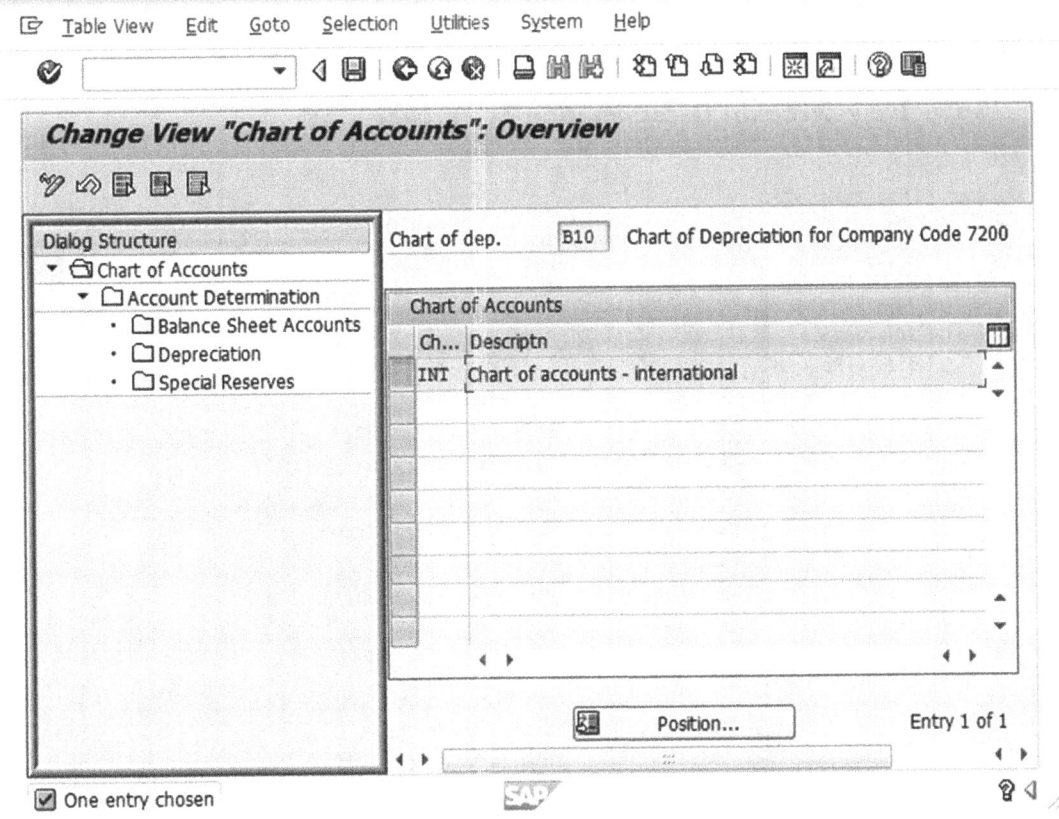

Figure 2-3. *The initial screen where you will assign general ledgers to asset accounting*

2. Select your INT Chart of Accounts and double-click the Account Determination folder. A list of the account determinations you defined in Chapter 1 in account determination section is displayed.

3. Search for the account determination AD1000 you defined earlier using the [Position...] button at the bottom of the screen. You will notice that your account determinations from AD10000 to AD8000 are displayed at the top of the displayed list of account determinations in the system, as in Figure 2-4. The next step is to assign G/L accounts in balance sheet accounts and depreciation to your depreciation areas in asset accounting.

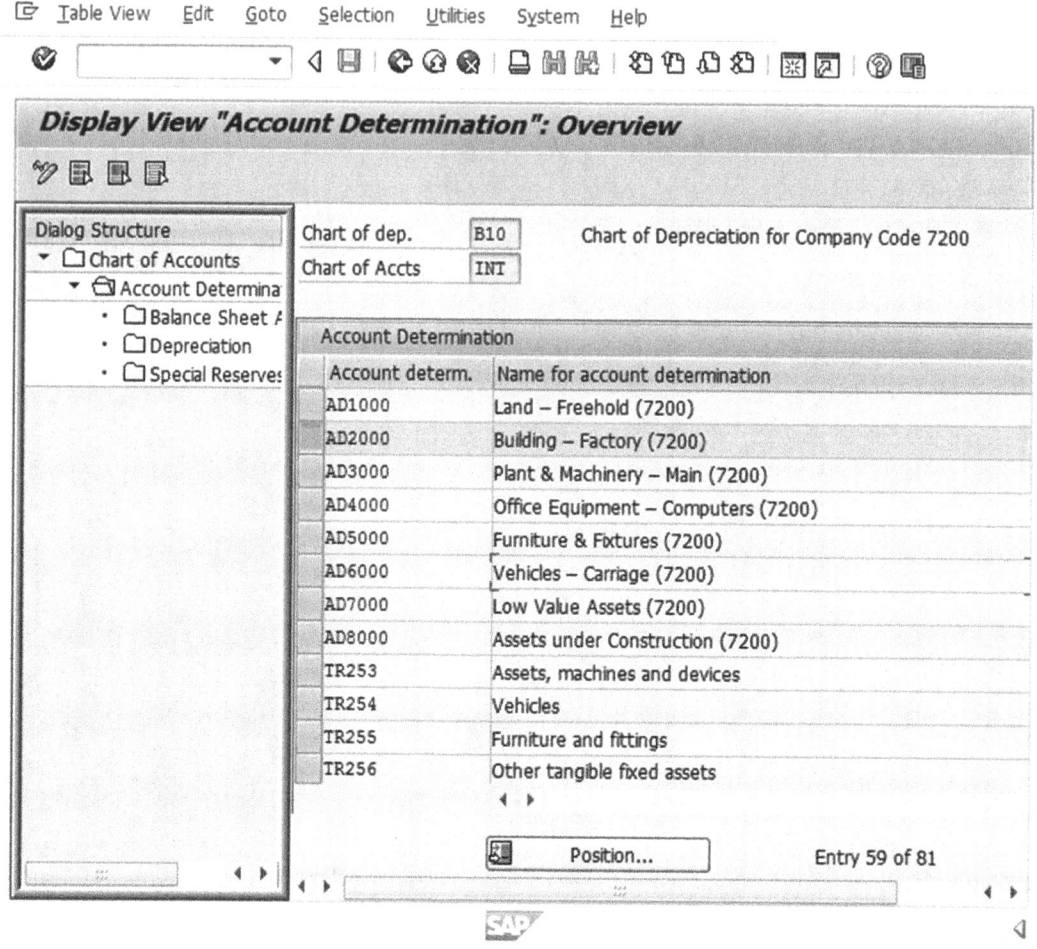

Figure 2-4. *The account determinations screen where you assign general ledgers to the appropriate account determination objects*

Balance Sheet Accounts

The accounts you assign to your depreciation areas in this step will allow asset accounting transactions to be posted to general ledgers in the balance sheet accounts.

1. To go to the screen where you will assign general ledgers to your depreciation areas in asset accounting, select AD2000 (Factory Building) from the list of your account determinations and double-click the Balance Sheet Accounts from the list of displayed objects in Account Determination. The Change View "Balance Sheet Accounts": Overview screen appears, displaying the possible depreciation areas you can assign G/L accounts. For example, depreciation area 01(Book depreciation) and 60(Book depreciation).

■ **Note**   Parallel accounting can be managed in asset accounting using depreciation areas. The depreciation area 01 is always the primary depreciation in asset accounting in an environment where parallel accounting is used. In this case, depreciation area 01 is posted to all ledgers. However, you will still need to assign the leading ledger to the depreciation area 01.

2.   Select the depreciation area 01 (Book Depreciation) and click the Details ⬚ button at the top left of the screen. The Change View "Balance Sheet Accounts": Details screen is displayed (see Figure 2-5). In this activity you will assign APC value and Asset Retirement accounts to the appropriate G/L accounts in Balance Sheet accounts. This will allow postings made to asset accounts to be posted to the G/L accounts that you assigned to the balance sheet accounts.

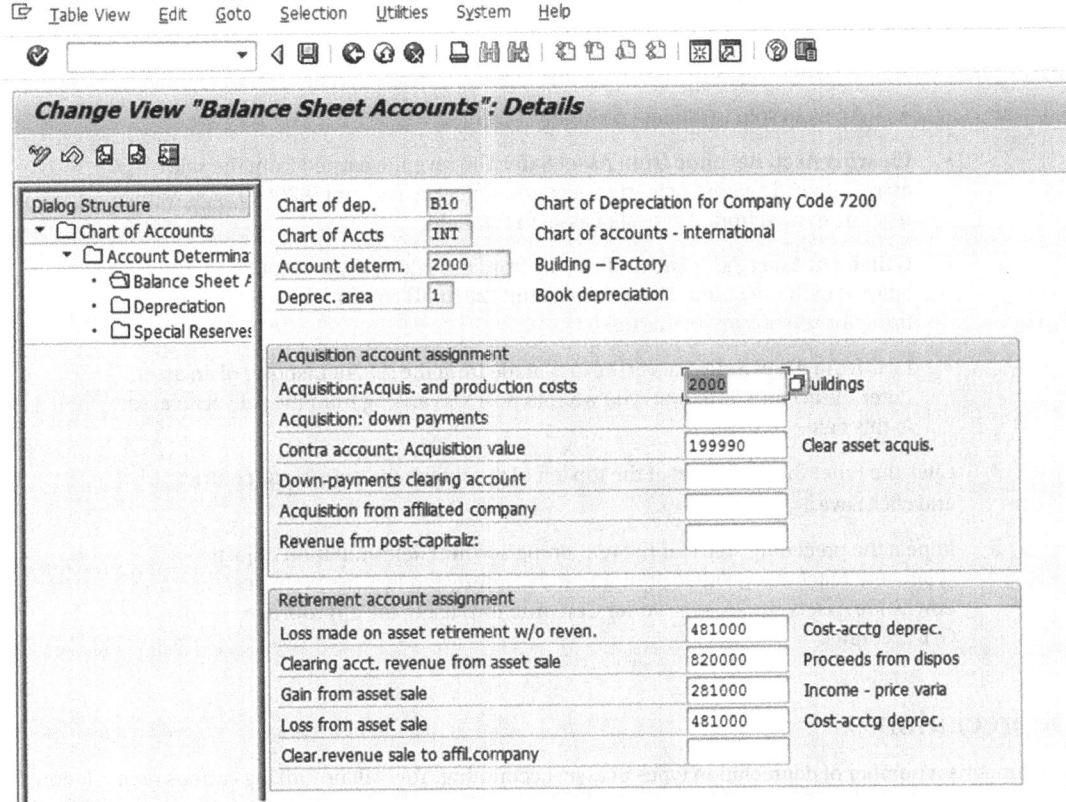

Figure 2-5. *Integration of G/L accounts in balance sheet accounts to asset accounting, showing the values entered in the following steps*

3. Update the following fields:

- **Acquisition: Acquis. and Production Costs:** This is an account for posting APC (Acquisition and Production Cost). Enter the general ledger account (**2000**) you want to post assets purchased or in-house asset production costs in this field. You can access the list of your general ledger accounts using the matchcode button by the field.

- **Contra Account: Acquisition Value:** This is the contra account for asset acquisition for posting values adjustments specific asset. Enter the account you want contra account (**199990**) for acquisition values in this field.

- **Loss Made on Asset Retirement w/o Revenue:** The removal of an asset or part of an asset from asset portfolio is often referred to as asset retirement. Enter the account you want post loss on asset retirement w/o revenue (**481000**) in this field. Losses arising from asset retirement with or without revenue are posted to this account. Asset retirement can arise under the following conditions:

  - An asset sold and revenue is earned

  - An asset is scrapped without revenue

  - An asset sold to affiliate company

- **Clearing Acct. Revenue from Asset Sale:** The revenue earned from the sale of asset is posted against a clearing account. Enter the account (**820000**) you want revenue earned from disposal of asset in this field.

- **Gain from Asset Sale:** The profit made from the sale or disposal of an asset is entered in this account. Enter the account (**281000**) you want to post gain made from the sale of asset in this field.

- **Loss from Asset Sale:** This is the loss made from the sale or disposal of an asset. Enter the account (**481000**) you want to post loss arising from the sale of an asset in this field.

4. Click the Enter the ✅ button at the top left of the screen to confirm your entries and click Save 💾.

5. Repeat the preceding steps for the remaining account determination objects (Plant and Machinery, Office Equipment, Furniture and Fixtures, Vehicles, Low Value Assets, and Assets Under Construction) using the appropriate G/L accounts.

Depreciation

SAP supports a number of depreciation types in asset accounting. You will be looking various depreciation types supported by SAP in detail in Chapter 4. In this step, you learn how to assign depreciation to G/L accounts. Then depreciation posted in an asset account will be posted to the G/L accounts assigned to this activity.

1. To go to the screen where you will assign G/L accounts for depreciation posting from asset accounting to FI, on the Change View "Balance Sheet Accounts": Details screen (Figure 2-5), double-click the Depreciation folder below the balance sheet folder. This will take you to the next screen where you will assign the G/L accounts for depreciation to the depreciation area.

The Change View 'Depreciation': Overview screen is displayed. You will noticed that the depreciation folder on the left pane is now open. On the depreciation list section, the depreciation areas available for the depreciation account determination are displayed (for example, depreciation areas 01 book depreciation, 20 Cost-accounting deprecation and 60 Book depreciation). You can assign G/L accounts to post depreciation to each of these depreciation areas. For illustration purposes, you will only be looking at how to assign G/L accounts to depreciation area 01 (Book depreciation). The same steps are applicable to the remaining depreciation areas.

2. To assign G/L accounts to your book depreciation, click 1-Book Depreciation from the list in the depreciation areas. Select Depreciation Area 01 (Book Depreciation) and click the Details ✪ button at the left of the screen. The Change View "Depreciation": Details screen comes up. On this screen you can assign the appropriate G/L accounts you want. Using the information found in Table 2-1, update Change View 'Depreciation': Details screen.

Table 2-1. *The Data to Update the Change View "Depreciation" Details Screen*

Fields	Values
Ordinary depreciation account assignment	
Acc.dep.accnt.for ordinary depreciation	2010
Expense account for ordinary depreciate.	55000
Unplanned depreciation account assignment	
Accumulated dep.account unpl.deprec.	2010
Expense account for unplanned deprec,	55000

3. Once you have assigned the appropriate G/L accounts, click the Enter ✅ at the top left of the screen to confirm your entries. Then save 💾 the account determination.

4. Repeat the preceding steps for the remaining account determination objects (Plant and Machinery, Office Equipment, Furniture and Fixtures, Vehicles, Low Value Assets, and Assets Under Construction) using the appropriate G/L accounts.

Specifying the Posting Key for Asset Posting

Posting key is defined using two characters. In order for the system to be able to carry out automatic posting when posting fixed asset accounts, the specification of posting key for asset posting must be in place. SAP comes with standard posting keys in the system. For example:

- G/L account posting from asset posting: Debit 40 and Credit 50

- Asset posting: Debit 70 and Credit 75

We recommend that you use the standard posting key specifications supplied by SAP because they are sufficient. Secondly, creating your own posting keys may be a daunting exercise and time consuming because you will need to change the settings in the associated tables. However, it is important to check the standard default values to make sure they meet your requirements.

1. To check the standard posting keys for asset posting, use this menu path: IMG: Financial Accounting (New) ➤ Asset Accounting ➤ Integration with the General Ledger ➤ Specify Posting Key for Asset Posting. The Configuration Accounting Maintain: Automatic Posts-Procedure screen is displayed in Figure 2-6, containing a list of procedures (e.g., Additional Accounts for Asset Accounting, Asset Posting, and G/L Account Posting from Asset Posting).

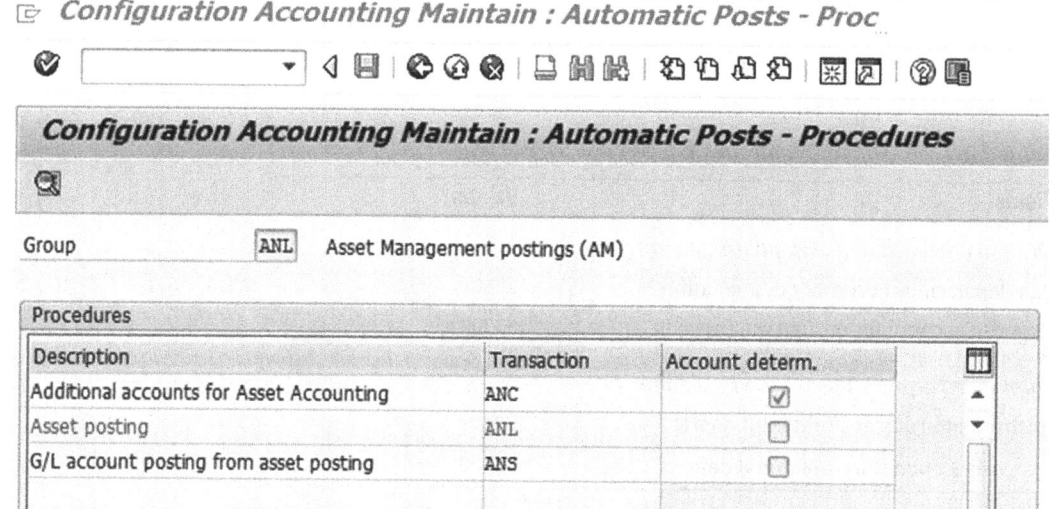

Figure 2-6. The list of procedures for automatic posting of asset accounts

2. To display the setting for asset posting, double-click asset posting from the displayed list of procedures on the screen. The Configuration Accounting Maintain: Automatic Posts – Posting Keys screen showing the default posting key values is displayed in Figure 2-7. It shows the appropriate posting keys for asset posting.

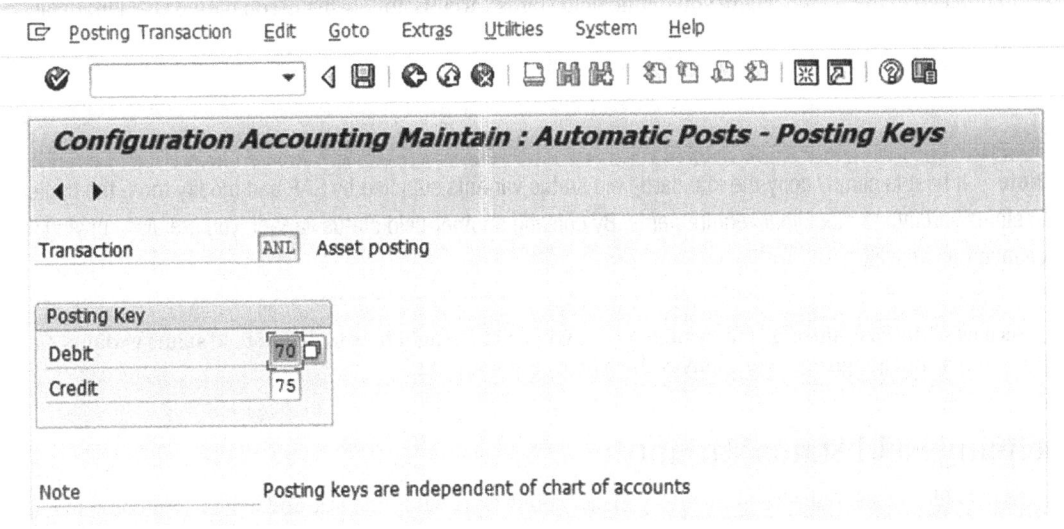

Figure 2-7. *The screen showing the default posting key values supplied by SAP*

3. To check the settings for G/L account posting whether they meet your requirements, use the Back ⟲ button at the top of the screen to return to the Configuration Accounting Maintain: Automatic Posts – Procedures screen. Double-click on G/L account posting for asset posting the list of displayed items on the screen. The Configuration Accounting Maintain: Automatic Posts – Posting Keys screen with default posting key values is displayed showing the appropriate posting keys for asset posting.

■ **Note**   The additional accounts for Asset Accounting that are displayed on the procedure list can only be used with the intercompany asset transfer function.

Changing the Field Status Variant of the Asset G/L Accounts

Field status variants are variants that hold the *field status groups* in SAP R/3. A field status group defines the screen layout for a general ledger account entry and controls document creation within a company code. Based on your specification, the field status groups determine which fields accept input during document entry, as well as whether a field should be inactive, be required, or be optional.

In SAP R/3, field statuses are defined as part of global settings, assigned field status groups and are independent of company codes (that is, they are available to all company codes in the client). Normally, field status variants are created when defining company code and it may not be necessary to define field status variant again in asset accounting if you have already defined field status variant in FI. However, SAP comes with standard field statuses with associated field status groups you can adapt and assigned to your company code. The field status group controls the appearance of certain data entry fields in the data screen for G/L accounts. When customizing the field status variant, it is important that you make sure that the group field indicators for asset and asset retirement are set as required entries for input.

To proceed to the screen where you define field status variants, follow the menu path: IMG: Financial Accounting (New) ➤ Asset Accounting ➤ Integration with the General Ledger ➤ Change the Field Status Variant of the Asset G/L Accounts. The Choose Activity screen pops up containing the list of field status activities to be performed is displayed in Figure 2-7.

■ **Note**   It best to simply copy the standard field status variants supplied by SAP and modify them the copied field status variants to meet your requirements. By copying another field status variant, you are also copying its account group as well.

As part of the customizing activity in this step, you will be taught how to define field status variants, field status groups, and assign your company code to field status variant.

Defining Field Status Variants

As part of field status variants customizing, you can define field status variants and assign your company code to the field status variant you have defined.

1. To proceed to the screen where you define field status variants, select Define Field Status Variants from the list of displayed activities in Figure 2-8 and click the ⟨🔍 Choose⟩ button at the bottom right of the screen. The Change View "Field Status Variants": Overview screen is displayed in Figure 2-9, containing the list of existing field status variants in the system.

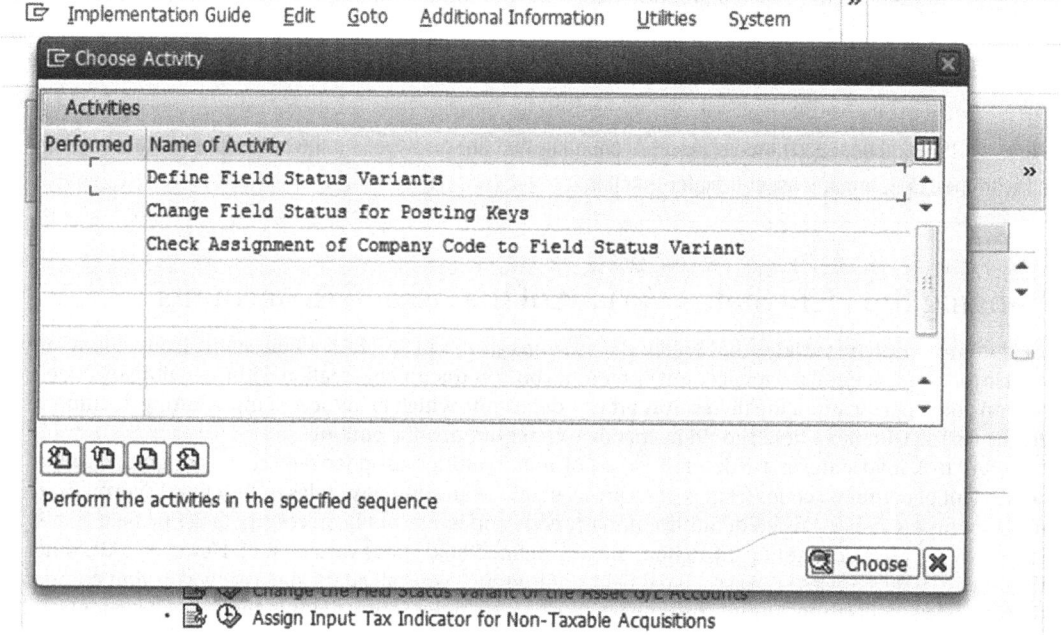

Figure 2-8. *The list of activities to be carried out as part of your field status configuration*

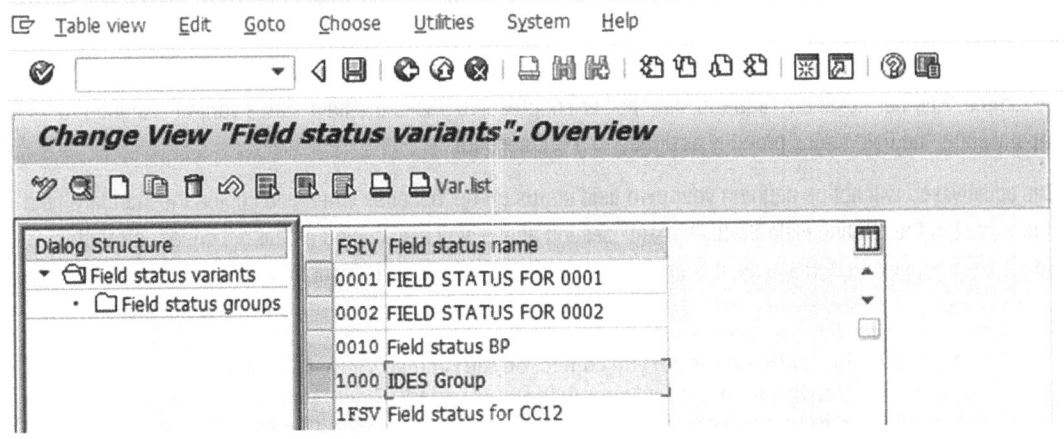

Figure 2-9. *The list of field status variants existing in the system*

The next step in this activity is to define your field status variant. You will define your field status variant by copying the standard field status variant supplied by SAP and modify them to meet your requirements. When you copy the standard field status variant, you are also copying the associated field status variant groups with it.

2.   Select the field status 1000 (IDES Group) from the list of displayed status group on the screen and click the Copy 🗐 button at the top left of the screen. The Change View "Field status variants": Overview of Selected Set screen appears, displaying the field status variant key and name of 1000(IDES Group) you copied. Change the field status key 1000 to your own field status key (**7200**) and change the field status name IDES Group to your field status name (**Field status for 7200**). We recommend that you use your company code as your field status key. This is important as it helps you to identify your field status variant with ease, especially in an environment where you have several field status variants in the system.

3.   Click the Enter ✅ button at the top left of the screen to confirm your changes. The Specify object to be copied screen pops up stating that "Entry 1 of the entries to be copied has dependent entries. You can copy the entry with all dependent entries, or just the entries".

4.   You have the option to copy all or only copy entry. Since you want to copy all the dependent entries as well, click the [copy all] button at the right side of the screen. The Information screen pops up notifying you of the "Number of dependent entries copied". Click the continue button at the bottom right of the screen. The Change View "Field status variants": Overview screen is displayed. You will notice that your Field status variant (7200-Field status variant 7200) is displayed on top of the existing field status variants displayed on the screen.

5.   Save 🖫 your field status variant.

■ **Note** As mentioned earlier, the field status variant holds the field status groups and the field status group holds the field attributes. The field status groups controls the input fields in the data screen for G/L accounts. For example, whether fields are required, optional, or suppressed. Unlike the field status variant assigned to company code, the field status group is assigned to a G/L account.

In this activity, you will not be defining your own field status group, because when you copied the standard field status variant in the "Define Field Status Variant" section above, you also copied all the dependent attributes (field status groups) with it. However, it is important to check the field status variant groups you copied.

6. To display the field status group you copied, on the Change View "Field status variants": Overview screen, select your field status variant (7200-Field status variant 7200) from the displayed list of field status variant and double-click the field status groups (this is a yellow folder on the left pane of the screen). The Change View "Field status groups": Overview screen appears displaying the copied field status group for a field status variant, as shown in Figure 2-10.

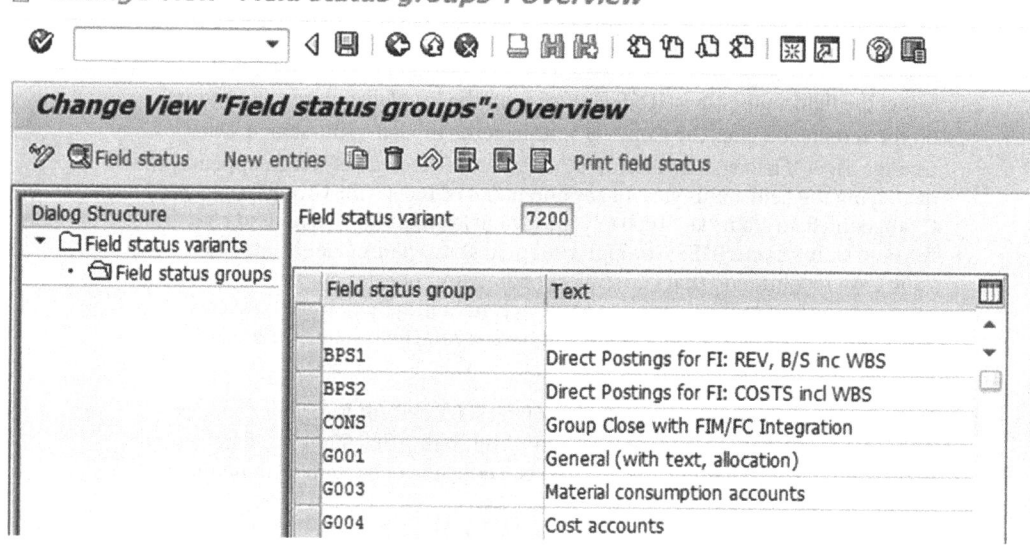

Figure 2-10. List of the field status groups you copied

Assigning Company Codes to Field Status Variants

In this step you assign your company code to the field status variant you previously defined in the "Defining Field Status Variants" section.

1. To assign company code to field status variant, use this menu path: IMG: Financial Accounting (New) ➤ Asset Accounting ➤ Integration with the General Ledger ➤ Change the Field Status Variant of the Asset G/L Accounts. The Choose Activity screen pops up containing the list of field status activities you can choose from.

2. Double-click the Check Assignment of Company Code to Field Status Variant from the displayed list of activities on the screen, the Change View "Assign Company Code-> Field Status Variant" Overview screen is displayed containing the list of company codes in the system (see Figure 2-11).

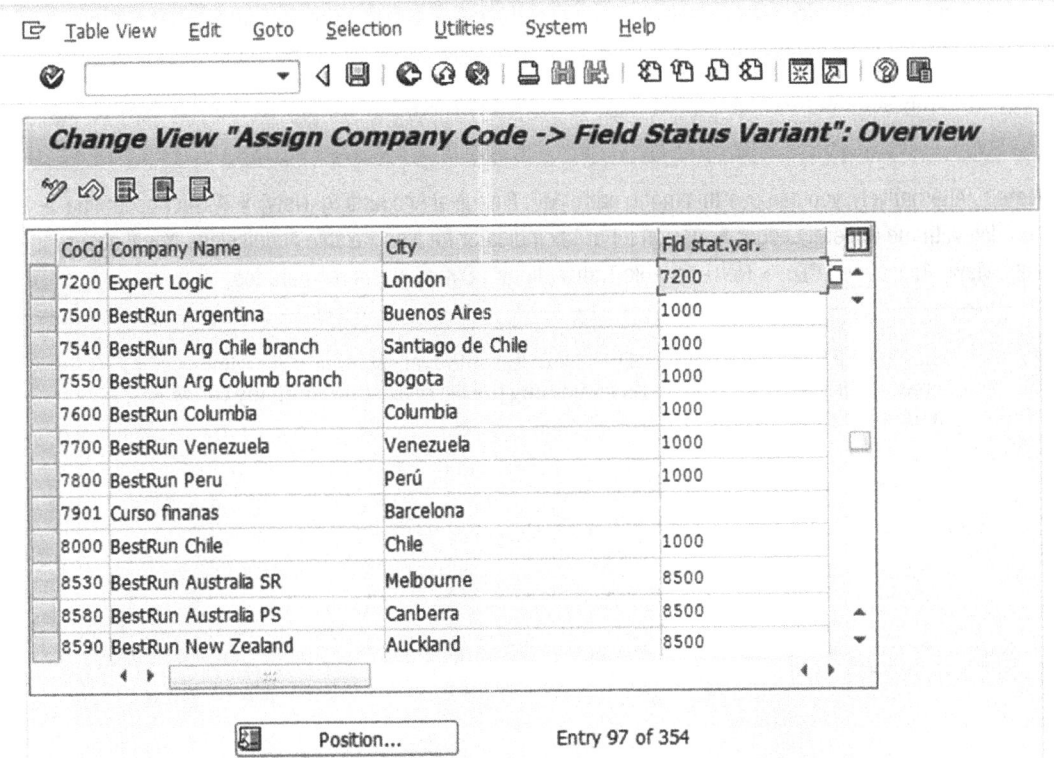

Figure 2-11. *The screen where the field status variant is assigned to a company code*

3. Using the [📋 Position...] button at the bottom of the screen, search for company code 7200. Your company code comes on top of the displayed company codes.

4. Enter your field status variant (**7200**) in the Fld Stat.Var. field to your company code.

5. Click the Enter ✅ button at the top left of the screen and then save 💾 your work.

Assigning Input Tax Indicator for Non-Taxable Acquisitions

You may sometimes have to report tax-exempt or non-tax sales/purchases that are posted to accounts that are tax relevant (for example, acquisition from in-house production are not subject to tax, but are relevant for tax purposes). As a result you have to specify zero input/output tax indicator per company code, which will allow you to post accounts that are tax relevant without actually calculating tax.

1. To assign taxable codes for non-taxable transactions, follow this menu path: IMG: Financial Accounting (New) ➤ Financial Accounting Global Settings (New) ➤ Tax on Sales/Purchases ➤ Posting ➤ Assign Tax Codes for Non-Taxable Transactions.

■ **Note**   Alternatively, you can use this menu path: IMG: Financial Accounting (New) ➤ Asset Accounting ➤ Integration with the General Ledger ➤ Assign Input Tax Indicator for Non-taxable Acquisitions. You'll access the Change View "Allocate Co.CD. -> Non –Taxable Transactions": Overview screen here too.

The Change View "Allocate Co.CD. -> Non –Taxable Transactions": Overview screen is displayed in Figure 2-12, containing the list of existing company codes in the system.

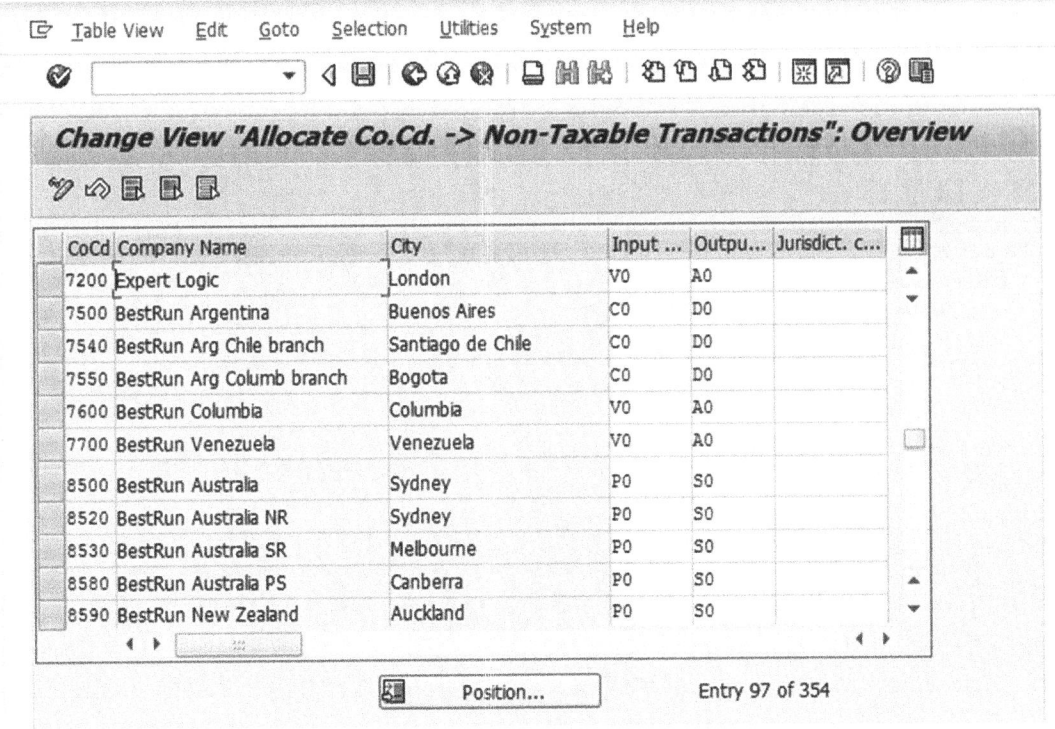

Figure 2-12. Assign input tax indicator for non-taxable acquisitions

2. Search for your company code (7200) using the [🔲 Position...] button at the bottom of the screen. Enter **V0** (Non-Taxable input tax code) in the Input Tax Code field and **A0** (Non-Taxable output tax code) in the Output Tax Code field for your company code.

3. Click the Enter ✅ button at the top left of the screen and then click Save 🖫.

Specifying Financial Statement Version for Asset Reports

In this activity, you assign financial statement versions to each of the depreciation areas in your company code. The specifications you perform in this step serve as the default financial statement versions for each depreciation area you specified. This allows the system to generate specific asset reports per depreciation area based on your specifications.

1. To go to the initial screen where you will specify financial statement version for asset reports, use this menu path: IMG: Financial Accounting (New) ➤ Asset Accounting ➤ Integration with the General Ledger ➤ Specify Financial Statement Version for Asset reports. The Change View "Company Code Selection": Overview screen containing a list of company codes in the system is displayed (see Figure 2-13).

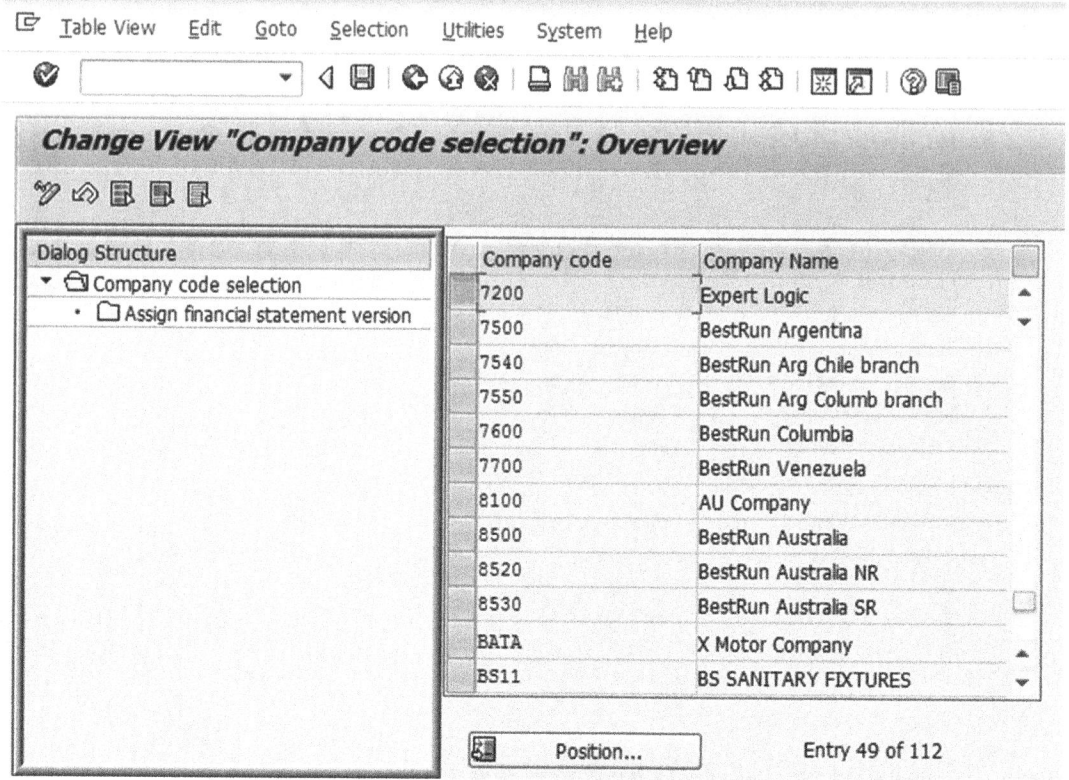

Figure 2-13. *The Change View "Company Code Selection": Overview screen*

2. To perform the specification of the financial statement version for asset reporting for your company code, on the Change View "Company code selection": Overview screen in Figure 2-13, search for your company code using the ![Position...] button at the bottom of the screen. Select your company code (7200) from the displayed list.

3. Double-click the Assign Financial Statement Versions folder. The Change View "Assign financial statement version": Overview screen (see Figure 2-14) is displayed showing the list of possible depreciation areas for your company code.

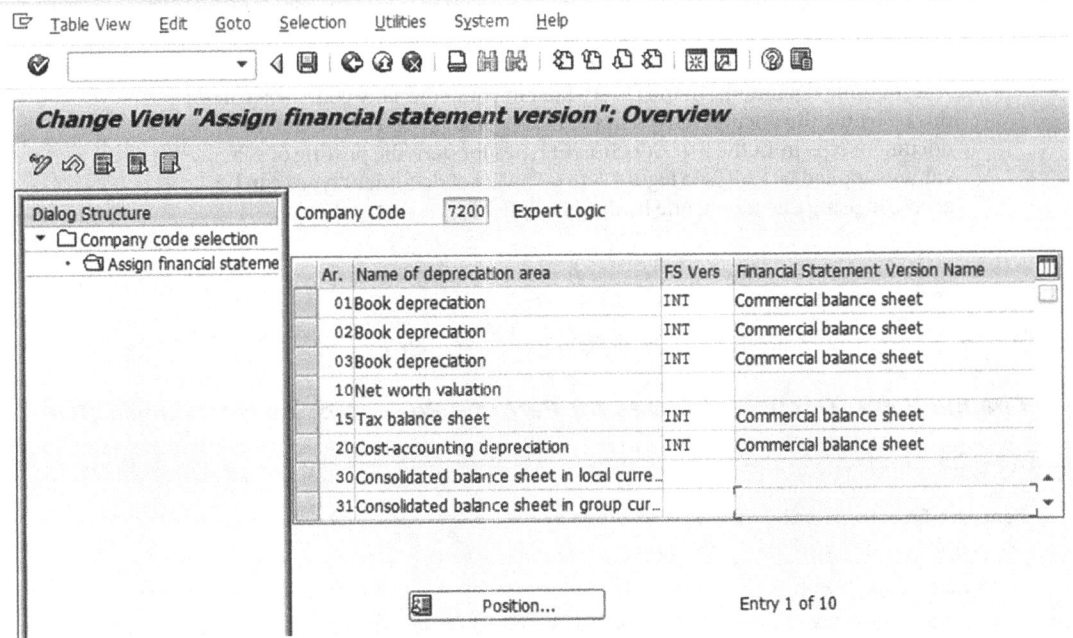

Figure 2-14. The Change View "Assign financial Statement Version": Overview screen

4. Enter the financial statement you want to use as default for asset reporting for each of the depreciation areas you want to include in the report, using Figure 2-14 as a reference.

5. Click the Enter ✅ button at the top left of the screen and save 🖫 your specifications.

Specifying the Document Type for Periodic Posting of Asset Values

In this step, you perform the specification of a default document type that will allow you to carry out periodic posting of asset balance sheet values from depreciation areas directly to the general ledger using the new APC posting run without using batch-input session. The document type you specify in this step is used only in the new report program for periodic posting of APC (Acquisition and Production Costs) values: RAPERB2000 (a standard executable ABAP report provided by SAP).

1. To specify the document type for periodic posing of asset balance sheet values, use this menu path: IMG: Financial Accounting (New) ➤ Asset Accounting ➤ Integration with the General Ledger ➤ Post APC Values Periodically to General Ledger Accounting ➤ Specify Document Type for Periodic Posting of Asset Values. The Change View "Document Types for Periodic Posting of Asset Values Overview screen appears, displaying the list of company codes in the system.

2. The next step is to assign the appropriate document type to THE company code. Search for your company code (7200) on the screen using the ▣ Position... button at the bottom of the screen, and enter the appropriate document type (AE – Accounting document) in the DocTy field in your company code. You can do this by typing the document type in the DocTy field, or you can select the document type from the list of document types for periodic posting of APC values supplied by SAP (see Figure 2-15). The list of document types can be accessed using the matchcode by the DocTy field.

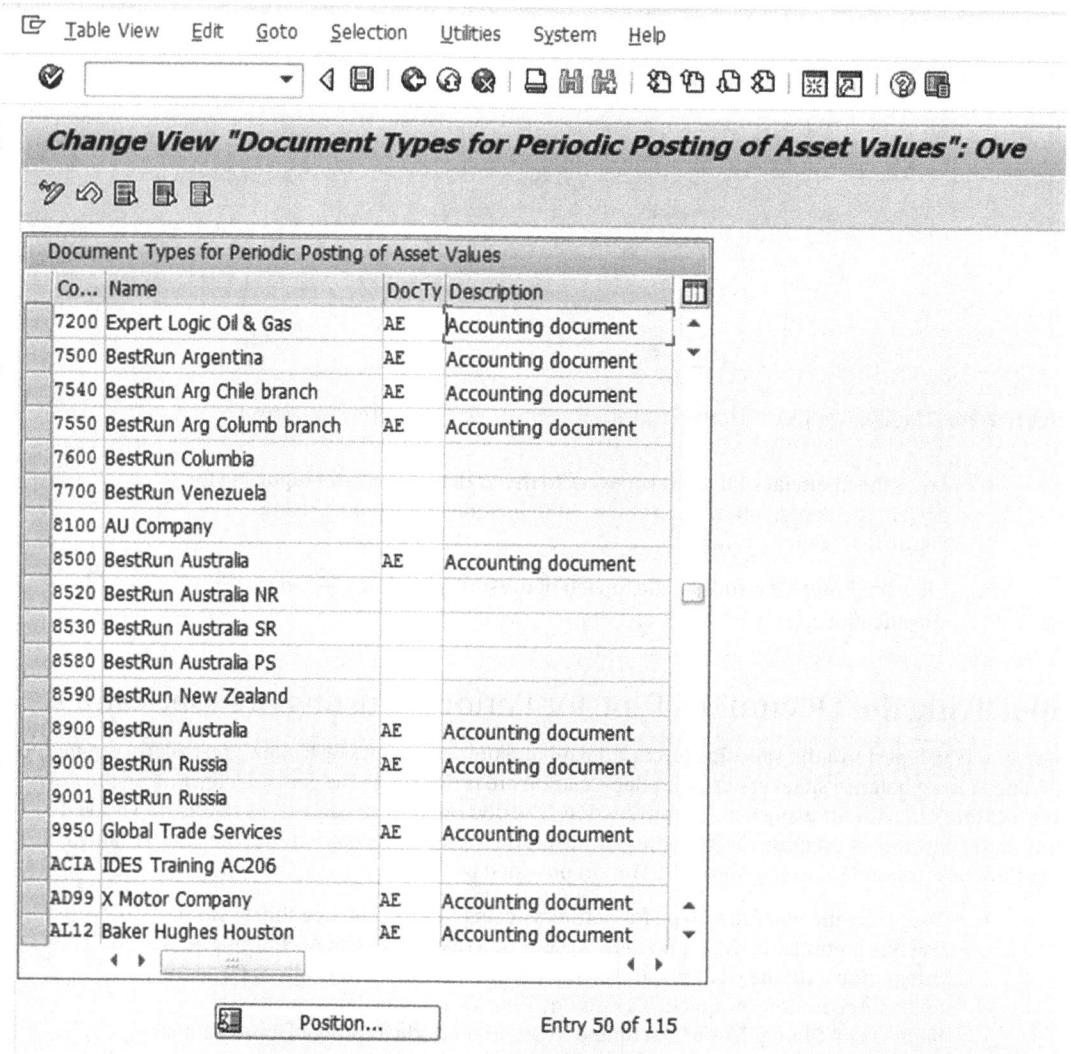

Figure 2-15. *The screen where you assign the document type for periodic posting of asset balance sheet values*

3. Click the Enter ✔ button at the top left of the screen and click Save 🖫.

Summary

The chapter looked the steps involved in the integration of asset accounting with general ledger in FI. You learned how depreciation areas are posted to general ledger in FI and went on to look at how to assign G/L accounts to the depreciation areas in the balance sheet accounts and depreciation. You then went on to look at how to specify posting keys for asset posting and G/L account posting from asset posting. You also learned how to define field status variant of the asset G/L accounts, define field status groups, and assign field status group to your company code. Afterward, you looked at how to assign input tax indicator for non-taxable acquisitions. You then looked at how to specify financial statement versions for asset reporting and, finally, you assigned financial statement versions to your depreciation areas and assigns document types to the company codes for periodic posting of asset balance sheet values.

In the next chapter, you will be looking at the valuation of fixed assets. You will look at how to set chart of depreciation, specify transfer of APC (acquisition and purchase costs), specify transfer of depreciation terms, set up areas for parallel valuation, specify maximum amount for low-value assets, specify other versions at the company code level, define depreciation area for foreign currencies, and define group assets.

CHAPTER 3

Valuation of Fixed Assets

This chapter looks at the steps involved in the configuration of the valuation of fixed assets in asset accounting and also explains the various steps involved in defining depreciation for foreign currencies in asset accounting. In this chapter, you will learn how to:

- Define depreciation areas in asset accounting
- Determine depreciation areas in the asset class
- Set up areas for parallel valuation
- Specify maximum amount for low-value asset
- Specify rounding of net book value and/or depreciation
- Specify other versions on company code level
- Specify other versions on depreciation area level
- Define depreciation areas for foreign currencies
- Specify the use of parallel currencies

Setting the Chart of Depreciation

The treatment and disclosure requirements of depreciation and valuation of assets varies from country to country. SAP comes with various charts of depreciation in an attempt to meet individual country-specific legal disclosure requirements. Therefore, charts of depreciation are always country-specific. Often, charts of depreciation are independent of other company codes outside the same country. All company codes in the same country are assigned the same chart of depreciation, since they fall under the same legal disclosure requirements and therefore need the same chart of depreciation. For example, if Company Code 1 and Company Code 2 are UK companies, they should be assigned to the same chart of depreciation for the UK. Likewise, all company codes operating in the United States can use the same chart of depreciation specifically for the United States, and so on.

Benefits of chart of depreciation include:

- The ability to define and manage assets' valuation and depreciation parameters in the same chart of depreciation.
- Asset valuation can be performed using parallel approaches to meet different purposes via depreciation areas such as balance sheet or cost accounting or tax purposes.

- Fiscal year adjustments can be performed to reflect certain depreciation calculations.

- Methods of valuation can be held in depreciation keys. SAP comes with most of the keys (you can change or add to these keys).

It is important to set the chart of depreciation in an environment where you have more than one chart of depreciation in the system. In order to indicate the chart of depreciation you want to customize, it is important to set appropriate chart of depreciation. The configuration you then carry out will be specific to the chart of depreciation you set. Based on the settings, the system can determine the chart of depreciation you are working on. For example, if you have only one chart of depreciation, the system will automatically use it. On the contrary, if more than one chart exists, the system will prompt you to specify which chart of depreciation you are using. The chart of depreciation you specify will remain active in the system until you specify another depreciation area.

To set chart of depreciation, use this menu path: IMG: Financial Accounting (New) ➤ Asset Accounting ➤ Valuation ➤ Set Chart of Depreciation. The Chart of Depreciation Selection screen is displayed in Figure 3-1.

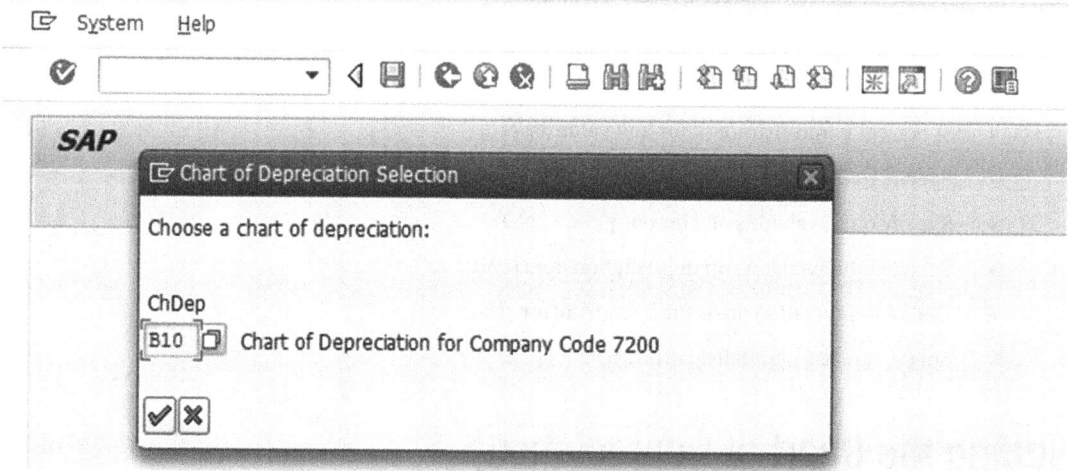

Figure 3-1. *Chart of depreciation selection screen*

Enter your chart of depreciation (B10) in the ChDep field (this is the chart of depreciation key you defined in Chapter 1 in the Copy Reference Chart of Depreciation/Depreciation Areas section). Then click the Enter button at the bottom-left side of the screen. This will take you back to the Display IMG screen. In the status bar at the bottom of the screen, the system will notify you that the chart of depreciation B10 was set.

Depreciation Areas

Depreciation was explained in depth in Chapter 1. In this step you will define depreciation areas for your asset accounting. During this customizing activity, you will also specify area type, specify transfer of APC values, specify transfer of depreciation terms, and set up areas for parallel valuation for your asset accounting according to IAS/IFRS standard.

Depreciation areas are important because they allow you to calculate various asset values in parallel for individual fixed assets for different purposes. For example, you may want to generate values for the balance sheet, which may be different from costing accounting for internal management purposes. The depreciation terms and values for asset valuation are managed in the depreciation area. You can create up to 99 depreciation areas in SAP ERP. Depreciation areas are grouped in the chart of depreciation according to country-specific requirements.

Defining Depreciation Areas

In this step, you define the depreciation areas and specify the area type that will allow you to calculate asset values in parallel for each asset for various purposes. SAP comes with various county-specific depreciation areas you can adopt and adjust to meet your requirements.

1. To define depreciation areas, use this menu path: IMG: Financial Accounting (New) ➤ Asset Accounting ➤ Valuation ➤ Depreciation Areas ➤ Define Depreciation Areas. The Choose Activity screen pops up with the option to define depreciation areas or specify area type (see Figure 3-2).

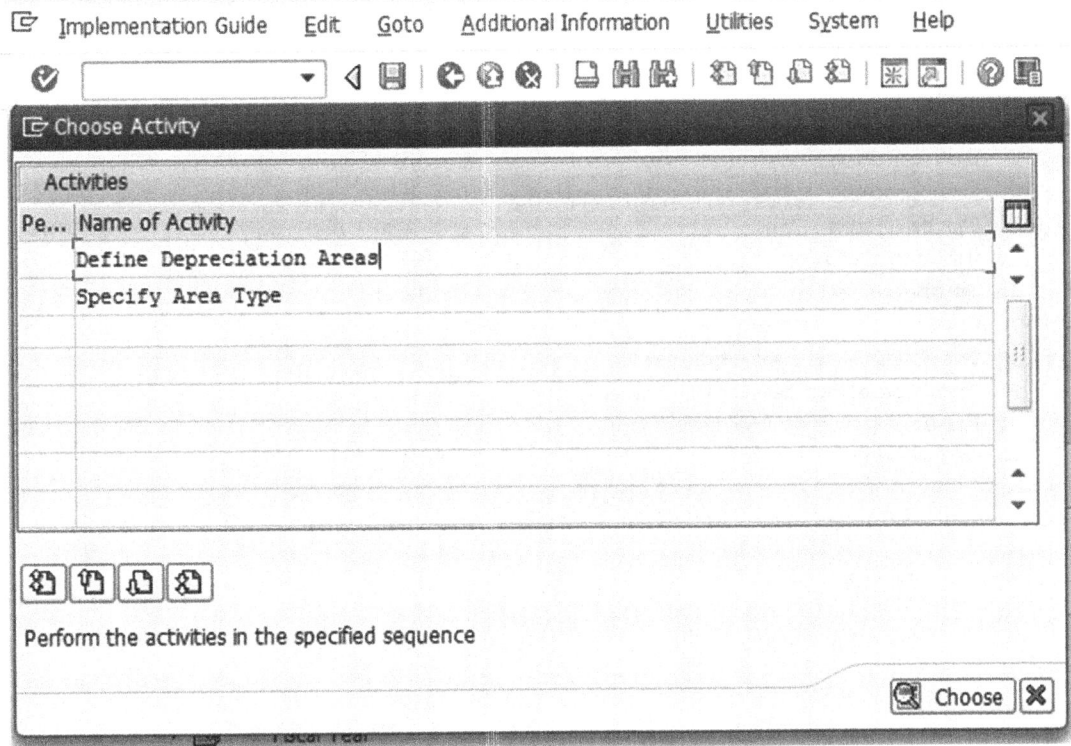

Figure 3-2. *The choose activity screen*

2. Select Define Depreciation Areas and click the [Q Choose] button at the bottom-right side of the screen. The Determine Work Area: Entry screen pops up. This screen will allow you to specify the chart of depreciation you want to define for your depreciation areas.

3. Enter your chart of depreciation (B10) in the Chart of Dep. field and click the [✔] Continue button at the bottom of the screen. You'll proceed to the screen where you will carry out the specification of the depreciation areas for your chart of depreciation. The Change View "Define Depreciation Areas": Overview screen appears (see Figure 3-3), showing the associated depreciation areas.

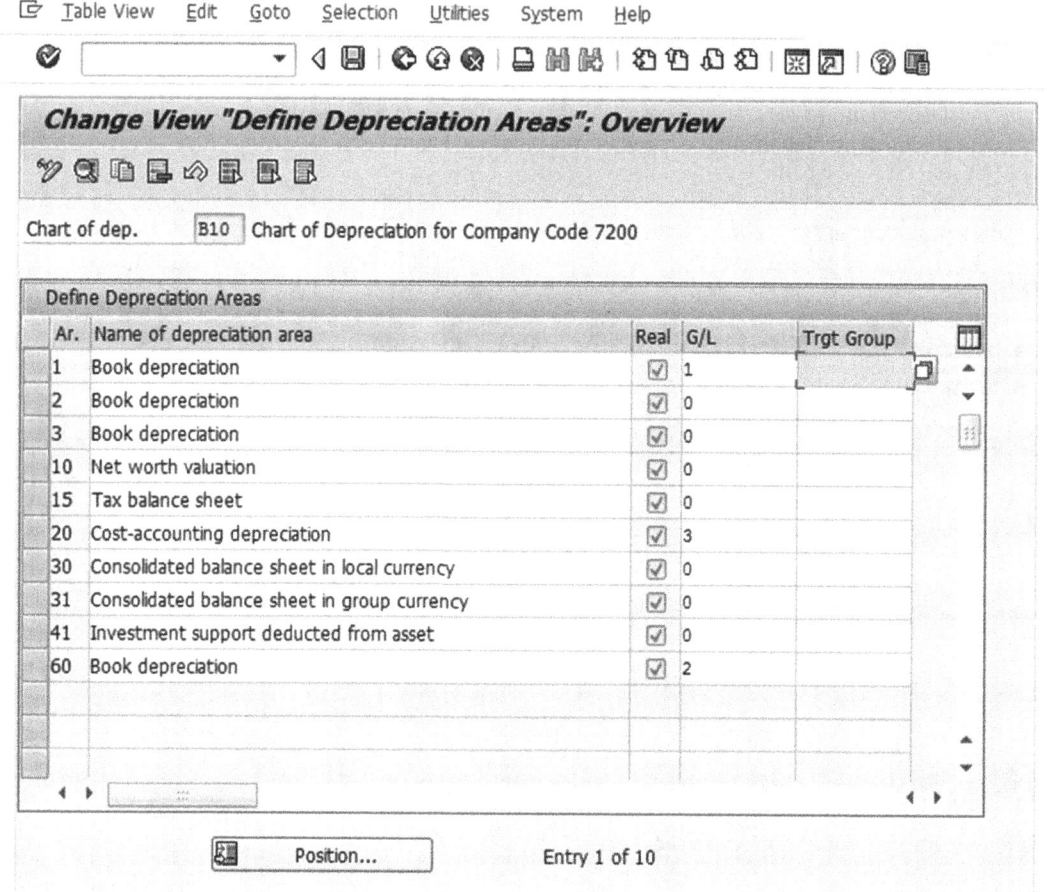

Figure 3-3. The Change View "Define Depreciation Areas": Screen

---

■ **Note**   You may not need to carry out any specifications in this activity, because the Standard Chart of Depreciation (1GB) for your country you copied in Chapter 1 contains the corresponding settings needed for the settings in this step.

---

4. Check the displayed chart of depreciation to see if it meets your requirements. You may also want to delete unwanted depreciation areas. To delete any unwanted depreciation areas, select the depreciation area you want to delete from the list of the displayed depreciation areas and click the Delete ■ button at the top-left side of the screen. Then save ■ your depreciation area.

Specify Area Type

SAP comes with standardization of depreciation areas you can assign to your depreciation area. You can access the list of standardization of depreciation areas supplied by SAP using the matchcode by the Type field for each depreciation area. The specification of area type will allow you to determine the valuation method applicable to each depreciation area. For example, when you specify the standardization of depreciation area 18 (balance sheet according to other guidelines, such as IAS) for Book depreciation area 01, the system will apply this specification strictly to depreciation area 01. Likewise, when you specify the standardization of depreciation area 04 (Net Worth Valuation) to a given depreciation area, the system will use the net worth in the valuation of an asset for the specified depreciation area.

1. The screen where you can specify area type for your depreciation area can be accessed on the Choose Activity screen shown previously in Figure 3-2 by double-clicking Specify Area Type from the displayed list on the screen. The Chart of Depreciation Selection screen then pops up. This screen will allow you to specify the chart of depreciation you are working on.

2. Enter your chart of depreciation (BT 10) in the Chart of Depreciation (ChDep) field.

3. Click the Continue ☑ button at the bottom-left side of the screen to proceed to the screen where you specify the area type for your depreciation areas. The Change view "Actual Depreciation Areas: Area Type": Overview screen is shown in Figure 3-4.

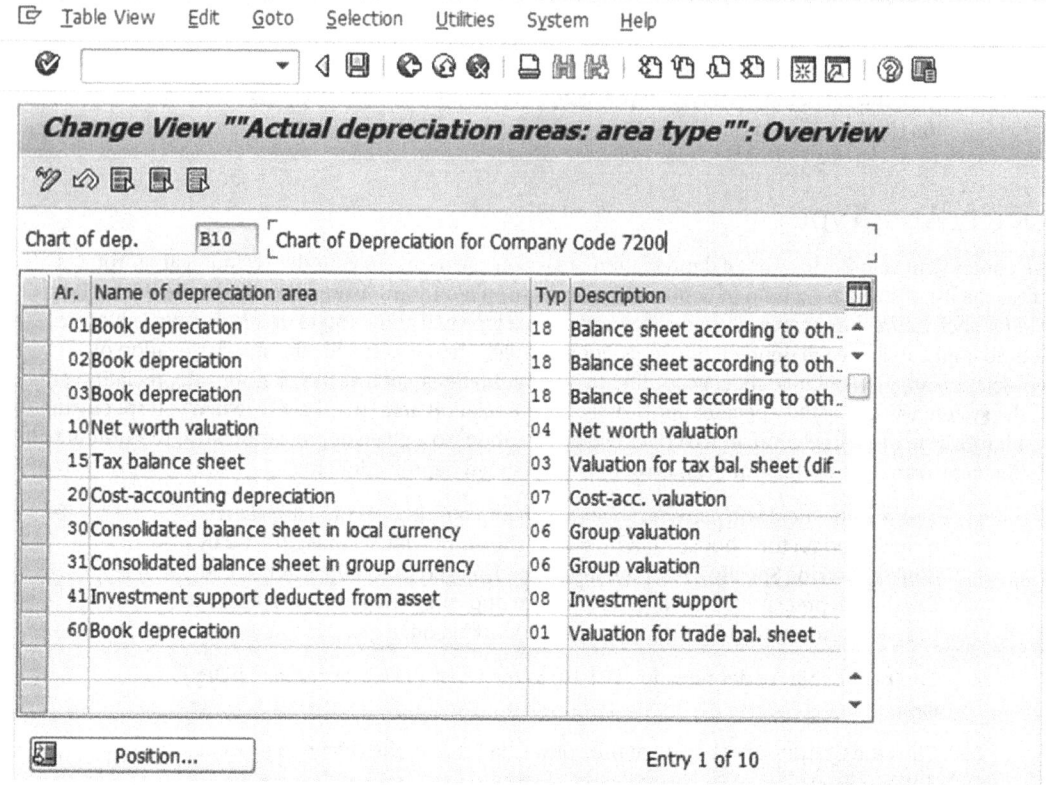

Figure 3-4. *The Change View ""Actual Depreciation Areas: Area Type"": Overview screen*

■ **Note**   On this screen, you will notice that the area types are defaulted. You can overwrite them by entering the area types of your choice in the type field.

You may not need to carry out any specifications in this activity because when you copied the standard chart of depreciation (1GB) for your country in Chapter 1, the area types for each depreciation areas were copied with the chart of depreciation.

Specify Transfer of APC Values

The standard system copies the asset balance sheet values from depreciation area 01 to all other depreciation areas during posting. (The only exceptions to this rule are areas for revaluation and for investment support, as well as derived depreciation areas.) Therefore, you only need to carry out this step if you want to copy posting values from a different depreciation area, *not* depreciation area 01.

In this step, you define transfer rules for posting acquisition values of depreciation areas. These transfer rules let you ensure that certain depreciation areas have identical acquisition values. For example, you can ensure that the depreciation areas holding foreign currency values use the same values in local currency.

In your customizing, you must ensure that of your country-specific chart of depreciation with the appropriate depreciation areas are defined based on the standard required transfer rules.

1. To go to the screen where you specify the transfer of APC values, use this menu path: IMG: Financial Accounting (New) ➤ Asset Accounting ➤ Valuation ➤ Depreciation Areas ➤ Specify Transfer of APC Values. The Change View "Depreciation areas: Rules for value takeover": Overview screen appears containing areas and chart of depreciation areas (see Figure 3-5).

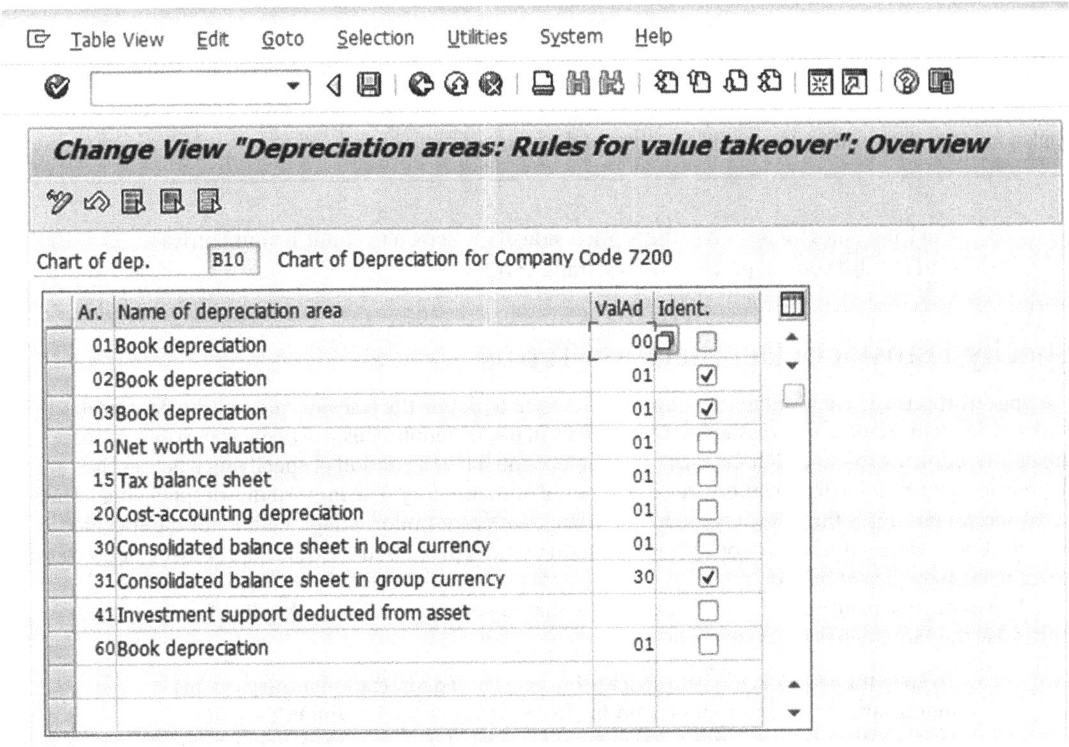

Figure 3-5. The Change View "Depreciation Areas: Rules for Value Takeover": Overview screen

2. Update the following fields:

    *   **ValAd:** This ensures that the acquisition costs are copied from a given depreciation area to the defined depreciation areas. For example, when you enter 01 as the acquisition value for book depreciation area 02, this will ensure that depreciation area 02 adopts the acquisition value from depreciation area 01.

■ **Note**   Depreciation area 31 (the consolidated balance sheet in group currency) should show depreciation area 30 (the consolidated balance sheet in local currency), so that they are valued uniformly to the book depreciation area. The only difference is the currency.

- **Ident.** By activating the identical check box, this will ensure that depreciation areas manage identical acquisition values.

■ **Note**   You may not need to carry out any specifications in this activity because when you copied the standard chart of depreciation for your country (1GB) in Chapter 1, the acquisition value transfer rules were copied for each depreciation areas with the chart of depreciation.

---

3.   Click the Enter ✅ button at the top-left side of the screen to confirm your entries and save 💾 your acquisition values' transfer rules.

Specify Transfer of Depreciation Terms

The specifications you carry out in this step will allow you to define the transfer rules for the depreciation terms of the depreciation areas assigned to your chart of depreciation. This will allow you to determine the depreciation area from which the terms are copied. You have the option of specifying whether the depreciation terms for a depreciation area are optional or mandatory. The importance of specifying transfer of depreciation terms is that it allows you to maintain identical or uniform depreciation for the specified depreciation areas, as you will not be able to maintain other depreciation terms for the copying depreciation areas in the asset master record.

As part of your customizing, you should ensure that the depreciation areas holding foreign currency values use the same values in the local currency.

1.   To go to the screen where you specify the transfer of depreciation terms, use this menu path: IMG: Financial Accounting (New) ➤ Asset Accounting ➤ Valuation ➤ Depreciation Areas ➤ Specify Transfer of Depreciation terms. The Change View "Depreciation Areas: Rules for Takeover of deprec. Terms": screen appears containing areas and chart of depreciation areas (see Figure 3-6).

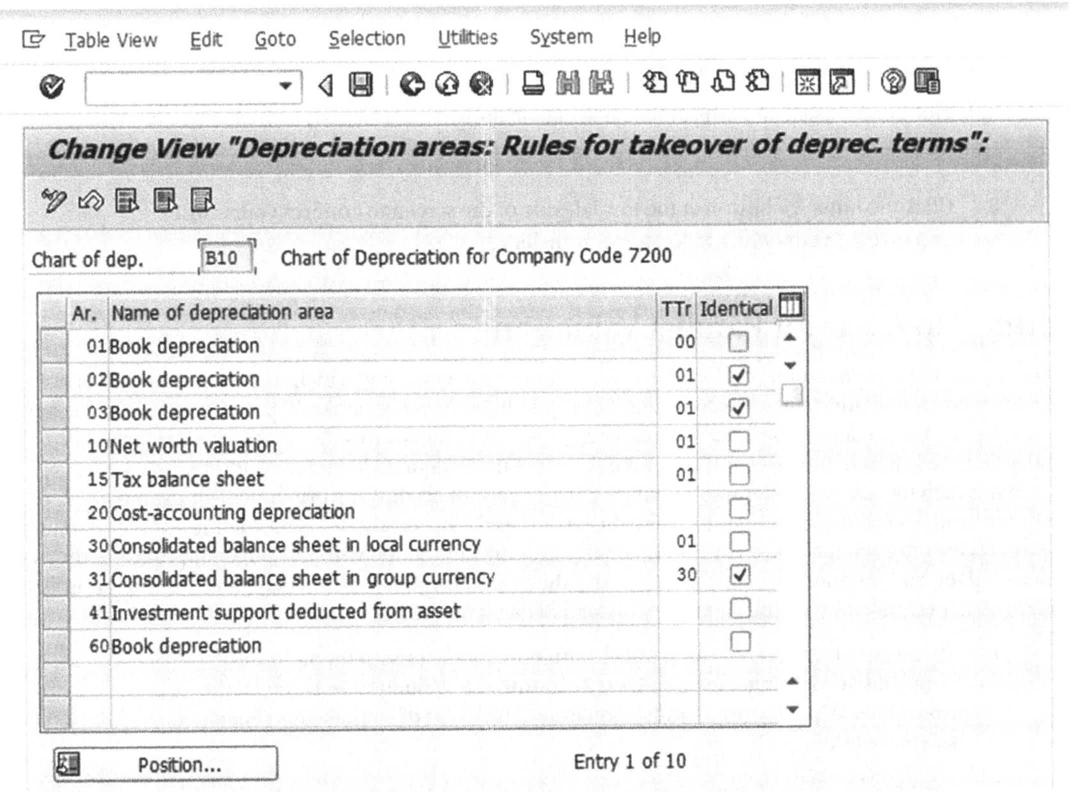

Figure 3-6. *The Change View "Depreciation Areas: Rules for Takeover of Deprec. Terms": screen*

2. Update the following fields:

- **TTr:** When you enter the depreciation area 01 (the primary depreciation area) in the depreciation term transfer field for other depreciation areas, the system will automatically copy the depreciation terms from area 01 to the specified areas.

■ **Note** The depreciation area 31 for consolidate balance sheet in group currency should show the depreciation area 30, so that they are valued uniformly to the book depreciation area. The only difference is the currency.

- **Identical:** The check box you activate will ensure that depreciation areas are managed in identical depreciation terms.

■ **Note**   You may not need to carry out any specifications in this activity because the standard chart of depreciation (1GB) for your country in Chapter 1. The area types for each depreciation area you copied holds the transfer rules for the depreciation terms of the depreciation areas.

---

3.   Click the Enter ✅ button at the top-left side of the screen to confirm your entries and save 💾 your depreciation terms transfer rules.

Setting Up Areas for Parallel Valuation

When setting parallel valuation you have to create additional accounting principles for one real and one derived depreciation area in asset accounting. The derived depreciation makes it possible to determine new asset value from a predetermined asset value. The derived depreciation applies mathematical formulas to ensure that the values of the asset subledger are the same in the general ledger accounting.

In this activity, you set up parallel valuation to meet certain accounting principles (for example, IAS or US GAAP) and disclosure requirements using the wizard tool. The wizard helps you define parallel valuation in asset accounting when you use the new general ledger in conjunction with the ledger approach in the new general ledger. You may not necessarily need to use the wizard if you have been using the account approach. You can also perform your settings manually instead of using the wizard.

1.   To create valuation areas for parallel valuation, follow this menu path: IMG: Financial Accounting (New) ➤ Asset Accounting ➤ Valuation ➤ Depreciation Areas ➤ Set Up Areas for Parallel Valuation. The Chart of Depreciation Selection screen pops up.

2.   Specify your chart of depreciation (B10) and click the Continue or Enter ✅ buttons at the bottom-left side of the screen to proceed to the wizard tool (the Set Up Parallel Valuation screen is shown in Figure 3-7).

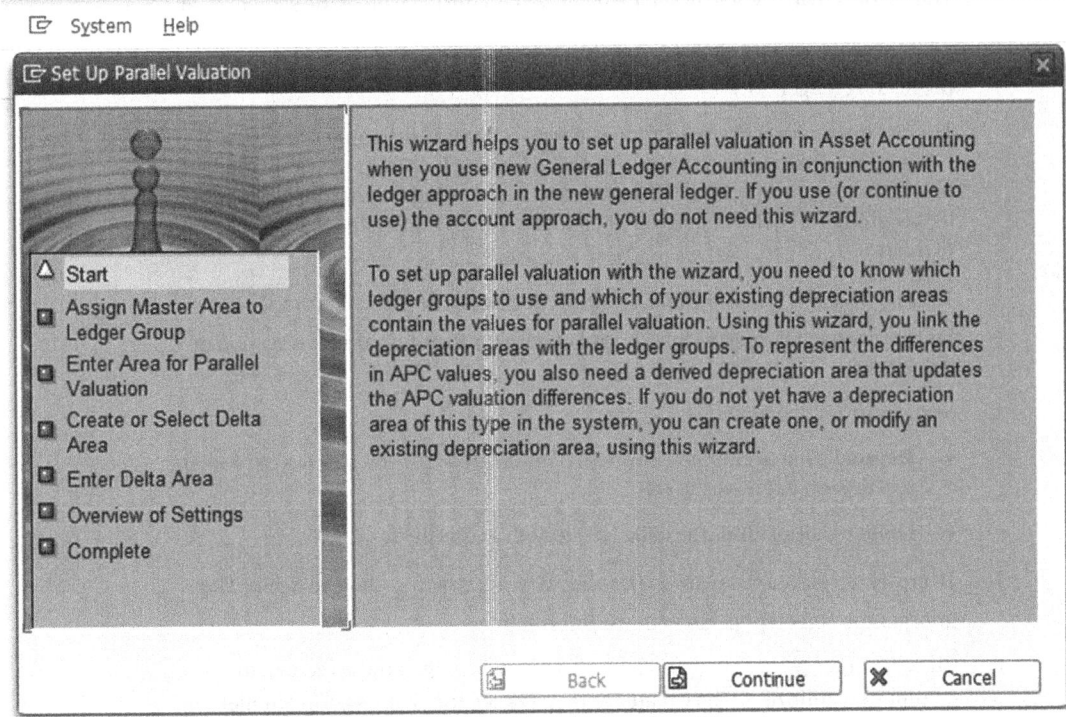

Figure 3-7. The initial wizard screen that will help you set up parallel valuation in asset accounting

---

■ **Note** Carefully read the note on the screen for further instructions on how to customize the settings for parallel valuation in asset accounting.

---

3. Click the Continue ⬛ Continue button at the bottom of the screen to assign a master area to the ledger group. The Control of Leading area of the Set Up Parallel Valuation screen comes up with this message:

    "Determine the chart of depreciation to be processed. For the leading depreciation area, you have to enter a ledger group that contains the leading ledger. If a ledger group with leading ledger is already set up, this is proposed. You change this assignment."

4. The list of activities you will set are displayed on the left side of the screen. Your chart of depreciation (B10) and the depreciation area (the master depreciation area 01) are defaulted by the system. Update the Ledger Group field by entering the leading ledger (0L).

    The bottom line is that you want to use the accounting principle LGAP (Local GAP) for the ledger group that contains the leading ledger. At the same time, use the accounting principle IAS (International Accounting Standards) for another ledger group for real and derived depreciation areas and assign the ledger group to them.

5. To enter areas for parallel valuation, click the Continue [⬚ Continue] button again to proceed to the Control of Area for Parallel Valuation section of the screen.

6. Update the following fields:

    • **Depreciation area:** Enter the depreciation area (30) you want to use for your real depreciation area in this field.

    • **Ledger group:** Enter the code (L5) for IAS in this field.

7. To create or select a delta area, click the [⬚ Continue] button again. The information screen pops up with the information.

8. Click the Enter [✔] button at the bottom-right side of the pop-up screen to continue customizing. The Create Delta Area? section of the Set Up Parallel Valuation screen comes up. This screen gives you the option to create new depreciation area or to using an existing depreciation area. Since in this activity you want to create the derived depreciation area, you will be creating a new depreciation area.

9. Select the Create New Depreciation Areas option and then click the [⬚ Continue] button. The Control of the Delta Area of the Set Up Parallel Valuation screen is displayed (see Figure 3-8). This is where you define your derived depreciation area.

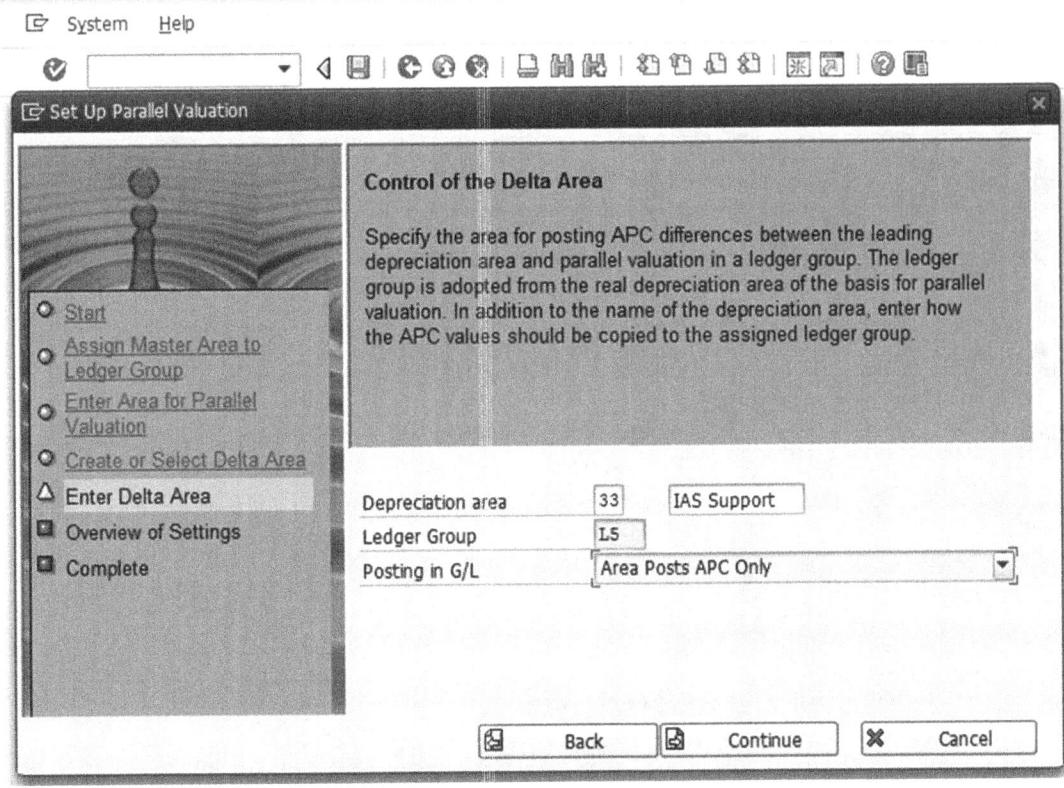

Figure 3-8. *The wizard screen where you specify the area for posting APC differences between the leading depreciation area and parallel valuation in a ledger group*

10. Update the following fields:

- **Depreciation area:** Enter a two-digit character you want to use as your derived depreciation area code (33) in this field and enter a short description that best describes your depreciation area. For example, IAS support.

- **Ledger group:** The ledger group (L5) is defaulted by the system. This is inherited from the settings on the Control of Area for Parallel Valuation section in the preceding setting.

- **Post in G/L:** The system defaults how APC should be copied to the assigned ledger group in this field. You can display the list of how the APC values should be copied to the assigned ledger group. However, we recommend that you stick to the default option (Area Post APC Only), as posting control is not allowed in the derived area.

11. Click the [🖫 Continue] button at the bottom of the screen and the Overview section of the Set Up Parallel Valuation screen comes up displaying your settings. See Figure 3-9.

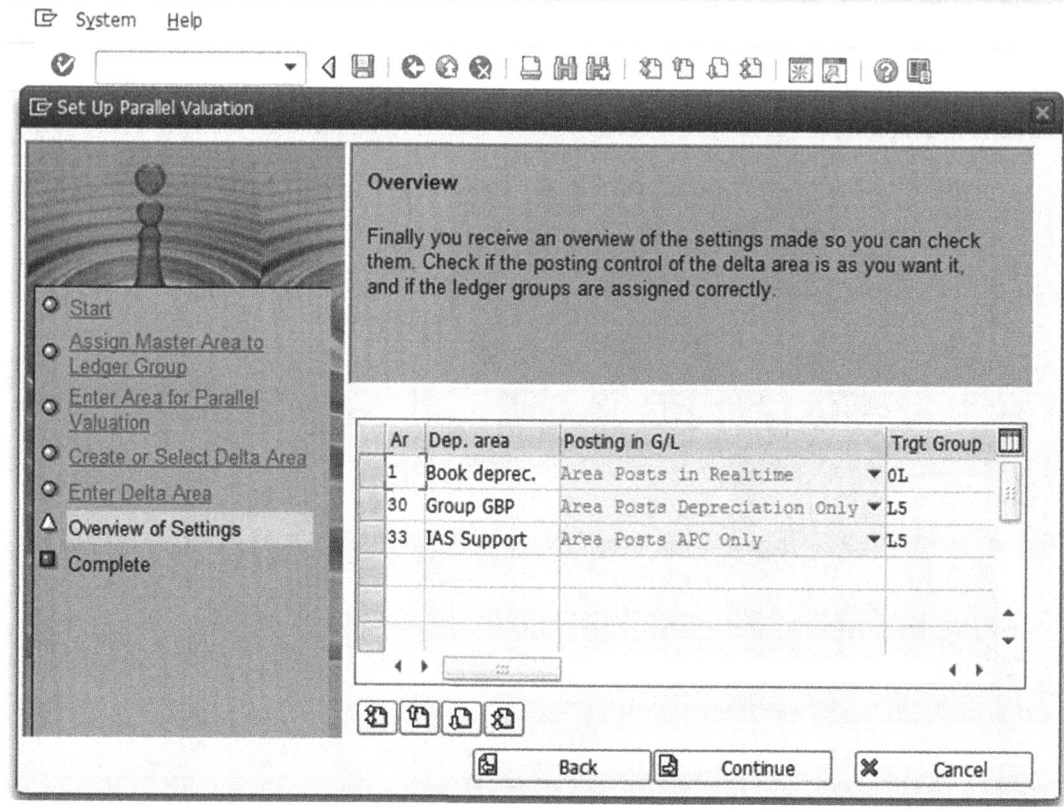

Figure 3-9. The wizard screen where you check your parallel valuation settings

12. If you're satisfied with the settings, click the [Continue] button. The complete section of the Set Up Parallel Valuation screen comes up with the following information "When you choose *Complete*, the settings you made are updated to the database."

The following additional modifications are made in the background:

- Posting control for the area for parallel valuation is set to Post Depreciation.

- The delta area updates real APC differences (no special depreciation logic).

- Both depreciation areas use the same accounts as the master depreciation area.

13. In certain cases, it might be necessary to change the intervals for depreciation posting and the other posting settings (transaction OAYR) of the depreciation area for parallel valuation in company code selection when defining posting rules. In addition, you should use report RAACCOBJ01 or transaction AACCOBJ to check if the account assignment types are maintained as you want for both depreciation areas.

14. Click the [Complete] button at the bottom of the screen. The Display IMG screen is displayed with a notification at the status bar at the bottom of the screen that the specification was saved.

Determining Depreciation Areas in the Asset Class

In this activity, you maintain the depreciation term for your asset class in the depreciation class. An asset in the asset class uses the same depreciation terms. The depreciation terms contain the depreciation key and the asset's useful life. The depreciation key holds the values needed for determining depreciation amount (depreciation key will be discussed in great detail in Chapter 4). The asset useful life is the estimated period an asset will be used for. Importantly, when you have maintained depreciation terms in the asset class, you do not have to maintain it again in the asset master record, rather they can be default values from the asset class.

1. To determine depreciation areas in the asset class, use this menu path: IMG: Financial Accounting (New) ➤ Asset Accounting ➤ Valuation ➤ Determine Depreciation Areas in the Asset Class. The Change View "Asset class": Overview screen is displayed. This screen contains the list of the asset classes.

2. Using the [⊞ Position...] button at the bottom-left side of the screen, search for your asset classes. Select the asset class you want to determine depreciation area (AS3000 Plant & Machinery) and double-click the Depreciation areas folder on the left pane of the screen. This will take you to the Change View "Depreciation Areas": Overview screen (see Figure 3-10). This screen contains the depreciation areas in the chart of depreciation that you assigned to the asset class for Plant and Machinery. On this screen, you will activate the depreciation areas you want to assign to the depreciation key and the asset's useful life, and specify the screen layout rule you are applying to each depreciation area. The screen layout dictates the field status in the asset master record. For example, the screen layout determines whether the input fields are required, are optional entry fields, or are suppressed.

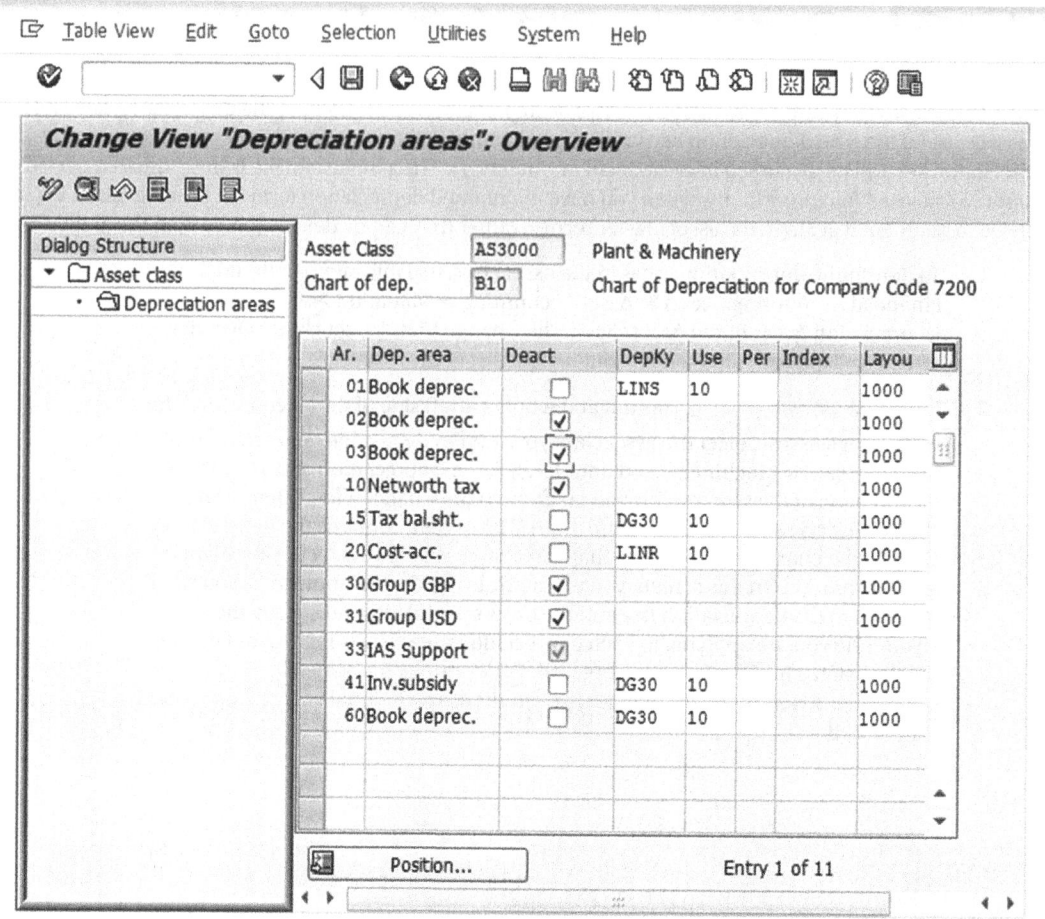

Figure 3-10. *The screen where you determine depreciation areas in the asset class*

3. Update the following items:

- **Deact:** Normally, the depreciation area is deactivated by the system automatically, so you should activate the book depreciation that you want to apply the depreciation terms. For this activity, activate the following depreciation areas by removing unchecking their check boxes:

    01 Book depreciation

    15 Tax balance sheet

    20 Cost accounting

    41 Investment subsidy

    60 Book depreciation

- **DepKy:** Enter the depreciation key you want the depreciation term to apply to each of the depreciation area in your asset class. SAP comes with standard depreciation keys you can use. You can access the list of supplied depreciation keys by SAP by using the matchcode by the depreciation key field. It is also possible to define your own depreciation key. We will be looking at defining depreciation keys and the various forms of depreciation methods in Chapter 4 when you learn to define the depreciation key.

- **Use:** Enter the useful economic life of the asset in this field. For example, it is assumed that you will use an asset for 10 years, after which point you will discontinue its use.

- **Layout:** Specify the screen layout (1000). SAP comes with a standard screen layout that you can use.

4. Click the Enter 🔘 button at the top-left side of the screen to confirm your entries and save 💾 your customizing.

Deactivating the Asset Class for the Chart of Depreciation

This function serves as control mechanism, as it allows you to lock asset classes for the chart of depreciation. For example, the asset class that you do not want to use can be locked and then unlocked at any time.

To deactivate asset class for chart of depreciation, use this menu path: IMG: Financial Accounting (New) ➤ Asset Accounting ➤ Valuation ➤ Determine Depreciation Areas in the Asset Class. The Change View "Lock Asset Class for Chart of Depreciation": Overview screen is comes up, displaying the list of asset classes in the system. Using the position button at the bottom of the screen, search for the asset class that you want to lock. Deactivate it by making sure that the Lock check box that's assigned to the asset class for the chart of depreciation is checked.

Amount Specifications (Company Code/Depreciation Area)

In this activity, you will customize these specifications for your company code and the depreciation area:

- Specify the maximum amount for low-value assets and asset classes
- Round the net book value and/or depreciation
- Specify memo value

Specify the Maximum Amount for Low-Value Assets and Asset Classes

In this step, you will carry out two specifications. First, you will specify what you consider to be the maximum amount for low-value assets (LVAs) and the maximum amount for LVAs for your company code. Based on your specifications, when you post asset acquisitions, the system will automatically check the maximum amount for LVAs against the value posted for LVAs.

To specify the maximum amount for LVAs and asset classes, use this menu path: IMG: Financial Accounting (New) ➤ Asset Accounting ➤ Valuation ➤ Amount Specifications (Company Code/ Depreciation Area) ➤ Specify Max. Amount for Low-Value Assets and Asset Classes. The Choose Activity screen appears, displaying the two specification options—Specify LVA Asset Classes and Specify Amount for Low Value Assets.

Specify LVA Asset Classes

The specification you carry out in this step will allow the system to check for low-value asset amounts and perform quantity checks.

1. On the Choose Activity screen, select Specify LVA Asset Classes from the displayed options and click the ⌗ Choose button at the bottom-right side of the screen. The Change View "Asset Class": Overview screen appears, displaying the list of asset classes in the system.

2. Using the button at the bottom of the screen, call up the asset class for the LVA asset (AS7000) that you defined in Chapter 1 in the "Asset Classes" section. Select your asset class and double-click the Low-Val. Asset check in the asset class, which is on the left pane of the screen. The Change View "Low-Val. Asset Check": Overview screen is displayed, as shown in Figure 3-11.

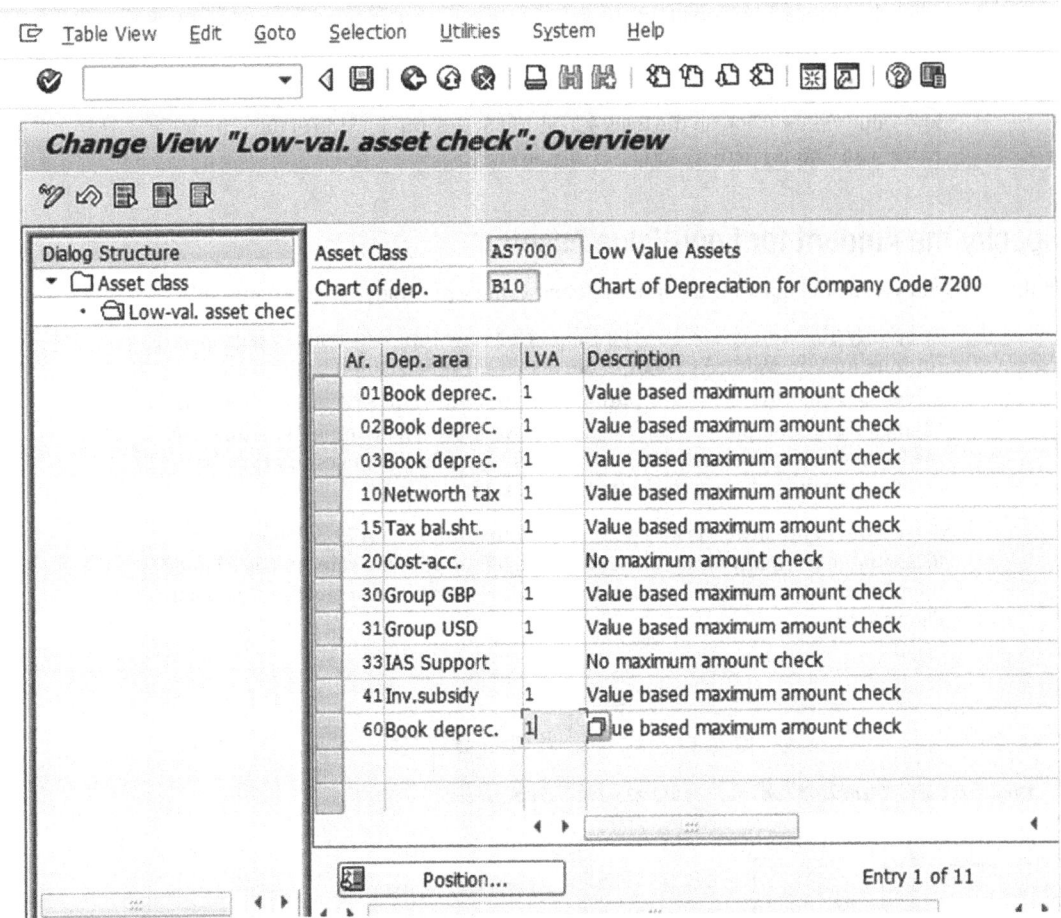

Figure 3-11. *The screen where you specify how you want the system to carry out the system maximum amount check for low-value assets*

3. Specify how you want the system to carry out the maximum amount check for the low-value asset. SAP comes with a standard low-val. check that you can choose from:

- **0 - No maximum amount check:** When you use this specification, no maximum check will be carried out by the system.

- **1 - Value based maximum amount check:** When you use this specification, the system will carry out a low-value asset check based on the asset acquisition amount.

- **2 - Check maximum amount with quantity:** When you use this specification, the system will perform a low-value asset check based on the asset quantity.

4. Click the Enter ✅ button at the top-left side of the screen to confirm your entries and save 💾 your customizing.

5. You now need to return to the Choose Activity screen to specify the amount for low-value assets. Click on the Back 🔙 button at the top-left side of the screen twice. The Choose Activity screen is displayed.

Specify the Amount for Low-Value Assets

In this step, you specify the maximum amount for low-value assets for your company code.

1. To specify the amount for low-value assets for your company code, select Specify Amount for Low-Value Assets from the displayed specification options on the screen and click the 🔲 Choose button at the bottom-right side of the screen. The Change View "Company Code Selection": Overview screen appears, displaying the list of company codes in the system. You can call up your company code (7200) using the button at the bottom of the screen.

2. Select your company code and double-click the Amount for Low-Value Assets folder in the company code selection on the left pane of the screen. The Change View "Amount for Low-Value Assets": Overview screen is displayed, as shown in Figure 3-12.

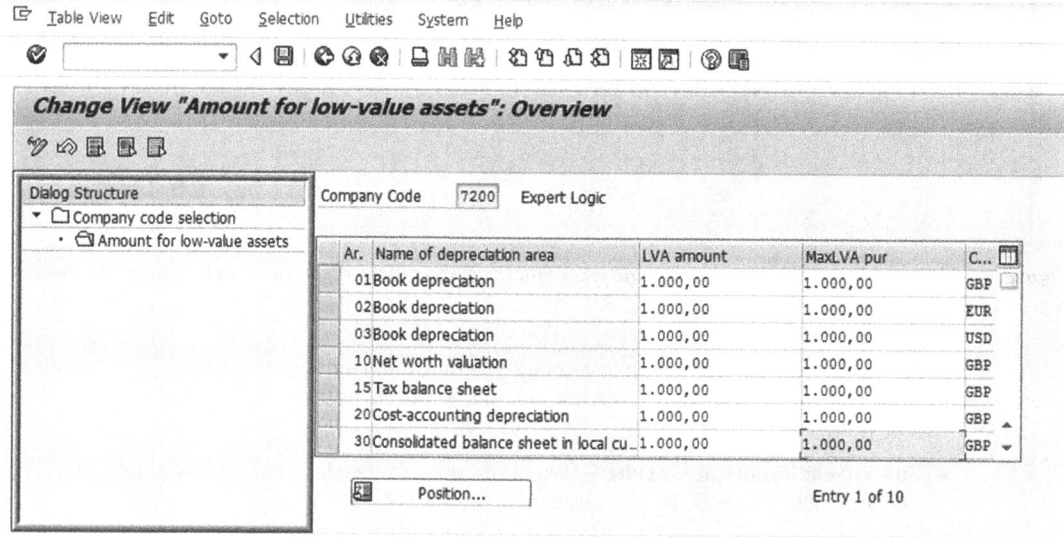

Figure 3-12. *The screen where you specify the minimum and maximum amount for low-value assets*

3. Specify your low-value amount for each depreciation area and the maximum low-value amount purchase for each depreciation area. You can use the specifications in Figure 3-12 as a guide.

4. Click the Enter ✅ button at the top-left side of the screen to confirm your entries and save 💾 your specifications.

Specify Rounding of Net Book Value and/or Depreciation

Two specifications are carried out in this activity. One for each company code and the other for each depreciation area. This specification will allow you to determine how the system will round decimal places for the net book values at year end and carry out the determination of automatic depreciation and replacement value for each depreciation area and each company code.

1.   To specify rounding of decimal places in the net book value, use this menu path: IMG: Financial Accounting (New) ➤ Asset Accounting ➤ Valuation ➤ Amount Specifications (Company Code/Depreciation Area) ➤ Specify Rounding of Net Book Value and/or Depreciation. The "Document Lines: Display Messages" screen appears, displaying a list of inconsistent rounding entries that were automatically corrected by the system (see Figure 3-13).

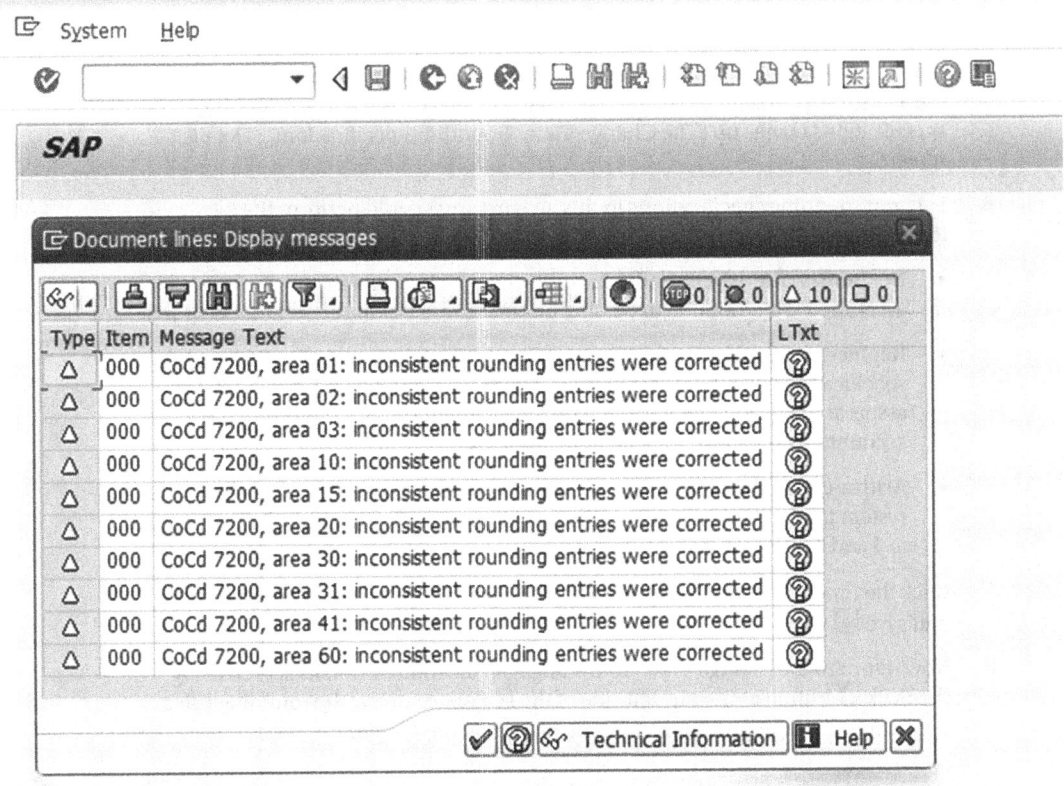

Figure 3-13.   *The screen displaying corrections to be made by the system to correct the rounding of decimal places for the Net Book Value*

2. Click the Continue ✅ button at the bottom of the screen to accept the proposed corrections to be made by the system for each of the depreciation areas for your company code. The Information screen pops up with a message that says "Changes have to be saved first".

3. Click the Continue ✅ button at the bottom-right side of the pop-up screen to initiate the saving process. The Change View "Company Code Selection": Overview screen appears displaying the company codes.

4. Using the [🔲 Position...] button at the bottom of screen, search for your company code (7200). Select your company code and double-click the Rounding Specifications folder on the left pane of the screen. The Change View "Rounding Specifications ": Overview screen appears displaying the depreciation areas for your company code.

5. The next step is to activate the rounding specifications for each of the depreciation areas. First, select the depreciation area (01 – Book depreciation) from the displayed list of depreciation areas. Click the Details 🔳 button at the top-left side of the screen. The screen where you will carry out your rounding specifications comes up (The Change View "Rounding specifications": Details screen).

6. For your rounding specifications in this activity, you should perform the following specifications:

   • **Net book value at year end:** This indicator specifies that net book value of an asset should be rounded to whole units of currency at the end of the fiscal year.

   • **Replacement value:** Select the check box for replacement value. This specification will allow the system to perform automatic rounding of fixed assets at the replacement value. The replacement value is important for cost accounting or to determine insurance values.

   • **Arithmetic Rounding:** Select the Arithmetic Value check box. This allows the system to automatically determine rounding rules. For example, 5.49 is rounded to 5 and 5.50 is rounded to 6.

7. Click the Enter ✅ button at the top-left side of the screen to confirm your entries and save 💾 your specifications.

8. Now return to the Change View "Rounding Specifications": Details screen using the Back ↩ button at the top-left side of the screen to specify the rounding rules for the remaining depreciation areas displayed on the screen.

Specify Memo Value

In this activity, you can specify the memo value for depreciation areas and specify asset classes without a memo value for each depreciation area for your company code. The memo value is the value that is not depreciated, so that memo posting for an asset that has already exceeded its planned useful life can be made. The planned depreciation per annum is the year that the asset is acquired and it's reduced by the memo value by the system.

You can access the screen where you can specify memo value using this menu path: IMG: Financial Accounting (New) ➤ Asset Accounting ➤ Valuation ➤ Amount Specifications (Company Code/ Depreciation Area) ➤ Specify Memo Value. You specify that asset classes without a memo value not be taken into account by using the indicator in the asset class.

We recommend that you not manage memo values, because the memo value functions are provided for the management of memo values from a previous system in FI-AA. Secondly, the system often takes the gross values into consideration and does not just adjust the remaining asset book value. This allows fully depreciated assets with a 0 book value to be disclosed legally in the balance sheet. The gross value is the asset acquisition amount and the adjusted amount. However, if you the specify memo value, it is compulsory that you make sure all the related assets have equivalent book value amounts as the memo value.

Defining the Fiscal Year

The *fiscal year* is normally your company code accounting year or annual accounting period. A *fiscal year variant* defines your company's accounting posting periods. A proper business accounting transaction normally covers a 12-month period. The normal rule is that business transactions are assigned to the period during which the transaction took place. The fiscal year variant is customized to match your company's fiscal year, which does not necessarily have to be the same as the normal calendar year (that is, January to December). SAP ERP is dynamic enough to fit into your company's calendar or fiscal year. For details on how to define the fiscal year, refer to our book entitled *SAP ERP Financial Accounting and Controlling Configuration and Use Management*.

In this activity, you'll make specifications for the fiscal year in asset accounting. You can define a different fiscal year for calculating depreciation in asset accounting from the FI fiscal year. You will look at how to specify other versions on company code levels and specify other versions on depreciation area levels.

To specify the fiscal year variant for asset accounting, use this menu path: Accounting (New) ➤ Asset Accounting ➤ Valuation ➤ Fiscal Year ➤ Fiscal Year Variants.

Specify Other Versions on Company Code Levels

In this step, you carry out the specifications of the fiscal year version for asset accounting on your company code only if the fiscal year you are applying to your asset accounting is different from your general ledger in FI's fiscal year. In practice, it is rare to use different fiscal years for asset accounting and for the general ledger in FI.

To access the specification of other versions on the company code level, use this menu path: Accounting (New) ➤ Asset Accounting ➤ Valuation ➤ Fiscal Year ➤ Fiscal Year Variants ➤ Specify Other Version on Company Code Level. The Change View "FI-AA Fiscal year version for company code": Overview screen appears. This is the screen where you assign the fiscal year variant for asset accounting to the general ledger in FI for your company code. Search for your company code from the displayed list of company codes (7200) by clicking the ⬛ Position... button at the bottom of the screen. Update the following field:

> **FV:** This is the field where you specify the fiscal year version of your asset accounting to the general ledger in FI. This specification will allow the system to use the specified fiscal year variant for posting asset values to the general ledger in FI. We advise that you leave this field blank, which means the system will automatically use the fiscal year variant you assigned to your company code in FI.

Specify Other Versions on Depreciation Area Levels

In this step, you assign the fiscal year version to each depreciation area for your company code. This specification will allow the system to apply the specified fiscal year to each depreciation area differently from the fiscal version for your company code.

To access the screen where you perform the specification, use this menu path: Accounting (New) ➤ Asset Accounting ➤ Valuation ➤ Fiscal Year ➤ Fiscal Year Variants ➤ Specify Other Version on Depreciation Area Level. The Change View "Company codes": Overview screen appears displaying the company codes in the system. Search for your company code (7200) from the list of the displayed company codes. Select your company code and double-click the Fiscal Year folder on the left pane of the screen. The Change View "Fiscal Year Variant": Overview screen appears displaying the depreciation areas defined for your company code. Update the following field:

> **Fyear version:** Enter the fiscal year version you want to apply for posting asset values to the general ledger in FI. You can access the fiscal year versions already in the system using the depreciation area's matchcode. We recommend that you leave this field blank for this activity. By leaving this field blank, the system will automatically use the fiscal year variant you assigned to your company code in FI.

Specifying Currencies in Asset Accounting

The currencies are represented in the SAP ERP company code currency and additional currency (parallel currency). In FI, you specify that the currency ledgers be managed for each company code. The currency for company code is often referred to as local currency or the national currency of the company code. All other currencies other than the company code currency are referred to as foreign currencies from the company code view. Foreign currencies allow you to manage ledgers in two parallel currencies (namely, group currency and hard currency) in conjunction with your company code currency. Group currency is used for consolidated financial reports and hard currency is used in countries with high inflation rates.

In this activity, you will define a depreciation area for foreign currencies for the valuation of fixed assets on the level of asset accounting and specify the use of parallel currencies for the legal consolidation of your fixed assets.

Define Depreciation Areas for Foreign Currencies

To manage asset values in a foreign currency FI-AA, it is important to define depreciation areas for foreign currencies. In asset accounting, you can manage depreciation areas in any currency specifically on group currency. This enables you to meet certain legal disclosure requirements relating to the legal consolidation of the corporate group activities and for the corporate group consolidation of financial statements. Particularly when the valuation of assets at the group level is completely different from the company code valuation, it is recommended that you use a separate depreciation area for group currency for coordinating the group activities and for historical management of values.

1. To define depreciation areas for foreign currencies, use this menu path: Accounting (New) ➤ Asset Accounting ➤ Valuation ➤ Currencies ➤ Define Depreciation Areas for Foreign Currencies. The Change View "Company Code Selection": Overview screen is displayed containing the list of company codes existing in the system.

2. To access the screen where you specify the currencies for each depreciation area, select your company code from the list of displayed company codes and double-click the Depreciation Area Currency folder in the Company Code selection on the left pane of the screen. The Change View "Depreciation Area Currency": Overview screen is displayed (see Figure 3-14) containing a list of depreciation areas for your company code.

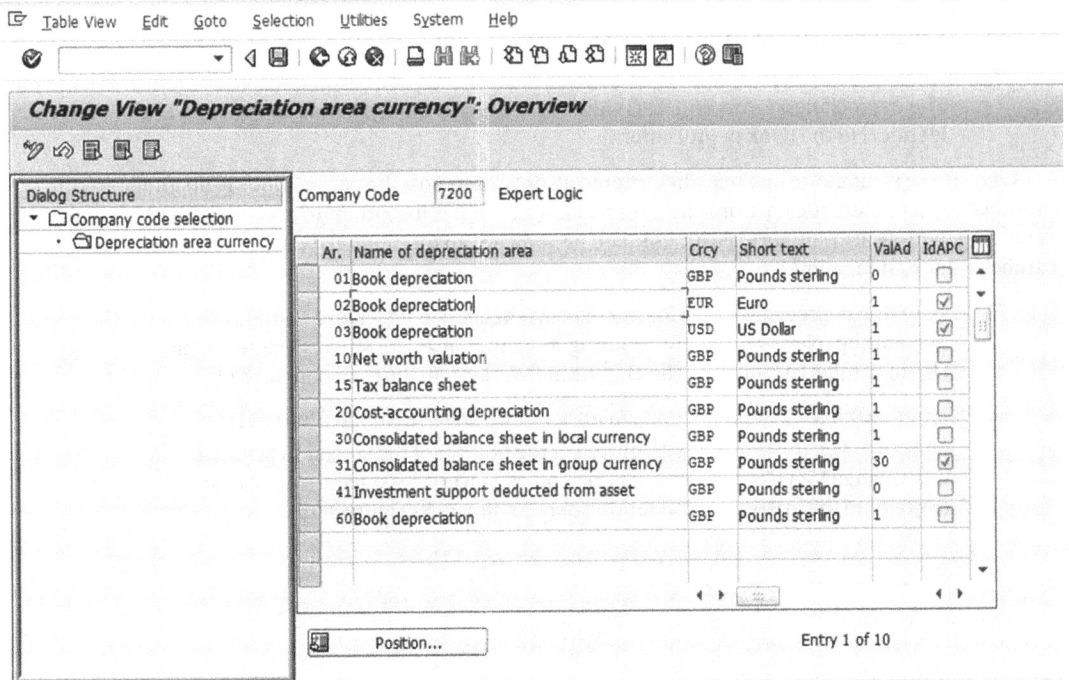

Figure 3-14. *The screen where you define depreciation area for foreign currencies*

3. Enter the currency you want to apply to each depreciation area in the Crcy (currency) field.

4. Click the Enter ⊘ button at the top-left side of the screen to confirm your entries and save 🖫 your specifications.

Specify the Use of Parallel Currencies

You can specify parallel currencies in addition to the company code currency in the asset accounting module. The foreign currency specifications can be used for the legal consolidation of fixed assets. Your specifications in this activity will allow you to post asset values within asset accounting and, at the same time, update values in several currencies. You can also make postings simultaneously in the FI document in parallel with the posted amount in the company code currency in FI. The following settings must be in place for this function to work effectively:

- The parallel currency you assigned to your company code must have the same currency type and the same currency of the depreciation area.

- The depreciation terms and APC values managed in the depreciation area must be identical to the book depreciation.

When these settings are in place, the system will be able to post the corresponding documents with additional values automatically from each depreciation area. It is important to note that the SAP asset accounting module also supports postings made periodically to the general ledger in FI (i.e., parallel currencies not posted online).

1. To define depreciation area for foreign currencies, use this menu path: Accounting (New) ➤ Asset Accounting ➤ Valuation ➤ Currencies ➤ Specify the Use of Parallel Currencies. The Determine Work Area: Entry screen pops up.

2. Enter the chart of depreciation you are working on (B10) in the Chart of Dep. field and click the Continue ✅ button at the bottom of the screen to proceed. The Change View "Set Up Parallel Currencies": Overview screen is displayed containing the existing depreciation areas, as shown in Figure 3-15.

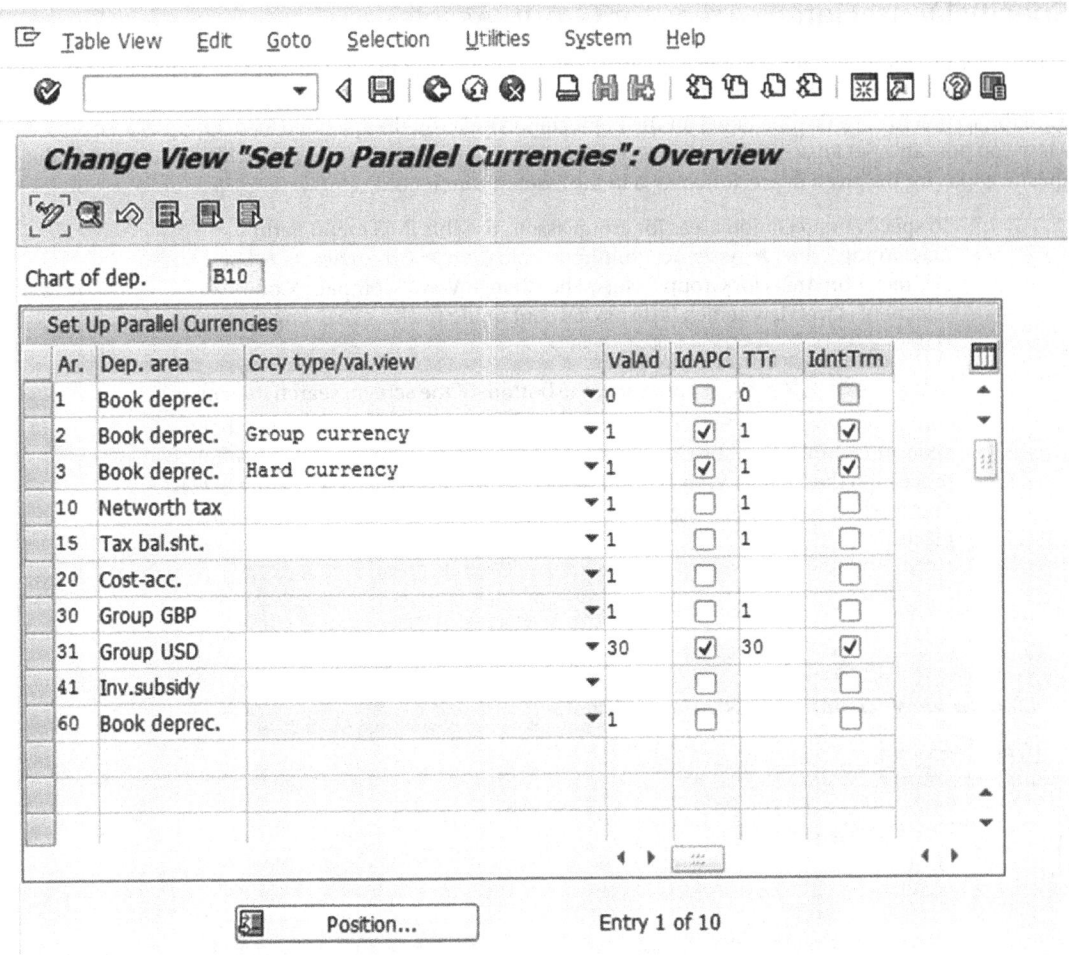

Figure 3-15. *The screen where you specify the use of parallel currencies for the depreciation area*

3. The system defaults the settings in this activity. Make sure the settings meet your requirements.

4. Click the Enter ✅ button at the top-left side of the screen to confirm your entries and save 🖫 your specifications.

Defining Group Assets

Depreciation calculation and posting of depreciation normally takes place at the level of individual assets. In some countries it is important to carry out special calculations to meet certain tax requirements. For example, in the United States certain tax reporting requirements are compulsory. Hence, these settings will be ideal for calculating depreciation at a higher level. To achieve this objective, you can group assets together into asset groups. For example, assets can be grouped together per depreciation area.

In this activity, you will be looking how to specify depreciation areas for group assets and how to specify asset classes for group assets.

Specify Depreciation Areas for Group Assets

In this activity, you specify the depreciation areas you want to assign to a group asset. This specification will allow you to determine the depreciation areas you want to manage on the asset group level. You may want the system to copy the line items for the depreciation areas on the specified asset group of asset, when you post an asset an acquisition to the related asset, but you first have to make this assignment in the specifications for the given depreciation area in the asset master record.

1. To specify depreciation areas for group assets, use this IMG menu path: Accounting (New) ➤ Asset Accounting ➤ Valuation ➤ Group Assets ➤ Specify Depreciation Areas for Group Assets. The Change View "Company Code selection": Overview screen is displayed containing the list of existing company codes.

2. Using the [Position...] button at the bottom of the screen, search for your company code (7200). Select your company code from the displayed company code and double-click the Group Assets folder in the Company code selection to proceed to the Change View "Group Assets": Overview screen (see Figure 3-16). This is where the actual assignment of group assets to depreciation areas takes place.

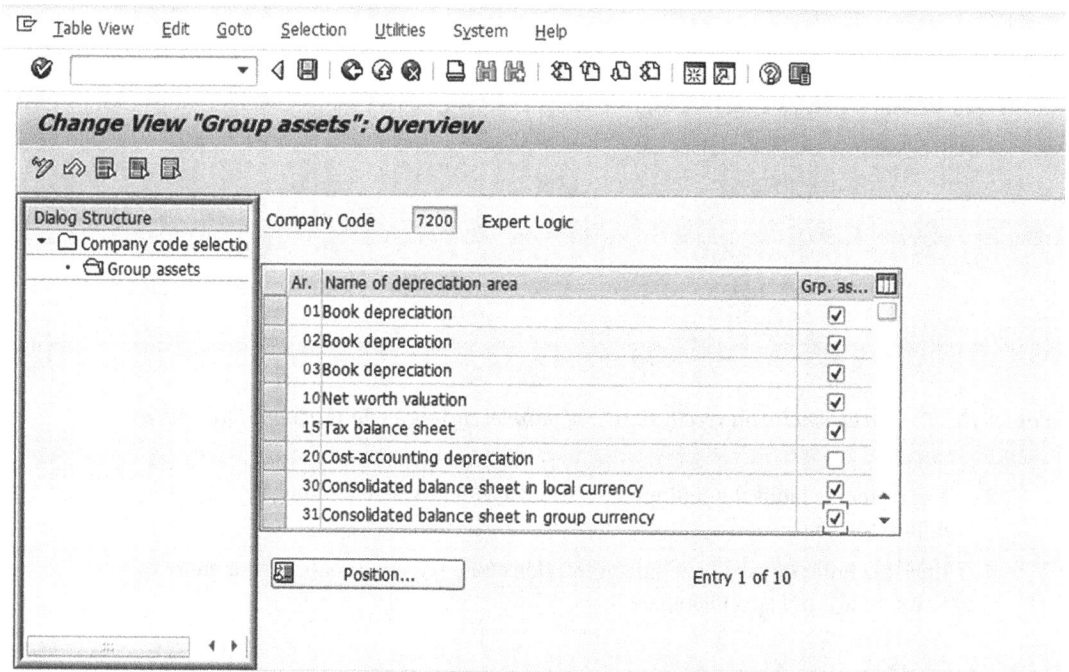

Figure 3-16. *The screen where you determine the depreciation areas you want to apply to group assets*

3.   Specify the book depreciation areas you want to apply to group assets by selecting the asset group of your choice. You can use the screen (Figure 3-16) as a guide.

4.   Click the Enter ✅ button at the top-left side of the screen to confirm your entries and save 💾 your specifications.

Specify Asset Classes for Group Assets

You may reserve some special assets specifically for group assets (i.e., set aside certain asset classes to be used in conjunction with group assets). The assets you specify for group assets in this activity cannot be used for normal assets.

To specify asset classes for group assets, use this menu path: Accounting (New) ➤ Asset Accounting ➤ Valuation ➤ Group Assets ➤ Specify Asset Classes for Group Assets. The Change View "Asset Class: Indicator for group assets only": Overview screen is displayed containing the list of existing asset classes in the system. Using the ▣ Position... button at the bottom of the screen, you can search for your asset classes. To specify certain asset classes for group assets, you should click the Class Consists Entirely of Group Assets check box shown in Figure 3-17 for the asset classes in question. For this activity, we recommend you leave the Class Consists Entirely of Group Assets check box unchecked (as shown in Figure 3-17).

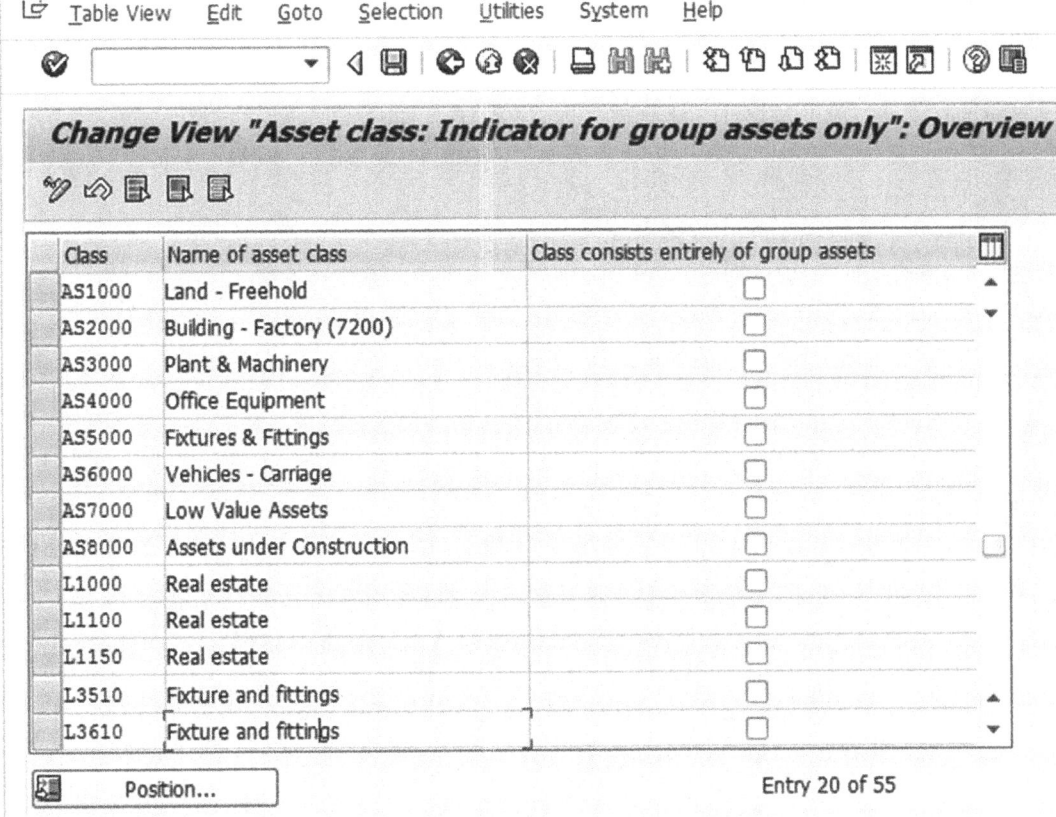

Figure 3-17. *The screen where you can activate asset classes for group assets*

Summary

This chapter looked the steps involved in the configuration of the valuation of fixed assets in asset accounting and explained the steps involved in defining depreciation areas for foreign currencies. In the process, you looked at how to set a chart of depreciation and the benefits of a chart of depreciation. You then learned about the customizing of depreciation areas. As part of the customizing steps involved in defining depreciation areas, you looked at how to specify area types for depreciation areas, specify transfer of APC values, and transfer of depreciation terms. We also showed you how to set up areas for parallel valuation using the wizard tool. Using the wizard tool, you saw how to assign a master area to a ledger group, enter an area for parallel valuation, create or select a delta area and, finally, saw the settings needed to carry out parallel valuation. We also took you through the steps involved in the amount specifications for your company code and depreciation areas by specifying maximum amount for low-value assets classes, rounding of netbook value, and specifying memo values.

As part of the valuation of fixed asset accounting configuration, we explained what fiscal year is and looked at how to define additional fiscal year variants in asset accounting at the depreciation level. You looked at how currencies are represented in the system and learned about depreciation area for foreign currencies, specifically the use of parallel currencies. Finally, you looked at how to specify depreciation areas for foreign currencies and asset classes for group assets.

In the next chapter, you will look at the configuration of depreciation in asset accounting. You will look at how to define ordinary depreciation, special depreciation unplanned depreciation, the valuation methods, and posting control. Further settings in asset depreciation include the definition of the cut-off value key, maximum base value, and the asset-specific base value percentages.

CHAPTER 4

■ ■ ■

Depreciation

This chapter explains the steps involved in configuring and defining depreciation in asset accounting. In this chapter, you will learn how to:

- Define ordinary depreciation

- Define special depreciation

- Understand planned and unplanned depreciation

- Define valuation methods

- Define a depreciation key

- Define the cutoff value key

- Specify asset-specific base value percentages

Defining Depreciation

Depreciation is simply a technical reduction in the book value of an asset due to wear and tear arising from its use over a period of time (often referred to as the useful economic life [UEL] of the asset). The UEL of an asset is the estimated period that the asset will be used. For example, the UEL of an asset may be 5 years, 15 years, or 20 years, etc. The UEL of an asset is determined based on the nature of the asset. Simply put, depreciation sets a fractional amount aside systematically over the UEL of the asset based on the asset's value.

The money set aside is often referred to as depreciation. Depreciation is treated in the accounts as an expense and it reduces the profit for the fiscal year. The depreciation you set aside annually is accumulated for the UEL and it is often referred to as provision for depreciation or accumulated depreciation. The essence of provision for depreciation is setting money aside for the replacement of the asset at the end of its UEL. When calculating depreciation, the various factors are taken into consideration: The value of the asset, the UEL of the asset and the expected value of the asset at the end of its UEL (scrap value). Depreciation calculation can be performed using various methods. For example, there is straight-line method, declining or reducing balancing depreciation, sum of the digit depreciation, etc. This section describes the types of depreciation supported by SAP ERP.

Planned Depreciation

Planned depreciation reduces the value of the asset systematically over a given planned period. This could be one month, one year, etc. The idea behind this concept is to depreciate the value of the asset systematically over its UEL based on plan defined parameters. This method will allow you to ascertain the value of the asset at any time during the economic life of the asset. Typical examples of planned depreciation are *ordinary depreciation* and *special depreciation*.

Ordinary Depreciation

Ordinary depreciation is the planned reduction of a specified given period. When customizing ordinary depreciation, you determine depreciation areas in which you want to manage ordinary depreciation and the general ledger accounts in which the ordinary depreciation is posted.

Determining Depreciation Areas

In this activity, you specify the depreciation areas you want to apply to ordinary depreciation. The value you specify in this step will be applicable to the respective depreciation area. When you enter corresponding depreciation terms in the asset master record, the system will not will issue an error message.

To determine depreciation areas for ordinary depreciation, use this menu path: IMG: Financial Accounting (New) ➤ Asset Accounting ➤ Depreciation ➤ Ordinary Depreciation ➤ Determine Depreciation Areas. The Change View "Specify Depreciation Areas for Ordinary Depreciation": Overview screen appears (Figure 4-1). It contains the list of depreciation areas you defined in Chapter 3 when defining depreciation areas.

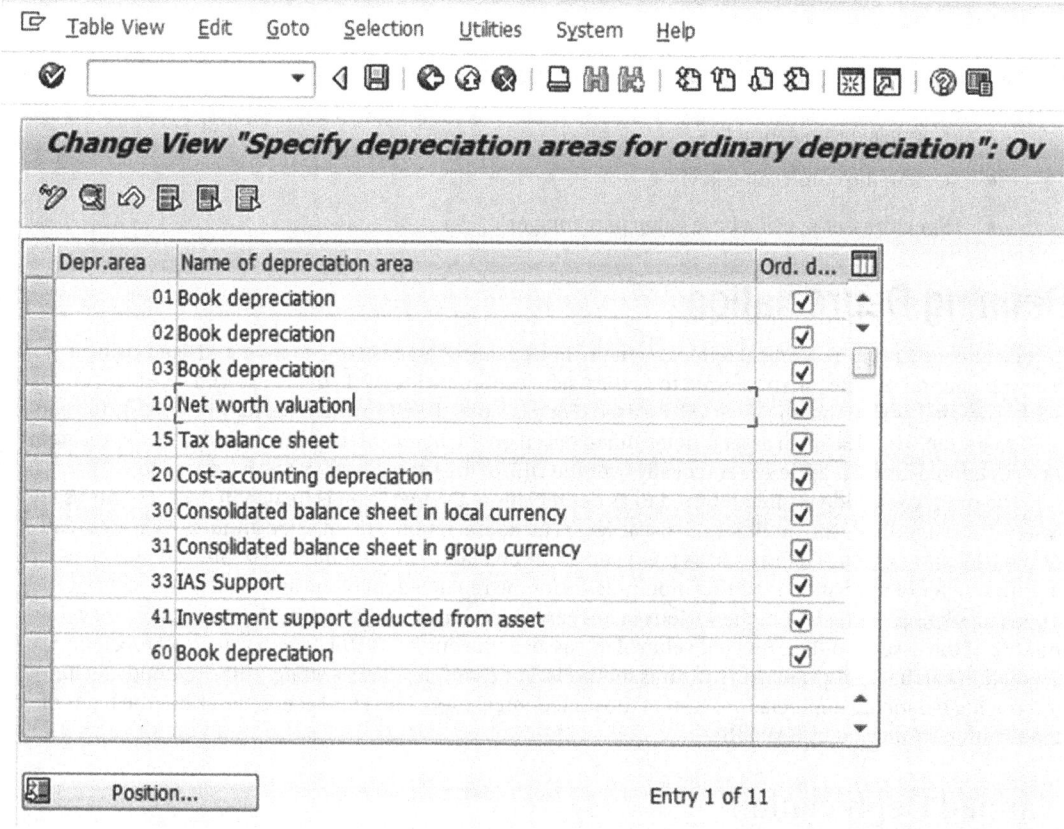

Figure 4-1. *The specification of depreciation areas for ordinary depreciation*

Specify the depreciation areas you want to manage in ordinary depreciation by clicking the Ord. Depreciation check boxes on the right side of the screen as shown in Figure 4-1. The next step in this activity is to determine the rule for the positive and negative amounts the ordinary depreciation is allowed to have in each depreciation area.

To proceed to the screen where you will carry out the specifications for the respective depreciation area, select a depreciation area (for example, 01 Book depreciation) from the list area and click the Details 🔍 button on the top-left side of the screen. The Change View "Specify Depreciation Areas for Ordinary Depreciation": Detail screen (Figure 4-2) is displayed. It contains four rules for positive/negative signs for ordinary depreciation options you can choose from. The system will automatically default to the Only Negative Values and Zero Allowed options. This option ensures that only negative depreciation amounts are allowed in the depreciation area in question if you want to calculate the negative depreciation or positive APC.

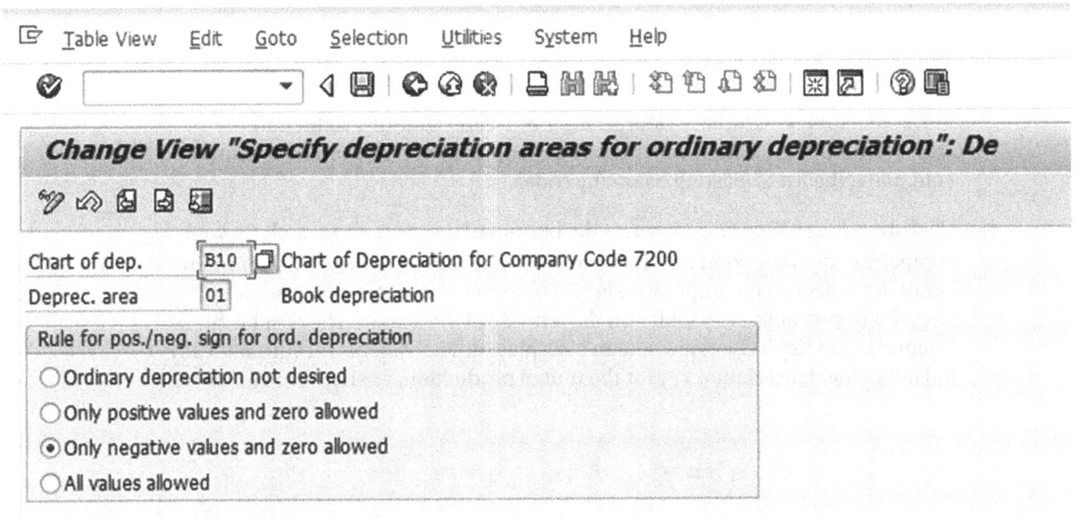

Figure 4-2. specification of the rule for positive/negative sign for ordinary depreciation

You can override the defaults by simply specifying the option(s) of your choice based on the requirements of your company. For example, if you want to calculate the positive depreciation of a positive APC, you can specify "Only Positive Values and Zero Allowed" as the rule. This specification will then allow the system to ensure that only positive depreciation amounts are allowed in the depreciation area.

Likewise, if you choose All Values Allowed as the rule for ordinary depreciation, this option will allow both positive and negative depreciation amounts in the respective depreciation area.

Assigning Accounts

Assigning accounts is the same as determining accounts. You covered this step in Chapter 2 in the "Assigning G/L Accounts" section. In this activity you determine the general ledger accounts in FI where ordinary depreciation in Asset Accounting are posted. You can assign the general ledger accounts for ordinary depreciation using the menu path: IMG: Financial Accounting (New) ➤ Asset Accounting ➤ Depreciation ➤ Ordinary Depreciation ➤ Assign Accounts.

Unit-of-Production Method of Depreciation

The unit of production depreciation method is quite different from the conventional methods of depreciation, which are based on the passage of time (estimated usage years of an asset). Rather, this method takes the movement of fluctuation in activity in a given period into consideration when calculating depreciation. Unit of production method of depreciation calculation is based on units of activity of expected output or an asset's usage. For example, the depreciation of a given asset is calculated on the basis of production output in a given period (i.e., in proportion to the estimated production capacity of the asset).

As part of the customizing of the unit-of-production method of depreciation, you will define the depreciation key for unit of depreciation and assign the estimated total number of units for the asset and the actual quantity produced for individual depreciation period. The system will then determine the depreciation amount using the total units, the actual units produced, and the APC or the net book value. APC is the acquisition cost of the asset or the replacement value and the net book value is APC less the provision for depreciation.

1. To define the depreciation key and specify the number of units for the depreciation keys for the unit of production method of depreciation, use this menu path: IMG: Financial Accounting (New) ➤ Asset Accounting ➤ Depreciation ➤ Ordinary Depreciation ➤ Define Unit-of-Production Depreciation. The Change View "Company codes": Overview screen is displayed containing the list of existing company codes.

2. Click the ⊞ Position… button at the bottom of the screen to search for your company code. Your company code will be displayed at the top of the company codes list. Select your company code (7200) from the displayed list and double-click the Depreciation key folder on the left side of the screen. The Display View "Depreciation Key": Overview screen is displayed. The system will automatically default to the depreciation key for the unit of production, as shown in Figure 4-3.

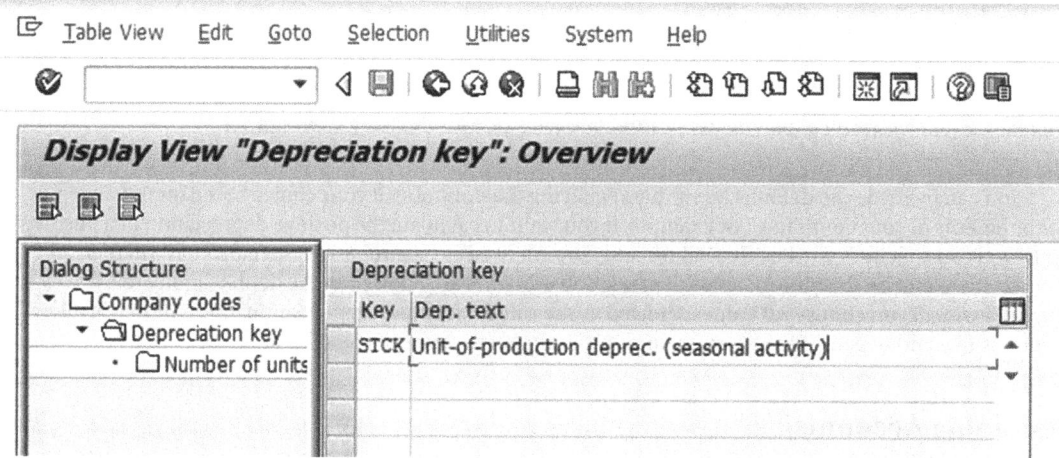

Figure 4-3. *The screen where you define depreciation keys for your unit of production depreciation*

■ **Note**   SAP provides a standard depreciation key (STCK) that you can use. The depreciation key uses a base (standard) method with unit of production.

If the depreciation key is not displayed, you can access the list of depreciation key in the system using the matchcode in the key field.

3. To assign a number of units to your depreciation key, select the depreciation key STCK-Unit-of-production deprec. (seasonal activity) and double-click the Number of Units folder on the left pane of the screen. The Change View "Number of units": Overview screen is displayed.

4. To enter data in the screen, click the [New Entries] button at the top-left side of the screen. The New Entries: Overview of Added Entries screen is displayed (Figure 4-4).

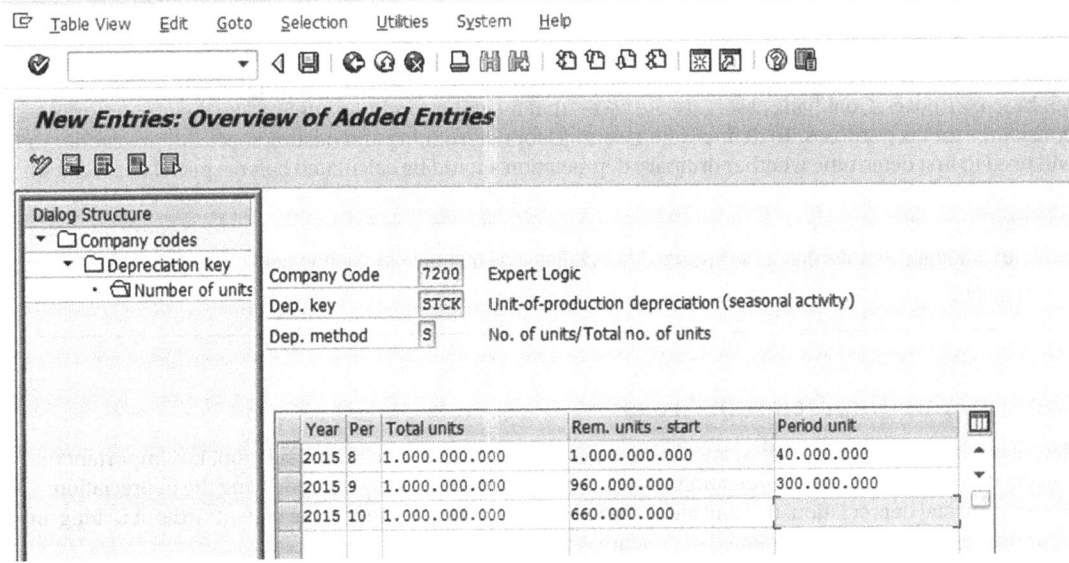

Figure 4-4. *Enter the units of production for your depreciation key (with values already entered)*

■ **Note**   This screen is initially blank.

5. Update the following fields:

- **Year:** Enter the accounting fiscal year (2015) the asset relates to.

- **Per:** Enter the related accounting period in this field. Accounting period is based on the number of months in an accounting year. This is usually 12 months. For example, if your accounting fiscal year is from January to December, January will be period 1, February will be period 2, March will be period 3, and so on.

- **Total Units:** This is the estimated production units of the asset with which the asset is depreciated.

▪ **Note**   The total number of units applied to the depreciation calculation for an individual period can be changed in any given period. The system then applies the new total number of units to calculate the depreciation.

Special Depreciation

In some cases, special depreciations are calculated purely for the wear and tear of qualifying assets for tax-based purposes. Qualifying assets are the assets that meet the conditions defined by the tax authority as considered for tax purposes. To define system settings for determining and posting special depreciation, you will need to first determine whether ordinary depreciation should be calculated before special depreciation.

▪ **Note**   Some countries don't use special depreciation, so you may not need to configure special depreciation.

Determining Depreciation Areas

Before you determine depreciation areas, you may want to manage special depreciation. It is important that you create at least a chart of depreciation of your own in asset accounting. By specifying the depreciation areas for special depreciation, this will allow the value type to be accepted by the system without issuing an error message when you enter related depreciation terms in the asset master record.

To determine the depreciation area for your special depreciation, use this menu path: IMG: Financial Accounting (New) ➤ Asset Accounting ➤ Depreciation ➤ Special Depreciation ➤ Determine Depreciation Areas. The Change View "Specify Depreciation Areas for Special Depreciation": Overview screen is displayed. It contains the list of depreciation areas in your chart of depreciation. Click the Special Depreciation check box for the appropriate depreciation areas in the depreciation area for special depreciation.

Click the Enter 🗸 button at the top left of the screen and save 💾 your work.

Calculating Ordinary Depreciation before Special Depreciation

The SAP system distinguishes between the depreciation types (ordinary depreciation, special depreciation, unplanned depreciation, and transaction reserves). There is no hard rule as to how the system determines the different types of depreciation. To specify that the system should calculate ordinary depreciation before special depreciation, use this menu path: Financial Accounting (New) ➤ Asset Accounting ➤ Depreciation ➤ Special Depreciation ➤ Calculate Ordinary Depreciation before Special Depreciation. When the change

View "Depreciation areas: Calculate sequence for depreciation screen is displayed, choose Ordinary Depreciation before Special Depreciation for the related depreciation areas.

Click the Enter 🗸 button at the top-left side of the screen and save 🖫 your work.

Unplanned Depreciation

Unplanned depreciation allows you apply an unplanned value adjustment due to an unforeseen occurrence of an event resulting in the permanent reduction in the value of an asset. For example, advancement in technology necessitates a drastic reduction in the value of an asset.

Determining Depreciation Areas

Before you determine depreciation areas, you want to manage your unplanned depreciation, because it is important that you create at least a chart of depreciation of your own. By specifying the depreciation areas for unplanned depreciation, this will allow the value type to be accepted by the system without issuing an error message when you enter related depreciation terms in the asset master record.

To determine depreciation area for your unplanned depreciation, use this menu path: IMG: Financial Accounting (New) ➤ Asset Accounting ➤ Depreciation ➤ Unplanned Depreciation ➤ Determine Depreciation Areas. The Change View "Asset Accounting: Define if Unplanned Deprec.Pos/Neg": Overview screen is displayed. It contains the list of depreciation areas in your chart of depreciation (Figure 4-5).

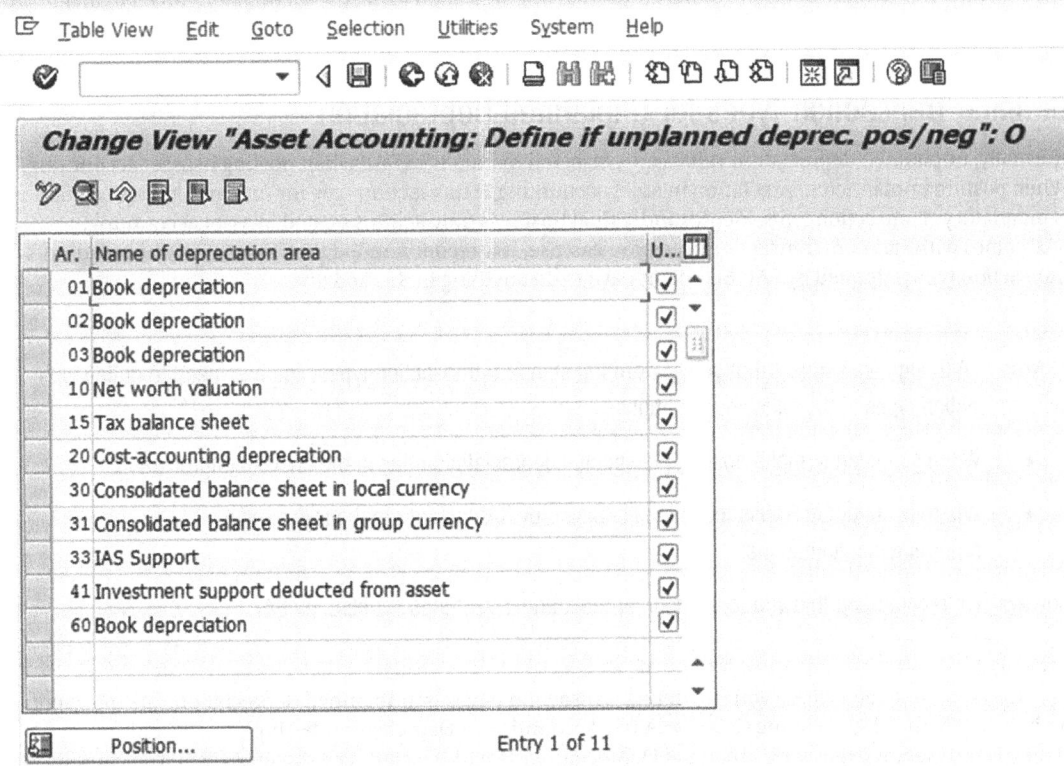

Figure 4-5. Defining the depreciation areas to manage in unplanned depreciation

Specify the depreciation areas you want to manage in unplanned depreciation by clicking the UDep check box on the right side of the screen. The next step in this activity is to determine the rule for positive and negative signs for the unplanned depreciation in each depreciation area.

To proceed to the screen where you will carry out the specifications for the respective depreciation areas, select a depreciation area (for example 01 Book depreciation) from the list of depreciation areas and click Details ☒ at the top-left side of the screen. The Change View "Asset Accounting: Define if unplanned deprec. Pos/neg": Overview screen is displayed containing four rules for the positive/negative sign for ordinary depreciation option you can choose from. The system automatically defaults to Only Negative Values and Zero Allowed. This option will ensure that only negative depreciation amounts are allowed in the depreciation area in question if you want to calculate the negative depreciation of a positive APC.

You can override the defaults by simply specifying the option of your choice based on the requirements of your company. For example, if you want to calculate the positive depreciation of positive APC, you can specify Only Positive Values and Zero Allowed as the rule for ordinary depreciation for the respective depreciation area. This specification will then allow the system to ensure that only positive depreciation amounts are allowed in the depreciation area.

Likewise, if you choose All Values Allowed as the rule for unplanned depreciation, this option will allow both positive and negative depreciation amounts in the respective depreciation area.

Assigning Accounts

We covered this step in Chapter 2 in the "Assign G/L Accounts" section. In this activity, you determine the general ledger accounts in FI where unplanned depreciation in Asset Accounting are posted. You can assign or determine the general ledger accounts for ordinary depreciation using the menu path: IMG: Financial Accounting (New) ➤ Asset Accounting ➤ Depreciation ➤ Unplanned Depreciation ➤ Assign Accounts.

Defining Transaction Types for Unplanned Depreciation

Normally, unplanned depreciation values are corrected manually in SAP when posting in asset accounting. When posting unplanned depreciation in asset accounting, a transaction type for unplanned depreciation is mandatory. Transaction types identify individual business transactions posted in asset accounting. SAP comes with standard transaction types you can use. It is recommended that you stick to the standard transaction types supplied by SAP. So do not have to do anything in this activity.

■ **Note**   Although we suggest that you stick to the standard transaction types, you may need to define your own transaction types in the following situations:

- When you need to make postings to specific depreciation areas in the chart of depreciation.

- When the standard transaction types supplied by SAP do not meet our desired requirements (limitations).

However, we recommend that you take a look at the standard settings supplied by SAP.

To get to the screen where you can define transaction types for unplanned depreciation, use this menu path: IMG: Financial Accounting (New) ➤ Asset Accounting ➤ Depreciation ➤ Unplanned Depreciation ➤ Define Depreciation Types for Unplanned Depreciation. The Choose Activity screen is displayed containing activities available in this activity, as shown in Figure 4-6.

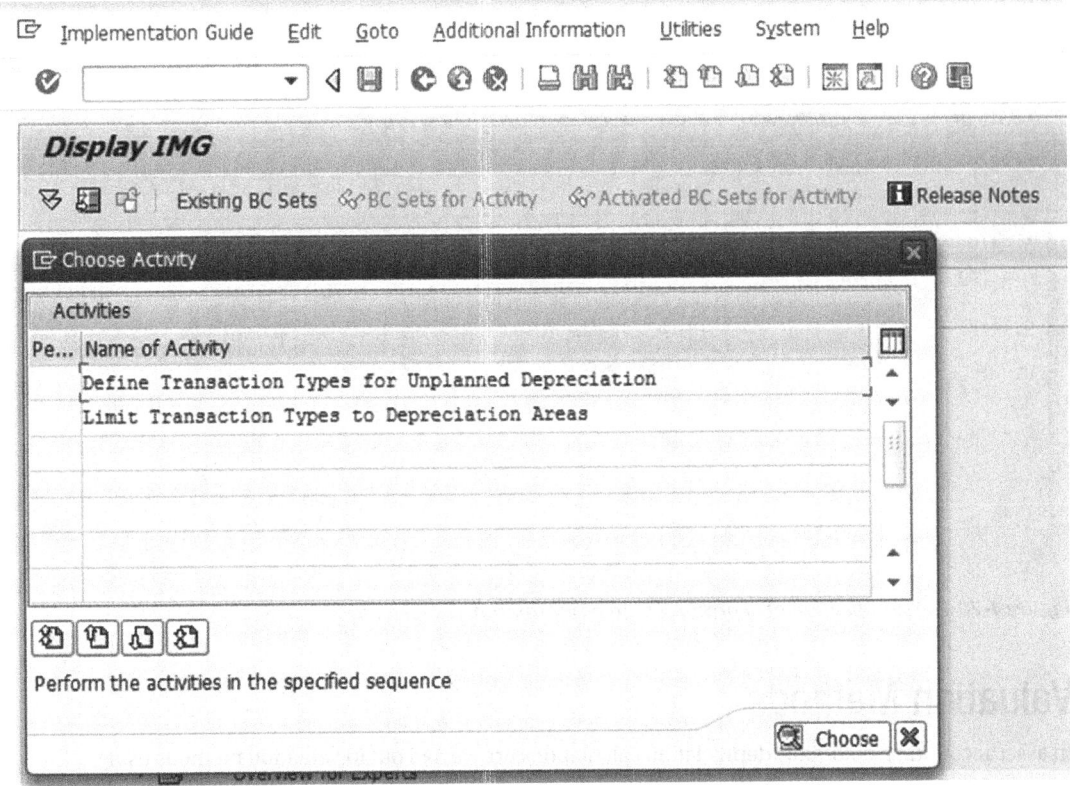

Figure 4-6. *The Choose Activity screen contains the activities for unplanned depreciation you can choose from*

To define/display transaction types supplied by SAP, select Define Transaction Types for Unplanned Depreciation from the list of displayed activities in Figure 4-6 and click the Choose button at the bottom-right side of the screen. The Change View "FI-AA Transaction Types": Overview screen appears containing a list of transaction types supplied by SAP.

To define a new transaction type to meet your requirements, on the top-left side of the Change View "FI-AA Transaction types": Overview screen, click the New Entries button. The Entries: Details of Added Entries screen will be displayed.

If necessary, you can limit your transaction types to a given depreciation area. To access the screen where you may define the limit for transaction types, select Limit Transaction Types to Depreciation Areas from the list of activities in Figure 4-6 and click the Choose button at the bottom-right side of the screen. The Change View "Transaction Type Select": Overview screen is displayed containing the list of existing transaction codes in the system. Click the Position... button at the bottom of the screen to search for the transaction type you want to limit to a depreciation area. The transaction type in question comes to the top of the transaction types list. Select it and double-click Depreciation Area Specification folder on the left pane of the screen. The Change View "Depreciation Area Specification": Overview screen is displayed. This is the initial screen for the specification of the depreciation area for your transaction type. Click the New Entries button at the top-left side of the screen to go to the input screen where you will carry out the specifications of the depreciation area for the transaction types for unplanned depreciation, as shown in Figure 4-7.

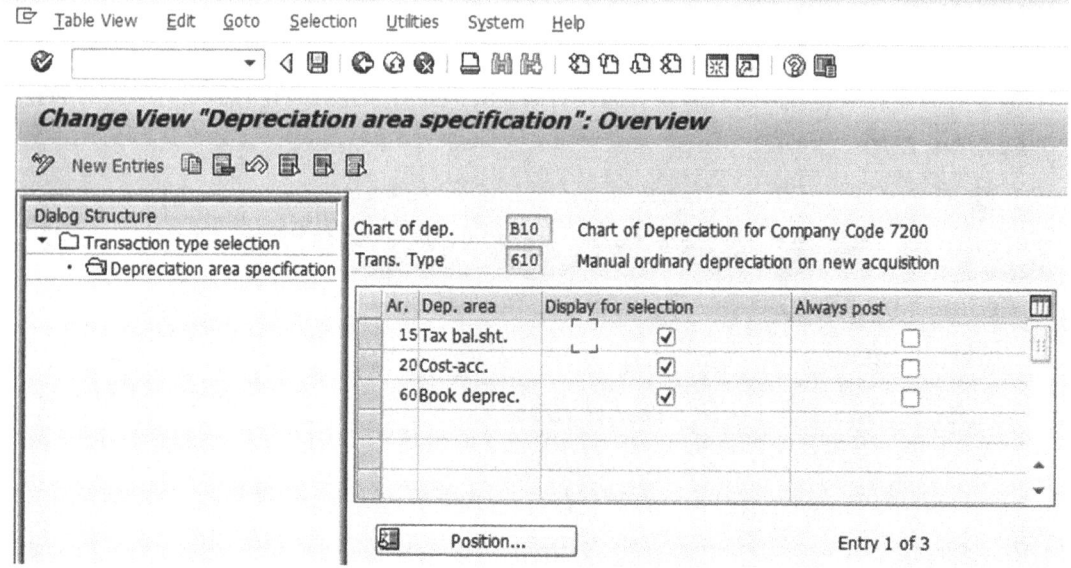

Figure 4-7. *The specification of depreciation areas for uplanned depreciation*

Valuation Methods

In asset accounting, automatic depreciation calculations are carried out in valuation methods using predefined depreciation keys that contain the calculation methods you define in this activity. In valuation methods, you define your own depreciation keys holding calculation methods and other control parameters used for the calculation of depreciation by the system. Most depreciation keys and calculation methods are supplied by SAP.

Depreciation keys are predefined keys that hold the calculation methods containing mathematical functions expressed in percentages used to calculate depreciation. This enables you to determine the value of assets at a specific time. Therefore, depreciation keys hold the calculation methods (mathematical formulas) used by the system for calculating depreciation and for the settings that control various types of depreciation, such as ordinary depreciation, special depreciation, scrap value (cutoff value), interest calculation, etc.

In this step, you will look at the calculation methods you can use to calculate depreciation in FI-AA.

Calculation Methods

The calculation methods are very important for defining depreciation methods, because they contain the parameters used by the system for automatic calculation of depreciation. The following depreciation calculation methods are represented in SAP:

- Base methods

- Declining-balance methods

- Maximum amount methods

- Multi-level methods

- Maintain period control methods

Defining Base Methods

Base methods are assigned to a depreciation key in SAP and are independent of the chart of depreciation (i.e., it is not country specific). SAP comes with various base methods that you can use or adapt to meet your requirements. The base methods supplied by SAP are generally sufficient. However, if you need to define one, follow these steps:

1. Follow this menu path: IMG: Financial Accounting (New) ➤ Asset Accounting ➤ Depreciation ➤ Valuation Methods ➤ Calculation Methods ➤ Define Base Methods. The Change View "Base Method": Overview screen is displayed containing the list of the existing base methods.

2. Click the New entries button at the top-left side of the screen to proceed to where you will enter the specifications for your base method. The Change View "Base Method": Details of Selected Set screen is displayed (Figure 4-8).

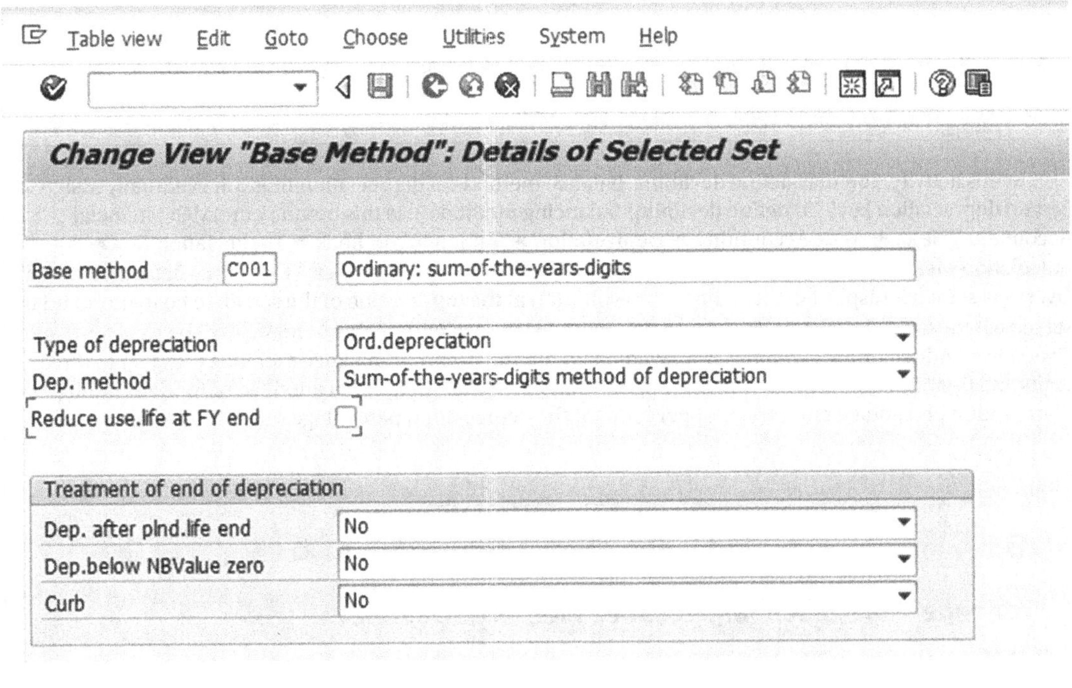

Figure 4-8. Defining a base method as the calculation method for your depreciation key

3. Update the following fields:

   • **Base method:** You can enter up to four digits as the base method code and a description for your base method in these fields. The code you enter in this field will serve as your base method identification code.

   • **Type of depreciation:** Enter the type of depreciation for your base method in this field. Using the drop-down arrow by the type of depreciation field, you can display the list of depreciation types you can choose from. For example, ordinary depreciation, special tax depreciation, and interest. Select Ordinary Depreciation from the list.

- **Dep. Method:** Using the drop-down by the Dep. Method field, select Sum-of-the-years-digits method depreciation from the list of displayed depreciation methods. The Sum-of-the-years-digits method depreciation is based on the concept of calculating depreciation based on the sum of the number of years contained in an asset useful economic life (UEL). This is often referred to as an accelerated depreciation technique. This method systematically allocates a higher depreciation amount to an asset in the earlier years of its useful life.

4. Click the Enter ❷ button at the top-left side of the screen to confirm if the system accepts your entries and then save 🖫 your work.

Defining Declining-Balance Methods

Declining-balance methods are calculated by applying a constant depreciation rate (for example, 10%, 15%, 20%, etc.) to the net book value (NBV) of an asset. This method is also referred to as accelerated depreciation in the sense that it allocates higher depreciation expenses to an asset in the earlier years of its life.

■ **Note**   You may not need to define your own calculation methods for declining-balance methods. The calculation methods supplied by SAP are usually sufficient.

In this activity, you may define declining-balance methods of depreciation that you eventually assign to certain depreciation keys. To define declining-balancing methods, use this menu path: IMG: Financial Accounting (New) ➤ Asset Accounting ➤ Depreciation ➤ Valuation Methods ➤ Depreciation Key ➤ Calculation Methods ➤ Define Declining-Balance Methods. The Change View "Declining-Balance Method": Overview screen is displayed. Click the ⟨New entries⟩ button at the top-left side of the screen to go to the standard screen where you will maintain the calculation methods for declining-balance methods. The New Entries: Overview of Added Entries screen is displayed. Maintain the declining-balance methods using up to three digits and their descriptions, as shown in Figure 4-9. Then specify a multiplication factor for determining the depreciation percentage rate and an upper limit for the depreciation percentage rate.

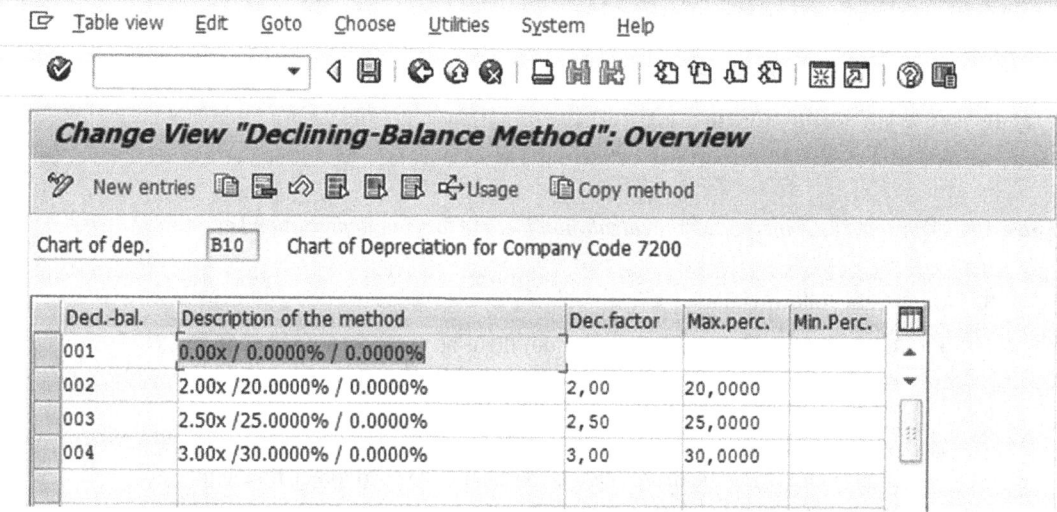

Figure 4-9. Specifying the declining-balance method for depreciation calculation

Defining Multi-Level Methods

A multi-level method is the process where you use a different percentage rate for depreciation for different years or periods. This method is more suitable when you may want to apply higher rate in the calculation of assets in the initial years and subsequently use a lower rate in the later years. For example, you can use a high rate in the earlier years when the asset is deemed to be more productive and a lower rate when the asset is deemed to be less productive as a result of wear and tear arising from the use of the asset.

SAP provides you with the flexibility to specify different rates of depreciation for different years or periods. Individual level represents the period of validity for each percentage rate of depreciation. At the end of the validity (year/period) of a percentage rate of depreciation, the system will automatically apply the next percentage rate of depreciation for the valid year/period (i.e., the next level). This is repeated systematically at the end of each year/period.

■ **Note**   SAP comes with standard multi-level methods you can use for the calculation of depreciation in most cases.

When defining multi-level methods for your depreciation calculation, you will carry out the following functions:

- Maintain the multi-level method using a three-digit character as your multi-level method identifier and a description.

- Enter the parameters of the multi-level method.

Complete the following steps to define multi-level methods:

1. Use this menu path: IMG: Financial Accounting (New) ➤ Asset Accounting ➤ Depreciation ➤ Valuation Methods ➤ Calculation Methods ➤ Define Multi-Level Methods. The Chart of Depreciation Selection screen pops up. This screen allows you to specify the chart of depreciation you are using for your multi-level method.

2. Enter your chart of depreciation (B10) in the ChDep field and click the Continue ☑ button at the bottom-left side of the screen. The Change View "Multilevel Method": Overview screen appears containing the existing multi-level methods.

3. Click the New entries button at the top-left side of the screen. The New Entries: Details of Added Entries screen is displayed (Figure 4-10). This is the where you maintain multi-level methods.

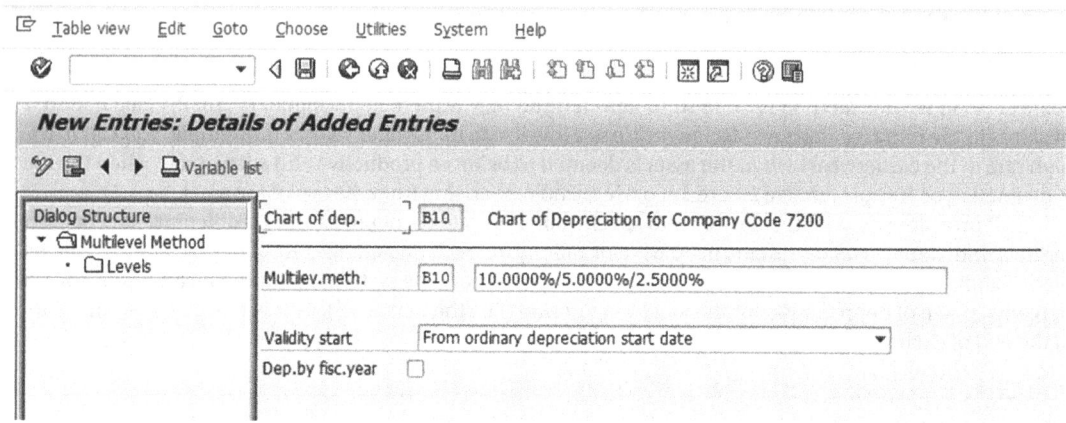

Figure 4-10. *Defining the settings for a multi-level method*

4.   Update the following fields:

- **Chart of Dep.:** The chart of depreciation you are using for your multi-level method is defaulted by the system from your specification when you specify the chart of depreciation (B10).

- **Multilev.Meth:** Specify the identification key (B10) you want to use for your multi-level method and enter a brief description that best describes your multi-level method.

- **Validity Start:** Here you have the flexibility of determining whether the defined validity period begins with:

  - Capitalization date

  - Ordinary depreciation start date

  - Special depreciation start date

  - Original acquisition data of AuC (asset under construction)

  - Changeover year

5.   Use the drop-down arrow by the Validity Start field to display the list of validity start options you can choose from. Select Ordinary depreciation Start Date from the list. This will allow you to calculate your depreciation using the multi-level method technique applying ordinary depreciation principles.

6.   Click the Enter ✓ button at the top-left side of the screen to confirm if the system accepts your entries. Then save ⊟ your work.

7.   The next step in this activity is to specify the levels for your multi-level method. To do this, double-click the Levels folder on the left pane of the screen. The Change View "Levels": Overview screen is displayed.

8.   Click the New entries button at the top-left side of the screen. The New Entries: Overview of Added Entries screen is displayed. This is where you specify the levels for your multi-level method. Update your screen as shown in Figure 4-11.

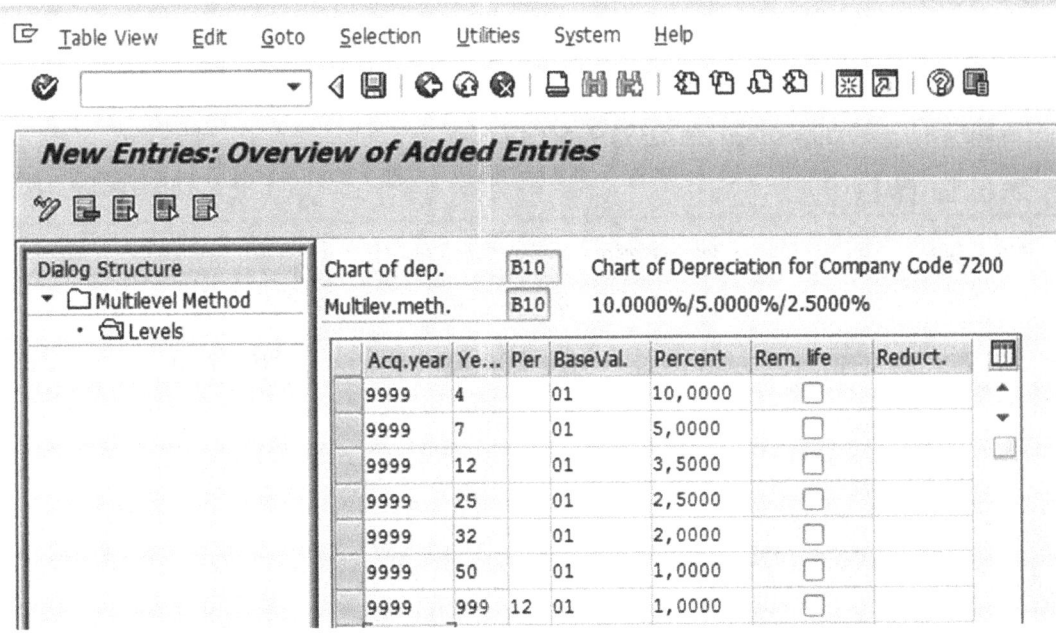

Figure 4-11. *The screen where you specify the levels for your multi-level method*

9. Click the Enter ✅ button at the top-left side of the screen to confirm if the system accepts your entries and then save 💾 your multi-level method.

Defining Maintain Period Control Methods

Maintain period control methods are important if you want to determine the depreciation start and end for your asset transactions. This can be achieved by maintaining an adequate period control method for at least the four following transaction categories:

- Acquisition transactions

- Subsequent additional acquisitions/post-capitalization

- Retirements

- Intracompany transfers

Follow these steps to specify period control methods:

1. Use this menu path: IMG: Financial Accounting (New) ➤ Asset Accounting ➤ Depreciation ➤ Valuation Methods ➤ Calculation Methods ➤ Maintain Period Control Methods. The Change View "Period Control": Overview screen is displayed.

2. Click the New entries button at the top-left side of the screen. Update the screen using the information in Figure 4-12.

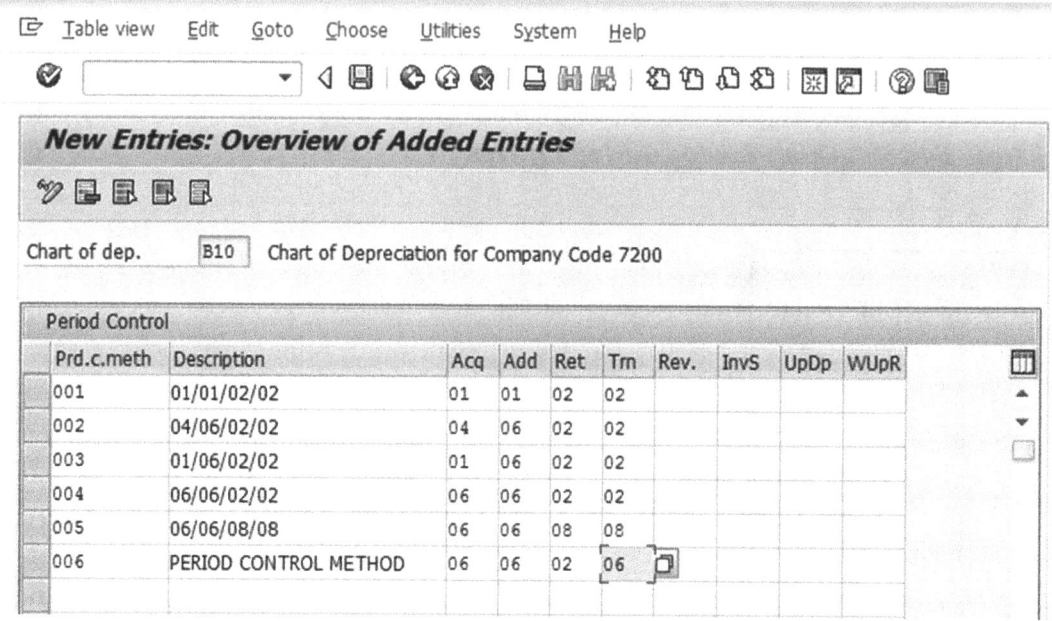

Figure 4-12. *Defining period control methods for your calculation method*

3. Click the Enter ✅ button at the top-left side of the screen to confirm if the system accepts your entries and then save 💾 your period control method.

Maintaining Depreciation Keys

A depreciation key contains the calculation methods and the parameter that controls ordinary and special depreciations. It also contains the parameter that controls other items like the scrap value of assets and the calculation of interest. Depreciation keys are maintained by assigning calculation methods to the depreciation keys. The duration of depreciation can be split into a number of phases in the system, so that when a changeover method is entered for a phase, the system moves automatically to the next phase when the conditions specified in the changeover method occur. The system then executes the depreciation calculation based on the calculation method for the phase.

When maintaining depreciation keys, you carry out the following functions:

- Define additional depreciation keys using four-digit characters as the depreciation key. This includes a short description that best describes your depreciation key.

- Assign calculation methods to the depreciation keys and activate the depreciation key.

■ **Note**   SAP comes with standard depreciation keys for different *depreciation types* that are sufficient for this activity.

To define depreciation key, follow these steps:

1. Use this menu path: IMG: Financial Accounting (New) ➤ Asset Accounting ➤ Depreciation ➤ Valuation Methods ➤ Depreciation Key ➤ Maintain Depreciation Key. The Change View "Depreciation Key": Overview screen is displayed containing the list of exiting depreciation keys in the system.

2. Click New entries button at the top-left side of the screen. The New Entries: Details of Added Entries screen is displayed (Figure 4-13). This screen will allow you to enter a depreciation key and a description.

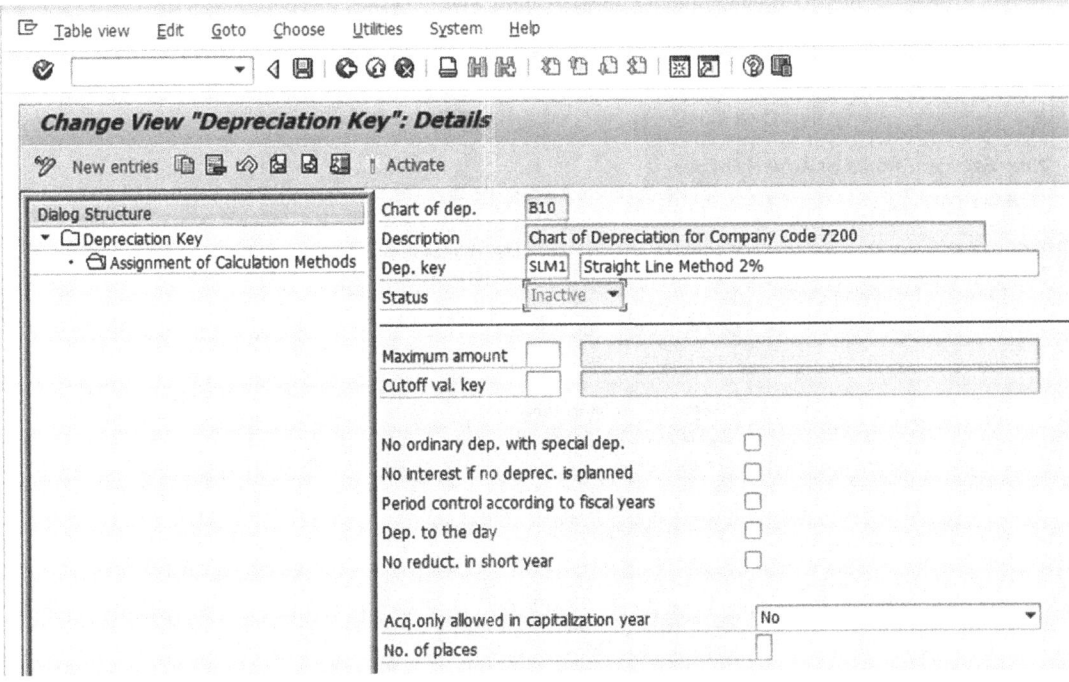

Figure 4-13. *Defining the straight line method for your depreciation key*

3. The chart of depreciation and its description are set by default by the system. Enter the depreciation key and a description in the Dep.Key field. For example, SLM1 (Straight Line Method 2%).

4. Click the Enter 🗸 button at the top-left side of the screen to confirm if the system accepts your entries and then save 🖫 your depreciation key.

■ **Note** You can create as many depreciation keys as you require for different depreciation methods. For example, the straight line method, declining balance method, and so on.

Assigning Calculation Methods

Once you have defined depreciation keys, the next step is to assign calculation methods to depreciation keys.

1. To assign calculation method to a depreciation key, double-click the Assignment of Calculation Methods folder on the left pane of the screen (see Figure 4-11). The Change View "Assignment of Calculation Methods": Overview screen is displayed.

2. Click the New entries button at the top-left side of the screen. The New Entries: Details of Added Entries screen appears (Figure 4-14). This is where you perform the assignment of calculation methods to depreciation keys.

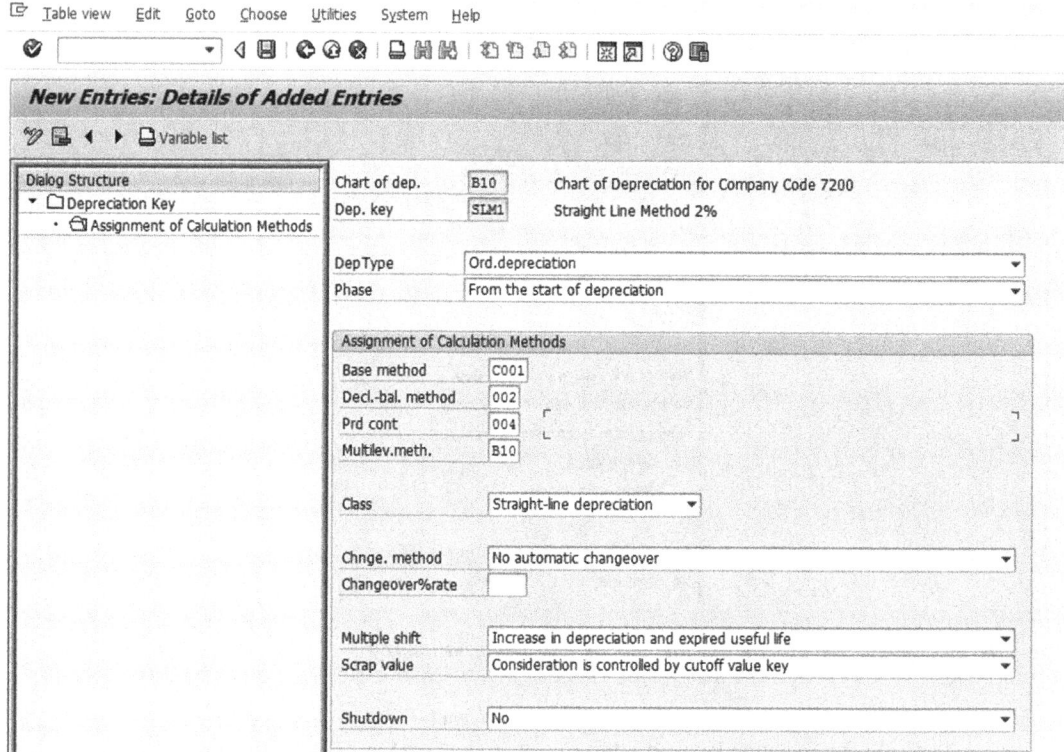

Figure 4-14. *Further specifications for your straight line method with values entered*

3. Update the following fields:

    - **Dep Type:** Enter the depreciation type you want to assign to your depreciation key in this field. You can assign up to three depreciation types to a depreciation key (for example ordinary depreciation, special tax depreciation, and interest). Using the drop-down menu by the Dep Type field, select Ordinary depreciation from the list.

    - **Phase:** Enter the phase you want to apply to your depreciation key in this field. You have up to three options you can choose from. Using the drop-down menu by the field, select From the Start of Depreciation.

    - **Assignment of Calculation Methods:** Enter the calculation method key you want to apply to your depreciation key for the base method, declining-balancing method, the period control method, and the multi-level methods in the respective fields.

4. Click the Enter 🗸 button at the top-left side of the screen to confirm if the system accepts your entries and then save 🖫 your work.

5. The next step is to activate the depreciation key. Click the ⟳ Back button twice to return to the Change View "Assignment of Calculation Methods": Overview screen. You will notice that the status is *inactive.*

6. Click the ⌊ Activate ⌋ button to activate the depreciation key. The system will notify you on the message bar that "Key SLM1 was activated successfully in chart of depreciation B10".

Customizing Period Control

This function dictates the time period that determines the start and end of the depreciation of asset acquisitions and retirements. SAP comes with standard control period, so you don't need to customize anything in this step. In period control, you can maintain period control, define calendar assignments, define time-dependent period controls, and generate period controls. To customize a period control, use this menu path: IMG: Financial Accounting (New) ➤ Asset Accounting ➤ Depreciation ➤ Valuation Methods ➤ Period Control ➤ Maintain Period Control. The Change View "Period Control": Overview screen appears containing the list of standard control period supplied by SAP, as shown in Figure 4-15.

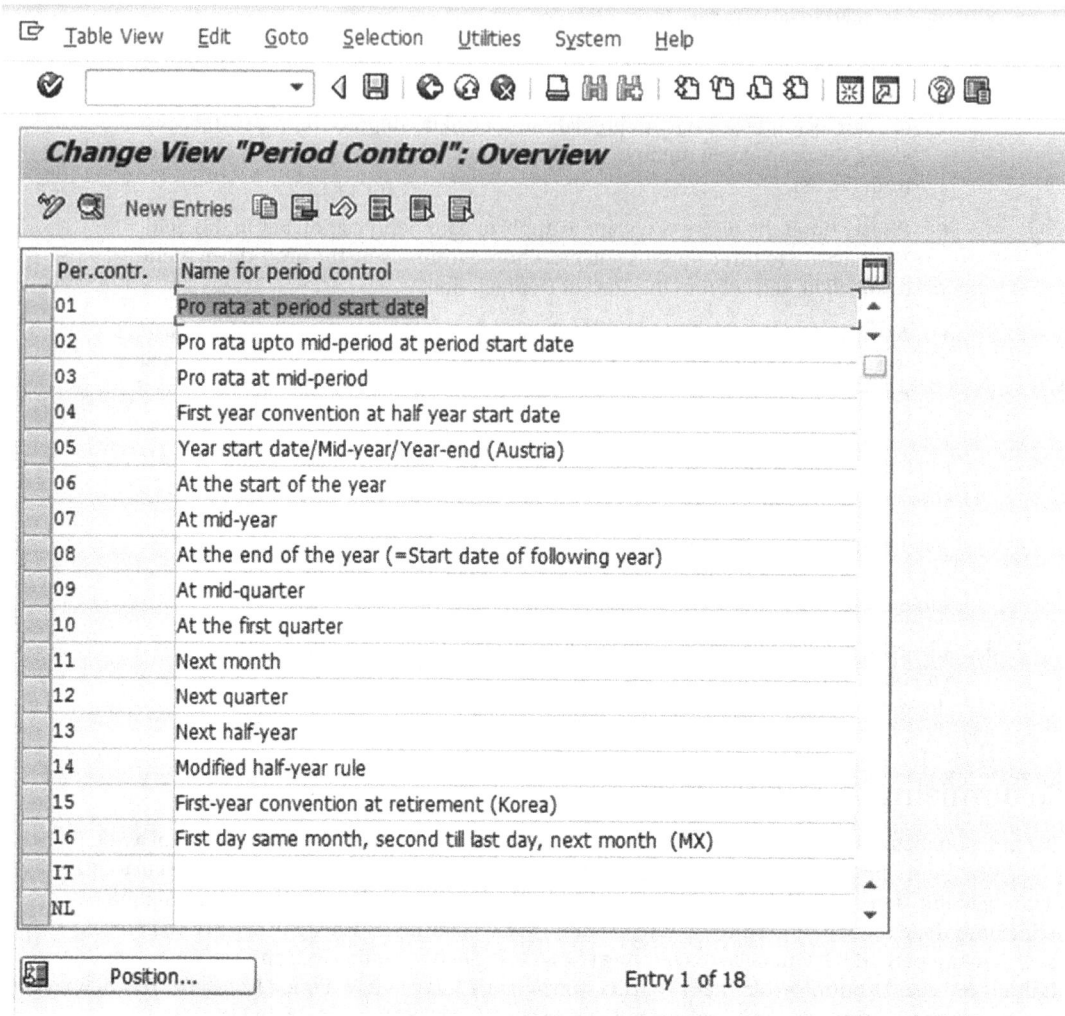

Figure 4-15. *Standard period control supplied by SAP*

■ **Note**   We recommend that you stick with the standard control periods supplied by SAP, as they are sufficient for your requirements.

Further Settings

In this activity, you can perform the following functions:

- Define the cutoff value key
- Define a maximum base value
- Specify asset-specific base value percentages

Defining the Cutoff Value Key

For some technical reasons or to meet legal requirements, it may become necessary to end the depreciation of some assets at a certain value level. For example, you can end the depreciation of assets before the net book value reaches zero. The point where you end the depreciation is referred as scrap value or cutoff value. SAP enables to define a cutoff value for each depreciation area. You can do this by entering an absolute scrap value in the asset master record or by specifying a cutoff percentage in the cutoff value (calculation) key.

SAP provides standard cutoff value keys you can adapt to meet your requirements by revising the time specifications of the scrap value keys that come with it.

1. You can define your cutoff value key using this menu path: IMG: Financial Accounting (New) ➤ Asset Accounting ➤ Depreciation ➤ Valuation Methods ➤ Further Settings ➤ Define the Cutoff Value Key. The Change View "Cutoff Value Keys": Overview screen is displayed, containing a list of cutoff values in the system.

2. Click the New entries button at the top-left side of the screen. The New Entries: Details of Added Entries screen is displayed. This is the screen where you specify the settings for your cutoff value key.

3. Enter a three-digit character as your cutoff value key identifier in the Cutoff Val. Key field.

4. Next, specify the date you want the system to start calculating the percentages for your cutoff key in the Start Date of Calculation of Percentages section of the screen. In this section, you have four options you can choose from:

    • FROM asset capitalization date

    • FROM ordinary depreciation start date for the asset

    • FROM special depreciation start date for the asset

    • FROM original acquisition date for asset under construction

    For the current activity, select FROM Asset Capitalization Date. This will allow the system to carry out calculations using the asset capitalization date.

5. Click the Enter ✅ button at the top-left side of the screen to confirm if the system accepts your entries. The system will issue a warning on the status bar at the bottom of the screen that says "Choose the key from the allowed name space".

6. Ignore the warning and click the Enter ✅ button again so the system will accept your entries. Save 💾 your work. The system will notify you on the status bar at the bottom of the screen that "data was saved".

7. Use the Back ⬅ button at the top of the screen to return to the Change View "Cutoff Value Keys": Overview screen.

8. Enter a description for your cutoff value key in the Name for Cutoff Value Key field, using Figure 4-16 as an example.

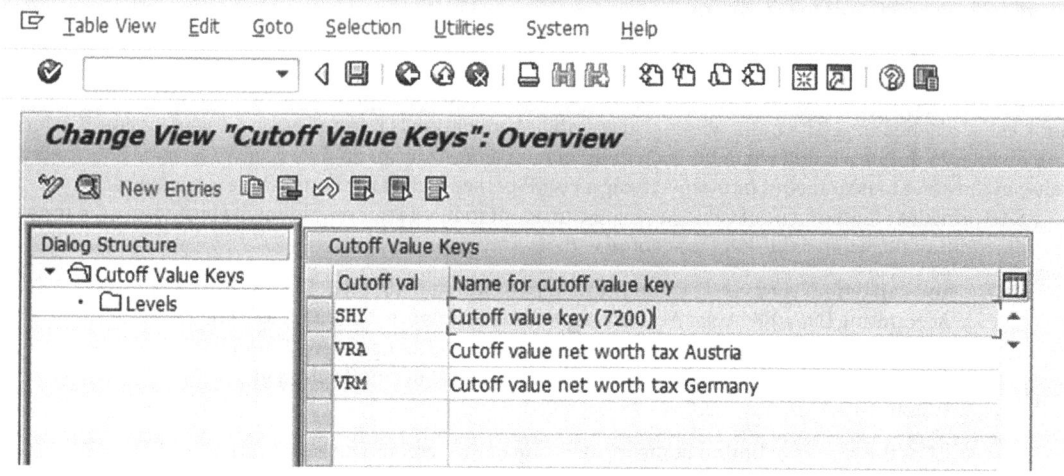

Figure 4-16. *The screen where you specify the settings for your cutoff value key*

9. Click the Enter ✅ button at the top-left side of the screen to confirm if the system accepted your entries and save 🖫 your work.

■ **Note** The key you defined may be overwritten by any subsequent upgrade. We advise that you document your change so that you can repeat it after an upgrade or release change if necessary. On the contrary, you can put the data in a change request, and then it can be exported before an upgrade or a release and imported again when needed after an upgrade or release change.

---

10. The next step in this activity is to specify the levels for your cutoff value key. To do this, select your cutoff value key and double-click the Levels folder on the left pane of the screen. The Change View "Levels": Overview screen is displayed.

11. Click the New entries button at the top of the screen. The New Entries: Overview of Added Entries screen appears (Figure 4-17).

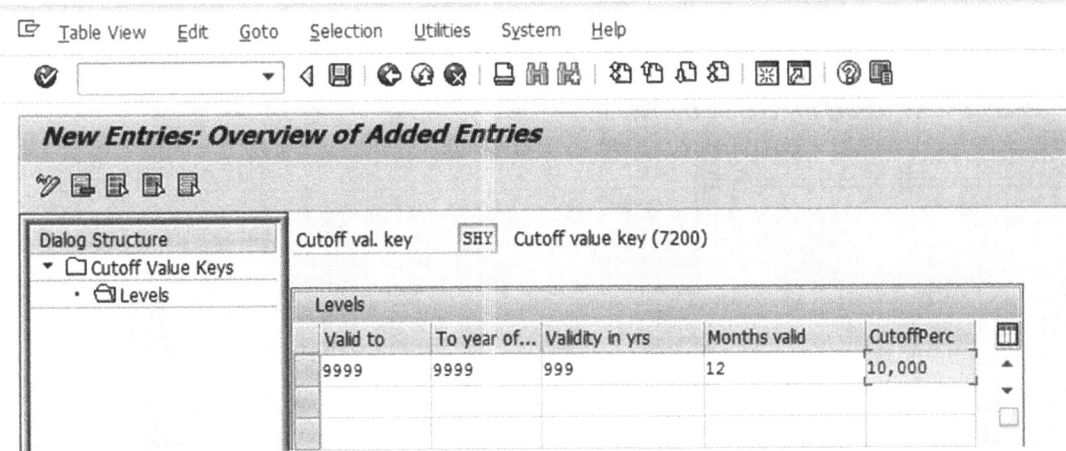

Figure 4-17. *specifying the validity period and cutoff percentage for the cutoff value key*

12.   Specify the Validity date and the Cutoff percentage.

13.   Click the Enter ✅ button at the top-left side of the screen to confirm your entries. Ignore any warnings and save 💾 your work.

Defining the Maximum Base Value

This step is not necessary if the limited acquisition value is not required as a base for calculating depreciation. Limited acquisition value simply indicates that the system uses the maximum amount as the base value for depreciation. When calculating depreciation, the system uses the acquisition value of the asset as the basis for calculating depreciation, if the value is below the specified maximum amount. On the other hand, if the asset acquisition value exceeds the specified maximum amount you specified as the base value, the system will automatically use the asset acquisition value as the basis for calculating depreciation.

Maximum base values are not delivered by SAP. To define maximum base values, use this menu path: IMG: Financial Accounting (New) ➤ Asset Accounting ➤ Depreciation ➤ Valuation Methods ➤ Further Settings ➤ Define Maximum Base Value. The Change View "Maximum base value": Overview screen is displayed.

Click the New entries button at the top-left side of the screen. The New Entries: Overview of Added Entries screen is displayed. This is where you will carry out the actual specifications for your maximum base value.

■ **Note**   You can limit your base values validity to company code, asset class, depreciation area, capitalization date, and maximum value.

Specifying Asset-Specific Base Value Percentages

This method is rarely used in most countries other than Japan. The settings in this step are specifically carried out to meet country-specific requirements for Japan. You can specify base value percentage rate as the base value for depreciation. To specify asset-specific base value percentages, use this menu path: IMG: Financial Accounting (New) ➤ Asset Accounting ➤ Depreciation ➤ Valuation Methods ➤ Further Settings ➤ Specify Asset-Specific Base Value Percentages. The Change View "Company Code": Overview screen is displayed, as shown in Figure 4-18.

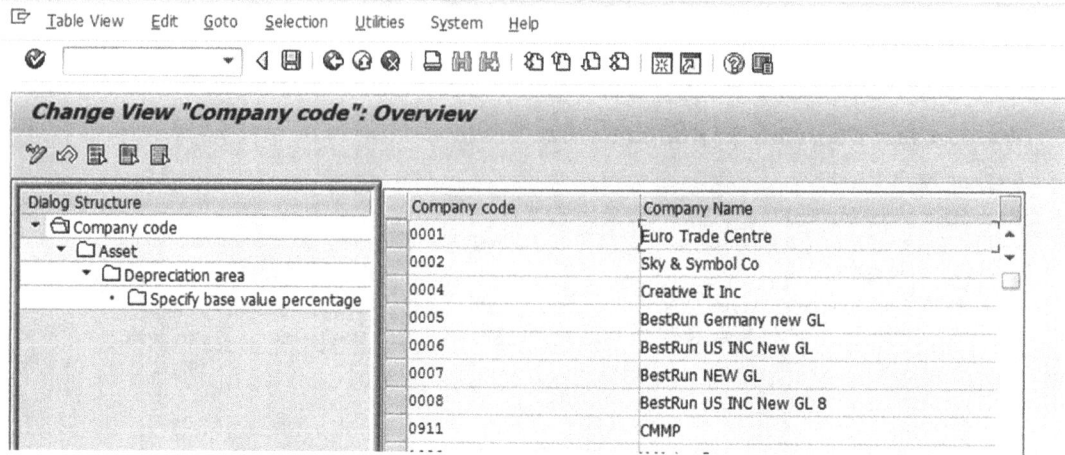

Figure 4-18. *The screen where you specify base value percentage*

On this screen you can specify base value percentage for your company code to meet your requirements.

Summary

This chapter defined depreciation and looked at the various depreciation methods supported by SAP (for example, planned and unplanned depreciation). Under planned/unplanned depreciation, you learned about ordinary depreciation. You then went through the steps involved in customizing depreciation areas. You went on to look at how to define unit of production depreciation. The next thing you did was look at what special depreciation is. Then you learned how to determine depreciation areas, calculate ordinary depreciation before special depreciation, and define transaction types for unplanned depreciation. You also looked at valuation methods represented by SAP and then went on to learn to define your own calculation methods and other control parameters specific to your calculation methods. This included defining various calculation methods (i.e. base methods, declining-balance methods, maximum amount methods, multi-level methods, and period control methods). You also looked at how to maintain depreciation keys and assign calculation methods to depreciation keys.

Finally, the chapter briefly touched period control and further settings in depreciation in asset accounting. This included how to define cutoff value keys, define a maximum base value, and specify an asset-specific base value key.

The next chapter looks at special valuation and the various activities involved in customizing special valuation. This includes the specifications involved in reserves for special depreciation, transfer of reserves (differed gain), investment support, and how to define investment support measures, and revaluation of fixed assets.

CHAPTER 5

■ ■ ■

Special Valuation

This chapter looks at the steps involved in the configuration of special valuation in Asset Accounting and also explains the various steps involved in defining special value adjustments to assets (investment support, special depreciation reserves) in asset accounting.

Some assets are classified as special assets and are treated differently by using a special valuation adjustment approach. In SAP, special valuation component plays an important role when calculating asset values for a specialized purpose. In this chapter, you will be defining system settings for:

> **Special valuation adjustments:** for example, reserves for special depreciation, investment support, and index series.

> **Special valuation purposes:** for example, cost accounting replacement values, interest, and revaluation of fixed assets

You will learn how to define the following aspects of special valuation:

- Reserves for special depreciation
- Transferred reserves (deferred gain)
- Investment support
- Revaluation of fixed assets

Reserves for Special Depreciation

In most countries, tax depreciation rates can be used for book depreciation. Hence, it is important to differentiate between tax depreciation and normal depreciation. For this reason, book depreciation is conducted based on the normal requirements and the allowed depreciation by tax law. The tax depreciation that exceeds the book depreciation is treated as special reserves and disclosed as liabilities in the balance sheet. Tax depreciation is an expense and is deductible from taxable income for a given period based on certain tax laws. The differentiation and disclosure of book depreciation and tax depreciation in a derived depreciation area in SAP is achieved using special reserves component. This is a common practice in Germany, for example.

In the next step, you will specify net reserves for special depreciation and assign accounts that special reserves are posted.

Specifying Gross or Net Procedure for Reserves

In this customizing step, you will specify whether the system should apply gross or net procedure to balance amounts when allocating or writing off reserves on the same asset in the same posting run against each other (net posting).

▪ **Note**   It is recommended that you use the net posting procedure because this meets legal requirements in most countries.

To specify net procedure for reserves for special depreciation, follow these steps:

1. Use this menu path: IMG: Financial Accounting (New) ➤ Asset Accounting ➤ Special Valuation ➤ Reserves for Special Depreciation ➤ Specify Gross or Net Procedure. The Change View "Company code selection": Overview screen is displayed.

2. Using the [▣ Position...] button at the bottom of the screen, look for your company code. Select your company code from the list of company codes and double click Net reserve for special depreciation folder in the Company code selection on the left pane of the screen. The Change View "Net reserve for special depreciation": Overview screen appears (Figure 5-1). This is the screen where you specify which depreciation areas you want to apply net procedure. On this screen you will notice that depreciation areas you specified in Chapter 3 in Set-Up Areas for Parallel Valuation (for example, depreciation area 33-IAS Support).

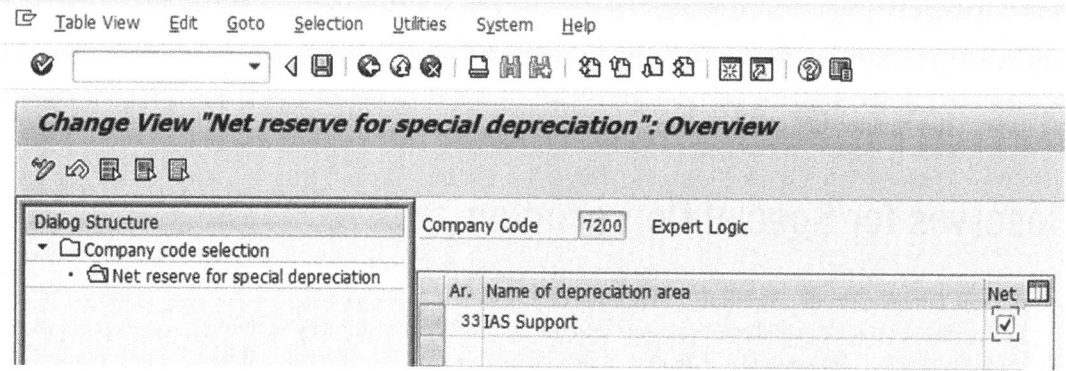

Figure 5-1. *The screen where you specify gross or net procedures for reserves for special depreciation*

3. Select the Net procedure checkbox, which will allow the system to determine whether to apply gross or net procedure to balance amounts when allocating or writing off reserves on the same asset in the same posting run against each other (net posting).

4. Click the Enter ✅ button at the top left of the screen and save 💾 your work.

Assigning Accounts

The next step in this activity is to carry out accounts determination of the general ledger that special reserves are posted:

1. To assign accounts reserves are posted, use this menu path: IMG: Financial Accounting (New) ➤ Asset Accounting ➤ Special Valuation ➤ Reserves for Special Depreciation ➤ Assign Accounts. The Chart of Depreciation Selection screen pops up. This screen will allow you to determine the chart of depreciation you are using for your account determination.

2. Enter your chart of depreciation (B10) in the ChDep field and click the Continue ☑ button at the bottom left of the screen. The Change View "Chart of Accounts": Overview screen is displayed containing your chart of accounts (Figure 5-2).

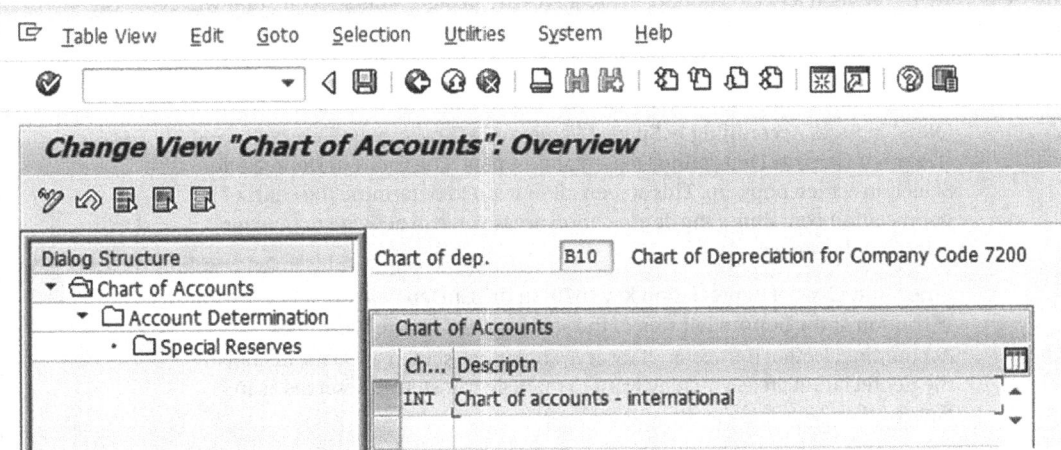

Figure 5-2. *The initial screen where you assign accounts to chart of accounts for your reserves for special depreciation*

3. Select your chart of accounts (INT-Chart of accounts—international) and double click the Account Determination folder in the chart of account on the left pane of the screen. The Change View "Account Determination": Overview screen appears containing all the account determination existing in the system (including the account determinations you defined in Chapter 1 in the Account Determination specification section.

4. Using the ☒ Position... button at the bottom of the screen, search for the account determination you want to use for your special reserves. Select the account determination (for example, in this exercise we used AD3000 Plant & Machinery) from the list of displayed account determination and double click Special Reserves folder in account determination on the left pane of the screen. The Change View "Special Reserves": Details screen is displayed. (Account assignment was covered in Chapter 2 in the Assigning G/L Accounts section.)

5. Enter the relevant general ledger accounts in the appropriate fields in the account assignment for special reserves sections of the screen.

6. Click the Enter ☑ button at the top left of the screen and save 🖫 your work.

Determining Depreciation Areas for Transferred Reserves (Deferred Gain)

Transferred reserves, as the name suggests, is a component that allows you to technically transfer all or part of deferred gain (sometime referred to as balancing charges or undisclosed reserves) generated from the sale of assets to newly acquired assets. The benefit of this technique is to use the gain from the sale to reduce the depreciation base of the acquired assets. On the contrary, if the reserves arising from the sale of asset are not applied to assets in the year in which they arise, because no new assets were acquired in that year, you can create a special reserve and carry the gain to the special reserve on the liability side of the balance sheet. The tax law in most countries allows this practice and the gains are not counted as part of profit made by the company. It is expected that the special reserves are transferred to newly acquired assets within a few years.

In this step you will specify the depreciation areas for which you want transfer reserves (deferred gain) and determine the general ledger accounts the reserves are posted. This specification will avoid the system from issuing error message when corresponding depreciation terms are entered into the asset master record:

1. To determine depreciation areas, use this menu path: IMG: Financial Accounting (New) ➤ Asset Accounting ➤ Special Valuation ➤ Transferred Reserves (Deferred Gain) ➤ Determine Depreciation Areas. The Chart of Depreciation Selection screen pops-up. This screen allows you to determine the chart of depreciation containing the depreciation areas you can activate to manage transferred reserves.

2. Enter your chart of depreciation key (B10) in the ChDep field and click the Enter ☑ button at the bottom left side of the screen. The Change View "Asset Accounting: Define if transfer of reserves pos/neg" screen appears, displaying the depreciation areas you may want to manage transferred reserves as in Figure 5-3.

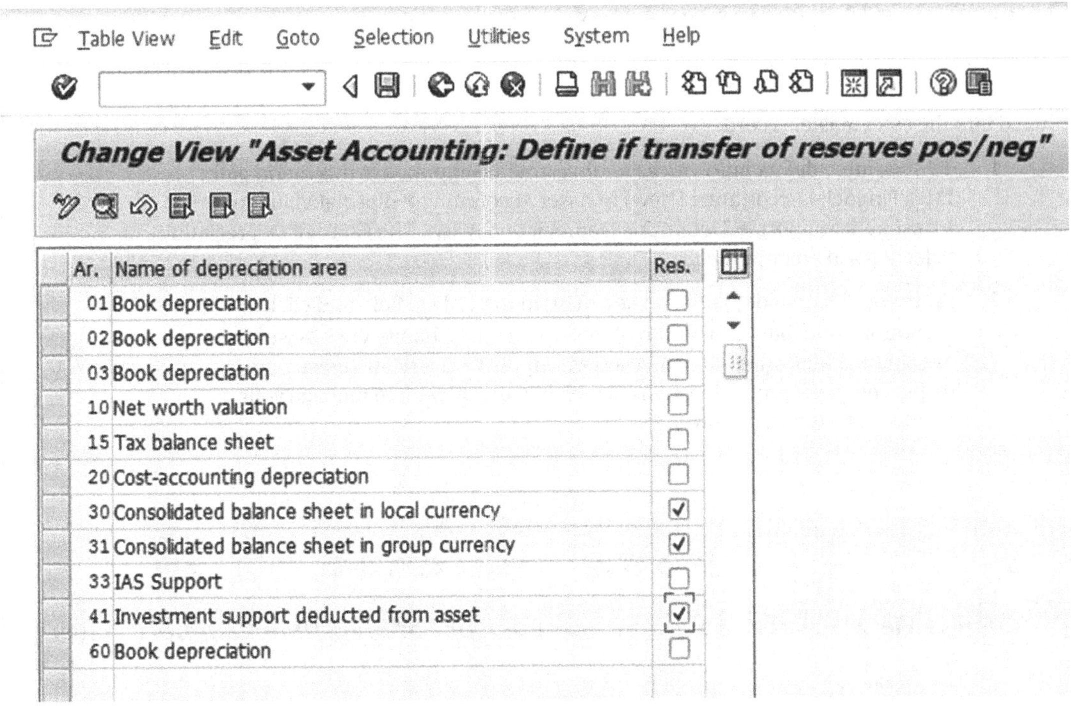

Figure 5-3. *The screen where you determine the depreciation areas where you want to manage your transfer reserves (deferred gain)*

3. Set the indicator(s) you want to manage transfer reserves in the depreciation areas in question.

4. Click the Enter ✅ button at the top left of the screen and save 💾 your work.

Investment Support

In some countries, the government gives incentives as subsidies for special investments based on stipulated conditions. This form of investment subsidy is technically referred to as "investment support." This subsidy simply reduces the Acquisition and Production Costs (APC) value or valuation adjustment. In practice, the investment support can either be treated as a reduction if the APC value in the balance sheet or disclosed separately valuation adjustment on the liabilities side of the balance sheet. The investment support component in SAP is specifically geared toward the management of government subsidies in order to meet legal treatment and disclosure requirements.

When defining investment support in SAP, you carry out the following steps:

- Determine the depreciation areas you want to manage investment support

- Define investment support measures

- Assign the account you want to post subsidies

Determining Depreciation Areas

In this step, you specify the depreciation areas in which you want to manage your investment support. This specification will stop the system from issuing error message when corresponding depreciation terms are entered into the asset master record:

1. To determine depreciation areas for investment support, use this menu path: IMG: Financial Accounting (New) ➤ Asset Accounting ➤ Special Valuation ➤ Investment Support ➤ Determine Depreciation Areas. The Chart of Depreciation Selection screen pops-up.

2. Enter your chart of depreciation key (B10) in the ChDep field and click the Enter button at the bottom left side of the screen. The Change View "Asset Accounting: Management of investment support": Overview screen appears, displaying the depreciation areas in which you may want to manage your investment support (Figure 5-4).

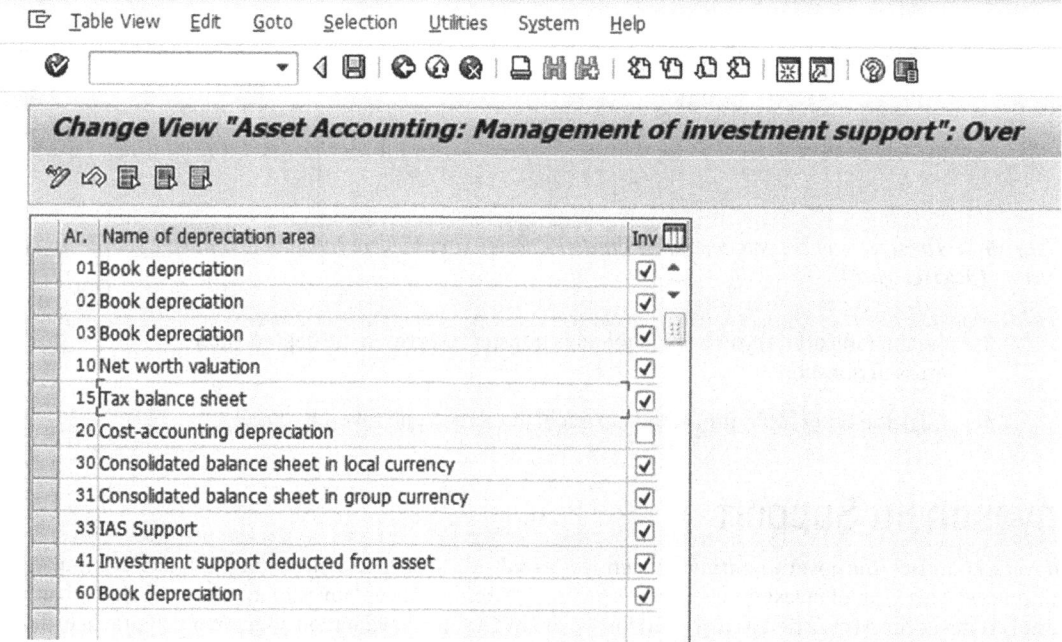

Figure 5-4. The screen where you specify the depreciation areas in which you want to manage investment support

3. Specify the depreciation areas you may want to manage investment support by selecting the checkbox for each depreciation each depreciation area as in Figure 5-4.

4. Click the Enter ✔ button at the top left of the screen and save 💾 your work.

Defining Investment Support Measures

The investment support measure is the component in SAP that holds the parameters which determines how investment support is managed in SAP. Subsidies can be used to reduce the acquisition and production costs (APC) of the asset in question on the asset side of the balance sheet or as valuation adjustment on the liabilities side of the balance sheet. In your configuration, you must decide whether the investment measure is managed on the liabilities side or as APC reduction on the asset side of the balance sheet.

■ **Note**   You should manage the investment support in the book depreciation area of your chart of depreciation if you chose to have the investment support reduce the APC value. On the contrary, if you chose to manage the investment support as an adjustment value on the liabilities side, then you should do this in the special depreciation area (and not in the book depreciation area). However, for reporting purposes you can also manage additional investment measure in other depreciation areas.

Follow these steps to define investment support measures:

1. Use this menu path: IMG: Financial Accounting (New) ➤ Asset Accounting ➤ Special Valuation ➤ Investment Support ➤ Define Investment Support Measures. The Chart of Depreciation Selection screen pops up. On this screen you determine the chart of depreciation to manage your investment support measure.

2. Enter your chart of depreciation key (B10) in the ChDep field and click the enter ☑ button at the bottom left side of the screen. The Change View "Investment Support Measure": Overview screen is displayed.

3. Click the New Entries button at the top left of the screen. The New: Details of Added Entries screen appears (Figure 5-5). This is the screen where you perform the actual specification of your investment measure.

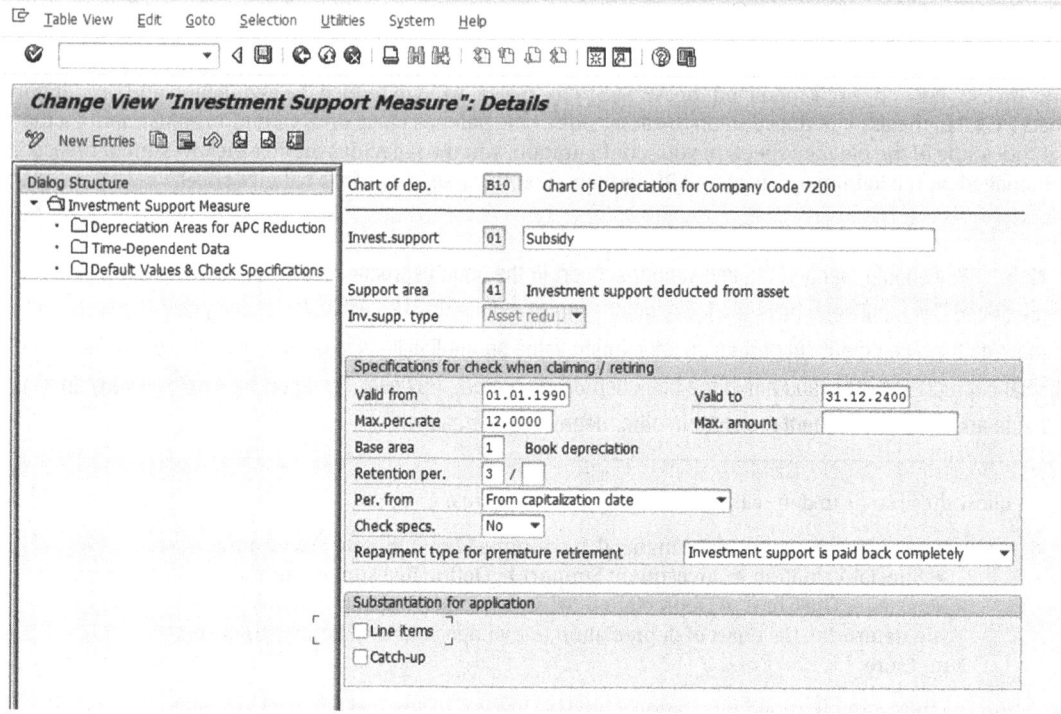

Figure 5-5. *The screen where you define investment support measures*

4. Update the following fields:

- **Chart of dep.:** This is defaulted by the system based on the specifications you made on the Chart of Depreciation Selection screen in Figure 5-5.

- **Invest.support:** This is defined by using a two-digit character (01) as the identification key for your investment support and a short text that best describes your investment support.

- **Support area:** You enter the depreciation area key of the depreciation area in which you want to manage the investment support (for example, depreciation area 41 – Investment support deduction from asset). You can access the list of depreciation key using the matchcode by the support area field. A Matchcode is a search function provided by SAP in the system, which allows you to search or look up items codes in the system.

- **Inv.supp. type:** Investment support type is defaulted by the system based from the settings that you made when specifying the depreciation areas that you want to carry out investment support. Setting determines how investment support measure should be carried out, either as a value adjustment on the liabilities side of the balance sheet or as a reduction of APC.

- **Valid from/Valid to**: Enter the date range you want the system to take into consideration in the treatment your support measure (i.e., start and end date).

- **Max.perc.rate:** Enter the maximum percentage rate for investment support in relation to the APC in this field. The system will automatically check the amount against the percentage when you are claiming investment support.

- **Max. amount:** It is also possible to specify maximum amount for investment support in conjunction with the maximum percentage rate. If this is the case, when you are claiming investment support, the system will automatically check the maximum percentage rate and the absolute maximum amount and use which ever ls lower.

- **Retention per.:** Enter the required period of retention of investment support in this field.

- **Per. from:** SAP comes with up to five period-from options you can choose from that you want to start the investment support calculation. To access the list of options you want to use as the start dates, click the pull down arrow by the per. from field. Choose "From capitalization date." This is the date the asset in question was acquired.

- **Repayment type for premature retirement**: This function allows to choose from four options. This is the indicator that controls the proportion of the investment support you claimed on a premature retired asset which need to be paid back within the specified retention period. For example, the "Investment support is paid back completely." This option will allow you to pay back the investment support received due to premature retirement of an asset. A premature retirement of an asset may arise due to the premature write-back of asset retirement for investment support valuation adjustment on the liabilities side.

5. Click the Enter ❤ button at the top left of the screen and save 💾 your work.

Assigning Accounts

In this step you are to carry out accounts determination of the general ledger for investment support measures.

1. To assign accounts investment support are posted, use this menu path: IMG: Financial Accounting (New) ➤ Asset Accounting ➤ Special Valuation➤ Investment Support ➤ Assign Accounts.

2. The Chart of Depreciation Selection screen pops up. Enter the chart of depreciation (B10) in the ChDep field and click the Continue ✅ button at the bottom left of the screen. The Change View "Chart of Accounts: Investment sup": Overview screen is displayed containing your chart of accounts (INT – Chart of accounts – international).

3. Select your chart of accounts (INT-Chart of accounts – international) and double click the Choose Account Determination folder in the chart of accounts on the left pane of the screen. The Change View "Accounts: Investment sup": Overview screen containing all the account determination existing in the system (including the account determinations you defined in Chapter 1 in the Account Determination specification section) appears (Figure 5-6).

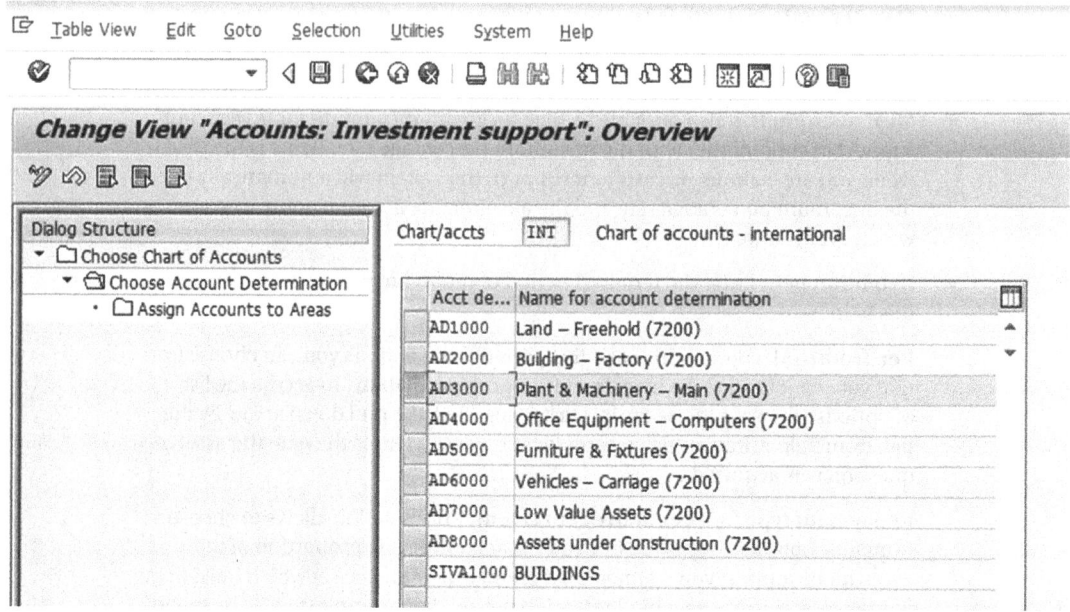

Figure 5-6. *The screen where you assign accounts that invest supports are posted*

4. Using the [▣ Position...] button at the bottom of the screen, search for the account determination you want to use apply investment support measures. Select the account determination (for example, in this exercise we used AD3000 Plant & Machinery) from the list of displayed account determination and double click Assign Accounts to Areas folder on the left pane of the screen. The Change View "Accounts: Investment sup": Overview screen appears, containing all the depreciation areas in your chart of depreciation.

5. Select the book depreciation that you want to manage investment support (41 – Inv. subsidy) from the list of displayed depreciation areas and click the Details ▣ button at the top left of the screen. The Change View "Accounts: Investment sup": Detail screen is displayed.

6. Specify the appropriate general ledger you want to post investment support.

7. Click the Enter ✅ button at the top left of the screen and save 🖫 your work.

Revaluation of Fixed Assets

An enterprise in most cases (depending on the activities of the enterprise) holds fixed assets for the purpose of producing goods or rendering services as opposed to be held as the primary object of business. A typical example of fixed assets that fell under this category include, properties, machineries, licenses/patents, and so on. Some of the assets held by an enterprise may appreciate (increase in value) or depreciate (reduction in value) in market value over time due to certain prevailing conditions (i.e., inflation, deflation, technological obsolesces, etc.). For example, in recent times we have seen high appreciation in market value of properties today as compared to the original value of the properties few years ago in most countries of the world due to inflation. In finance in order for the asset in question to be disclosed in the balance sheet at its true value, it is important to revise the value of the asset to be in line with the prevailing fair market value using the revaluation of fixed assets technique.

To avoid the abuse of revaluation of fixed assets, the finance regulatory bodies in several countries have come up with various accounting standards and GAAPs to ensure uniform standards applied consistently in the treatment of fixed assets revaluation.

In order to be able to account for revaluation of fixed assets arising from an inflation-related increase or reduction in the value of fixed assets. Revaluation of fixed assets is important for one of these reasons:

- For management internal reporting to aid decision making

- Proper accounting treatment for tax requirements

SAP provides the following functions for the treatment of revaluation of fixed assets:

- Index replacement values

- Revaluation for the balance sheet

Index Replacement Values

Apart for being able to determine the historical APC of an asset, the system uses index series to determine the asset replacement values. The determined asset replacement value is then uses as a base for calculating depreciation in Asset Accounting.

The replacement value may be used under the following conditions:

- In a high inflation environment. For example, a country where interest rate is significantly high. It makes sense to use replacement value as a basis for determining depreciation.

- For cost accounting purposes, it is ideal to consider price changes of investment goods as a reasonable pricing policy.

- For a comparison of companies with similar real estate, the use replacement value as the basis of depreciation is an important reserves policy.

The index series you specify will allow the system to automatically take periodic value changes into consideration when depreciation that is asset-specific or class-specific is posted. When you cost your own product price, it is advisable to take normal price rate rise into consideration by simply transferring the depreciation derived from the replacement value to controlling. When defining index replacement values in Asset Accounting you carry out the following steps:

- Determine the depreciation areas for indexed replacement values

- Define index series

Determining Depreciation Areas

In this activity, you will specify the depreciation areas that you want to manage replacement values:

1. To determine depreciation areas for indexed replacement values, use this menu path: IMG: Financial Accounting (New) ➤ Asset Accounting ➤ Special Valuation ➤ Revaluation of Fixed Assets ➤ Indexed Replacement Values ➤ Determine Depreciation Areas. The Change View "Asset Accounting: Management of replacement values": Overview screen (Figure 5-7).

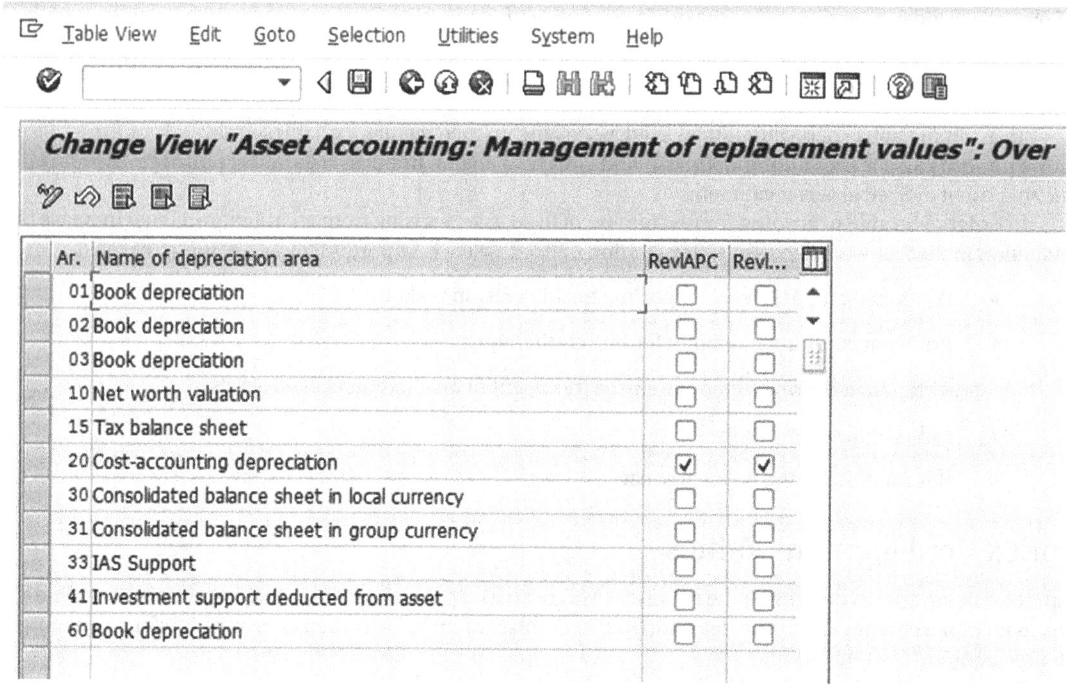

Figure 5-7. *The screen where you specify the depreciation areas that you want to carry out the management of index replacement values*

2. Specify the book depreciation you want to replacement values as in Figure 5-7.

3. Click the Enter ✔ button at the top left of the screen and save 🖫 your work.

Defining Index Series

If you want to calculate depreciation replacement values, you definitely need index figures. You need to define index series and historical index figure for your index series. For the system to calculate replacement value, you need to maintain index figures which starts at the time the oldest asset with an index series was acquired, up to the takeover time of the old assets data:

1. To define index series, use this menu path: IMG: Financial Accounting (New) ➤ Asset Accounting ➤ Special Valuation ➤ Revaluation of Fixed Assets ➤ Indexed Replacement Values ➤ Define Index Series. The Change View "Index series": Overview screen is displayed containing the list of index series supplied by SAP in the system.

2. Click the New Entries push button at the top left of the screen. The New Entries: Details of Added Entries screen comes up (Figure 5-8). This is the screen where you specify the details for your index series.

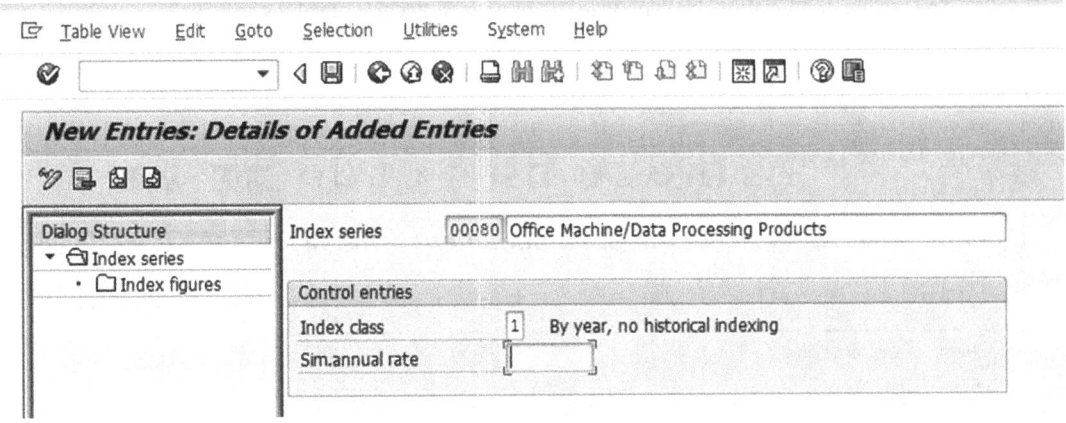

Figure 5-8. *The screen where you define index series for index replacement values*

3. Update the following fields:

    - **Index series:** You can enter up to five-digit character as your index series and a descriptive name for your index series (for example, 00080 – Office Machine/ Data Processing Products).

    - **Index class:** Specify the appropriate index class for your index series (i.e., whether the index series should be year-dependent or age-dependent) and whether the replacement value should be calculated on historical bases. For this activity we used '1- By year, no historical indexing'. You can use the matchcode by the index class field to display the standard index class supplied by SAP in the system.

4. Click the Enter ✅ button at the top left of the screen and save 💾 your work.

■ **Note**   The maintenance of current index figure is a part of period processing in the application menu of the FI-AA system.

Revaluation for the Balance Sheet

In this activity you determine depreciation area and define revaluation measures for your Asset Accounting.

Determining Depreciation Areas

In this step, you will specify the depreciation areas that you want to manage replacement values:

1. To determine depreciation areas for revaluation for the balance sheet, use this menu path: IMG: Financial Accounting (New) ➤ Asset Accounting ➤ Special Valuation ➤ Revaluation of Fixed Assets ➤ Revaluation for the Balance Sheet ➤ Determine Depreciation Areas. The Change View "Asset Accounting: Management of replacement values": Overview screen.

2.   Specify the depreciation area you want to manage replacement values as in Figure 5-9.

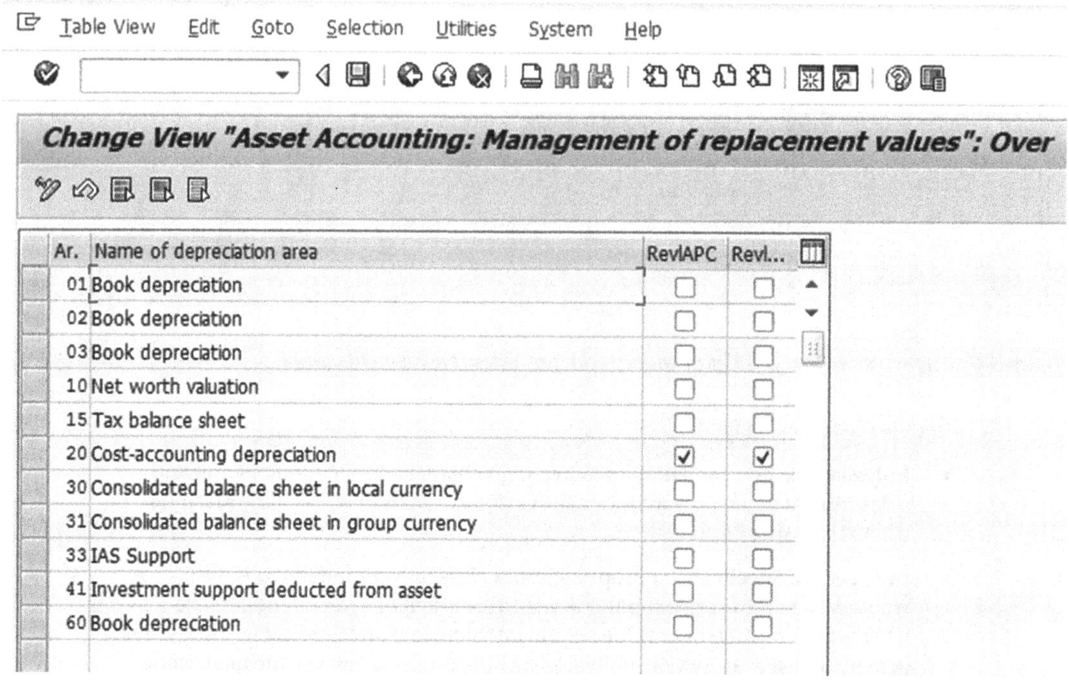

Figure 5-9. *The screen where you determine the depreciation you want to manage replace values*

3.   Click the Enter ✅ button at the top left of the screen and save 💾 your work.

Defining Revaluation Measures

In this activity, you will define the revaluation measures for the revaluation for balance sheet.

1.   To define the revaluation for balance sheet, you may use the menu path: IMG: Financial Accounting (New) ➤ Asset Accounting ➤ Special Valuation ➤ Revaluation of Fixed Assets ➤ Revaluation for the Balance Sheet ➤ Determine Depreciation Areas. The change View "Revaluation Measure": Overview screen is displayed. This is the initial screen where you define revaluation measure for balance sheet.

2.   Click the New Entries button at the top left of the screen. The New Entries: Details of Added Entries screen appears. This is the screen where you will enter the specification for revaluation measure.

3.   You define the revaluation measures using up to two-digit characters as your revaluation key and a shot description of your revaluation measure. In the date specifications section of the screen, enter a date in the Date field (could be the posting date or the asset value date of the revaluation) and in the area specifications section, enter the appropriate depreciation area in the Base area field (this is the base area for calculating revaluation) and revaluation area in the Revaluation field using Figure 5-10 as a reference.

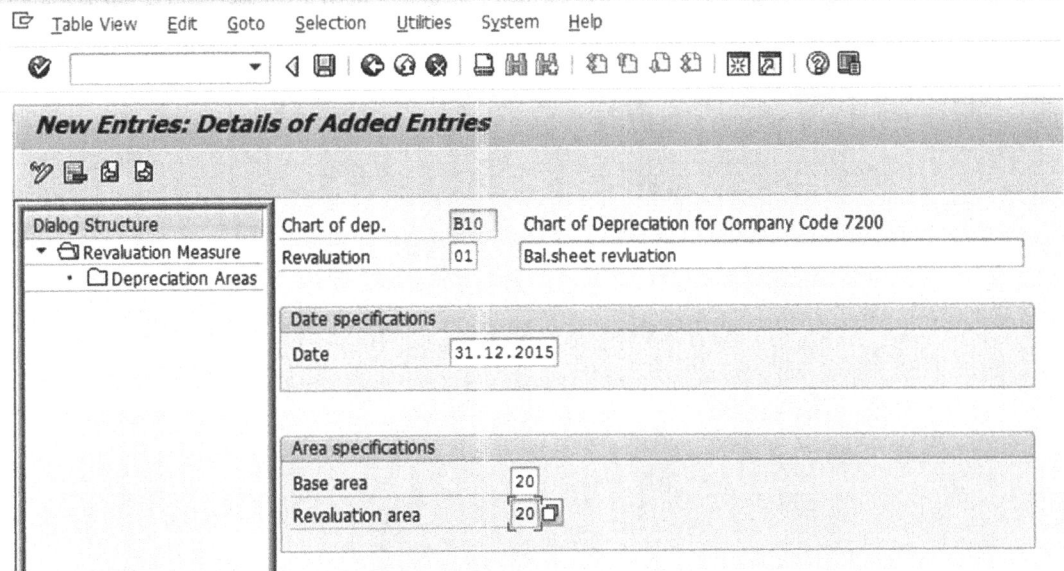

Figure 5-10. *The screen where you carry out specification of revaluation measure*

4.   Click the Enter ⊘ button at the top left of the screen and save 💾 your work.

Summary

In this chapter, we started with how assets are classified and treated using special valuation adjustment components. We explained how permitted book depreciation that exceeds the book depreciation are treated as special depreciation and disclosed in the liabilities side in the balance sheet. We then taught how to customize the specification of gross or net procedure and how to assign accounts that they are posted in general ledger. The thing we looked at was transferred reserves (differed gain). In doing this, we looked at the customizing steps involved in determining depreciation areas. Thereafter, we looked at what investment support and took you through the steps involved in defining investment support by looking at how to determine the depreciation areas for managing investment support, how to define investment support measures, and how to assign them investment support measures to the accounts where you want to post subsidies. We went on to look at the purpose of fixed assets revaluation. For example, for management internal reporting to aid management decision making and for proper accounting treatment for tax requirements.

Finally we looked at the function provided by SAP for the treatment of fixed assets. These include index replacement values and revaluation for balance sheet. In index replacement values, we looked at the purpose of index replacement values as replacement values and various conditions for when replacement values may be used, for example, in a high inflation economy, for cost accounting purposes, and for real estate valuation in order to show a fair market value. We then finally briefly looked at the revaluation for the balance sheet.

In the next chapter we will be looking at the customizing steps in defining master data in FI-AA. This will include defining screen layout for asset master data, screen layout for asset depreciation areas, and how to specify tab layout for asset master record. We will then go on to look at how to create a master record for assets, group assets, and subnumbers. Finally, we will then look at how to change assets and group assets master records, respectively.

▓ ▓ ▓

CHAPTER 6

Customizing Master Data

This chapter looks at the steps involved in the configuration of master data in Asset Accounting and also explained the various steps involved in customizing master data in asset accounting.

In this chapter, you will learn what master data is and how to:

- Define screen layouts for asset master data

- Define screen layouts for asset depreciation areas

- Specify tab layouts for asset master record

- Define substitution for mass changes

- Maintain a depreciation key

- Create a master record for assets, group assets, and subnumbers

- Change assets and group assets master records

- Display master records

What Is Master Data?

Master data in Asset Accounting is critical data about the fixed assets held in the system that remains relatively unchanged over a period of time. Using master data in Asset Accounting you can create, change, and display asset data.

The master asset master record holds the basic asset master data, which contains the specific information about the fixed assets. This includes the general information about the asset (such as the asset description, asset main number text, account determination, etc.), the time-dependent aspects (such as business area, cost center, plant, location, functional area, and real estate key), investment measures, trading partner, net worth valuation, real estate, and similar rights, and so on. And the calculation aspect of the master data for calculating the fixed assets APC and depreciation (for example, the depreciation key, the asset useful life, the depreciation methods, the asset scrap value, etc.).

In SAP FI-AA, you can customize the settings for needed for master data. In this chapter we will be looking at how to define screen layouts and create asset master records.

Screen Layout

Screen layout holds the screen layout rules that allow you to define the structure of your asset master records. In SAP FI-AA, the master records come with a large number of fields to meet varied needs. Some of the fields may not be need for your own use, so it is important that during the customizing of master data, you maintain your master record by carrying out the following specifications to meet your requirements:

- Define a screen layout for asset master data
- Define a screen layout for asset depreciation areas and
- Specify a tab layout for asset master record

Defining the Screen Layout for Asset Master Data

Here you define the screen layout for asset master data. Your specifications allow you structure the asset master record in the asset class for each asset class individually. The importance of the screen layout for asset master data is that the specification you make controls the field group features in the asset master record.

■ **Note**   SAP comes with defined screen layout you can use as reference when defining your screen layout for asset master data. We recommend that you look the predefined screen layout supplied by SAP in the system, before attempting to define your own screen layout.

To define screen layout for asset master data, perform the following steps:

1. Use this menu path: IMG: Financial Accounting (New) ➤ Asset Accounting ➤ Master Data ➤ Screen Layout ➤ Define Screen Layout for Asset Master Data. The Choose Activity screen comes up with activities you can choose from (Define Screen Layout for Asset Master Data and Create Screen Layout Rules for Asset Master Record).

2. Select Define Screen Layout for Asset Master Data from the displayed activities and click the [Q Choose] button at the bottom right of the screen. The Change View "Screen layout": Overview screen appears containing a list of screen layout for asset master records already in the system. You have already defined some screen layout for asset master records in Chapter 1 when you defined asset classes.

3. Using the [彩   Position...] button at the bottom of the screen, search for your screen layout for asset master records.

■ **Note**   You can only define the screen layout for the asset master record for each asset class individually.

---

4. Select your first screen layout as in Figure 6-1.

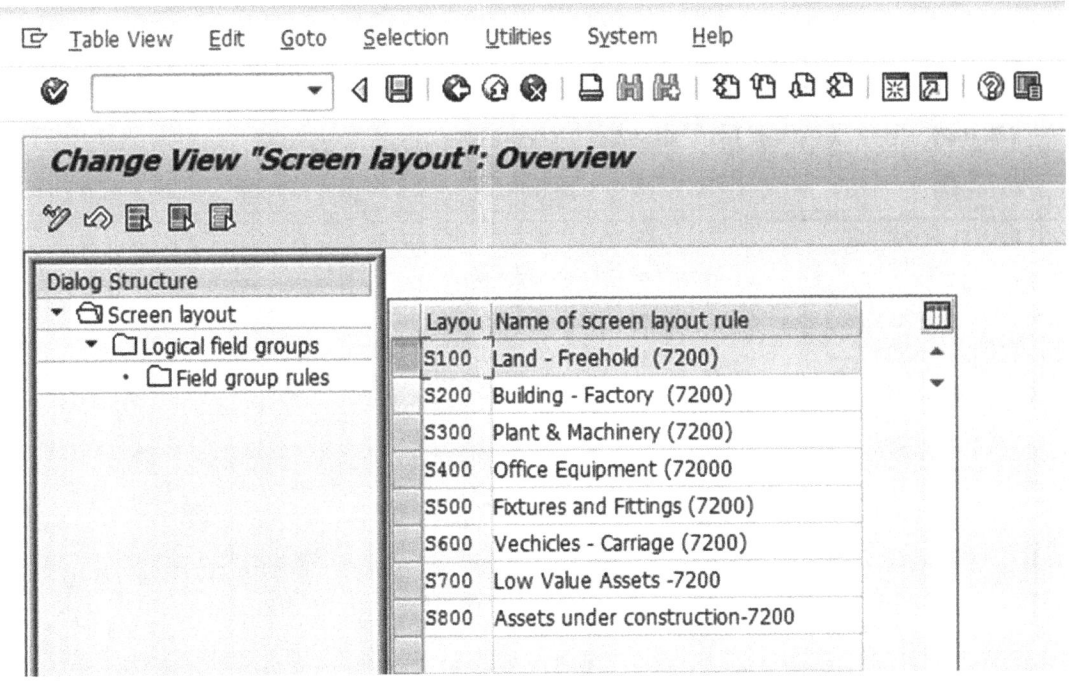

Figure 6-1. The list of screen layout for asset master records

5. Double-click the Logical field groups folder in the screen layout on the left pane of the screen. The Display View "Logical field groups": Overview screen appears. SAP provides a list of field groups with appropriate field group rules, which are sufficient for your requirements (Figure 6-2).

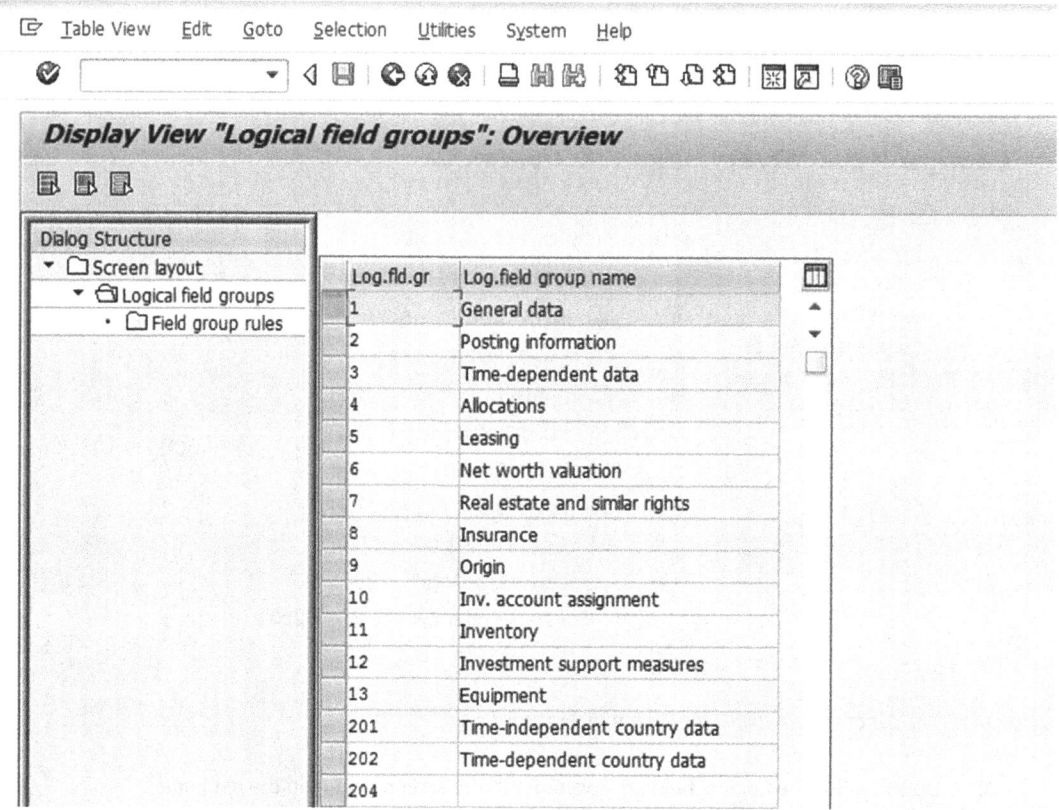

Figure 6-2. *The list of logical field groups you can define field group rules*

6. To specify the field group rules, select a field group (General data) and double-click the Field group rules from the Logical field groups on the left pane of the screen. The Change View "Field group rules": Overview screen is displayed (Figure 6-3), showing field group and the specifications of how input fields will be structured in the asset master record, for example, whether a field should be required entry, optional, display or hide suppressed, and the maintenance level (the level at which a field is maintained in the asset master record).

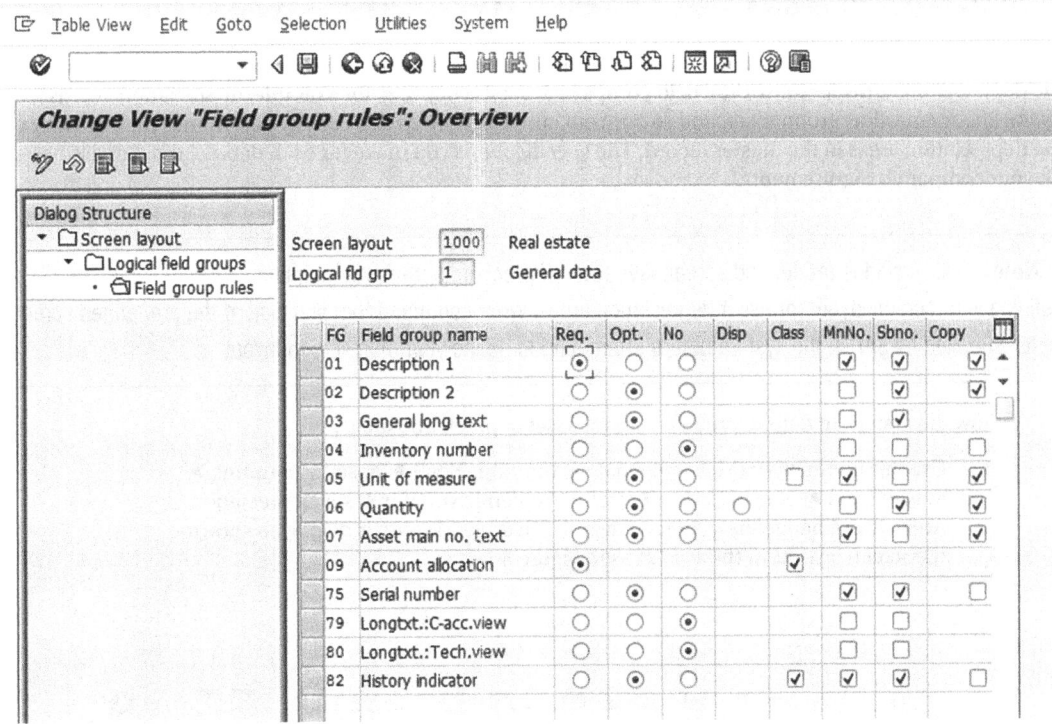

Figure 6-3. *The screen where you can define the fields that are required, optional, or suppressed during data entry for asset master record*

7. On this screen you will define the screen layout control for the master record by carrying out the following specifications:

- The characteristics of the master record screen. This is the part of the screen where you specify which field in the master record should be required for input, optional, or suppressed.

- The maintenance level of the master record screen. This is the other part of screen where you define the maintenance level for a field, for example, the main asset number and the asset subnumber. This setting will allow the field to receive a default value from the asset class. However, the default value can be over written during the master data maintenance.

- The final specification is to define the master record can be copied; for example, you can use the master record as a reference master record when creating a new master record.

8. On the completion of your specifications, click the Enter ✅ button at the top left of the screen and save 💾 your field group rules.

Defining the Screen Layout for Asset Depreciation Areas

Like the screen layout for asset master data, you will also in this step define the screen layout control for the depreciation terms for individual field groups in Asset Accounting, for example, depreciation key, asset useful life, scrap value, group asset, and so on. Your specifications in this activity determines the structure of the depreciation areas in the master record. The specifications you make for each depreciation area is based on your company's requirements.

■ **Note**   SAP provides predefined screen layout for depreciation areas you can use as reference when defining your screen layout for asset depreciation areas. We recommend that you look at the predefined screen layout supplied by SAP in the system before attempting to define your own screen layout.

Follow these steps to define screen layout for asset depreciation areas:

1.   Use this menu path: IMG: Financial Accounting (New) ➤ Asset Accounting ➤ Master Data ➤ Screen Layout ➤ Define Screen Layout for Asset Depreciation Areas. The Change View "Screen layout": Overview screen is displayed showing the screen layouts in the system as in Figure 6-4.

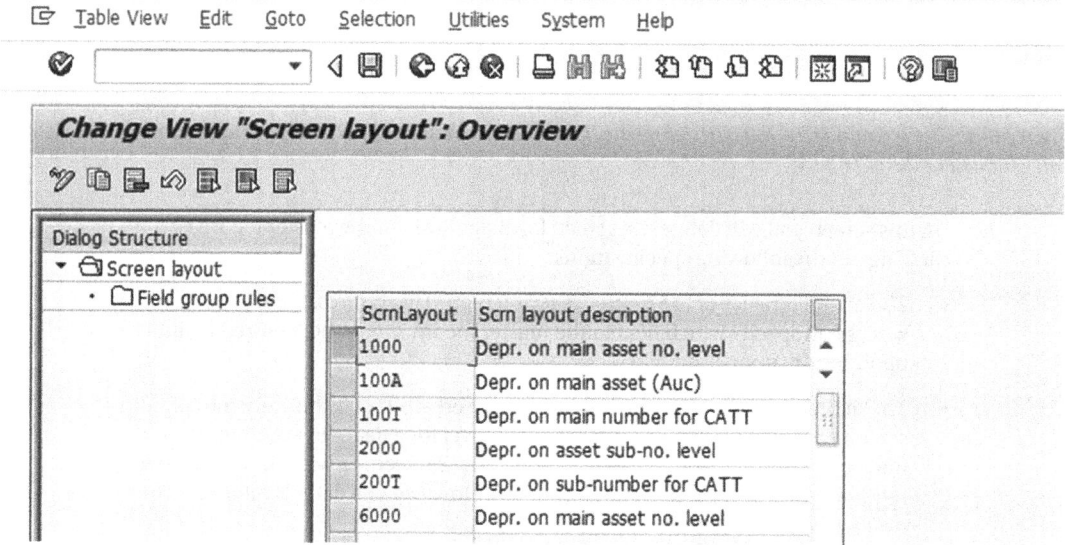

Figure 6-4.   *The list of screen layout for asset depreciation master records*

2.   Select the screen layout (1000) from the displayed list of screen layout and double-click the Field group rules folder on the left pane of the screen. The Change View "Screen layout for": Overview screen comes up in Figure 6-5.

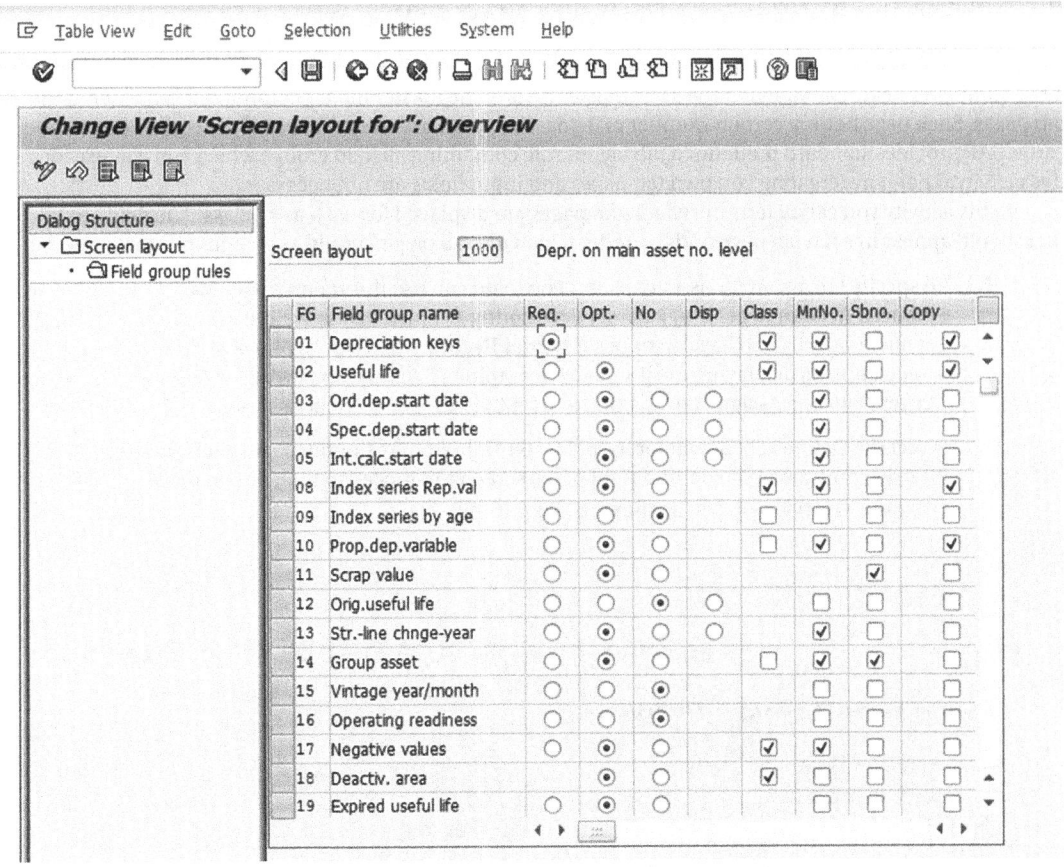

Figure 6-5. *The screen where you can define the fields that are required, optional, or suppressed during data entry for asset depreciation master record*

3. On this screen, you will define the screen layout control for the asset depreciation areas you are using in the master record by carrying out the following specifications:

   • The characteristics of the master record screen. Specify the field in the master record that should be required for input, optional or suppressed.

   • At the maintenance level of the master record screen, specify the main asset number and the asset subnumber. This specification will allow the field (for example depreciation key) to receive a default value from the asset class. However, the default value can be over written during the master data maintenance.

   • Finally, specify whether the master record can be copied.

4. Click the Enter 🗹 button at the top left of the screen and save 🖫 your field group rules.

Specifying the Tab Layout for Asset Master Records

Data relating to assets are stored in master record via several input fields. In order to be able to manage the large number of fields contained in the asset master record, the master record component is divided into tab pages. Each page holds a certain number of fields. Tab pages use the principle of the conventional index cards. SAP provides standard predefined tab layout rule containing all field groups which you can use for this activity. Therefore, creating you own tab pages and input fields are not necessary.

In this activity you can determine which tab pages are displayed for each asset class. The field groups that should appear in each tab page and the order which the tab pages should appear in the master record.

1. To specify tab layout for asset master record, you can use this menu path: IMG: Financial Accounting (New) ➤ Asset Accounting ➤ Master Data ➤ Screen Layout ➤ Specify Tab Layout for Asset Master Record. The Choose Activity screen appears displaying the list of activity otpions (Define Tab Layout for Asset Master Data and Assign Tab Layouts to Asset Classes) you can choose from.

2. Select the Define Tab Layout for Asset Master Data from the options and click the ⬚ Choose button at the bottom right of the screen to proceed to the Change View "Layout": Overview screen as shown in Figure 6-6.

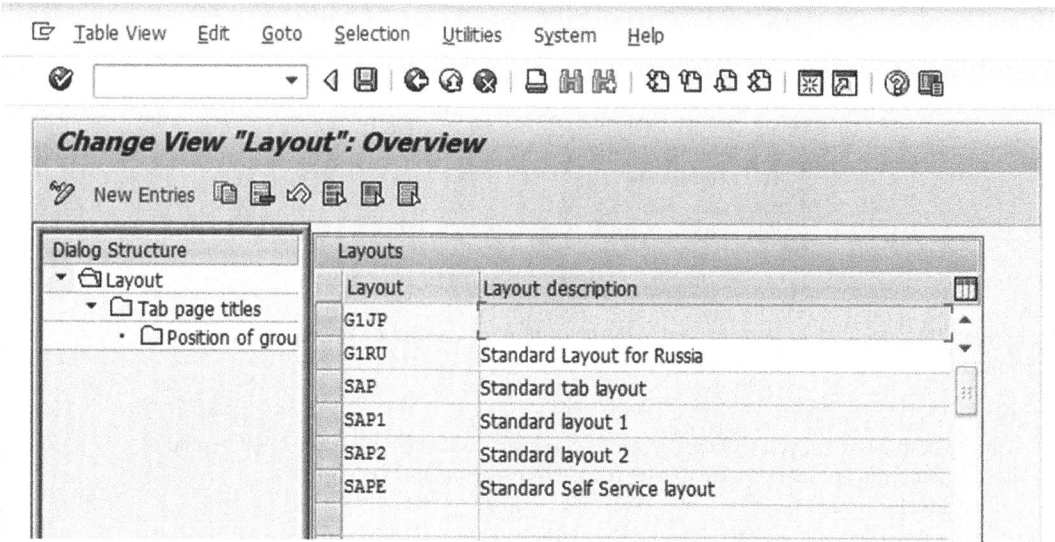

Figure 6-6. *The Standard tab layout rules supplied by SAP in the system*

■ **Note** The Change View "Layout": Overview screen contains the standard tab layout rules supplied by SAP for this requirements. We recommend that you stick to these standard predefined screen layout rules as they are sufficient for this customizing requirments.

Creating a Master Record

Because we have completed defining the control parameters for an asset master record, the next step is to look at how to create the asset master record.

Asset Master Record contains two parts:

- The part that hold general data, which relates to general information about the asset, which seldom change

- The part that holds data for calculating Asset Values. Here you make specifications for depreciation terms in the asset master record for each depreciation area in the chart of depreciation. This section of the master record contains an overview of the depreciation areas. There is also a detailed display for each depreciation area. The depreciation areas that are not needed for specific asset can be deactivated at the asset level.

In this activity we will be creating a master record for assets, group assets, and subnumbers and taking a look at how to change/edit and display asset master record.

Creating Assets

Use the following steps you can create an asset in the asset master data:

1. Use this menu path: Accounting ➤ Financial Accounting ➤ Fixed Assets ➤ Assets ➤ Create ➤ Asset. The Create Asset: Initial screen is displayed (Figure 6-7).

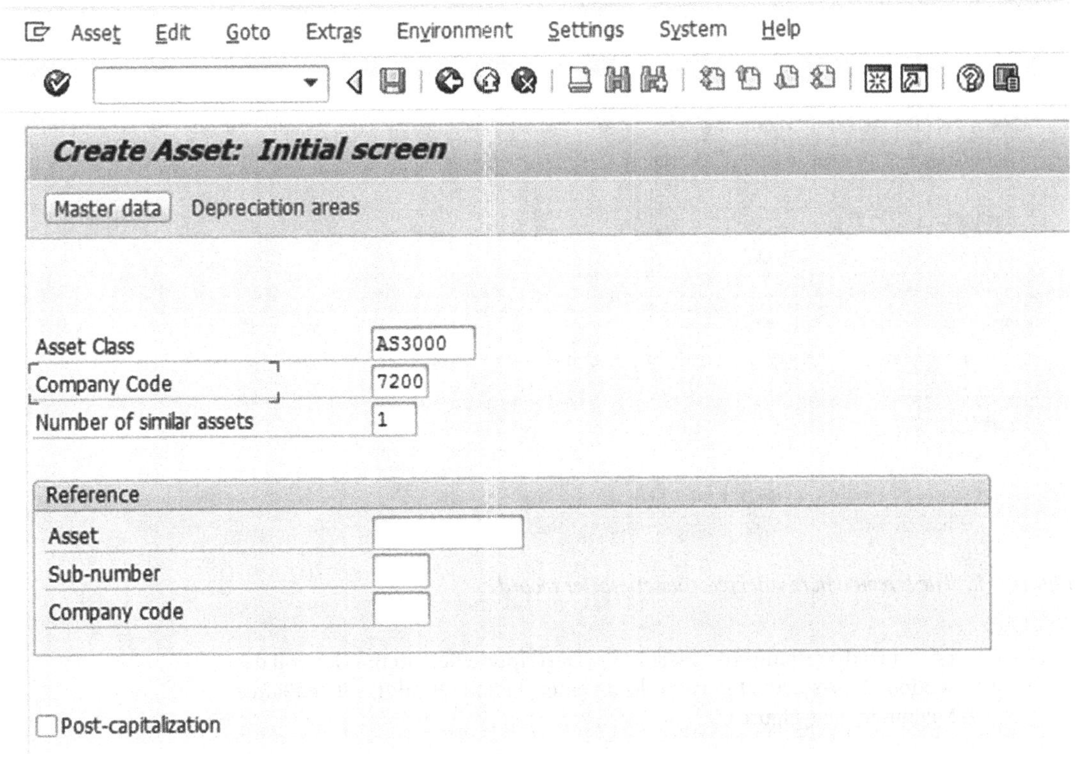

Figure 6-7. *The asset initial screen where you can specify the asset class you want to create its master record*

2. Update the following fields using Figure 6-7 as a reference:

- **Asset Class:** For each master record, you must assign one asset class. Enter the appropriate asset class (for example AS3000 for Plant & Machinery) for the asset in question you are creating the master record in this field (You can refer to chapter one on more details on asset classes.) You can access the list of asset class in the system, use. To access the list of asset class in the system you can use the matchcode by the asset class field.

- **Company Code:** Enter your company code (7200) in this field. This is the company code you want to manage the asset master record.

- **Number of similar assets:** This is defaulted by the system. This function will allow you to create multiple identical assets in a single master data transaction.

3. To specify the general data for the asset master record, click the [Master data] button at the top left of the screen. The Create Asset: Master data screen is displayed (Figure 6-8).

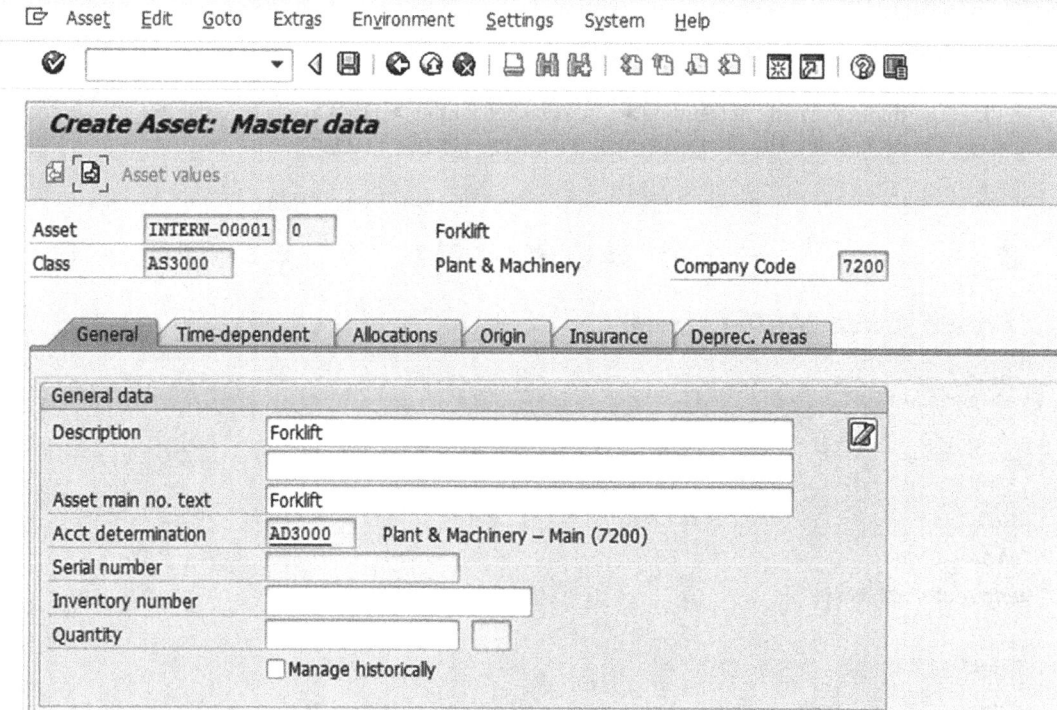

Figure 6-8. *The screen where you create asset master record*

4. Enter text describing your asset in the Description field in the General date section of the screen, for example, an asset class for Forklift will be Plant & Machinery (see Figure 6-8).

5. Click the Time-dependent tab somewhere at the middle of the screen to move to the nest page of the screen. Update the following fields:

- **Business Area:** Business area is a specific business segment of operation of an organizational unit, entrusted with the responsibility of external accounting that relates specifically to its own activities in an enterprise. Enter the appropriate business area key (1000) for your asset master record in this field. This entry will allow every posting to an asset balance sheet to be automatically posted by the system to this business area. So you do not need to manually make account assignment for a business area.

- **Cost Center:** Enter the cost center (1100) that you want to manage your asset master record in this field. Cost center is used for internal purpose to records costs with reference to plan values. For internal accounting purposes, it is important to assign asset costs to cost centers. You can assign individual asset in Asset Accounting to exactly one cost center.

6. Click the Deprec. Areas tab to call up the valuation page of the screen. The list of depreciation areas with the assigned depreciation keys and the asset useful life you performed in the customizing of determine depreciation area in the asset class in Chapter 3 are defaulted by the system.

7. Specify the depreciation start date by entering the date you want the ordinary depreciation of assets to commence in the ODep Start field for each depreciation area, as in Figure 6-9.

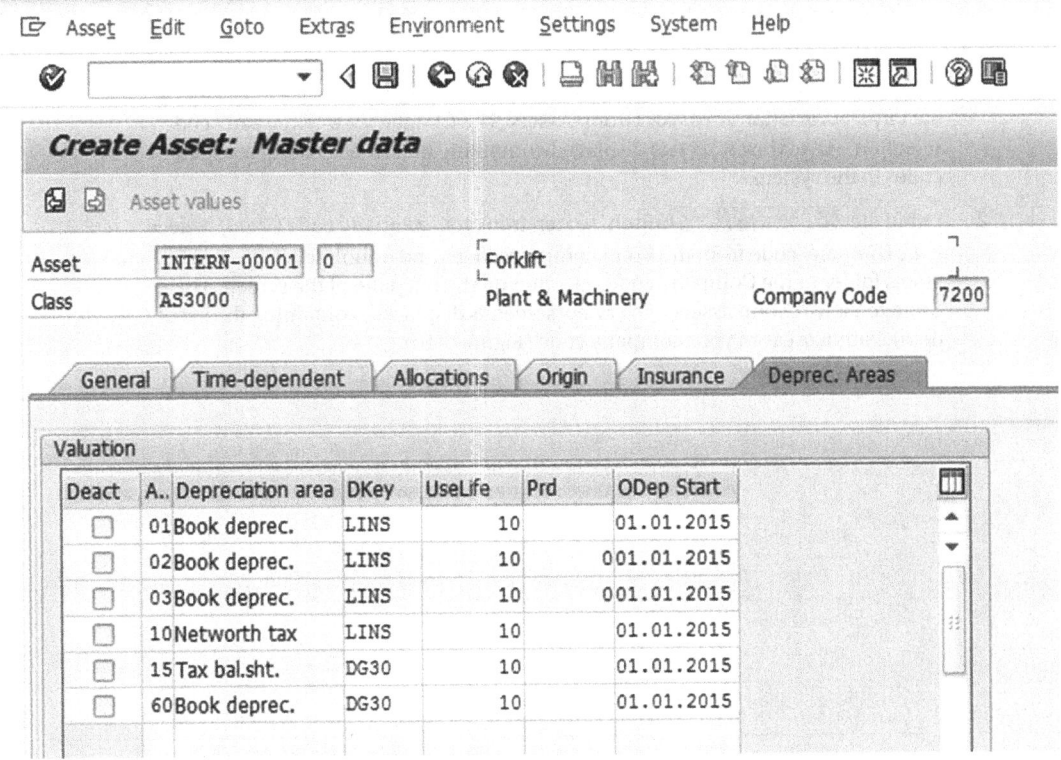

Figure 6-9. *The area of the asset master record where you specify the depreciation key, the asset useful life, and ordinary depreciation date for each depreciation area for depreciation calculation*

8. Click the Enter ✅ button at the top left of the screen and save 🖫.

9. Repeat the same process for the remaining asset classes.

Specifying Depreciation Areas for Group Assets

Normally, depreciation is calculated for each asset at the level of individual asset in FI-AA for each asset main number or subnumber. The asset main number is a unique number that identifies an asset, whereas the asset number allows you to identify the individual subassets separately. This is the case in an environment where you have an asset consisting of several component assets.

The group assets specification allows you to group several assets together for the calculation and posting of depreciation. In some countries, in order to meet certain tax disclosure requirements, such as for Asset Depreciation Rang (ADR) in the United States, SAP FI-AA Group assets component allows you to calculate asset depreciation at a higher level to meet these requirements, rather than calculating depreciation at individual asset level. (ADR is an accounting method businesses can use for calculating asset depreciation, which is generally acceptable by IRS for determining asset classes and year of acquisition.)

■ **Note** In SAP FI-AA, the asset group is represented with a separate master record different from the normal master record.

Before managing group asset, first you must specify each depreciation area that you want to manage on group asset level in your company code:

1. To specify depreciation areas for group assets, use this menu path: IMG: Financial Accounting (New) ➤ Asset Accounting ➤ Valuation ➤ Group Assets ➤ Specify Depreciation Areas for Group Assets. The Change View "Company code selection": Overview screen is displayed containing the list of existing company codes in the system.

2. Using the ▣ Position... button, search from you company code (7200). Select your company code from the list of company codes and double-click the Group assets folder in the Company code selection on the left pane of the screen. The Change View "Group assets": Overview screen is displayed, containing the list of depreciation areas in your company code (Figure 6-10).

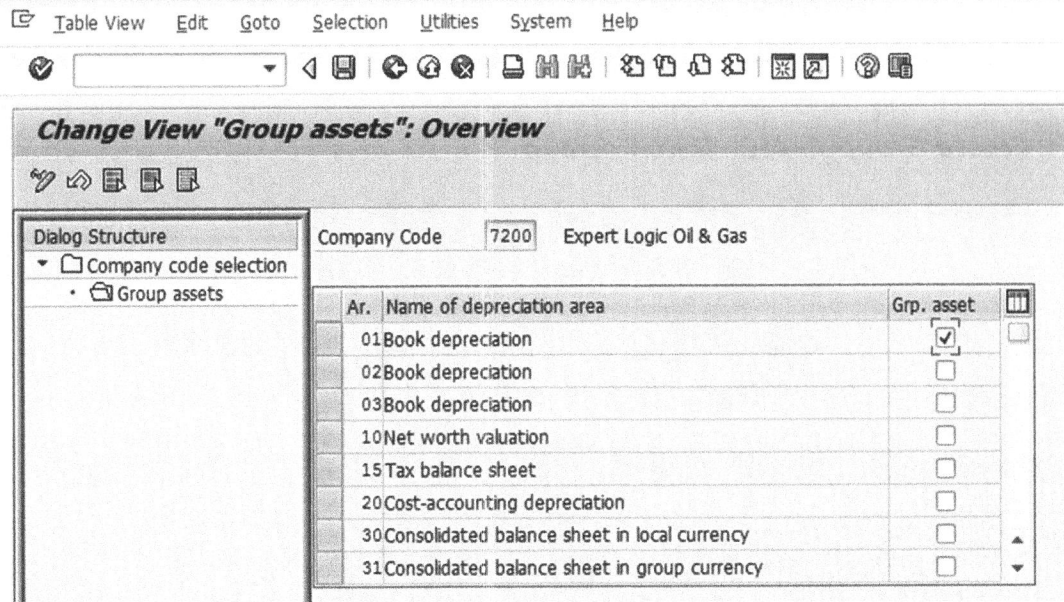

Figure 6-10. *The screen where you specify the depreciation area you want to manage group asset*

3. Indicate the depreciation areas for which you want group assets are to be managed as in Figure 6-10.

4. Click the Enter ✅ button at the top left of the screen and save 💾 your specifications.

The next step is to create the master record in fixed asset accounting where you will manage your group assets.

Creating Group Asset in Asset Master Data

Complete the following steps to create a group asset in the asset master data:

1. Use this menu path: Accounting ➤ Financial Accounting ➤ Fixed Assets ➤ Asset ➤ Create ➤ Group Assets. The Create Group Asset: Initial screen is displayed in Figure 6-11.

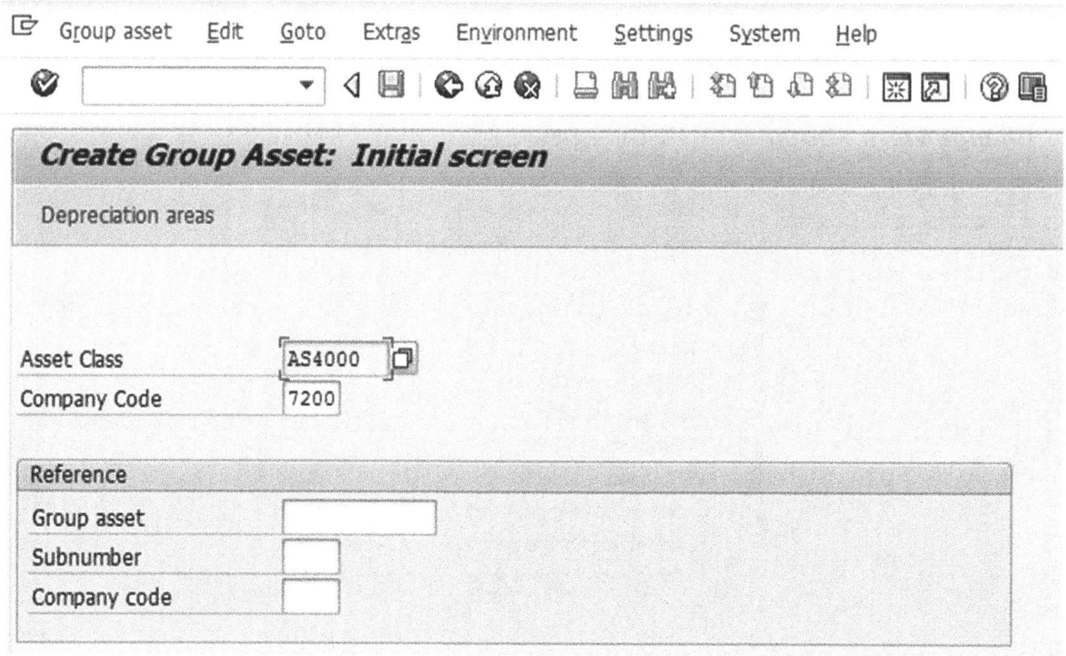

Figure 6-11. *The initial screen where you creat group asset*

2. Enter the data for your asset group in the following fields:

- **Asset Class:** Enter the asset class you want to manage your group assets on in this field. For example, assume that you want to manage real estate in group assets, use the appropriate asset class (AS4000). You can access the list of existing assets classes in the system using the matchcode by the asset class field.

- **Company Code:** Enter the company code (7200) you want use for your group assets in this field.

3. Click the [Depreciation areas] button at the top left of the screen. This will take you to the Create Group Asset: Master data screen where you will enter the information for your group asset.

4. In the General tab section of the screen, enter a text for your group asset description in the description field as shown in Figure 6-12.

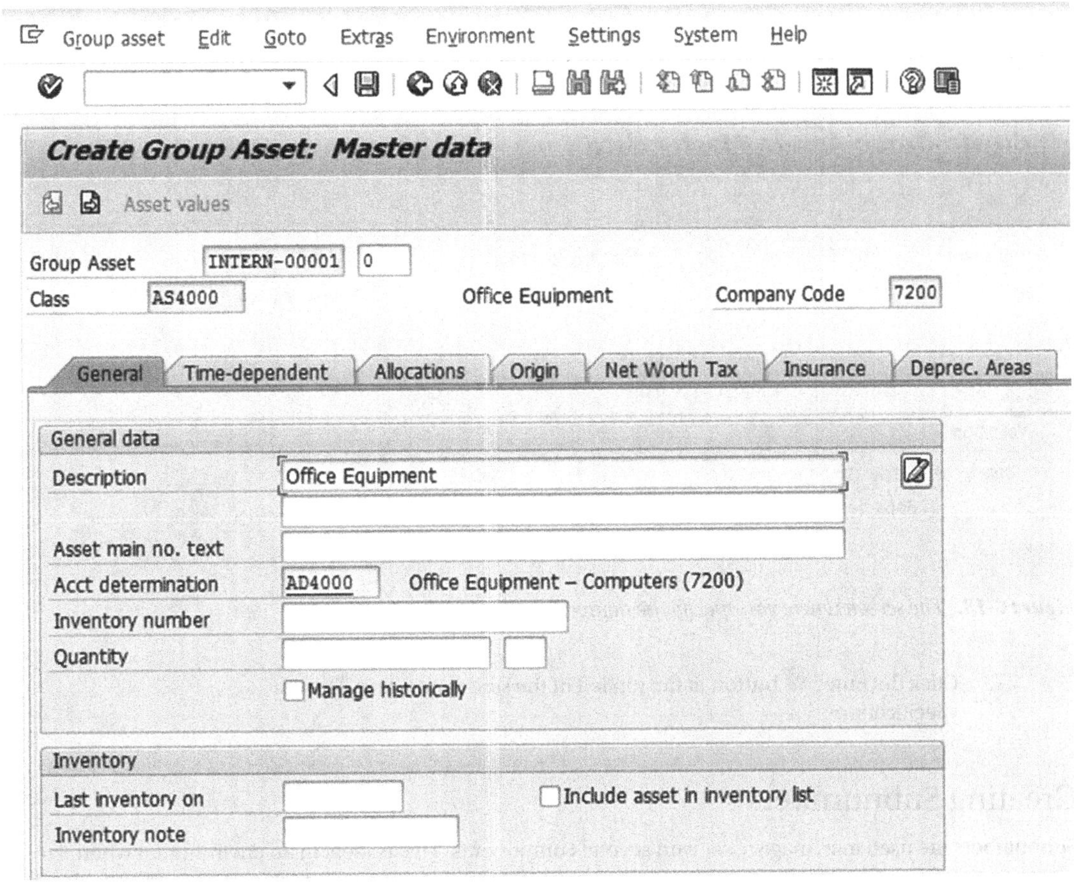

Figure 6-12. *The screen where you create group asset for the master data*

5. Click the time-dependent tab at the top of the screen to proceed to the time-dependent section of the screen. On this screen, enter the business area (1000) in the business area field and the cost center (1100) in the corresponding cost center field.

6. The next step is to specify the start date for depreciation. Click the Deprec. Areas tab to go to the depreciation areas of the screen. On this screen enter the date you want the system to start calculating depreciation, as shown in Figure 6-13.

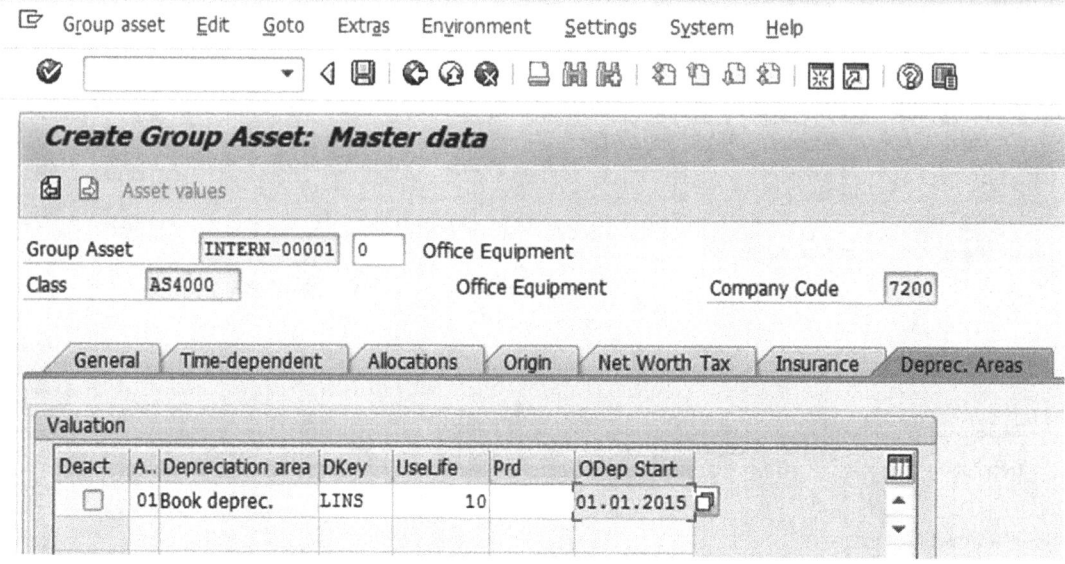

Figure 6-13. *The screen where you specify the depreciation start date*

7. Click the Enter ⊘ button at the top left of the screen and save 🖫 your specifications

Creating Subnumbers

Subnumbers are used to manage asset with several components. This is ideal in an environment where an asset has several components and the management want to be able to control each component individually, although for external and tax reporting purposes, it may be ideal to depreciate the entire asset uniformly. By contrast, for cost accounting purposes, the subassets are usually depreciated individually. You can create a subnumber for each asset or group asset.

Creating a Subnumber for Assets

To create a subnumber for an asset, complete the following steps:

1. Use this menu path: Accounting ➤ Financial Accounting ➤ Fixed Assets ➤ Asset ➤ Create ➤ Subnumber ➤. Asset. The Create Subnumber: Initial screen is displayed in Figure 6-14, which you can use as a reference.

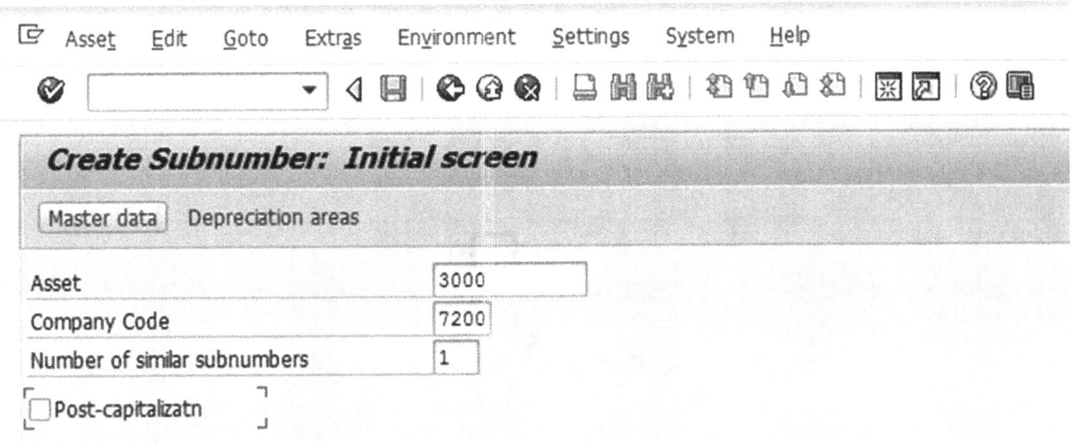

Figure 6-14. *The initial screen where you specify the asset main number you want to create subnumber for the asset component*

2. Update the following fields:

- **Asset:** Enter the main asset number of the asset in question with different asset components you want to create asset subnumbers in this field

- **Company Code:** Enter the company code the asset belongs in this field

- **Number of similar subnumbers:** This is automatically defaulted by system

3. Click the [Master data] button at the top left of the screen to proceed to the screen where you will create the master record for your asset component. The Create Asset: After data screen is displayed.

■ **Note** The system will automatically inherit the attributes of the main asset number (for example, the asset description, business area, cost center, depreciation areas, etc.).

---

4. The asset description is defaulted. You can overwrite the asset description. (For example, for we changed Forklift in the description field to Forklift Accessories-1, as can be seen in Figure 6-15.)

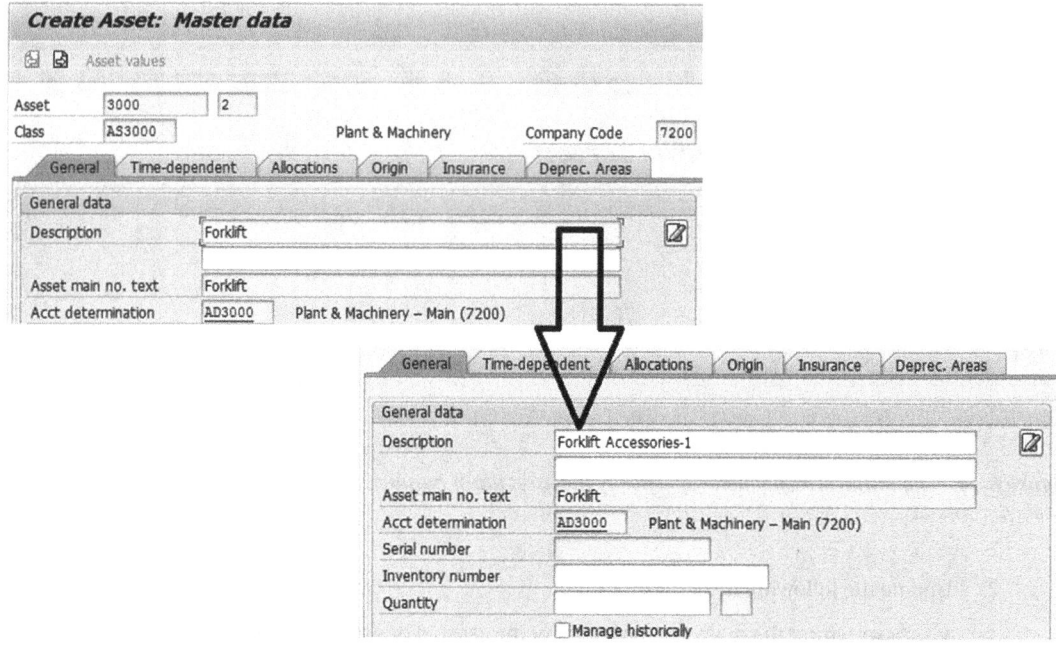

Figure 6-15. *Specifying the asset component description*

5. Click the Enter 🗸 button at the top left of the screen and save 💾 your specifications. The system will notify you that "The asset 3000 2 is created" on the status bar at the bottom of the screen.

Creating a Subnumber for Group Assets

The same principle for creating subnumbers for individual assets is used when creating a subnumber for asset group. To create subnumber for an asset group, you can use this menu path: Accounting ➤ Financial Accounting ➤ Fixed Assets ➤ Asset ➤ Create ➤ Subnumber ➤. Group Asset. The Create Group Asset Sub-number: Initial screen is displayed. Specify the Group Asset key and the company code you are managing your group asset. Click the Depreciation areas button at the top left of the screen. The Create Asset: Master data screen is displayed, defaulting all the attributes of the group asset. You can overwrite the asset description to reflect the asset component in the group asset master record.

Changing Asset Master and Group Asset Master Records

You can change asset master record and group asset master record, respectively, in Asset Accounting.

Changing an Asset Master Record

To change asset master record, you can use these steps:

1. Use this menu path: Accounting ➤ Financial Accounting ➤ Fixed Assets ➤ Asset ➤ Change ➤ Asset. The Change Asset: initial screen is displayed. This is the screen where you specify the asset master data that you want to change.

2. Enter the main number (3000) of the asset you want to change in the Asset field and the company code (7200) the asset in question relates to in the Company Code field.

3. Click the Master data button at the top left of the screen. This will take you to the Change Asset: Master data screen where you can carry out appropriate changes in the asset master data.

4. After making your changes, click the Enter ✅ button at the top left of the screen and save 💾 your changes.

Changing a Group Asset Master Data

You can also make changes in the group asset master data.

1. To do so, use this menu path: Accounting ➤ Financial Accounting ➤ Fixed Assets ➤ Asset ➤ Change ➤ Group Asset. The Change Group Asset: Initial Screen is displayed as shown in Figure 6-16.

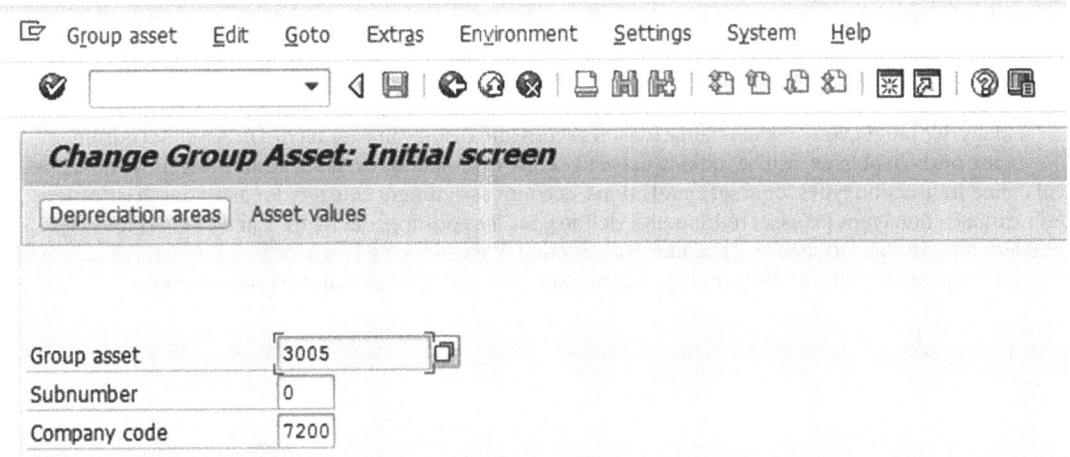

Figure 6-16. *The initial screen where you make make changes to the group asset master data*

2. Enter the group asset (3005) you want to change in the group asset field (you can access the list of assets groups using matchcode) and your company code (7200) in the company code field. Click the Depreciation areas button at the top left of the screen to proceed to the Change Group Asset: Master Data screen where you can carry out changes in the group asset master data.

3. You can change the depreciation key, useful life, and ordinary depreciation start date by overwriting the content of each field.

4. Click the Enter ✅ button at the top left of the screen and save 💾 your changes.

Displaying an Asset Master Record

In this activity, we look at how to display the asset master record in Asset Accounting.

To do so, you can use this menu path: Accounting ➤ Financial Accounting ➤ Fixed Assets ➤ Asset ➤ Display ➤ Asset. The Display Asset: Initial screen is displayed. Enter the main asset number (3000) you want to display the master record in the Asset field and the company code the asset belongs to in the Company Code field. Then click the ⬚Master data button at the top left of the screen. The display Asset: Master data screen is displayed showing the asset information in the asset master data.

⬛ **Note**   You can also display further data about the asset (for example depreciation areas and asset values) by clicking on the respective push button somewhere at the top of the screen.

Summary

In this chapter, we talked about master data and its importance in Asset Accounting. We then talked briefly about various screen layouts provided by SAP in the system and their uses. We then took you through the customizing steps involved in defining screen layout for asset master data, depreciation areas, and how to specify tab layout for asset master record. We then went on to look at how to create master record. In so doing, we looked how to define the control parameters for asset master record for asset and group assets. As part of the master record customizing, we looked at how to define subnumbers for assets components for asset and group assets.

Finally, we taught you how to change master record and display master record in Asset Accounting.

In the next chapter, we will be looking at ow to define transactions in Asset Accounting. In so doing, we will define transaction types for asset acquisitions, account assignment category for asset purchase orders, define transaction types for asset retirements, define gain/loss posting, define transaction types for asset transfers, and capitalization of assets under construction. We will then go on to look at how to post asset acquisition, post capitalized assets under construction, post asset transfer, and asset retirement.

CHAPTER 7

■ ■ ■

Customizing Transactions

This chapter looks at steps involved in customizing transactions. You learn how transactions are posted in asset accounting. In this chapter, you will learn how to:

- Define transaction types for acquisitions
- Define the account assignment category for asset purchase orders
- Define transaction types for retirements
- Define transaction types for write-ups due to gain/loss
- Define transaction types for transfers
- Specify posting variants for retirement transfers
- Post asset acquisitions
- Capitalize assets under construction
- Perform asset transfers
- Carry out asset retirement
- Post fixed assets

Transactions

Customizing transactions is important for posting transactions in asset accounting. To post asset acquisitions, asset retirements, and asset transfers in asset accounting, you need to define the important transaction types for each posting activity for asset accounting. Transaction types are used to distinguish various transactions posted in the account. In this activity, we will be looking at how to define transaction types for asset acquisition, asset retirements, and asset transfers.

Asset Acquisitions

Asset acquisition transactions can either be an external acquisition (with a vendor or from an affiliated company) or in-house production. It is important that you define transaction types for asset acquisition that will differentiate asset acquisitions from other transactions when posting them in the system.

Defining Transaction Types for Acquisitions

You can define transaction types for asset acquisitions and limit transaction types to certain depreciation areas in this customizing step. If you limit transaction types to certain depreciation areas, the system will generate a popup window, which will only propose the depreciation areas that can posted during transaction posting. You do not need to do anything in this step. SAP comes with standard transaction types, which are usually sufficient for these requirements.

■ **Note** We recommend that you use the standard transaction types supplied by SAP, as they are almost always sufficient for your requirements. Secondly, defining your own transaction types may be cumbersome and time consuming, as you will also need to define the associated tables.

To define transaction types for asset acquisitions, follow these steps:

1. Use this menu path: IMG: Financial Accounting (New) ➤ Asset Accounting ➤ Transactions ➤ Acquisitions ➤ Define Transaction Types for Acquisitions. The Choose Activity screen is displayed (Figure 7-1), showing the activities you can choose from.

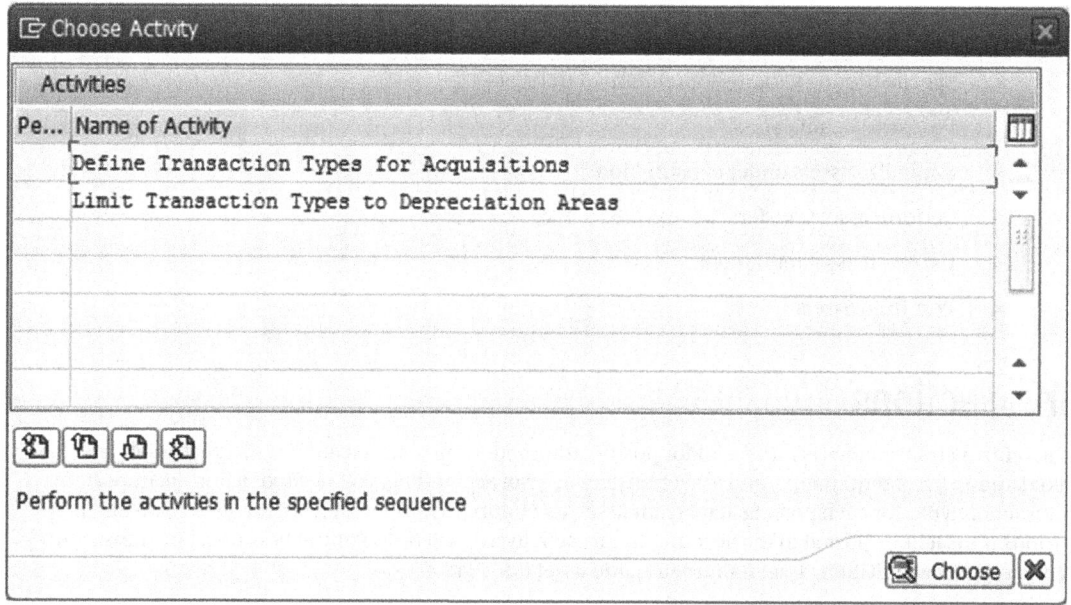

Figure 7-1. *The screen where you can choose the activity you want to carry out when customizing transaction types for asset acquisition*

2. Choose Define Transaction Types for Acquisitions from the activities on the screen in Figure 7-1. Click the [🔍 Choose] button at the bottom-right side of the screen. The Change View "FI-AA: Transaction Types": Overview screen is displayed, showing the list of transaction types in the system.

3. To define your own transaction type, click the [New Entries] button at the top-left side of the screen. The Change View "FI-AA: Transaction Types": Details screen appears, as shown in Figure 7-2.

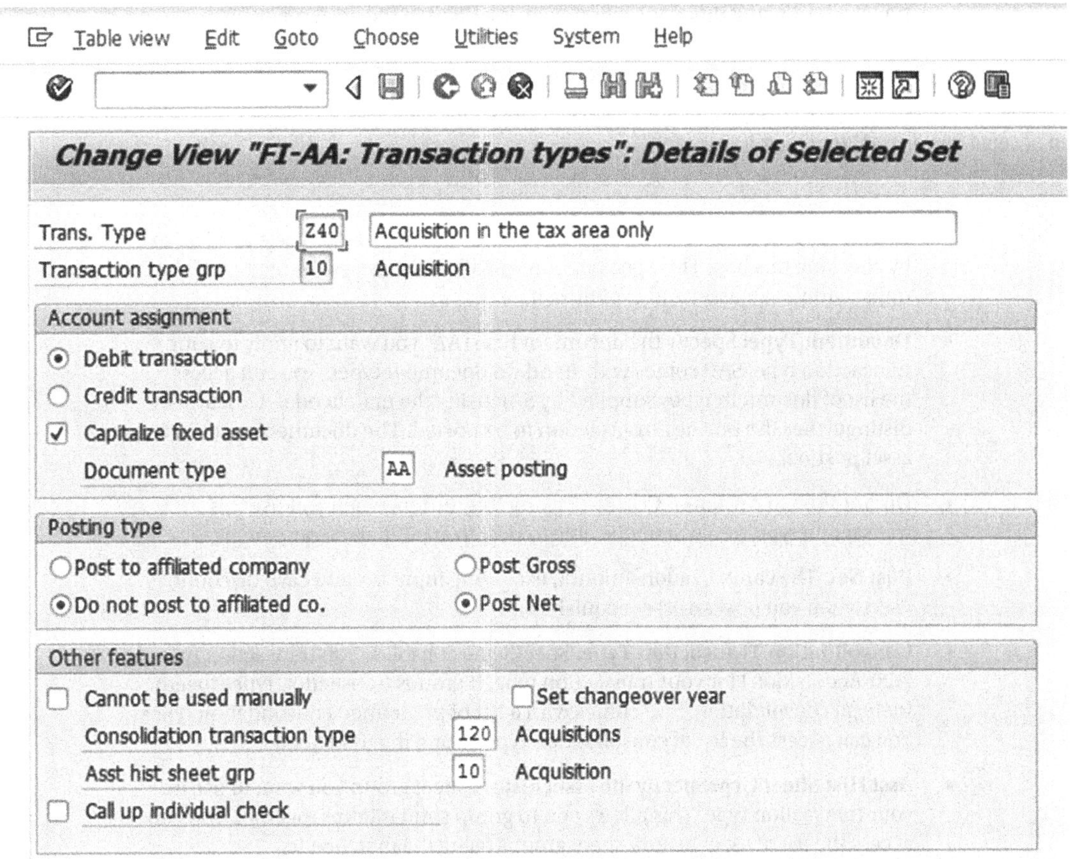

Figure 7-2. The screen where you carry out the actual specifications for the transaction types for asset acquisition

4. Update the following fields:

- **Trans. Type:** You can enter up to a three-digit character as your transaction type key and short text describing your transaction type.

- **Transaction Type Grp:** You specify the transaction type group you want to assign your transaction type. SAP comes with a list of transaction type groups you can choose from. You can access the supplied transaction type groups by using the matchcode next to the Transaction Type Grp field.

- **Debit Transaction:** By selecting this button, the system will automatically post transactions using this transaction type as a debit in the account.

░ **Note**   It is also possible to specify that transactions should be posted as credits to the account by selecting an account assignment for credit transaction.

- **Capitalize Fixed Asset:** You may instruct the system to capitalize a fixed asset by checking this box. This specification will allow the system to recognize the transaction as an asset and capitalize it.

- **Document Type:** Specify the document type (AA) you want to apply to your transaction type. SAP comes with standard document types. You can access the list of document types supplied by SAP using the matchcode. A document distinguishes the business transaction to be posted. The document type AA is for asset posting.

- **Do Not Post to Affiliated Co.:** By clicking this button, when you use this transaction type, you will not be able to post to an affiliated company.

- **Post Net**: The capitalization amount, excluding input tax and cash discount, is used when you post an asset acquisition.

- **Consolidation Transaction Type:** Specify the consolidation transaction type (120-Acquisition) for your transaction type. It groups transaction types together for legal consolidation. SAP comes with a list of predefined consolidation types. You can access the list of consolidation types using the matchcode.

- **Asst Hist Sheet Grp:** Specify the asset history sheet group you want to use for your transaction type. This allows you to group similar items together. You can access the list of asset history sheet groups using the matchcode.

5. Click the Enter 🟢 button at the top-left side of the screen and then click Save 💾.

Defining the Account Assignment Category for Asset Purchase Orders

SAP comes with settings for account assignment categories you can use your asset purchase order. When processing purchase orders in material management (MM), you can post asset acquisitions. Purchase orders can also be posted using account assignment to an asset. Based on the settings of the account assignment category, when you post goods receipt (GR) or invoice receipt (IR), the system will automatically capitalize the asset in question.

■ **Note**   Make sure that you have already created the asset in order to make this account assignment.

The account assignment category is entered in the system when you create a purchase order. For example, account category A informs the system that the transaction is a fixed asset purchase order. Secondly, you should also specify in the account assignment category whether you want the system to valuate GR.

■ **Note**   We recommend that you use the standard categories provided by SAP instead of creating new ones.

To define an account assignment category for an asset purchase order, perform the following steps:

1. Use this menu path: IMG: Financial Accounting (New) ➤ Asset Accounting ➤ Transactions ➤ Acquisitions ➤ Define Account Assignment Category for Asset Purch. Orders. The Change View "Account Assignment Categories": Overview screen is displayed, showing the list of account assignment categories.

2. Click the New Entries button at the top-left side of the screen. The Change View "Account Assignment Categories": Details of Selected Set screen is displayed (see Figure 7-3).

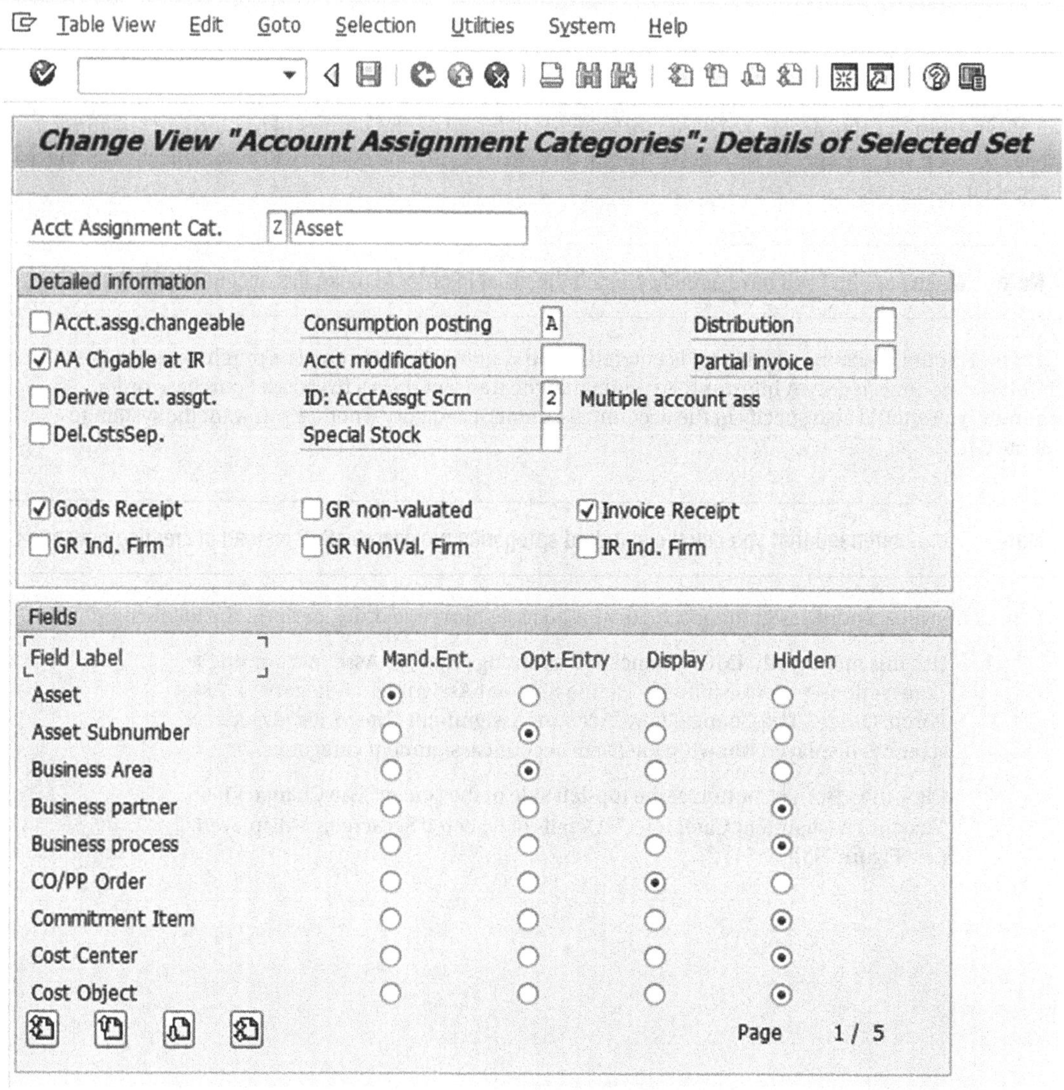

Figure 7-3. *The screen where you define the account assignment category for asset purchase orders*

3. The screen is divided into the two sections:

- The Detailed information section. This section contains the general information about the account assignment category.

- The Fields section. This section allows you to define the field structure. For example whether a field is mandatory, optional, displayed, or hidden.

Update the appropriate fields and click the appropriate check boxes and radio buttons, as shown in Figure 7-3.

4. Click the Enter 🗸 button at the top-left side of the screen and then save 🖫.

Assigning Accounts

Account assignment was covered in Chapter 2, when we defined how depreciation areas post to the general ledger. Basically, the account you assigned in this customizing step will allow the system to post asset transactions to the general ledger in FI.

1. In order to define general ledger accounts for asset acquisition, you can use this menu path: IMG: Financial Accounting (New) ➤ Asset Accounting ➤ Transactions ➤ Acquisitions ➤ Assign Accounts. The Chart of Depreciation Selection screen pops up. This screen allows you to specify the chart of depreciation for account determination.

2. Enter your chart of depreciation (B10) in the Chart of Depreciation field and click the Enter ☑ button at the bottom-left side of the screen. The Change View "Chart of Accounts": Overview screen is appears containing your chart of accounts (INT – Chart of accounts – international).

3. Select the chart of depreciation and double-click the Account Determination folder in the chart of accounts on the left pane of the screen. The Change "Account Determination": Overview screen containing a list of account determination in the system appears.

4. Click the 🔲 Position... button at the bottom of the screen to search for your account determinations (you created account determination in Chapter 1 in the "Specifying Account Determination" section). You have to assign accounts you want to post asset transactions to each account determination individually.

▪ **Note**   You don't need to do any account assignment in this step, because you already did this in Chapter 2.

Asset Retirements

When an asset is retired, it simply means the asset is removed from the asset portfolio. The removal of asset can be complete or removal from the asset portfolio. Retirement can be performed in the following ways:

- Asset sold for a profit to a customer (this is a customer with a customer account in the system) or to someone else (not a customer account in the system)

- Asset retirement by scrapping

- Asset sold to an affiliated company

Defining Transaction Types for Retirements

Transaction types play a significant role in asset retirement, especially when differentiating between the business transactions that led to asset retirement. In this activity, you can define transaction types for posting fixed asset retirements, to limit transaction types to depreciation areas, or to define transaction types for subsequent costs/revenues.

When you limit transaction types to depreciation areas, only the depreciation areas you specified are proposed for posting by the system. When posting transaction, the system will generate a popup window, displaying the depreciation areas that can be posted.

■ **Note**   You do not need to perform any customizing in this step, because SAP comes with standard transaction types that are sufficient for this requirement.

To define asset retirement transaction types, follow these steps:

1. You can define transaction types for asset retirements, using this menu path: Financial Accounting (New) ➤ Asset Accounting ➤ Transactions ➤ Retirements ➤ Define Transaction Type for Retirements. The Choose Activity screen appears showing activities you have available for this activity.

2. Select the Define Transaction Types for Retirements from the list of displayed options and click the ⬛ Choose button at the bottom-right side of the screen. The Change View "FI-AA: Transaction Types": Overview screen appears with the list of transaction types for retirements in the system.

3. To define a transaction type, click the New Entries button at the top-left side of the screen. The New Entries: Details of Added Entries screen is displayed. This is the screen where you set the transaction type for retirement.

4. Update the following fields:

    • **Trans. Type**: You can enter up to a three-digit character as your transaction key and include a short description of your transaction type.

    • **Transaction Type Grp:** Enter an appropriate transaction type group (20-Retirement) that relates to your transaction type. You can access the list of transaction type groups supplied by SAP using the matchcode.

    • **Deactivate Fixed Asset:** Deactivating fixed asset will prevent posting to the asset using this transaction type.

    • **Document Type:** Enter the document type (AA – Asset Posting). You can access the list of document types supplied by SAP using the matchcode.

    • **Do Not Post to Affiliated Co.:** When you use this transaction type, you will not be able to post to an affiliated company.

    • **Consolidation Transaction Type:** Specify the consolidation type for asset retirement (140 – Retirement). You can access the list of consolidation transaction types supplied by SAP using the matchcode.

    • **Asst Hist. Sheet Grp:** Enter the asset history sheet group (20 – Retirement) from the list supplied by SAP.

5. Click the Enter ✅ button on the top-left side of the screen. The screen expands to include a Transfer/Retirement/Current Acquis. section of the screen, as shown in Figure 7-4.

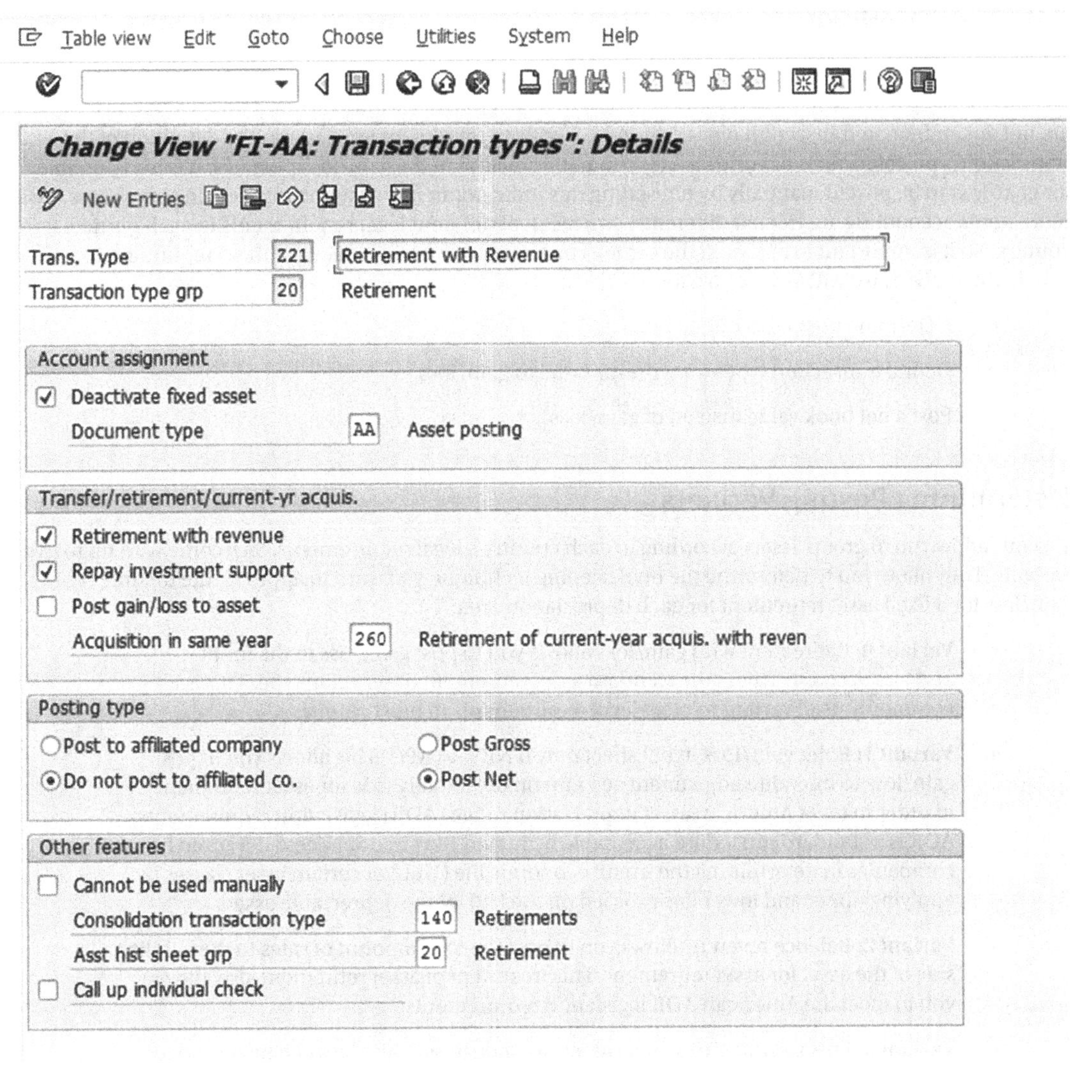

Figure 7-4. The screen where you define transaction types for asset retirements

6. Update the following fields in Transfer/Retirement/Current-Yr Acquis. section of the screen:

- **Retirement with Revenue:** The removal of an asset or part of an asset from the asset portfolio earning revenue.

- **Repay Investment Support:** The investment support provided for asset retirement for the transaction type is prepared for a refund.

- **Acquisition in Same Year:** Retirement of an asset in the same year as acquisition.

7. Click the Enter 🗸 button at the top-left side of the screen to confirm if the system accepted your entries and then save 🖫 your transaction type.

Gain/Loss Posting

When transaction types are used, the system will automatically create gain or loss posting in addition to the revenue clearing entry when you use the standard transaction types. However, the gain and loss posting are not dependent on transaction types. The gain/loss from retirement indicator in the definition of the transaction type determines or controls the automatic creation of the gain/loss postings. It is also possible for gain/loss to be posted manually by not setting this indicator in this customizing step. In some cases, asset retirements accounting are treated differently as a result of different legal requirements in each particular country. So it is important to carry out the settings necessary to meet the needs of these requirements.

In this activity, we will look at how to:

- Determine posting variants
- Define transaction types for write-ups due to gain/loss
- Post a net book value instead of gain/loss

Determining Posting Variants

Variants allow you to group assets according to each country's legal requirements. SAP come with up to five variants. They allow you to determine the bookkeeping technique you want to apply for the treatment of gain/loss for a fixed asset retirement for each depreciation area:

- **Variant 0:** Retirement with gain/loss allows you to post gain/loss to the profit and loss account. This is the standard asset retirement transaction type. This is a commonly used variant to meet legal requirements in most countries.

- **Variant 1:** Enter gain/loss in bal.sheet only if NBV <= APC. This allows you to post gain/loss to the value adjustment account on the liability side for asset retirement in order to meet American asset depreciation range (ADR) legislation requirements. ADR is a standard procedure acceptable by Inland Revenue Services (IRS) used by companies in determining the useful economic life (UEL) of certain asset classes by applying upper and lower limits based on the UEL of the depreciable assets.

- **Variant 2:** Balance revenue allows you to post the total amount of sales to the liability side of the asset for asset retirement. This treatment of asset retirement also allows you to meet the American ADR legislation requirements.

- **Variant 3:** Post gain/loss to special assets for gain/loss. Gain/loss can be posted to special assets for gain/loss at asset retirement.

- **Variant 4:** Enter gain/loss in the bal.sheet even if over APC. This allows you to post gain/loss arising from the retirement of assets even if it exceeds the acquisition and production cost of the asset.

To specify transaction type you want to use to manage posting variants, use the following steps:

1. To determine posting variants, use this menu path: Financial Accounting (New) ➤ Asset Accounting ➤ Transactions ➤ Retirements ➤ Gain/Loss Posting ➤ Determine Posting Variants. The Chart of Depreciation Selection screen pops up.

2. Enter your chart of depreciation key (B10) in the ChDep field and click then the Continue ✅ button at the bottom-left side of the screen. The Change View "Transaction type selection": Overview screen appears containing the list of transaction types.

3. Click the ⬚ Position... button at the bottom of the screen and search for the transaction type you want to manage. To go to the screen where you will carry out your specifications, select the appropriate transaction type (for example, Z21 – Retirement with Revenue) and double-click the Special Treatment of Retirement folder in the Transaction type selection on the left side of the screen. The Change View "Special treatment of retirement": Overview screen is displayed.

4. Click the New Entries button at the top-left side of the screen. The New Entries: Overview of Added Entries screen appears (Figure 7-5).

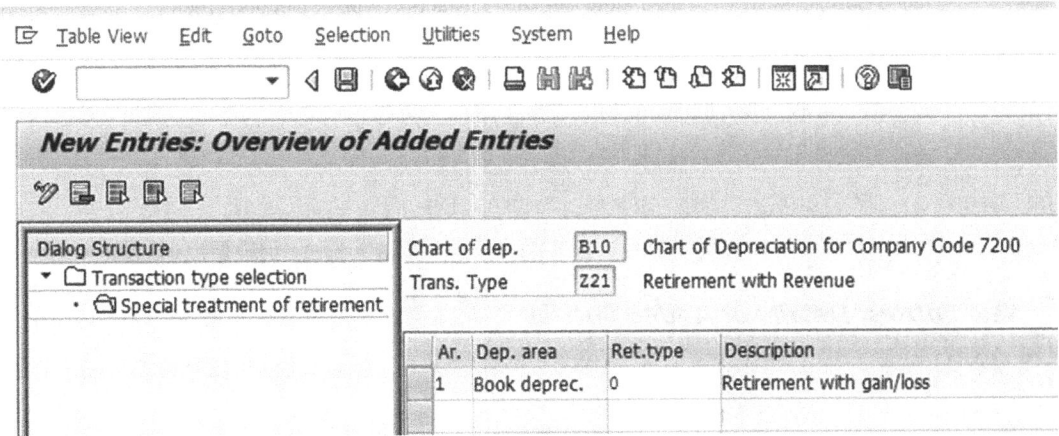

Figure 7-5. *The screen where you specify the retirement type for asset retirement with gain/loss*

5. Update the following fields:

   - **Ar.:** Enter the depreciation area you want to use to manage retirements in the Area field. For example, 01- Book Depreciation. You can access the list of book depreciations you defined in Chapter 1 using the matchcode.

   - **Ret.Type:** Enter the retirement type you want to use to treat the retirement of assets.

6. Click the Enter ✅ button at the top left side of the screen to confirm if the system accepted your entries and then save 🖫.

Defining Transaction Types for Write-Ups Due to Gain/Loss

This is another method of asset retirement in FI-AA. This step is essential only when you want to post gain/loss on special assets, rather than posting gain/loss to the profit and loss account. This method is applicable in certain countries (for example, the United States). SAP comes with standard transaction types for gain/loss (770). It is strongly recommended that you stick to this transaction type and it is not necessary to create your own transaction type in this step. However, we will be taking you through the customizing steps involved in transaction types for write-ups due to gain/loss for illustrative purposes only.

1. Transaction types for write-ups due to gain/loss can be defined using this menu path: Financial Accounting (New) ➤ Asset Accounting ➤ Transactions ➤ Retirements ➤ Gain/Loss Posting ➤ Define Transaction Types for Write-Ups Due to Gain/Loss. The Change View "FI-AA: Transaction types": Details screen appears.

2. Click the New Entries button at the top-left side of the screen to proceed to the data entry screen, as shown in Figure 7-6.

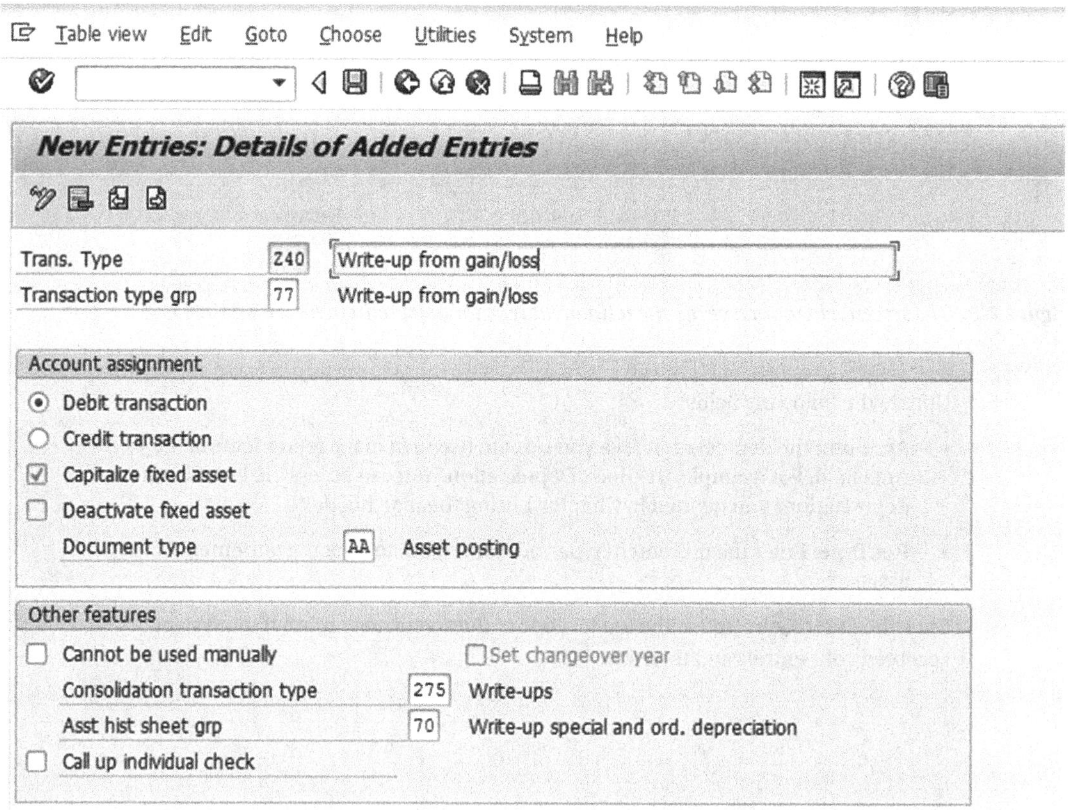

Figure 7-6. *The screen where you perform the specifications for transaction types for write-ups due to gain/loss*

3. Update the following fields:

- **Trans. Type:** Enter a key as your transaction type identifier and a short description for your transaction type.

- **Transaction Type Grp:** Using the matchcode, enter the transaction type group want to assign to your transaction type. For example, 77 – Write-up from gain/ loss.

- **Debit Transaction:** This selection will allow postings to be made to the debit side when posting transactions using this transaction code.

- **Capitalize Fixed Asset:** Transactions are recognized and capitalized when this check box is checked.

- **Document Type:** SAP comes with standard document types you can use from. To access the document types supplied by SAP, you can use the matchcode by the document type field.

- **Consolidation transaction type:** Specify the consolidation transaction type (275 Write-ups) for your transaction type.

- **Asst. Hist. Sheet Grp:** Enter the asset history sheet (70 – Write-up special and ord. depreciation).

4. Click the Enter ⊘ button at the top-left side of the screen and click Save 💾.

Posting Net Book Value Instead of Gain/Loss

This setting is only necessary if you want to post the net book value (NBV) of the asset at asset retirement, instead of posting gain/loss to the profit and loss account. In this activity, you specify the company code you want to use to manage NPV at asset retirement.

You can specify the company code using this menu path: Financial Accounting (New) ➤ Asset Accounting ➤ Transactions ➤ Retirements ➤ Gain/Loss Posting ➤ Post Net Book Value Instead of Gain/ Loss. The Change View "FI-AA: "Posting Remaining Value"": Overview screen appears, displaying the list of company codes. Click the ▣ Position... button at the bottom of the screen to search for the company code (7200) you want. You do this by clicking the Post Net Book Value Indicator check box for the appropriate company code.

Asset Transfers

Assets can be transferred using intracompany or intercompany asset transfer methods. By using the intracompany asset transfer method, an asset or an asset component is simply transferred in the same company code to a different asset master record. One of the following factors may necessitate the need to carry out intracompany asset transfers:

- When you mistakenly create an asset in a wrong asset class, because an asset class cannot be modified in the asset master data. The only way to remedy this error is to transfer it in the company code to which the asset relates in the appropriate master record.

- When an asset component is transferred between assets in the same company code.

- When an asset under construction is transferred to a finished asset.

We will be looking at intercompany asset transfers in detail in the "Intercompany Asset Transfer" section.

In this activity, we will be looking at how to:

- Define transaction types for transfers

- Specify the posting variant for retirement transfers

Defining Transaction Types for Transfers

In this customizing activity, you define transaction types for asset retirement transfers, for asset acquisition transfers and limit transaction types to depreciation areas. By limiting a transaction type to a depreciation area, the transaction type in question can only be applicable to the assigned depreciation area. In this situation, the transaction posting is carried out from the sending company's (the company carrying out the transfer) viewpoint.

There are two basic transaction types represented in SAP for transfers between assets. Namely:

- For asset retirement from a sending asset. A sending asset is the asset making a transfer to another asset (the receiving asset)

- For asset addition to a receiving asset

■ **Note**   SAP comes with standard transaction types sufficient for this function, which you can adapt to meet your requirements.

To define your transaction types for asset transfers, perform these steps:

1.   Use this menu path: Financial Accounting (New) ➤ Asset Accounting ➤ Transactions ➤ Transfers ➤ Define Transaction Types for Transfers. The Choose Activity -screen pops up with a list of activities you can carry out, as shown in Figure 7-7.

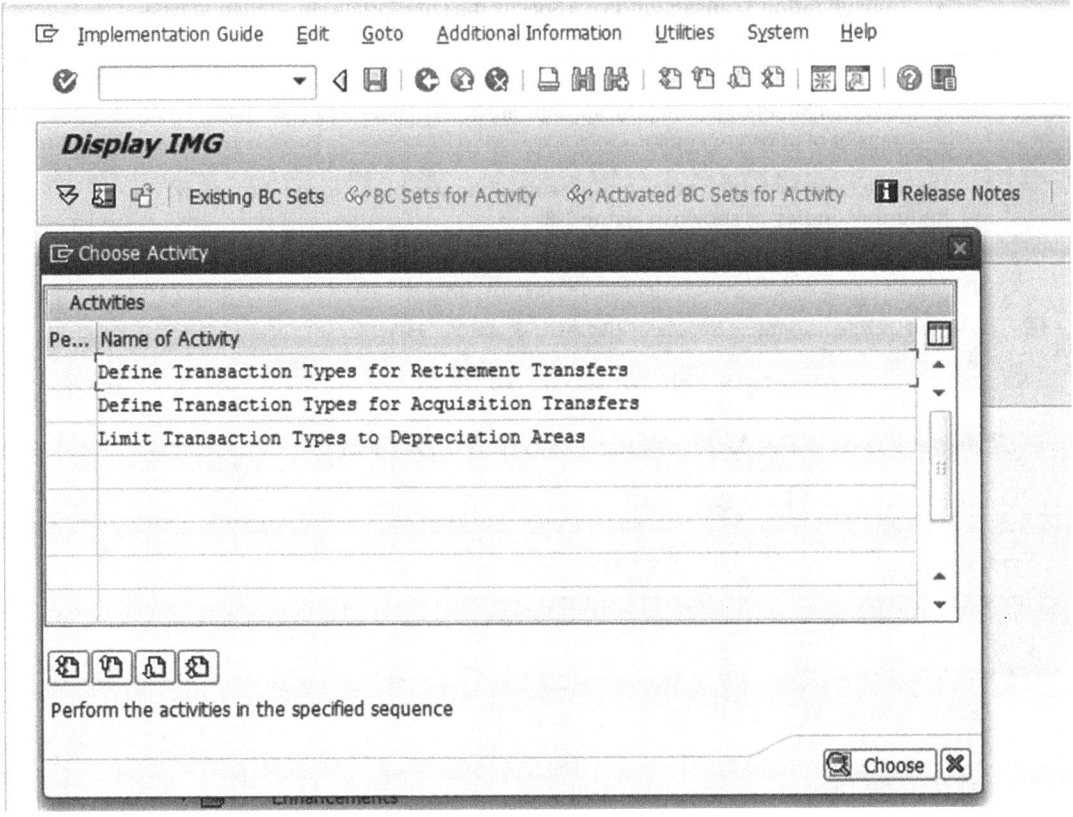

Figure 7-7. *The activity screen containing the list of transaction types for retirement and acquisition transfers*

2. Select Define Transaction Types for Retirement Transfers from the list of activities displayed on the screen and click the ⌕ Choose button at the bottom-right side of the screen. The New Entries: Details of Added Entries screen appears. This is the where you perform the transaction type for retirement transfers specifications.

3. Update the following fields:

    -   **Trans. Type:** Enter a transaction type key and a description.

    -   **Transaction Type Grp:** Enter the transaction group (30- Retirmt transfer of prior-yr-acquis.) you want to manage.

    -   **Credit Transaction:** This selection will allow postings to be made to the credit side when posting a transaction using this transaction code.

    -   **Document Type:** Enter the appropriate document type (AA – Asset Posting).

    -   **Do Not Post to Affiliate Co.:** When you set this function, you will not be able to post to affiliated companies by using the transaction type.

    -   **Post Net:** When you choose this function, the system will allow post net amounts.

- **Consolidation Transaction Type:** Specify the appropriate consolidation type (170- Transfer). You can access a list of consolidation transaction types supplied by SAP using the matchcode.

- **Asst Hist Sheet Grp:** Enter the appropriate asset history sheet group (30 – retirmt transfer of prior-yr-acquis).

4. Click the Enter ✅ button at the top-left side of the screen to expand the screen for further entries, as shown in Figure 7-8.

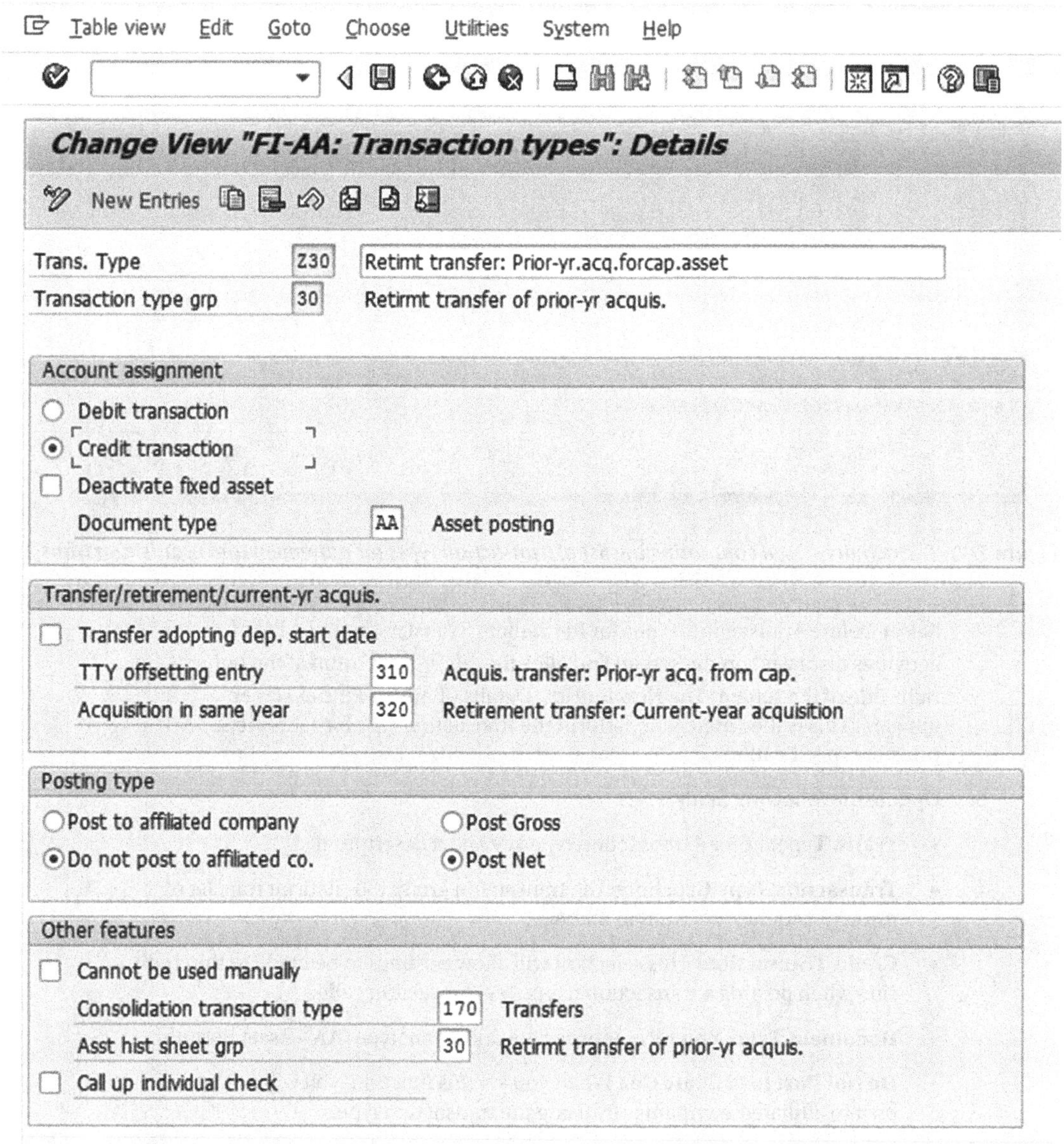

Figure 7-8. The screen where you specify transaction types for asset retirement transfers

5. Update the following fields in the Transfer/retirement/current-yr acquis. section of the screen, which you can see in Figure 7-8:

   - **TTY Offsetting Entry:** Enter the transaction type offsetting (310 – Acquis. transfer: Prior-yr acq. From cap.). This specification will allow the system to make an offsetting entry of acquisition transfer, using the prior year acquisition from capitalization.

   - **Acquisition in Same Year:** Enter the appropriate acquisition in the same year (320 – Retirement transfer: Current-year acquisition). This specification will allow the system to make an asset retirement transfer, using the current year of the asset acquisition.

6. Click the Enter ✅ button at the top-left side of the screen and then save 💾.

Specifying the Posting Variant for Retirement Transfers

The specification you perform in this step enables you to determine how you want to treat asset retirement transfers in each depreciation area in the chart of depreciation for your company code. It is important to define different transaction types to post fixed asset APC retirements and the retirement of proportional value adjustments for asset retirement. You have two options for specifying posting of variant for retirement transfers:

- The asset retirement transfer is carried out using the asset APC and proportional value adjustment

- The transfer of asset acquisition and production costs (APC) with proportional value adjustment or transfer of APC without proportional value adjustment is carried out

The transfer of asset APCs without the proportional value adjustment option is accepted by the IRS in the United States for grouping assets to meet ADR requirements.

■ **Note**   The standard transaction types are sufficient for this requirement. You don't need to do anything in this activity. We recommend that you use the standard transaction types for this requirement.

Follow these steps to specify posting variants for retirement transfers:

1. Use this menu path: Financial Accounting (New) ➤ Asset Accounting ➤ Transactions ➤ Transfers ➤ Define Transaction Types for Transfers. The Change View "Transaction Type Selection": Overview screen appears, displaying the list of transaction types supplied by SAP.

2. The next step is to specify the depreciation areas you want manage the transfer of APC only for this transaction type. To do this, select the transaction type you want to use from the list of transaction types displayed and double-click the Special Handling of Transfer Posting in Transaction Type selection on the left pane of the screen. The Change View "Special Handling of Transfer Posting": Overview screen appears, showing the list of depreciation areas you defined for your chart of accounts.

3. Set the Trans. APC check box for each depreciation area on the right side of the screen, as shown in Figure 7-9.

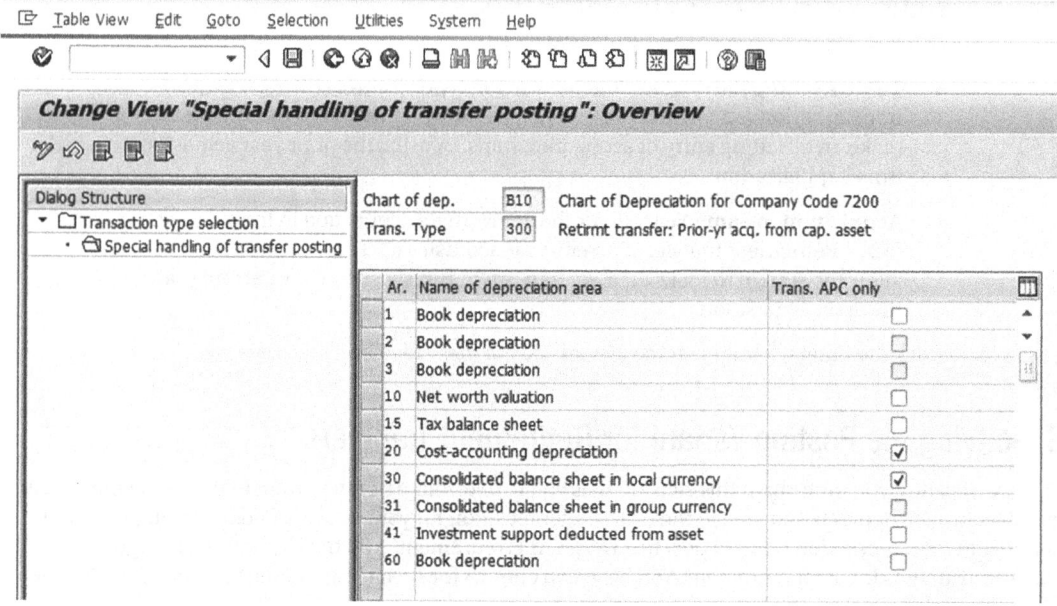

Figure 7-9. *The screen where you activate the APC transfers*

4. Click the Enter ✅ button at the top-left side of the screen and then save 🖫.

Intercompany Asset Transfers

Intercompany asset transfers, simply put, are transfers of assets between two company codes in the same corporate group. Unlike intracompany transfer, the assignment of the asset cannot be changed through maintenance in the asset master record. For intercompany transfer transactions, you need another asset master record in the receiving company code. The receiving company code is the company to which the asset is being transferred. You can post intercompany code asset transfers two ways in SAP:

- Automatic intercompany transfer
- Manual intercompany transfer

As part of automatic asset transfers, you define the control parameters that allow the automatic intercompany asset transfers by carrying out the following settings:

- Define cross-system depreciation areas
- Define transfer variants

During document posting, you only post asset transfer on the sender company code and the system automatically executes the posting in the target (receiving) company code.

Defining Cross-System Depreciation Areas

The cross-system depreciation areas control the transfer of values during intercompany asset transfer. The company codes involved in asset transfer may not have the same chart of depreciation. However, they may have depreciation areas in their chart of depreciations that have the same function with different keys. In this activity, you define cross-system depreciation to ensure that the depreciation areas with the same function are assigned even though they have different charts of depreciation. Your assignment will allow all the depreciation areas to use a common key that's valid in all clients. When customizing, you specify individual transfer methods in a transfer variant for each cross-system depreciation area and assign the local settings to the cross-system depreciation areas.

1. You can define cross-system depreciation areas using this menu path: Financial Accounting (New) ➤ Asset Accounting ➤ Transactions ➤ Intercompany Asset Transfers ➤ Automatic Intercompany Asset Transfers ➤ Define Cross-System Depreciation Areas. The Choose Activity screen pops up with the following activities:

   • Define Cross-System Depreciation Areas (this is optional)

   • Assign Local to Cross-System Depreciation Areas

2. Click Define Cross-System Depreciation Areas and then click the ![Choose] button at the bottom-right side of the screen. The Change View "Define Cross-System Depreciation Areas": Overview screen is displayed. The system supplies defaults for the cross-system areas.

3. Enter a short description and a name for your cross-system areas for each area.

4. Click the Enter ✓ button at the top-left side of the screen and save 🖫.

Assigning Local Settings to Cross-System Depreciation Areas

This is simply assigning the cross-system area to each depreciation area in the charts of depreciation defined for your company code.

1. To assign local settings to cross-system depreciation areas, use this menu path: Financial Accounting (New) ➤ Asset Accounting ➤ Transactions ➤ Intercompany Asset Transfers ➤ Automatic Intercompany Asset Transfers ➤ Define Cross-System Depreciation Areas. The Choose Activity screen pops up with options to choose from.

2. Select Assign Local to Cross-System Depreciation Areas from the displayed options on the screen and click the ![Choose] button at the bottom-right side of the screen. The Chart of Depreciation Selection screen pops up.

3. Enter the chart of depreciation key (B10) to which you want to assign cross-system depreciation areas in the ChDep field and click the Continue ✅ button at the bottom-left side of the screen. The Change View "Assignment of Depr.Area to Cross-System Depreciation Area screen appears (see Figure 7-10).

Change View "Assignment of depr. area to cross-system depreciation are

Chart of dep.　　B10　　Chart of Depreciation for Company Code 7200

Ar.	Dep. area	Crs-sys.ar	Short description	ValAd	IdAPC
1	Book deprec.			0	☐
2	Book deprec.			1	☑
3	Book deprec.			1	☑
10	Networth tax			1	☐
15	Tax bal.sht.	15		1	☐
20	Cost-acc.	20		1	☐
30	Group GBP			1	☐
31	Group USD			30	☑
33	IAS Support			0	☐
41	Inv.subsidy	41		0	☐
60	Book deprec.	1		1	☐

Figure 7-10. The screen where you assign cross-system areas to the sending company depreciation areas

4. Assign the cross-system depreciation areas to each depreciation area you want to manage, as shown in Figure 7-10.

5. Click the Enter 🗸 button at the top-left side of the screen and save 🖫.

Capitalization of Assets under Construction (AuC)

An asset can be acquired externally or produced in-house. Assets you produced in-house are often referred to as assets under construction (AuC). Assets under construction are a special form of fixed assets; they require different accounting treatments and disclosures in the balance sheet. The fixed assets of this nature usually fall under two phases: the *construction phase* and the *useful life phase* (when the asset is completed and put into use). In each of these phases, assets are shown as different items in the balance sheet. The transaction of an asset from assets under the construction phase to the useful life phase is referred to as *capitalization* of assets under construction.

In the customizing steps involved in the capitalization of assets under construction, we will look at the following activities:

- Allowing transfer transaction types for asset classes

- Defining cost elements for settlements to CO receivers

- Defining/assigning settlement profiles

Allowing Transfer Transaction Types for Asset Classes

In this activity, you carry out the specifications of asset classes for each transaction type group for making asset transfer of assets under construction to completed assets. SAP provides the following transaction type groups you can specify for asset classes. These transaction type groups and their individual characteristics cannot be changed:

> 15 – Down payment

> 16 – Down payment balance from previous years

> 38 – Retirement transfer prior year acquisitions – AuC summary

> 39 – Retirement transfer current year acquisition - AuC summary

In order to specify the asset classes that allow the system to transfer AuC to completed assets, follow these steps:

1. Use this menu path: Financial Accounting (New) ➤ Asset Accounting ➤ Transactions ➤ Capitalization of Assets under Construction ➤ Allow Transfer Transaction Types for Asset Classes. The Display View "Transaction Type Group Selection": Overview screen appears, containing the list of transaction type groups supplied by SAP.

2. In this step, you will need to perform the specification of asset classes for each transaction type group. Select the first transaction type group (15 – Down payment) from the displayed transaction groups on the screen and double-click the Specification of Asset Classes folder in the Transaction Type Group selection on the left pane of the screen. The Change View "Specification of Asset Classes": Overview screen appears.

3. Click the ⬜New Entries button at the top-left side of the screen. The New Entries: Overview of Added Entries screen appears. This is the screen where you specify the asset classes for the transaction group.

4. Enter the asset classes for AuC in the asset class fields (4000 – Asset under Construction and 4001 – Asset under Construction in investment measures), as shown in Figure 7-11. You can access the list of asset classes in the system using the matchcodes next to the class fields.

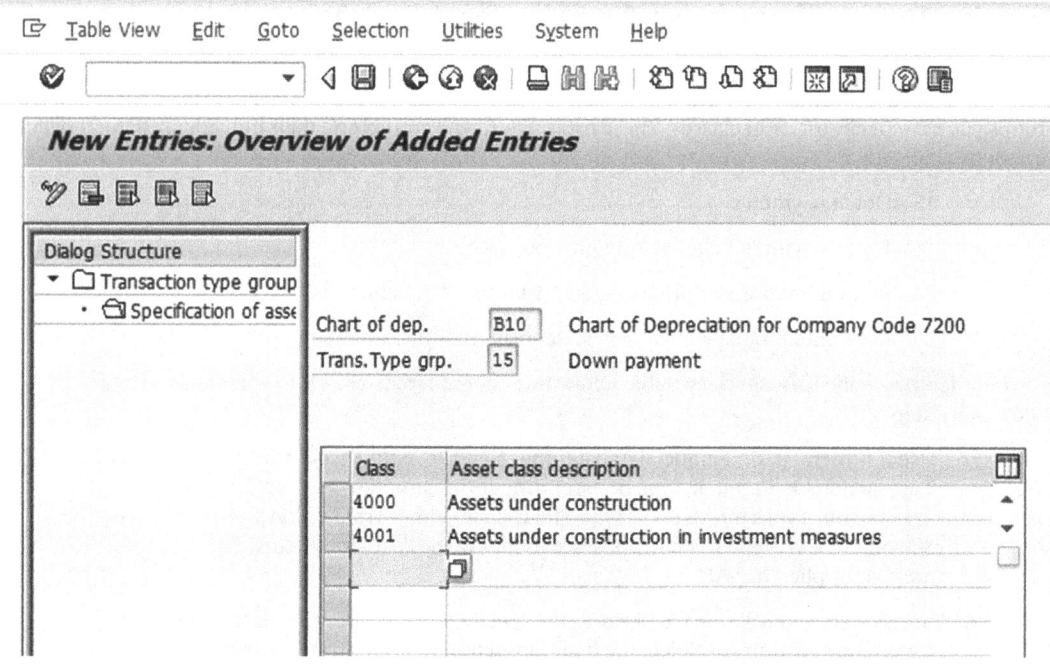

Figure 7-11. *The screen where you specify asset classes for transaction group*

5. Click the Enter ⊘ button at the top-left side of the screen and save 🖫 your specifications.

Determining Cost Elements for Settlements to CO Receivers

To be able to determine cost elements for the settlement of assets under construction to the controlling (CO) receivers (i.e., the cost centers), this customizing is important. Controlling is nothing other than management accounting. Management accounting is the gathering, analyzing, and interpretation of financial data to provide management with information on which to base managerial decisions. It is important that you specify the cost element to which the line item of asset under construction is to be settled to the CO receivers. A cost center is a function in an organization that incurs its own costs and the cost element reconciles cost postings between FI and CO.

You can determine the cost element for settlement to cost receiver using the following procedure:

1. Use this menu path: Financial Accounting (New) ➤ Asset Accounting ➤ Transactions ➤ Capitalization of Assets under Construction ➤ Allow Transfer Transaction Types for Asset Classes. The Chart of Depreciation Selection screen pops up.

2. Specify the chart of depreciation you are using to manage the cost element for the settlement to Co receiver by entering your chart of depreciation (B10) in the ChDep field. Click the Continue ☑ button at the bottom-left side of the screen. The Change View "Chart of Accounts": Overview screen appears showing the chart of accounts (INT – Chart of accounts – international) assigned to your chart of depreciation.

3. Select the appropriate chart of depreciation you are using for your account determination and double-click the Account Determination folder in the Chart of Accounts on the left pane of the screen. The Change View "Account Determination": Overview screen appears, containing the list of account determinations in the system.

4. Click the ⊞ Position... button at the bottom of the screen and search for your account determinations (remember that you created some account determinations in Chapter 1). Select the account determination (AD3000 – Plant & Machine) you are applying to the cost element and double-click the Assign Accounts to Areas folder in the Account Determination on the left pane of the screen. The Change View "Assign Accounts for Areas": Overview screen appears, showing the depreciation areas.

5. Select the depreciation area you want to assign (1 – Book depreciation) from the list and then click the Details 🔍 button at the top-left side of the screen. The Change View "Assign Accounts to Areas": Details screen appears (Figure 7-12).

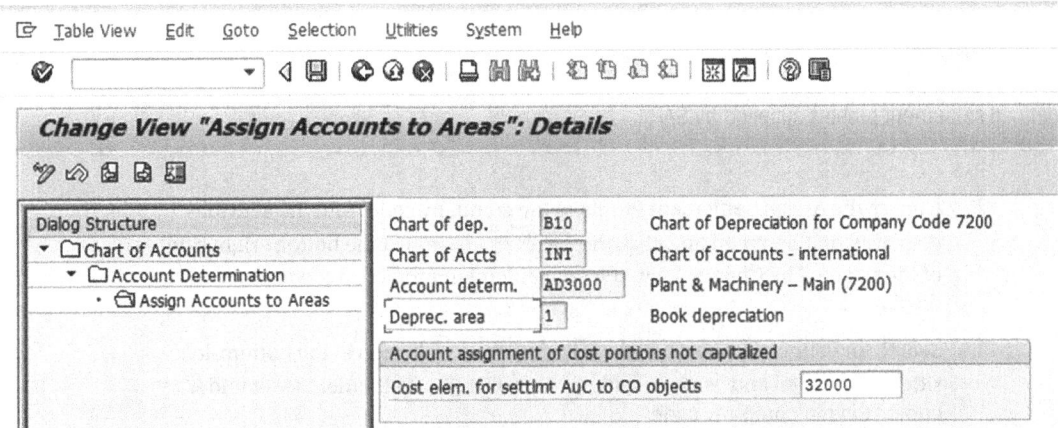

Figure 7-12. *Assignment of accounts to controlling objects*

6. You will notice that the chart of depreciation key, the chart of accounts, account determination, and depreciation you selected are defaulted by the system. Enter the account you are using for the cost element for settlement of assets under construction to controlling in the Cost elem. for settlmt AuC CO Object field. You can access the list of accounts in the system using the matchcode.

7. Click the Enter 🗸 button at the top-left side of the screen and save 💾 your specifications.

Defining/Assigning Settlement Profiles (TC: OAAZ)

In this activity, you will be looking at how to define/assign settlement profiles and maintain number ranges for settlement documents.

Settlement profiles are defined so you can enter a settlement rule for a sender. A sender is the object or the cost center releasing its costs to be settled to the receiver(s). A settlement profile will allow you to settle the cost each time to one cost center or G/L account.

The settlement profile you defined in this activity for assets under construction is assigned to your company code. During settlement of asset under construction in your company code, the system will automatically use this key as a basis for settlement of asset under construction.

To define/assign settlement profiles, you can use these steps:

1. Use this menu path: IMG: Financial Accounting (New) ➤ Asset Accounting ➤ Transactions ➤ Capitalization of Assets under Construction ➤ Define/Assign Settlement Profiles. The Choose Activity screen pops up with the following options:

    - Define the settlement profile

    - Assign the settlement profile to the company code

░ **Note** You do not need to define the settlement profile in this activity. Instead, you should use the pre-defined settlement profiles supplied by SAP.

---

2. Choose the Assign Settlement Profile to the company code from the activities displayed on the screen and click the ▨ Choose button at the bottom-right side of the screen. The Change View "FI-AA: Settlement profile": Overview screen is displayed.

3. Search for your company using the ▨ Position... button at the bottom-left side of the screen and assign a settlement profile (A1- Settlement asset under const.) to your company code.

░ **Note** You can access the list of the standard settlement profiles for assets under construction provided by SAP using the matchcode.

---

4. Click the Enter ✔ button at the top-left side of the screen and save 💾 your assignment.

Fixed Asset Posting

Fixed asset posting is carried out on the user side of the system. Users can post asset acquisitions, asset transfers, asset retirements, assets under construction, asset capitalization, reverse documents, etc. in SAP.

Asset Acquisition

The Asset Accounting component supports various business processes, ranging from the acquisition of assets and/or the capitalization of products or services produced in-house in the system. Asset acquisition can be posted in the system in asset accounting via integration with accounts payable (AP) without reference to a purchase order, or via clearing offsetting without reference to accounts payable and without reference to a purchase order, or it can be posted in material management (MM), either upon good receipt or invoice receipt with reference to the asset.

External Acquisitions

This business process is the purchasing of assets from a business partner. Assets acquired externally can be posted in the system in different ways in asset accounting:

- With the vendor
- Acquisition with an automatic offsetting entry

Asset Posting with a Vendor (TC: F-90)

This is possible in asset accounting with integration to accounts payable, without reference to a purchase order. This function allows you to post the asset acquisition and the associated business partner simultaneously in a single transaction. This appears to be the most effective way of posting assets acquisition externally.

Follow these steps to post an external acquisition with a vendor:

1. Use this menu path: Accounting ➤ Financial Accounting ➤ Fixed Assets ➤ Posting ➤ Acquisition ➤ External Acquisition ➤ With Vendor. The Acquisition from Purchase w. Vendor: Header Data screen appears.

■ **Note**   To avoid having problems posting asset acquisitions, make sure that you have defined the document number ranges in FI for Documents in Entry View and Documents in General Ledger View for the current fiscal year. Secondly, you need to specify the amount of authorization for customer/vendor line items in your company code (7200) for the user group you assigned in FI. We recommend that you refer to our book entitled *SAP ERP Financial Accounting and Controlling: Configuration and Use Management.*

---

2. Update the fields using the data in Table 7-1.

Table 7-1. *Data to Update the Acquisition from Purchase with Vendor: Header Data Screen*

Field	Value	Description
Document Date	Today's date	This is usually the invoice or document date.
Posting Date	Today's date	This is the date the document is posted into the system.
Company Code	7200	Your company code is usually defaulted by the system. Otherwise, you have to enter it manually yourself.
Currency/Rate	GBP	If a document has been posted before, the system will automatically default a currency code.
PsKy	31	Posting key for vendor.
Account	100544 – Truck Supplies Inc.	Enter the related vendor's account number. You can access a list of your vendor using the matchcode.

3. Click the Enter button at the top-left side of the screen. The Enter Vendor Invoice: Add Vendor Item screen appears (see Figure 7-13).

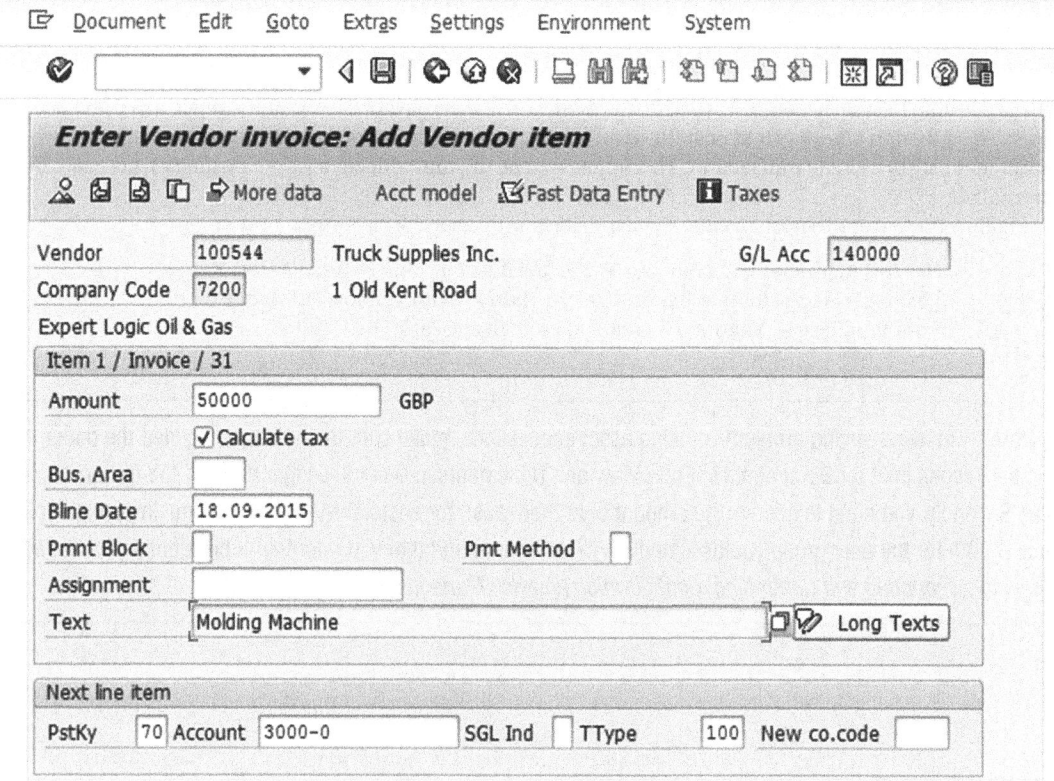

Figure 7-13. *The screen where you enter the vendor's invoice into the system*

4. Update the fields using the data in Table 7-2, and as shown in Figure 7-13.

Table 7-2. *The Invoice Data to Update the Enter Vendor Invoice: Add Vendor Item Screen*

Field	Value	Description
Amount	50000	Enter the asset purchase price.
Calculation Tax	Select	Set the calculate tax check box to instruct the system to carry out tax calculations.
Bline Date	Today's date +14 days	Enter a baseline date. This is usually a future date for which terms of payment apply.
Text	Molding Machine	
PsKy	70	Debit asset (this is the posting key for posting asset acquisitions supplied by SAP).
TType	100	This is the asset transaction type for external asset acquisitions supplied by SAP.

5. Click the Enter ✅ button at the top-left side of the screen. The Vendor invoice: Add Asset item screen appears.

6. Update the fields using the data in Table 7-3.

Table 7-3. *The Invoice Data to Update the Enter Vendor Invoice: Add Asset item Screen*

Field	Value	Description
Amount	*	Enter the asset amount or the * symbol in the amount field. This will call up the amount of asset entered in the previous screen.
Tax code	B1	Enter the tax code for input tax related to asset transaction. This will allow the system to use the tax percentage rate assigned to the tax code you entered to be applied for tax calculation.
Text	Molding Machine	Enter a description of your asset.

▓ **Note**　We covered how to define tax code in our book *SAP ERP Financial Accounting and Controlling: Configuration and Use Management.* Again, you may want to use it to learn how to calculate tax.

7. Click the Enter ✅ button at the top-left side of the screen to confirm your entries.

8. To see the transactions you entered in the system, you have to display the transactions by selecting ⌐Document⌐ in the menu bar and clicking Simulate on the drop-down menu. The Enter Vendor invoice: Display Overview screen appears, displaying your transactions, as shown in Figure 7-14.

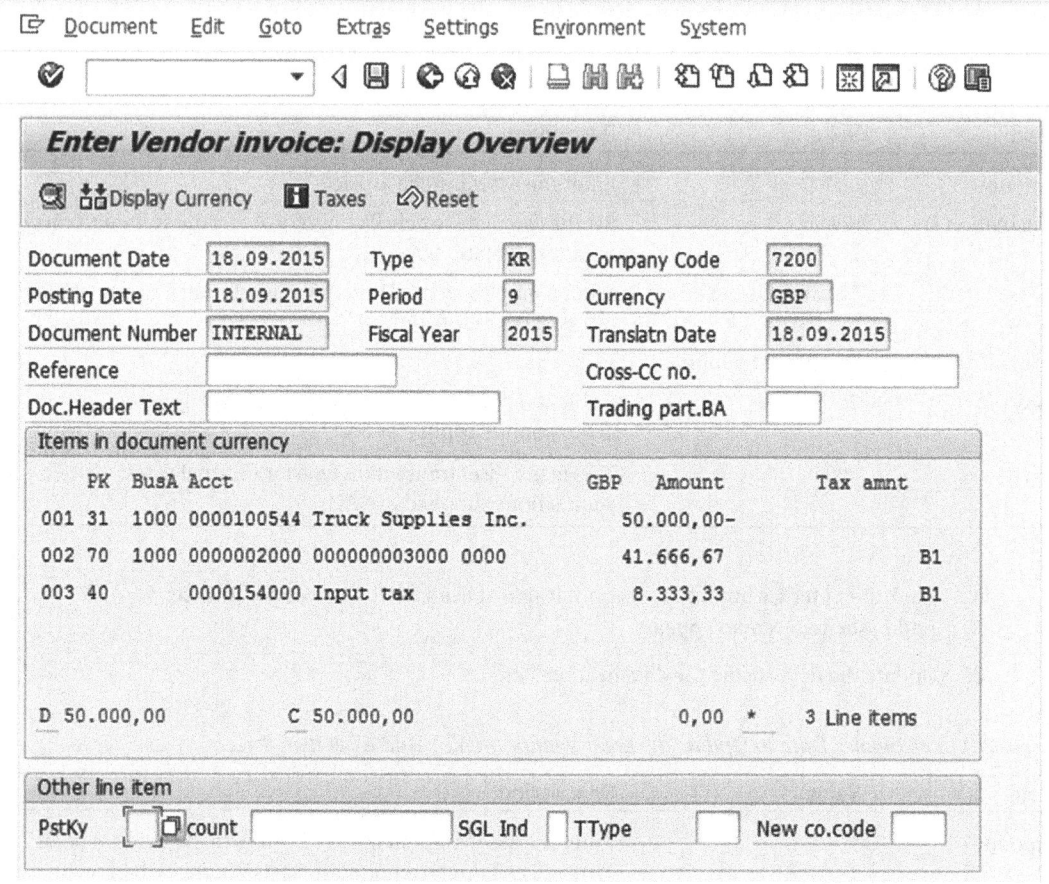

Figure 7-14. The Overview screen displays the invoice data of the asset you entered in the system

9. If you are satisfied with the displayed entries, post ▣ your entries.

■ **Tip**   As part of your exercise in this activity, enter more asset acquisitions at your discretion.

Acquisitions with Automatic Offsetting Entry (TC: ABZON)

This function allows you to perform automatic posting against clearing accounts for fixed asset acquisition simultaneously.

1. To post acquisition with automatic offsetting entry, you can use this menu path: Accounting ➤ Financial Accounting ➤ Fixed Assets ➤ Posting ➤ Acquisition ➤ External Acquisition ➤ Acquis. w/Autom. Offsetting Entry. The Enter Asset Transaction: Acquis. w/Autom. Offsetting Entry screen appears.

2. Using the data in Table 7-4, update the screen.

Table 7-4. *The Data to Update the Enter Asset Transaction: Acquis. w/Autom. Offsetting Entry Screen*

Field	Value	Description
New asset	Select	You have the option of choosing an appropriate button, whether the asset is an existing or new asset.
Description	Wheel Alignment Machine	Enter a description that best describes your asset.
Asset Class	AS3000	Enter the asset class the asset is related to.
Cost Center	1100	Center the related cost center you want the asset to be posted.
Document Date	Today's date	Enter the document date. This is usually date on the document.
Posting Date	Today's date	Today's date is defaulted by the system.
Asset Value date	Today's date	Enter the asset value date.
Amount posted	10000	Enter the value of the asset (i.e., asset cost).
Text	Wheel Alignment	Enter a short description of the asset.

░ **Note**   Here it assumed that this transaction relates to new asset.

---

3.   Click the 〔🖳 MasterData〕 button on the screen to proceed to the next screen, where you will enter additional information about the asset. The Create Asset screen pops up with most of the items defaulted. The defaulted items are inherited from the previous screen (Enter Asset Transaction: Acquis. W/Autom. Offsetting Entry screen).

░ **Note**   You may update the fields that you think are required. For example, the business area.

---

4.   Click the 〔Additional data〕 button at the bottom-left side of the screen for further data entry in the Asset master data. The Create Asset: Master data screen is displayed.

5.   Update the fields as shown in Table 7-5. Most of the fields on this screen are defaulted from entries in the previous screen. Enter the date you want the asset to be capitalized in the posting information section.

Table 7-5. *The information to Enter Further Data Entry in the Asset Master Data*

Field	Value	Description
Capitalized on	Enter earlier date.	Enter the date you want to capitalize the asset. As part of this exercise, in order to see how depreciation calculated on this asset, enter a date three months earlier than today's date.

6. Click the Deprec. Areas tab in order to assign an Ordinary Depreciation Start date to each depreciation area, as shown in Figure 7-15.

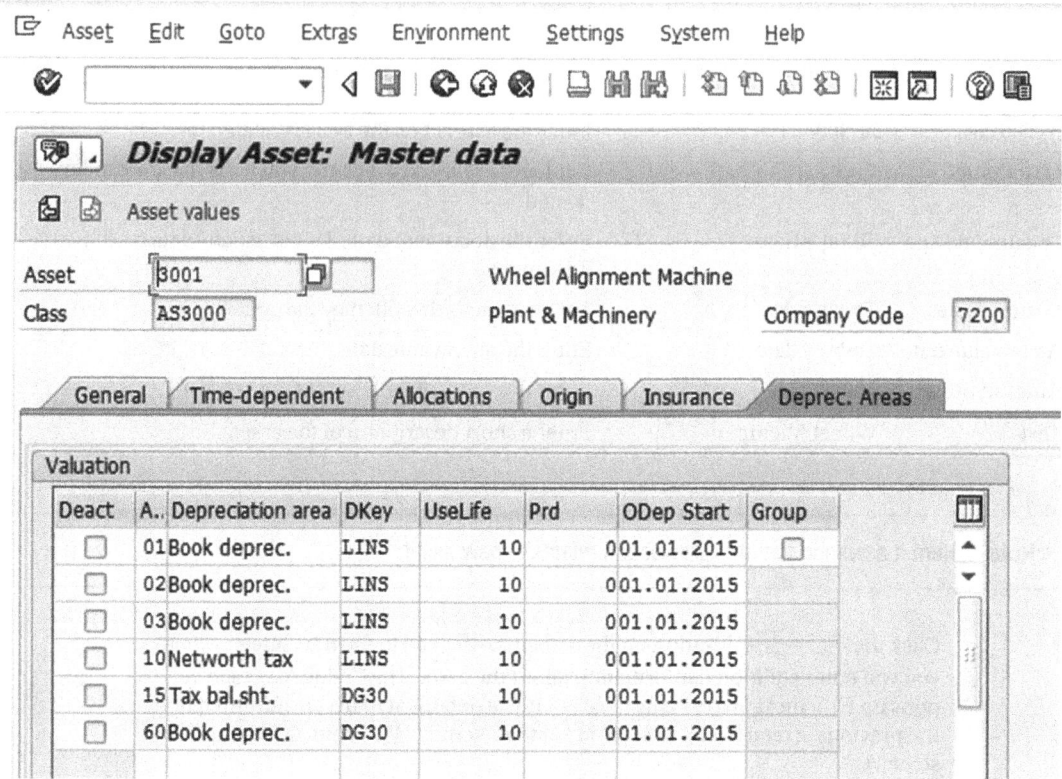

Figure 7-15. *The screen where you assign the ordinary depreciation start date to each depreciation area*

7. Click the Enter ✅ button to verify your entries and click the Back 🔙 button to return to the Enter Asset Transaction: Acquis. W/Autom. Offsetting Entry. The Create Asset screen pops up again.

8. Click the Continue ✅ button to close the screen.

9. The Enter Asset Transaction: Acquis. W/Autom. Offsetting Entry screen is displayed. You may want to see your entries before posting. To do this, click the ⎣Asset values⎦ button at the top-left side of the screen. The Asset Explorer appears with your entries, as shown in Figure 7-16.

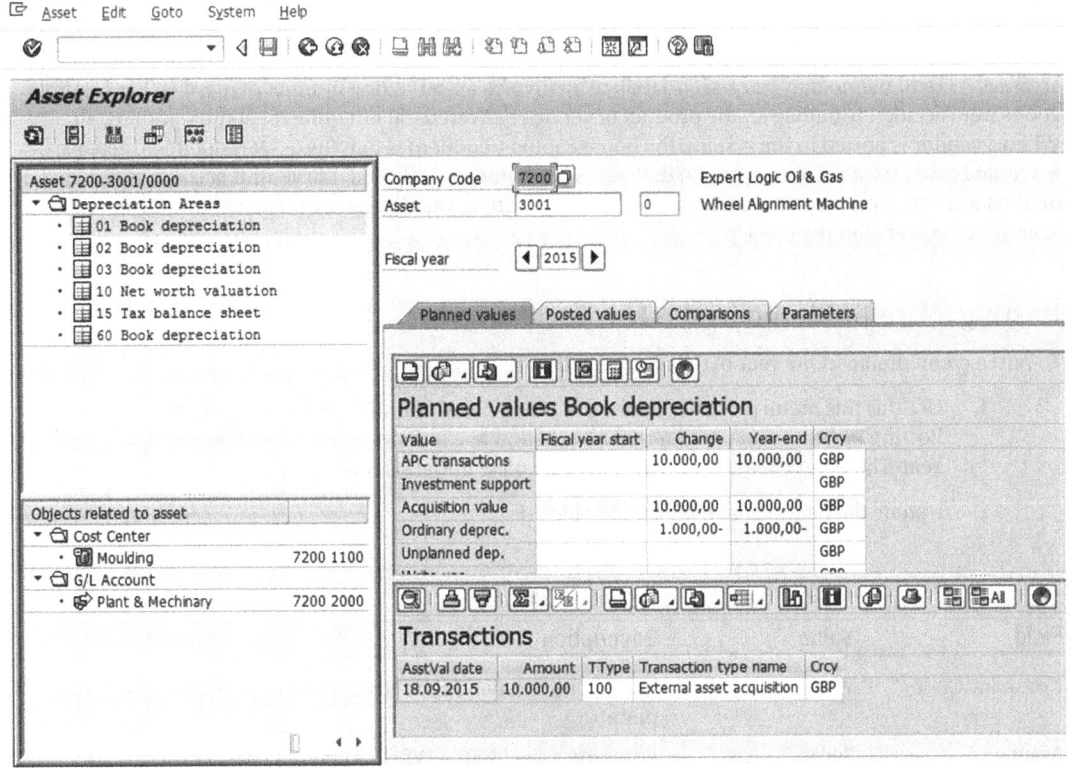

Figure 7-16. *The screen where you display the values of a fixed asset, including APC values and depreciation*

10. If you are satisfied with your entries, click the Back 🔄 button at the top-middle side of the screen to return to the previous screen and post 🖫 your work. The Document Lines Display messages screen pops up with your posting information, as shown in Figure 7-17.

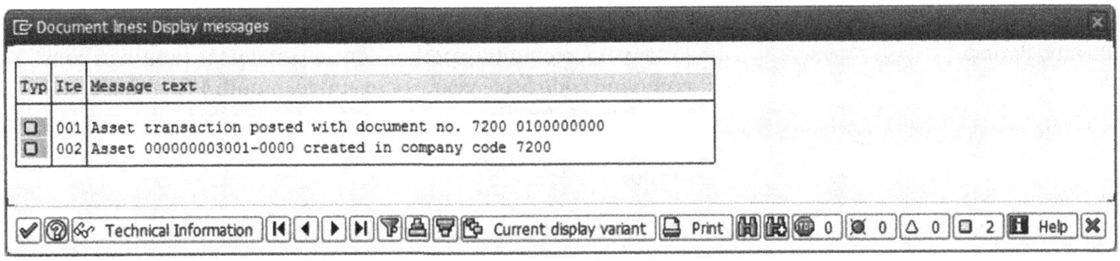

Figure 7-17. *The document line items display screen*

11. Click the Continue ✅ button at the bottom-left side of the screen to close it.

Credit Memos

A credit memo is an acceptable systematic way of reducing the original acquisition and production costs of an asset. A credit memo may be raised to reduce an invoice amount for a number of reasons. For example, goods were accidently damaged, the product or service delivered did not quite meet the standard, etc. When a vendor is posted in the system, the bookkeeping treatment is that the asset is debited (increase in asset) and the vendor account is credited. When a credit memo is posted, the vendor account is reduced. It's debited with the credit memo and the asset is credited. Credit memos can be posted in the current invoice year or in the year after the invoice.

Posting a Credit Memo in the Invoice Year

To post a credit memo in the year of the invoice, follow these steps:

1. Use this this menu path: Accounting ➤ Financial Accounting ➤ Fixed Assets ➤ Posting ➤ Acquisition ➤ External Acquisition ➤ Credit Memo ➤ . . . in Invoice Year. The Enter Credit Memo in Year of Invoice: Initial screen appears.

2. Update the fields using the data in Table 7-6.

Table 7-6. *The Data to Post a Credit Memo in the Invoice Year*

Field	Value	Description
Company Code	7200	Enter your company code the asset you are posting the credit memo.
Asset	3001	Enter the asset (3001 – Wheel Alignment Machine) you are posting the credit memo against. You can access the list of assets you posted in the system using the matchcode by the Asset field.
Subnumber	0	The subnumber is defaulted by the system automatically.
Document Date	Today's date	This system defaults today's date as the document date. You can overwrite the date by entering another date. The document date is usually the date on the document.
Posting Date	Today's date	Posting date is also defaulted by the system as today's date. This is the date that the document was posted in the system. This date can be overwritten.
Posting Period	9	Enter your accounting period. This is usually the month in your company code fiscal year. For example, month 1 is January, month 2 is February, and so on. This is the case if your fiscal year starts in January. Otherwise, month 1 will be the starting month of your fiscal year.
Transaction Type	105	Credit memo in acquisition year. This is defaulted by the system.

3. Click the Enter ✅ button at the top-left side of the screen. The Create Asset Transaction: credit memo in acquis. Year screen appears.

4. Enter amount on the credit memo document (500) in the Amount Posted field in the posting data section of the screen. You might want to enter additional details by entering a short description (for example, "memo") in the Text field.

■ **Note** The Asset value date, the offsetting G/L account the credit memo is posted to, and the document type are all defaulted by the system.

5. You can display the document line items by clicking the Simulate ▦ button at the top-left side of the screen. The Document Header Info section of the screen appears, displaying the document line items, as shown in Figure 7-18.

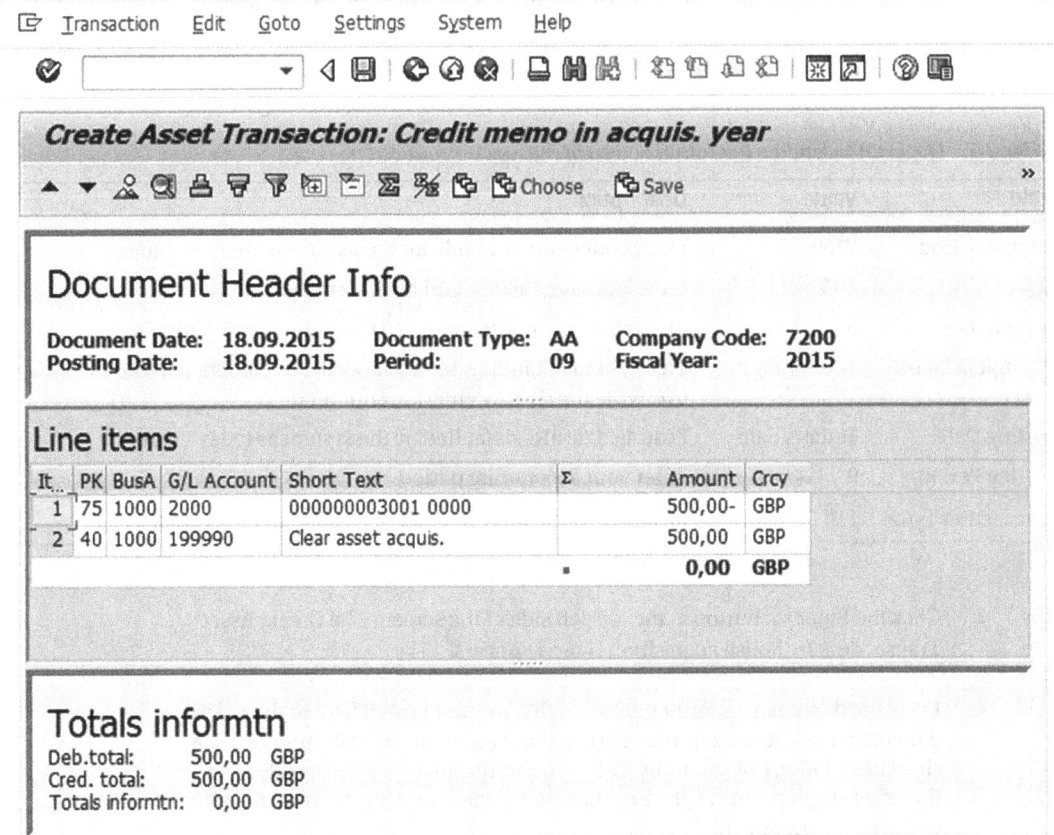

Figure 7-18. *Credit memo document header information and line items display*

6. If you satisfied with your entries, you may post your entries by clicking the Post ▦ button. The system will notify you in the status bar at the bottom of the screen that the asset transaction has been posted.

Posting a Credit Memo in the Next Year

To post a credit memo in the year after the invoice, you can use this this menu path: Accounting ➤ Financial Accounting ➤ Fixed Assets ➤ Posting ➤ Acquisition ➤ External Acquisition ➤ Credit Memo ➤ . . . in Next Year.

In-House Production

In-house productions are assets produced by your company.

To post acquisitions from in-house productions, follow these steps:

1. Use this menu path: Accounting ➤ Financial Accounting ➤ Fixed Assets ➤ Posting ➤ Acquisition ➤ External Acquisition ➤ In-House Production. The Acquisition from In-House Production: Initial screen is displayed.

2. Update the screen using the data in Table 7-7.

Table 7-7. *The Data to Update the Initial Screen of the Assets Produced In-House*

Field	Value	Description
Company Code	7200	Enter your company code for the asset you are managing.
Asset	8000	Enter the asset (3000 – Forklift Accessories - 1).
Subnumber	0	The subnumber is defaulted by the system automatically.
Document Date	Today's date	This system defaults today's date as the document date. You can overwrite the date by entering another date.
Posting Date	Today's date	Posting date also defaulted by the system as today's date.
Posting Period	9	Enter your accounting period.
Transaction Type	110	In-house acquisition year. This is defaulted by the system.

3. Click the Enter ✅ button at the top-left side of the screen. The Create Asset Transaction: In-house acquisition screen appears.

4. Enter the document amount (20000) in the Amount Posted field in the posting data section of the screen. You also can enter additional details by entering a short description (for example, "AuC") in the Text field. The Asset value date, the offsetting accounting, the in-house acquisition, and the document type are defaulted by the system.

5. You may want to display the document line items by clicking the Simulate 🔳 button at the top-left side of the screen. The Document Header Info section of the screen appears, displaying the document line items.

6. Post 💾 your in-house acquisition.

Capitalizing Assets under Construction (AuC)

Assets produced in-house, like normal assets, incur costs at the production stage. Costs of production arising from assets produced in-house are capitalized in accounting at the completion of the asset. Assets produced in-house go through different phases of production, which are disclosed in the balance sheet. The change of an asset from one phase to another during the asset production is referred to as *capitalization* of AuC.

The AuC master record can be managed in two ways: as a normal asset record or as a master record with line item management. An AuC is capitalized and transferred to a completed asset by distribution/settlement. This will enable the system to use different transaction types to segregate transactions related to the current year from the previous years. AuC can be capitalized as a lump sum or with line item settlement. Line item settlement allows you to decide which line item to settle at any given time. You may not need to necessarily settle all the line items at the same time. Secondly, you can settle some line items completely.

■ **Note**   To settle an asset to another asset/object, you must assign a distribution rule to the asset master record.

AuC - Distribute (TC: AIAB)

This is the aspect of AuC component where line item settlement is performed using distribution rules. A combination of distribution rules is referred to as *distribution rule group*. By using a distribution key and receiver, you can assign distribution groups to line items. The amount of AuC can be distributed systematically using:

- Percentage rates
- Equivalent quantities or the amount being settled to respective receivers

---

■ **Note**   A receiver is that part of the AuC capitalization that needs to be settled to capitalized assets. On the other hand, other costs that do need not to be capitalized as part of the asset are treated as expenses and settled as adjustment postings to respective cost centers on a fiscal year basis.

Use the following steps to distribute AuC:

1. Use this menu path: Accounting ➤ Financial Accounting ➤ Fixed Assets ➤ Posting ➤ Capitalize Asset u, Const. ➤ Distribute. The Settlement AuC: Initial screen is displayed.

2. Enter your company code (7200) in the Company Code field and the code (8000) of AuC you want to settle in the Asset field.

3. Click the Enter 🗸 button and the Execute ⊕ button at the top-left side of the screen. The Settlement AuC: Line item list screen appears, showing the AuC line items that you may want to settle, as shown in Figure 7-19.

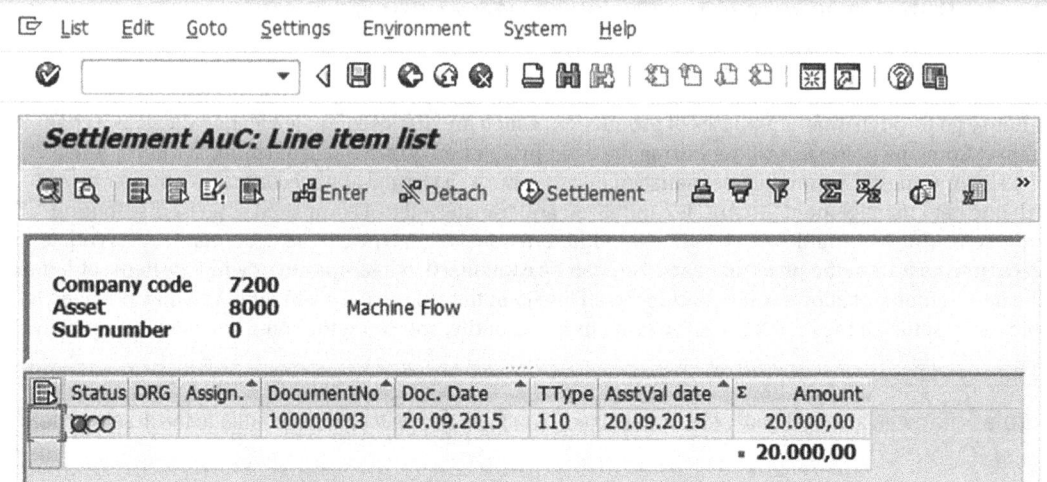

Figure 7-19. *The screen where the settlement of AuC settlement is performed*

4. In this activity, you want to settle the Machine Flow to Forklift Accessories-1 assets at 100% settlement. You will notice that the status of each item that is not settled is red. First, select the item you want to settle from the displayed items on the screen. To assign an object to the distribution rule group you want to settle it to, click the ⏎Enter button at the top-middle side of the screen to proceed to the Maintain Settlement Rule: Parameters screen.

5. Update the following fields:

   - **Description:** Enter a short description (asset settlement) for your asset distribution rule.

   - **Settlement profile:** Enter the settlement profile (10 – All receiver) you are applying to your settlement rule. This function will allow you to display all possible receivers you can choose from. You can access the list of settlement profile entries provided by SAP.

6. Click the Overview 🔏 button at the top-left side of the screen. The Maintain Settlement Rule: Overview screen is displayed, as shown in Figure 7-20. This is the screen where you specify the settlement rule.

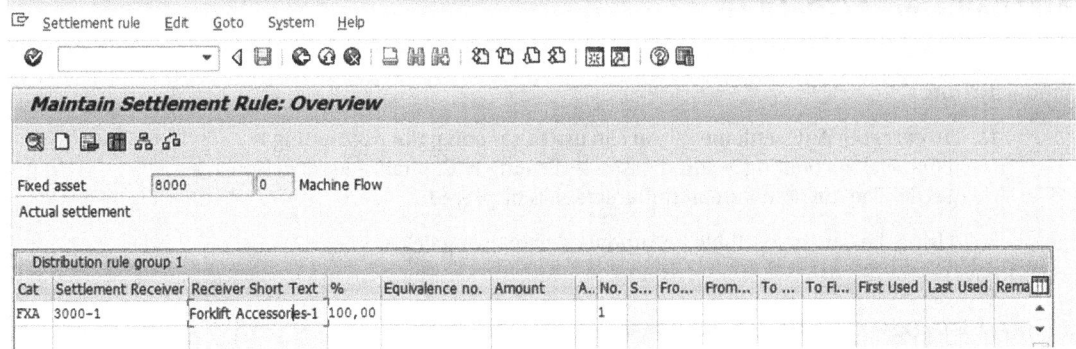

Figure 7-20. *Maintaining a settlement rule*

7. Update the screen using the data in Table 7-8.

Table 7-8. *Data to Update the Maintain the Settlement Rule Overview Screen*

Field	Value	Description
Cat.	FXA (Asset)	Enter the account assignment category you want to use to distribute the cost of the asset to the receiver. You can access the list of account assignment categories using the matchcode.
Settlement Receiver	3000-1 (Forklift Accessories – 1)	Enter the asset that you want to use as the settlement receiver.
%	100	Enter the percentage that you want to settle. In the case, you want to make full settlement (100%).
Receiver Short text	Forklift Accessories -1	The receiver short test is defaulted from the settlement receiver number by the system.

■ **Note**   You can also use the amount of the asset as your settlement costs rather than using percentages. If this is what you choose to do, leave the percentage field blank and enter the settlement amount in the Amount field.

8. Click the Enter ✅ button at the top-left side of the screen to confirm your entries and click the Back 🔙 button to return to the previous screen, called Settlement AuC: Line Item List.

9. You will now notice that the status of your asset settlement has turned green. You may now save 💾 your work.

AuC Settlement (TC: AIBU)

AuC settlement transaction is in a productive mode, but you should perform a test run before you carry out a productive run.

1. To carry out AuC settlement, you can use this menu path: Accounting ➤ Financial Accounting ➤ Fixed Assets ➤ Posting ➤ Capitalize Asset u, Const. ➤ Settle. The AuC Settlement: Initial screen is displayed.

2. Using the data in the Table 7-9, update the following fields.

Table 7-9. *The Data to Update the AuC Settlement Initial Screen*

Field	Value	Description
Company Code	7200	Enter the company code you want to use to settle the AuC.
Asset	8000	Enter the Asset you want to settle to the receiving asset.
Document Date	Today's date	This is defaulted by the system.
Asset val. Date	Today's date	Enter today's date as the Asset Value date.
Posting Date	Today's date	This date is also defaulted by the system.
Period	9	The system automatically defaults the period from the posting date and the fiscal year/posting period that you configured earlier.
Text	AuC Settlement	Enter text describing your transaction.
Document Type	AA	Since this transaction relates to asset settlement, enter the document type for asset posting. You can access the list of transaction types using the matchcode.
Test Run	De-Select	This is defaulted by the system. If you want to perform a productive run, you should de-select test run. It is advisable to perform a test run before carrying out a productive run.
Detail list	Select	

3. Click the Enter ✅ button at the top-left side of the screen to confirm your entries and then click the ⊕ Execute button at the top of the screen. The AuC settlement: Initial Screen appears, as shown in Figure 7-21.

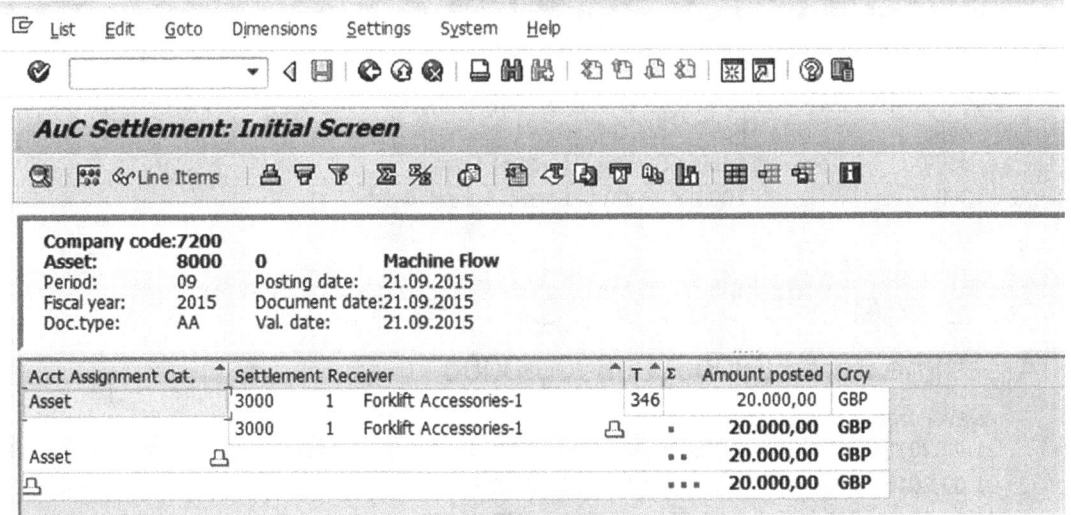

Figure 7-21. *The initial screen for AuC settlement*

4. To display line items of the settlement you performed, click 🔗Line Items . The AuC Settlement: Initial Screen appears containing the assets posted, as shown in Figure 7-22.

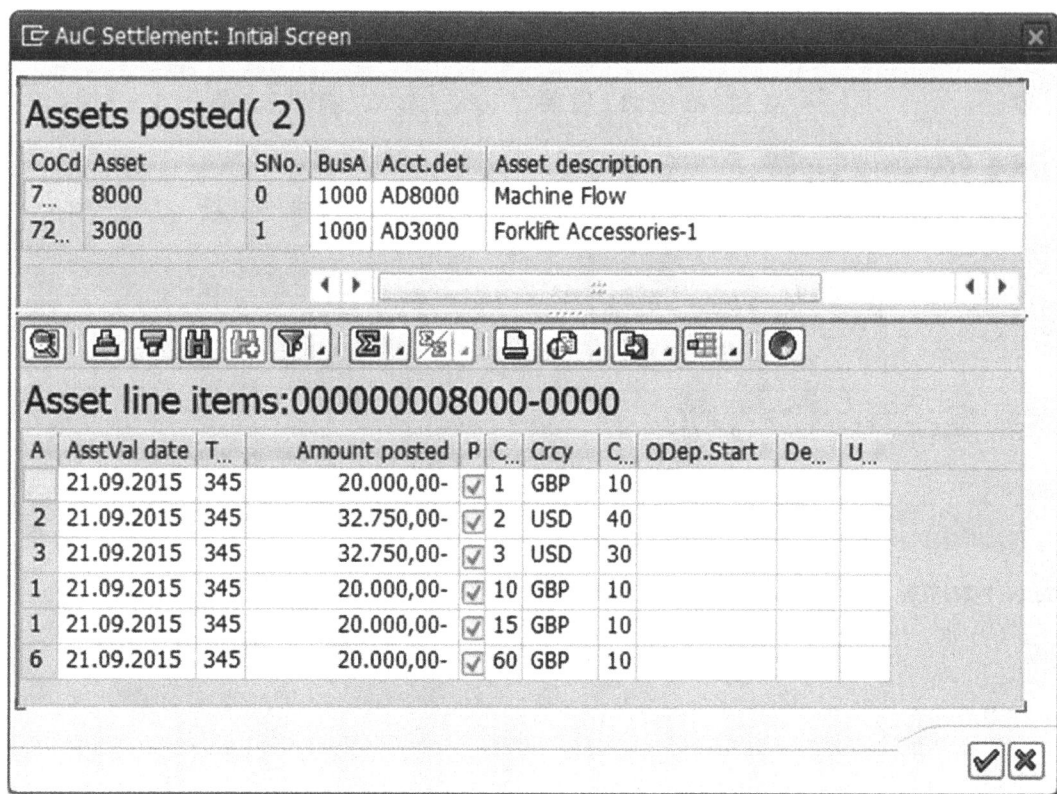

Figure 7-22. Displaying the list of AuC settlements

Reverse Settlement of AuC. (TC: AIST)

It is possible to reverse the settlement of AuC. To do this, first you have to execute a productive settlement.
To be able to reverse a settlement of AuC, do the following:

1. Use this menu path: Accounting ➤ Financial Accounting ➤ Fixed Assets ➤ Posting ➤ Reverse Document ➤ Capital Asset u. Const. The Reversal of Settlement of AuC: Initial Screen is displayed.

2. Update the fields using the data in Table 7-10.

Table 7-10. *The Data to Update the Reversal of Settlement of AuC Initial Screen*

Field	Value	Description
Company Code	7200	Enter the company code that you want to carry out the settlement reversal for.
Asset	8000	Enter the settled asset that you want to reverse.
Document date	Today's date	Enter the document date of the transaction that you want to reverse. For this exercise, use today's date.
Posting date	Today's date	This is the date the document reversal was posted. This will be today's date.
Period	9	This is determined by the system from the document/posting date.
Test Run	De-activate	If you want to perform a test run before performing a productive run, check the Test Run check box. Otherwise, make sure it is de-selected. It is advisable to always perform a test run before performing a reversal.

3. Once you have updated the required field, click the 🔵Execute button at the top-left side of the screen. The Reversal of Settlement of Au: Initial Screen is displayed showing the line items of Settlement of AuC that you have revered.

4. Click the Save button 🖫 at the top of the screen. The system will then notify you that the asset transaction has been posted.

Transfers

There are two types of asset transfers in the SAP R/3 system:

- Intracompany transfers (transfers with a company code)
- Intercompany transfers

Transferring Within a Company Code (TC: ABUMN)

Intra-company transfers are SAP R/3 components that allow you to transfer assets or a part of an asset from the sending asset to a different asset (receiving asset) master record within the same company code. Intra-company asset transfer is possible when one of the following conditions is present:

- When an asset is mistakenly created in a wrong asset class. Since it is not possible to change the asset class in the master record, the only option is to transfer the asset to another master record in the same company code.
- When an asset is split up or a component of the asset is moved to another asset.
- When an AuC is settled and transferred to a normal asset.

Transferring within a company code can be carried out in asset accounting by following these steps:

1. Use this menu path: Accounting ➤ Financial Accounting ➤ Fixed Assets ➤ Posting ➤ Transfer. ➤ Transfer within Company Code. The Enter Asset Transaction: Transfer within Company Code screen appears.

■ **Note** Partial transfer is carried out before depreciation is posted. Whereas, in the case of a full transfer, depreciation is posted before transfer.

---

2. Update the fields on the screen using the data in Table 7-11.

Table 7-11. *Data to Make Partial Transfer of One Asset to Another*

Field	Value	Description
Asset	3000	Enter the asset number you want to transfer to another asset. You can access the list of assets in your company code using the matchcode.
Document date	Today's date	Enter the associated document date.
Posting date	Today's date	Enter the date the asset in question is posted.
Asset Value date	Today's date	Enter the asset value date.
Text	Forklift Accessories - 2	This is the description of the asset you want to transfer to another asset.
Existing asset	Activate and enter asset number (8000)	It is assumed that you are transferring an existing asset (3000) partially to an existing asset (8000). Therefore, activate the Existing Asset radio button and enter the number of the existing assets you are transferring here.

■ **Note** It is assumed that you are make a partial transfer of an amount of 1000 acquired in the current year from the asset (3000-2 Forklift Machine Flow) to an existing asset (8000 – Machine Flow).

If you are making full transfer, save your work at this point. You don't need to go to the partial transfer screen.

---

3. Click the Enter 🗸 button at the top-left side of the screen and choose the Partial Transfer tab on top. This will take you to the partial transfer part of the screen.

4. On this screen, you have three options you may want to use for your transfer. You can perform your transfer using the amount posted, percentage rate, or quantity. Update your screen using the data shown in Figure 7-23.

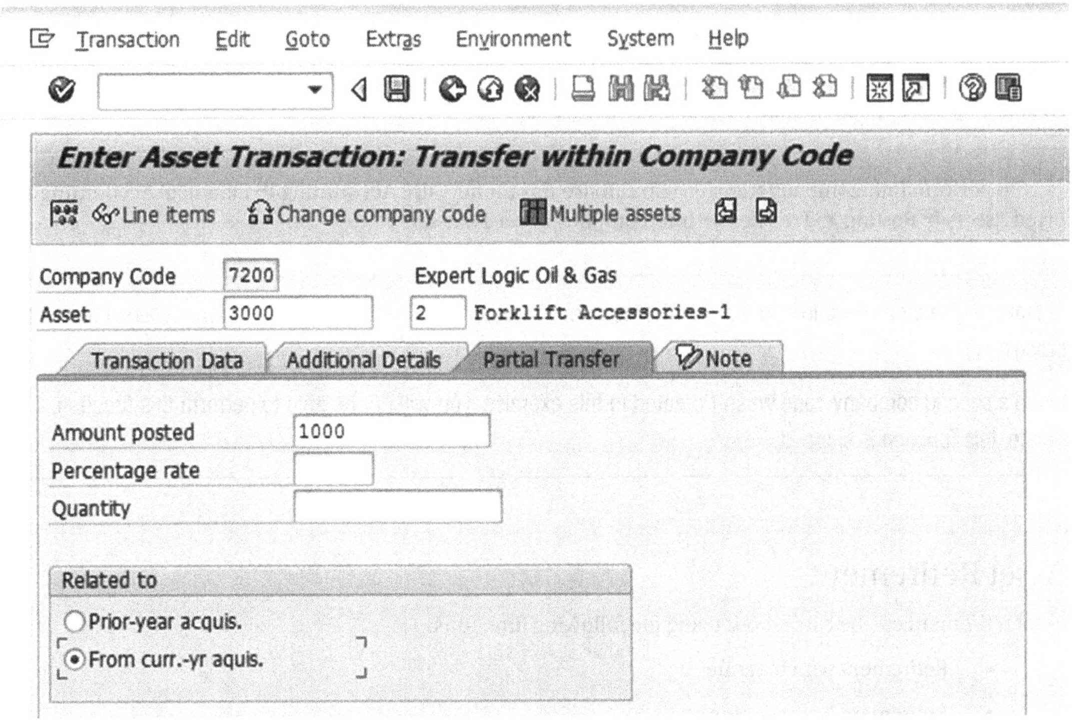

Figure 7-23. The transfer of an asset transaction within a company code

---

▓ **Note**   You can display your entries before posting by clicking the Simulate ▦ button at the top-left side of the screen or you can display line items using the ⌖Line Items button at the top-left side of the screen.

---

5.   Click the Enter ✅ button on the top-left side of the screen and save 🖫 your entries.

Intercompany Transfers (TC: ABT1N)

Intercompany transfer is when an asset is transferred between two company codes in the same corporate group. You can carry out intercompany transfer when one of the following conditions is satisfied:

- An asset's location has changed, which means the original asset must be assigned to a new company code.

- Changes in organizational structure have necessitated the change to an original asset.

■ Note In both cases, the system will not allow you to carry out asset assignment to the company codes involved through master record maintenance. For each asset, you need a new master record in the receiving company code. For a partial transfer, you need an existing asset.

To perform intercompany transfer, you can use this menu path: Accounting ➤ Financial Accounting ➤ Fixed Assets ➤ Posting ➤ Transfer. ➤ Intercompany Asset Transfer.

■ Note The steps for carrying out an intra-company transfer are similar to the intercompany asset transfer process.

Since a second company code wasn't created in this exercise, you will not be able to perform this function. Hence, this function is skipped.

Asset Retirement

Asset retirement can be carried out using the following functions:

- Retirement with revenue
- Retirement by scrapping

Asset Retirement with Revenue

This is the aspect of asset retirement by sale to a business partner. This method of asset retirement is represented in two ways in the SAP R/3 system:

- Asset sale with customer
- Asset sale without customer

Asset Sale with Customer (TC: F-92)

Here, the system allows you to carry out entry postings to account receivable (AP), sale of asset account in the GL, and asset retirement simultaneously.

Let's assume that the Wheel Alignment Machine, which was acquired for $10,000, is sold for $12,000. Use the following procedure to perform asset sale with a customer:

1. Use this menu path: Accounting ➤ Financial Accounting ➤ Fixed Assets ➤ Posting ➤ Retirement. ➤ Retirement w/Revenue ➤ With Customer. The Asset Retire. from Sale w/Customer: Header Data screen appears. The system defaults the following fields: Transaction Type, Company code, Posting Date, Currency/ Rate, Posting Period, and the Posting Key.

2. Using the data in Table 7-12, update the following fields.

Table 7-12. *The Data to Update the Asset Retirement from Sales with Customer Header Data Screen*

Field	Value	Description
Document Date	Today's date	This is date on the document related to the retired asset.
Account	600000	Search for the related customer using the search function and enter the customer account number.

3. Click the Enter ✅ button at the top-left side of the screen to move to the next screen. For the Enter Customer Invoice: Add Customer item, enter the data in Table 7-13.

Table 7-13. *The Data to Update the Enter Customer Invoice Add Customer Item Screen*

Field	Value	Description
Amount	12000	This contains the proceeds received from the asset disposal.
Calculate tax	Select	When this check box is selected the system will perform tax calculation on the asset sales proceed.
Text	Wheel Alignment Machine	Enter a short description of asset retired.
PstKy	50	The will allow the system to perform credit posting to the GL account related to the asset.
Account	820000	The G/L account that the asset disposal proceeds are posted.
TType	210	Retirement of current year acquis. With revenue.

4. Click the Enter ✅ button to proceed to the next screen, which is the Enter Customer Invoice: Add G/L account item screen.

5. Update the fields using the data in Table 7-14.

Table 7-14. *The Data to Update the Enter Customer Invoice: Add G/L Account Item Screen*

Field	Value	Description
Amount	12000	This contains the proceeds received from the asset disposal.
Tax code	A2	This is the tax code for output tax.
Profit Center	1200	The profit center to which the asset disposal proceed is posted.
Asset Retirement	Select	Although the system will automatically default asset retirement, make sure that the Asset Retirement check box is selected.
Text	Wheel Alignment Machine	A short description of the retired asset.

181

6. Click the Enter ✅ button and the Create Asset Retirement screen pops up. You will notice that some fields inherit values that you entered in the previous screen.

7. Update the fields using the data in Table 7-15.

Table 7-15. *The Date to Update the Create Asset Retirement Screen*

Field	Value	Description
Asset	3001 – Wheel Alignment Machine	Enter the asset you want to retire. You can also use the matchcode to search for the exact asset that you want to retire.
Asset value date	Today's date	Enter today's date as the asset value date.
Complete retirement	Tick	It is possible to retire an asset partially or completely, depending on the nature of transaction related to the asset. In this exercise, it is assumed that this asset is to be retired completely. Click the Complete Retirement check box so the system will perform 100%-complete asset retirement on this asset.

8. Click the Enter ☑ button at the bottom of the screen to close the Create Asset Retirement screen.

9. To display your entries, on the Enter Customer Invoice: Add G/L account item screen, click Document on the menu bar and choose Simulate from the drop-down menu. The Enter Customer Invoice: Display Overview screen appears, displaying the transactions. (The transactions displayed will include the profit realized from the asset disposal.)

▪ **Note** You will notice that there is a gain from the disposal of this asset.

---

10. If you are satisfied with the displayed transactions, you can click the Enter ✅ button at the top-left side of the screen and post 💾 your transaction.

Asset Sale Without Customer (TC: ABAON)

This function is carried out when an asset is sold for cash or to a one-time customer. Let's work through this step, by carrying out a partial asset retirement for the Machine Flow without a customer:

1. To perform an asset sale without customer, you can use this menu path: Accounting ➤ Financial Accounting ➤ Fixed Assets ➤ Posting ➤ Retirement ➤ Retirement w/Revenue ➤ Asset Sale Without Customer. The Enter Asset Transaction: Asset Sale Without Customer screen is displayed.

2. Update the following fields using the data in Table 7-16.

Table 7-16. *The Data to Update the Enter Asset Transaction for Asset Sale Without Customer*

Field	Value	Description
Asset	8000	Enter the asset number you want to retire. It is also possible to use the matchcode to search for the appropriate asset.
Document Date	Today's date	This is date on the document related to the retired asset.
Posting Date	Today's date	This is the date the document is posted into the system.
Asset Value Date	Today's date	Use today's date as the asset value date.
Text	Machine Flow	Enter text describing the asset.
Specification for Revenue		
Manual Revenue	Select and enter amount (20000)	The system automatically defaults the Manual Revenue radio button. This will allow you to enter the revenue generated from the asset sale. Enter the asset sale proceeds.

3. Click the Enter ✅ button and choose the Partial Retirement tab. The page to enter partial retirement details is displayed.

4. Update the fields using the data in Table 7-17.

Table 7-17. *The Data to Update Partial Retirement Details Screen*

Field	Value	Description
Amount Posted	20000	Enter the amount of proceeds related to the partial asset sale.
Form curr-yr acquis.	Select	When this radio button is selected, the system will carry out the partial asset retirement from the current year asset acquisition.

5. In order to display the data you entered in the system, click the Enter ✅ button and choose the 🎲 Simulation button, or click the Extras button on the menu bar and select Simulate from the drop-down menu. The Enter Asset Transaction: Asset Sale without Customer screen appears, displaying your entries.

6. If you are satisfied with your transaction, you can post 💾 your transaction.

Asset Retirement by Scrapping (TC: ABAVN)

This component is used when an asset is removed completely or partially from an asset portfolio. An asset is scrapped with no revenue earned. Let's assume that you want to partially scrap an asset (the forklift) by 40%.

1. To perform asset scrapping, you can use this menu path: Accounting ➤ Financial Accounting ➤ Fixed Assets Posting ➤ Retirement ➤ Asset Retirement by Scrapping. The Enter Asset Transaction: Asset Retirement by Scrapping screen is displayed.

2. Update the fields using the data in Table 7-18.

Table 7-18. *The Data to Update the Enter Asset Transaction for Asset Retirement by Scrapping Screen*

Field	Value	Description
Asset	3000	Enter the asset you want to scrap. It is also possible to use the matchcode to access the appropriate asset you want to scrap.
Document Date	Today's date	This is date on the document related to the retired asset.
Posting Date	Today's date	This is defaulted by the system. You can override this by manually entering a posting date.
Asset Value Date	Today's date	Use today's date as the asset value date.
Text	Forklift	Enter short text describing the asset.

3. Click the Enter ✅ button and choose the Partial Retirement tab at the top of the screen. The page to enter partial retirement by scrapping details is displayed.

4. Update the fields using the data in Table 7-19.

Table 7-19. *The Perform Partial Retirement by Scrapping Screen*

Field	Value	Description
Percentage rate	40%	You have the choice of entering a partial amount you want to scrap the asset for in the Amount posted field or entering a percentage rate in the Percentage rate field.
Form curr-yr acquis.	Select	When this radio button is selected, the system will carry out the partial asset retirement from the current year's asset acquisition.

5. In order to display the date you entered, click the Enter ✅ button and then the 🔲 Simulation button, or click Extras on the menu bar and choose Simulate from the drop-down menu. The Enter Asset Transaction: Asset Retirement by scrapping screen appears (Figure 7-24).

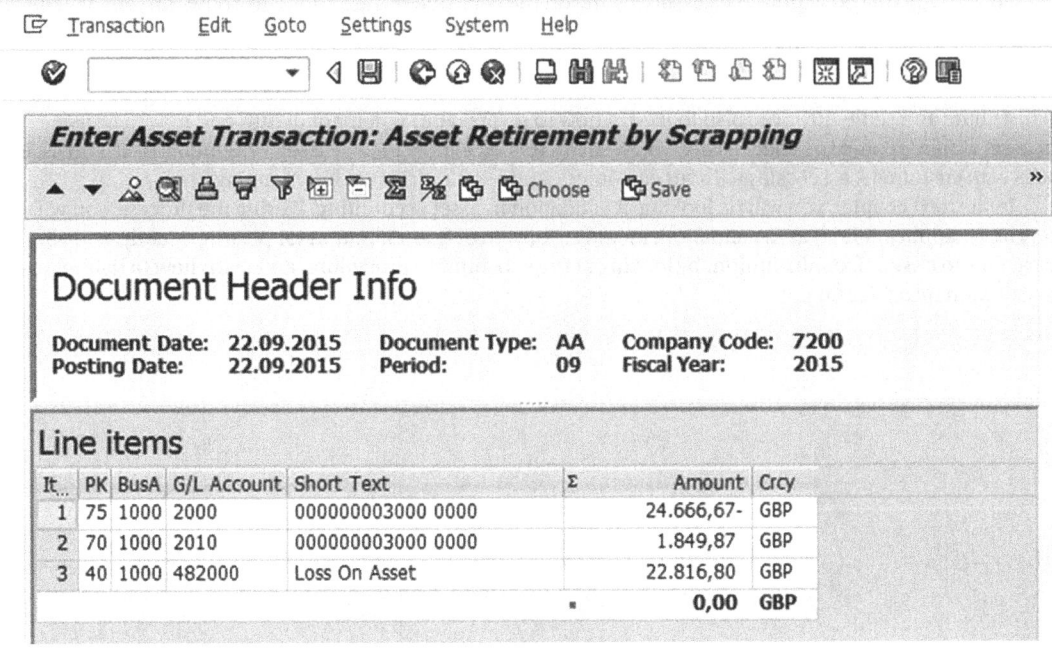

Figure 7-24. *Line items display of asset retirement by scrapping*

6. If you are satisfied with the displayed line items, you can post 💾 your work.

Summary

This chapter talked briefly about transactions involved in posting assets and asset acquisitions in asset accounting. You then went on to look at how to define transaction types for asset acquisitions, account assignment category for asset purchase orders, and how to assign accounts to acquisition transactions. You then went on to look at how to define asset retirements at the following asset retirement levels:

- Assets sold with revenue to a customer and without a customer

- By scrapping

- When an asset is sold to an affiliate company

You then learned about the transaction types for retirements as they relate to gain/loss posting. You then looked at how to determine posting variants and how to define transaction types for write-ups due to gain/loss when an asset is retired.

You learned about asset transfers and learned how to define transaction types for asset transfers. You also looked at how to specify variants for asset retirement transfers. You also looked at the steps involved in defining cross-system depreciation areas and learned how to assign local assets to cross-system depreciation areas. You looked how to capitalize assets under construction (AuC) and how to determine cost elements for settlement of the controlling receiver. You then looked at how to define settlement profiles and assign settlement profiles to a company code.

Finally, you looked at how to fix asset posting on the user side of the system. In doing this, you looked at how to post assets with vendor and acquisition of assets with automatic offsetting entries. You then went on to look at how to post credit memos for asset acquisitions in the current year and in the next year, post in-house productions, and capitalize assets under construction. In the capitalization of AuC, you looked at how to distribute and settle AuC. You also looked at how to reverse the settlement of AuC and how to transfer an asset within a company code. Lastly, you went on to look at how to post asset retirements based on asset sales with customers, asset sales without customers, and asset retirement by scrapping.

In the next chapter, you will be looking at validation in asset accounting. During the process, you will look at the application areas in validation, including how to define validation for posting. Finally, you will learn how to customize substitution, by looking at the substitution procedure, and learn how to define substitution in accounting.

■ ■ ■

CHAPTER 8

Customizing Validation and Substitution

This chapter looks at validation and substitution and the customizing steps involved in the configuration of validating and substituting in asset accounting. In this chapter, you learn how to:

- Define an application area for validation and understand what validation is

- Define validation for posting

- Define an application area for substitution and understand what substitution is

- Define substitution in an accounting document

Validation in SAP

This section first looks at validation in SAP generally and then goes through the practical details of working with validation in SAP.

What Is Validation?

Validation is a control component in SAP that allows the system to perform checks on the integrity of the data as it's being entered in the system to ensure that required conditions are met based on the defined validation rules. The validation rule is a control mechanism containing the rule manager that carries out checks on data entered into certain fields. The rule manager validates the data you enter in certain fields according to the defined conditions. If these conditions are not met, the system will issue an error message and reject your entry.

You can define validation rules using Boolean logic (which allows you to reduce values of variables to true or false). This makes it possible for the system to check the validation rule to ensure it is syntactically correct. Validation is maintained in an application area in asset accounting. SAP comes with standard validations in the system. You can create your own validation without having to make changes to the standard validations. In SAP, a validation can consist of up to 999 steps. Therefore, it is possible that before data is posted in the system, it can be validated against any Boolean statement. You can use a:

- **Prerequisite statement.** This statement determines conditions that are met before the validation can be carried out. If the prerequisite statement is false, the transaction continues without validation.

- **Check statement.** Unlike the prerequisite statement, the check statement checks whether values entered meet the defined conditions. If the check statement is true, the values are accepted and the transaction continues. If the check statement is false, the system will issue an error message.

It is possible that you may want to create a user-defined Boolean statement for certain entries in a different way not represented by the standard system. You can do this by creating your own validation without making changes to the existing standard system. Validations are created and maintained in the application areas.

Defining Validations for the Asset Master Data in the Application Area

The application area contains the list of application areas (for example, Asset Accounting, Cost Accounting, Financial Accounting, etc.), and this is where the validation, substitution, or rule can be created or maintained.

To define validation for your asset master data, you perform the following steps:

1. Use the menu path: Financial Accounting (New) ➤ Special Purpose Ledger ➤ Tool ➤ Maintain Validation/Substitution/Rules ➤ Maintain Validation. The Change Validation: Overview screen appears showing the application area and the list of application areas where you can define validation.

2. Click the area by the Asset Accounting folder to expand the hierarchy to the desired event, as shown in Figure 8-1.

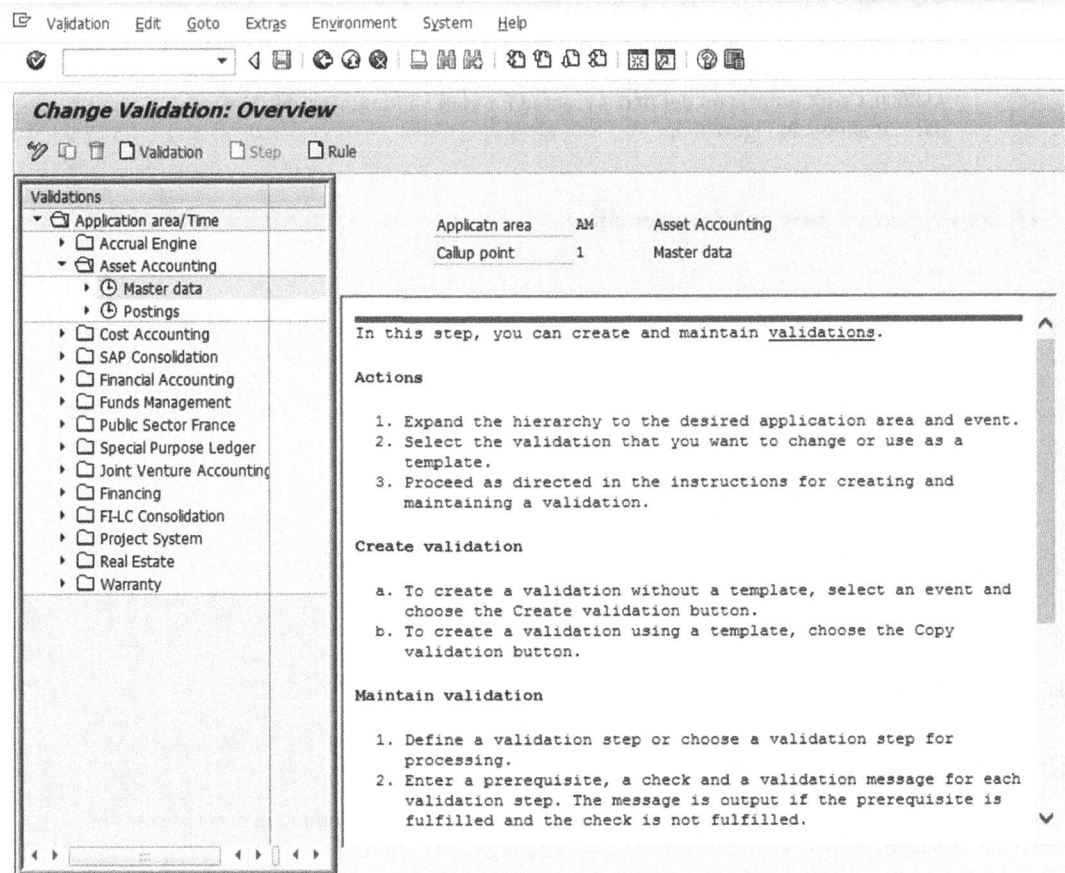

Figure 8-1. *The initial screen where you customize the validation in asset accounting*

■ **Note** You have two options when creating validation. You can create validation using a template or create it without a template. In this activity, you will only be looking at how to create a validation without a template. If you want to use a template, click the Copy Step 🗔 button at the top-left side of the screen.

3. Select Master Data from the hierarchy and click the ☐ Validation button at the top-left side of the screen. The Create Validation: New validation (Header data) screen appears.

4. Enter an identifier key and a short description that best describes your validation (AA-VAL3 – Asset Class AS3000) in the Validation Name fields.

5. Click the ☐ Step button at the top-left side of the screen. The Create Validation: AA-VAL3 – Step 001 – Overview screen appears.

6. Enter a short description (Asset Class, Cost Center) in the Validation Step field for your validation and click the Enter ✅ button at the top-left side of the screen. You will notice on the left pane that a Validation folder (AA-VAL3 – Asset Class AS3000, Cost Center) you defined is created for your validation under Master data, as shown in Figure 8-2.

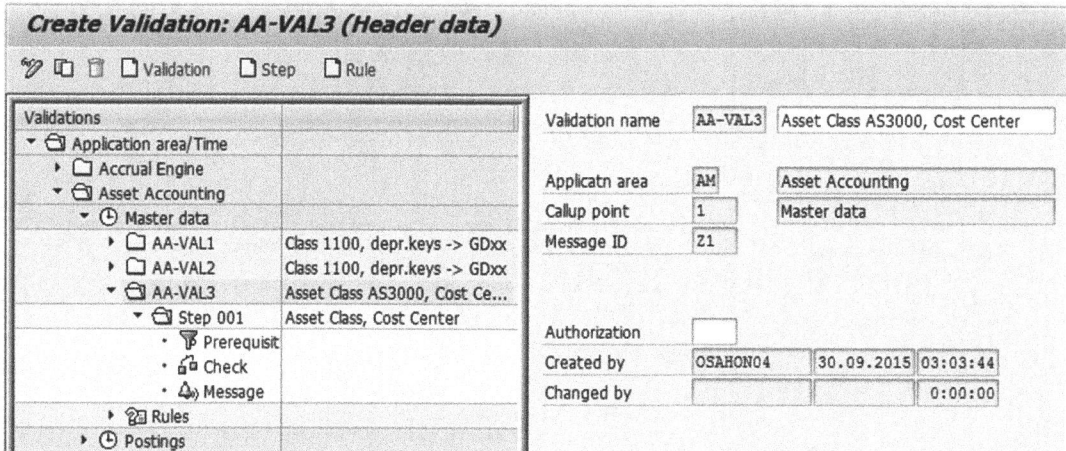

Figure 8-2. *Creating validation for the Asset Class*

Creating a Validation Rule

The validation rule holds the rule manager that performs checks on data entered in defined fields for accuracy. The following steps are performed when creating validation rule:

- Prerequisite
- Check
- Message

Defining Prerequisites

The next step in this activity is to define prerequisites for your validation rule.

1. Select the ▼ Prerequisite icon in Step 001 in your valuation (AA-VAL3) on the left pane of the screen. The Create prerequite: AA-VAL3 Step 001 screen appears displaying the list of structures that you can choose from.

2. Double-click the technical name (Structure ANLA – Asset Master Record Segment) from the displayed list strucure. The Asset Master Record Segment technical Name list is displayed.

■ **Note**   In this activity, you will create validation rule for the Asset Class AS3000 that you created in Chapter 1.

---

3. To create validation rule for asset class, double-click the technical name (ANLA-ANLKL) from the displayed asset master record segment. You will notice that the technical name (ANLA-ANLKL)for the asset class is copied into the upper pane of the screen.

4. Click the equals sign ⬚ button on the right pane of the screen. Then click the [Constant] button on the right pane of the screen. The Enter Constants dialog box pops up. Enter the asset class (AS3000) you are using for your validation in the Asset Class field. You can access the list of asset classes using the matchcode by the Asset Class field. You will notice that the validation rule you defined is displayed on the upper pane of the screen, as circled in Figure 8-3.

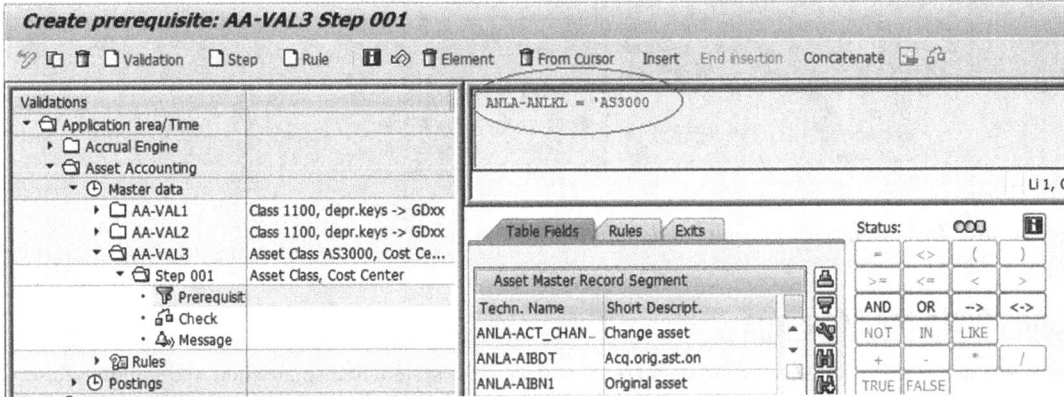

Figure 8-3. *Defining the prerequiste for your validation rule*

Defining the Validation Check

The next step is to define a check for your validation.

1. Select ⬚ Check in Step 001 in your valuation (AA-VAL3) on the left pane of the screen. The Create Check: AA-VAL3 Step 001 screen is displayed.

■ **Note** In this activity it assumed that you want to use the cost center 1100 for your asset class.

---

2. To create check for your validation, double-click the technical name (Structure ANLA – Asset Master Record Segment) from the list structure. The list of asset master record segment technical names is displayed. Search for cost center using the Find 🔲 button in the middle-right side of the screen, then double-click the technical name (ANLZ-KOSTL – Cost Center) from the list of depreciation terms. The technical name (ANLZ-KOSTL) is copied into the upper pane of the screen.

3. Click the equals sign ⬚ button on the right pane of the screen. Then click the [Constant] button on the right pane of the screen. The Enter Constants dialog box pops up.

4. Enter the cost center (1100) you are using for the asset class for your validation. You can access the list of cost centers in the system using the matchcode by the Cost Center field. The validation rule you defined is displayed on the upper pane of the screen, as circled in Figure 8-4.

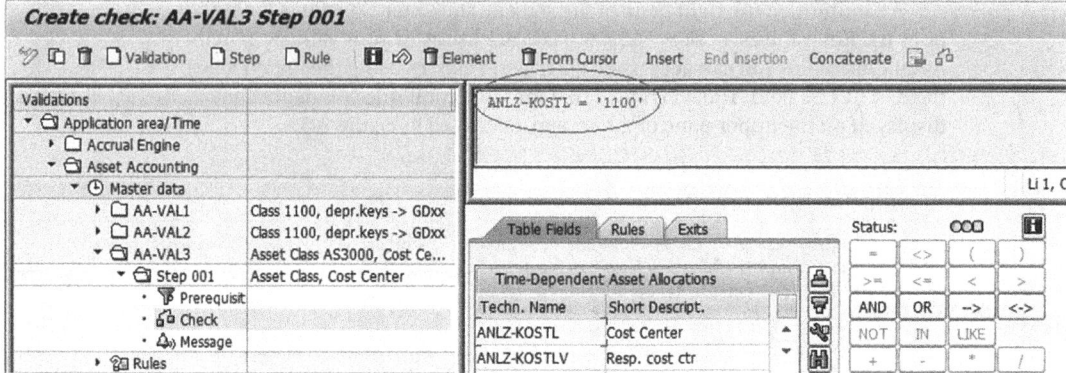

Figure 8-4. *Defining a check for your validation rule*

Specifying the Message

The next step is to specify an appropriate message you want the system to display when a condition is false. SAP comes with a list of standard message types you can choose from. For example:

A – Cancel

E – Error

W – Warning

I – Information

In this activity, you will be specifying the error message.

▧ **Note**   You can also define a custom message if you choose to.

---

1. Click the ⚠ Message icon on Step 001 in your valuation (AA-VAL3) on the left pane of the screen. The Create Validation: AA-VAL3 – Step001 – Message screen is displayed, as shown in Figure 8-5.

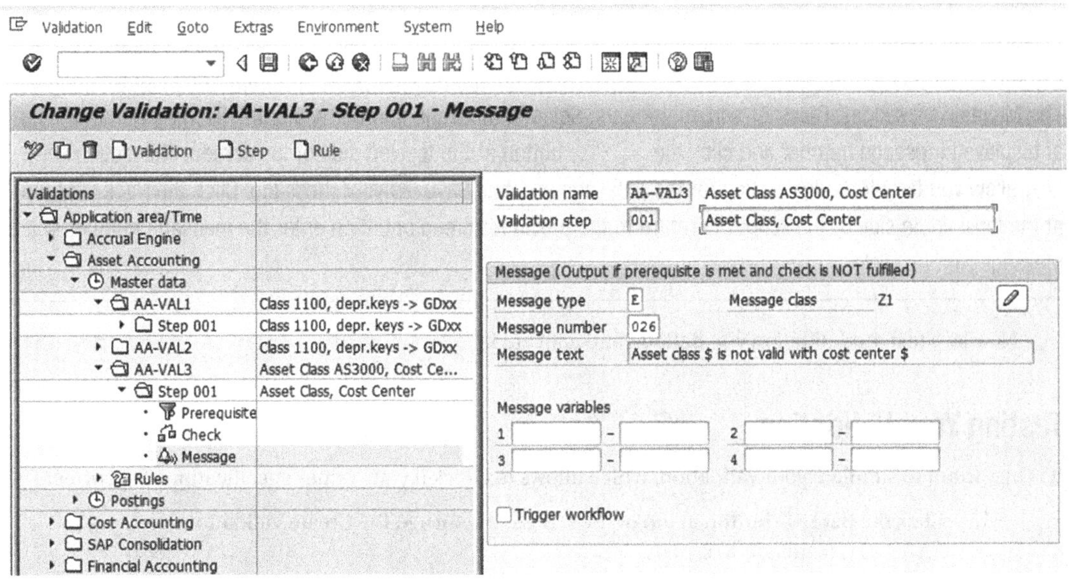

Figure 8-5. *The screen where you specify an error message for your validation*

2. Update the following fields:

    - **Validation Step:** The system defaults to step 001. Enter a brief description for your validation steps (for example, Asset Class, Cost Center).

    - **Message Type:** Enter the message type (E – Error) you are applying to your validation step in this field. SAP comes with four standard steps you can choose from. You can access these standard steps using the matchcode by the Message Type field.

    - **Message Number:** Enter the message number (26 – Asset Class is not valid with cost center) that best meets your requirement in the Message Number field in the Message (Output if prerequisite is met and check is Not fulfilled) section of the screen (you can access the list of message numbers in the system using the matchcode).

3. Click the Enter ✅ button at the top-left side of the screen and save 💾 your configuration.

■ **Note**   To create your message, click the ⬚Environment⬚ button at the menu bar at the top of the Create Validation: AA-VAL3 – Step 001 – Message screen. A drop-down menu appears. Click ⬚Maintain messages⬚ from the displayed items. The Maintain Messages: Class Z1 screen appears. Select a message number without a discription from the list of displayed message number and click the ⬚Individual maint.⬚ button at the top-left side of the screen. This action will now allow you to enter a description for the message number. Save 💾 your message. Click the Back 🔙 button at the top-middle side of the screen to return to the previous screen and then enter the message number in the Message Number field.

Now let's test the validation you defined and activate it.

Testing Your Validation

It is important to simulate your validation, which allows to check if your values specifications are correct.

1. Click the Back 🔙 button at top of the screen to return to the Create Validation: AA-VAL3 (Header data) screen.

2. Click ⬚Validation⬚ at the menu bar, at the top-left side of the screen.

3. Click Simulate on the drop-down menu. The Simulation: Validate AA-VAL3 – Data input screen is displayed.

4. Enter the values for asset class and cost center that you specified for validation in the respective fields, as shown in Figure 8-6. You can access each value using the matchcode by each value field.

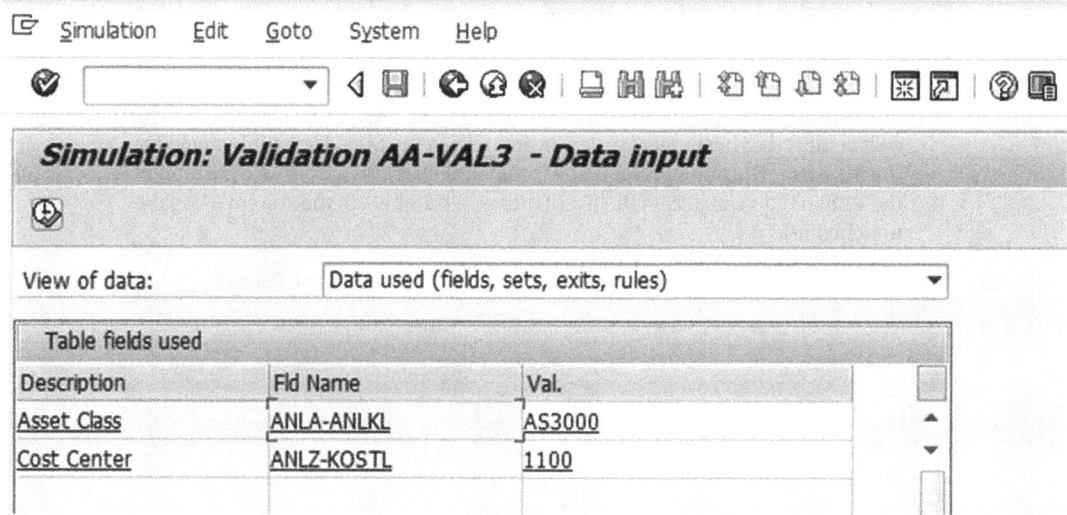

Figure 8-6. *Validation simulation to check if your values specifications are correct*

5. Click the Execute ⊕ button at the top-left side of the screen. The Simulation: Validation AA-VAL3 screen is displayed with the result of your validation condition and check, as shown in Figure 8-7.

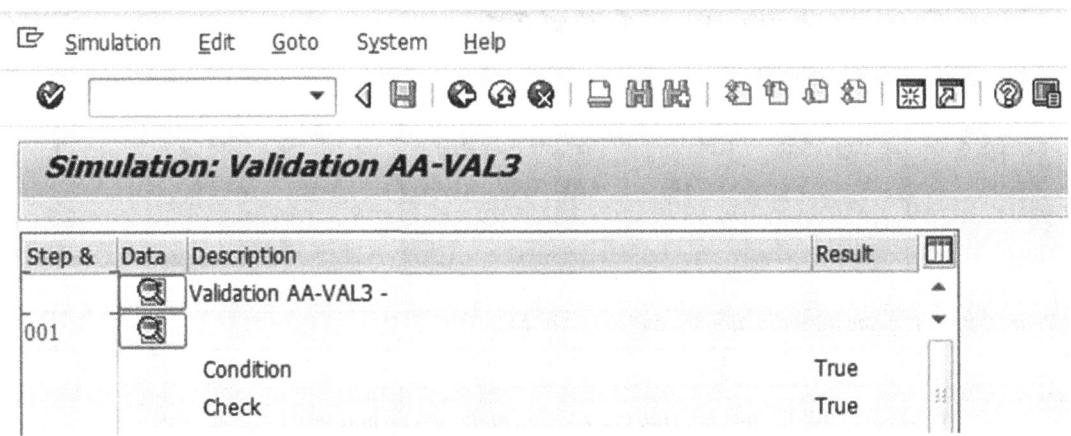

Figure 8-7. *The screen showing the result of the validation condition you defined*

The final step in this activity is to activate the validation you created.

Activating Your Validation

To be able to use your validation, first you have to activate it. Validations are activated in the application area where you are using it. In this activity, since you are using validation in asset accounting, you must activate it there.

1. To activate validation, you can use this menu path: To define validation for posting use the transaction cod: GGB4. The Select Action: Valid./Subst. Menu screen appears with the select action button to choose from.

2. Click the ⌷ Activate valdatn/substn button. The Activation of Validation/Substitution screen appears.

3. Select Asset Accounting from the displayed list of application areas and click the ⌷ Validation button at the bottom of the screen in the Activation Objection section of the screen. The Selection: Asset Accounting screen pops up.

4. Make sure that the Master Data radio button is activated and click the Continue ☑ button at the bottom-right side of the screen. The Change View "Validation for Master Data (Asset Accounting)": Overview screen appears. This is the screen where you a specify company code for your activation and activate your validation.

5. Click the ⌷New Entries⌷ button at the top-left side of the screen. The New Entries: Overview of Added Entries appears.

6. Update the screen using the values shown in Figure 8-8.

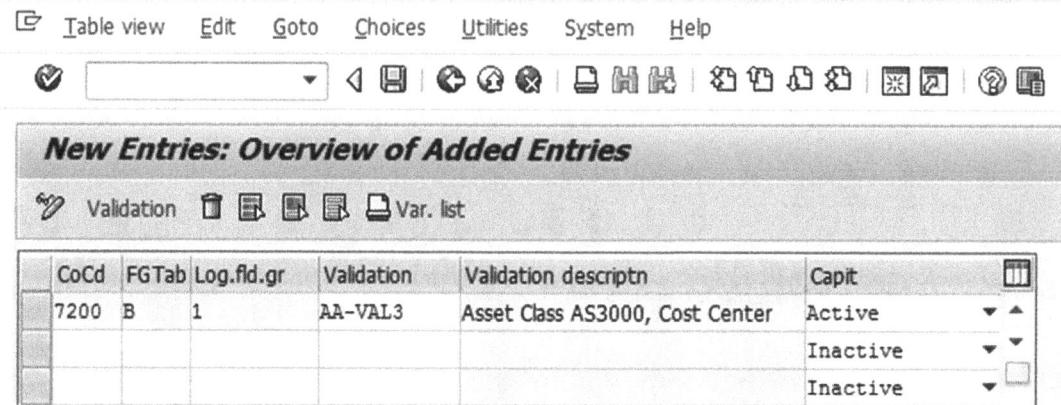

Figure 8-8. Activating the validation in your company code

7. Click the Enter ✅ button at the top-left side of the screen and save 💾 your work.

Now let's create an asset master record to see how the validation you created works.

Creating an Asset Master Record

To see how validation works, we advise that you create one or more asset master records using asset class AS3000 and use a different cost center number instead of the cost center 1100 you specified in the validation you created. When you do this, an error message is displayed on the status bar at the bottom of the screen: "Asset Class is not valid with cost center". You will not be able to complete your transaction.

■ **Tip** We covered how to create an asset master record in Chapter 6. You can use the steps outlined in Chapter 6 as a reference.

Substitution in SAP

This section explains what substation is and then steps through its practical applications in SAP.

What Is Substitution?

Substitution, like validation, is a control mechanism with similar structure, but it functions differently from validation. When data is entered in the system, the substitution rules check to see if defined conditions are met and carry out a substitution. In other words, the substitution rule substitutes the data entered in the system by the users with other data, according to the defined substitution rule using the integration manager if the specified conditions are met (for example, if A is entered during the transaction, the system should substitute it with B). Integration manager uses the conditions in the rule manager to perform substitution. Substitution is defined using Boolean logic and the substitution process contains up to 999 steps.

You can define a substitution rule for mass change of assets, when creating assets, changing business areas, changing cost centers, and so on, within the asset master data. Before data is posted in the system, the values can be substituted using a Boolean statement.

The Substitution Procedure

The substitution procedure involves the substitution steps containing the following statements:

- **Prerequisite Statement.** Determines the conditions that must be fulfilled before substitution can be carried out. If the condition is false (i.e. the conditions are not satisfied), the transaction is carried out without performing the substitution. If the conditions are true (i.e. the conditions are satisfied), the substitution is performed.

- **Substitution Value(s).** This could be a numerical value, a string of letters, or a string of alphanumeric characters that replace the value for the substitution.

Defining Substitution for Asset Master Data

You define substitution in SAP using Boolean statements. Conditions are linked together in Boolean statements using operators (for example, AND and OR). In order to remove the complications involved in customizing substitution, you will be working through an example, as depicted in Figure 8-9.

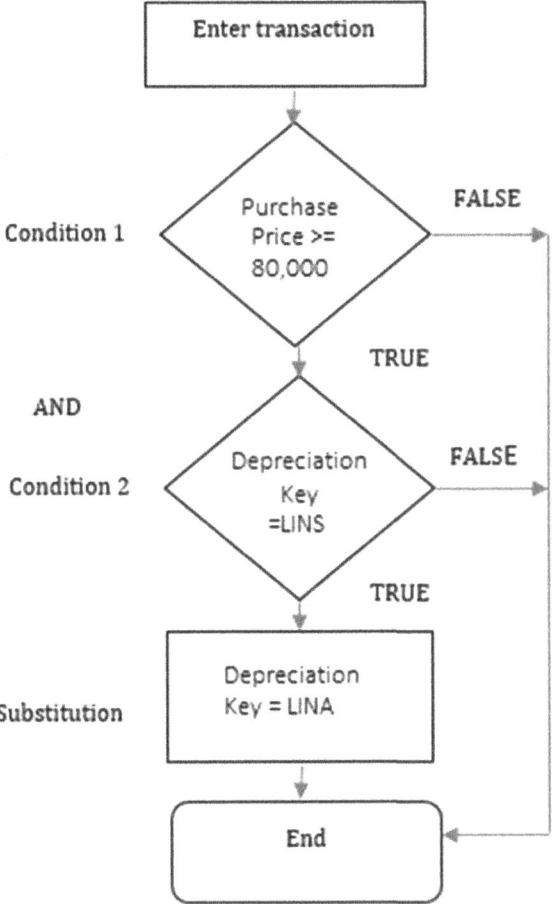

Figure 8-9. *Flow chart diagram depicting the steps involved in defining substitution*

When an asset is acquired and entered into the system, you want the system to check the defined conditions in the Boolean statement (if condition 1 is true, check condition 2; if condition is true, perform substitution). For example, if asset acquisition price is >=80,000 (condition 1) and the depreciation key =LINS (condition 2), substitute depreciation key with LINA and end.

To define a substitution for asset master data, follow these steps:

1. Use the menu path: Financial Accounting (New) ➤ Special Purpose Ledger ➤ Tool ➤ Maintain Validation/Substitution/Rules ➤ Maintain Substitution. The Change Substitution: Overview appears, displaying a list of the application area on the substitution section of the screen.

2. Click the arrow next to the Asset Accounting folder to expand the hierarchy.

3. Select ⊙ Master data from the displayed items and click the ☐Substitution button at the top-left side of the screen. The Create Substitution: New Substitution (Header Data) appears.

4. Enter an identifier key (AA-SUB1) and a short description (Purchase Price, Depr. Key) of your substitution in the Substitution field.

5. Click the Enter ✅ button at the top-left side of the screen for the system to accept your entries. You will notice that a folder AA-SUB1 (Purchase price, Depr. Key) is created for your substitution on the left pane of the screen for the Master Data.

6. Click the ☐Step button at the top-left side of the screen. The Substitutable field (Class 030) screen pops up with list of substitutable fields you can use.

7. Search for the field you are using for substitution (AFASL – Dep.key) by scrolling on the right side of the screen or click the Find button at the bottom-right side of the screen. Select the appropriate substitutable table key (ANLB) and the substitution field key (AFASL) from the displayed list, as shown in Figure 8-10.

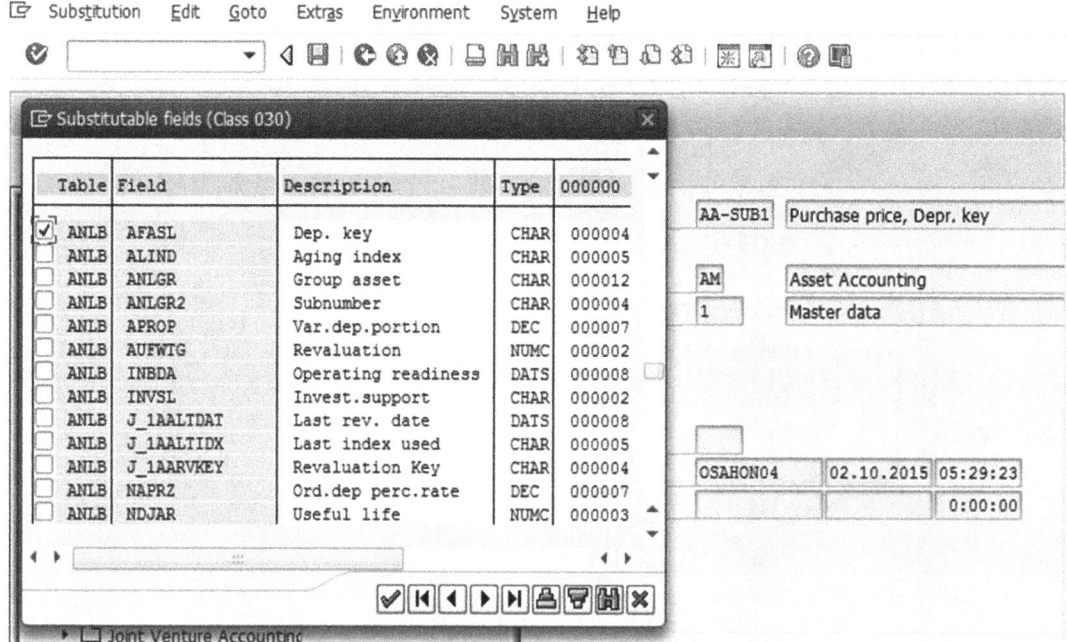

Figure 8-10. *The screen displaying the standard substitution tables and fields in the system*

Tip Take note of the substitution table key (ANLB) and field (AFASL). You will need them later in this chapter when activating your substitution (ANLB).

8. Click the Continue ☑ button at the bottom-right side of the screen to proceed to the next screen, where you define the steps for your substitution. The Entering the Substitution Method screen pops up. The system automatically defaults to a method (Constant Value).

9. Click the Continue ☑ button at the bottom-right side of the screen. The Create Substitution: AA-SUB1 – Step 001 – Overview screen appears. The system defaults the substitution (AA-SUB1 – Purchase price, Depr. Key) and the step key (001) you created.

10. Enter a short description (Depr. Key) for your step in the Step field at the top-right side of the screen.

11. The next step in this activity is to define the prerequisite for your substitution. On the left pane of the screen, click the ▼ Prerequisite button for the Step 001. The Create prerequisite: AA-SUB1 Step 001 screen appears containing the list of structures.

12. Double-click the Structure ANLA – Asset Master Record Segment) from the displayed technical name list. The Asset Master Record Segment section containing the list of technical names you use for your substitution is displayed.

13. First, let's define Condition 1 for your substitution:

    a. Click the open bracket ☐ button on the right pane of the screen, then search for ANLA-LKAUF (Purch.price) from the displayed technical names and double-click on it. You will notice that the technical name (ANLA-LKAUF) is copied to into the upper-right section of the screen, as shown in Figure 8-11.

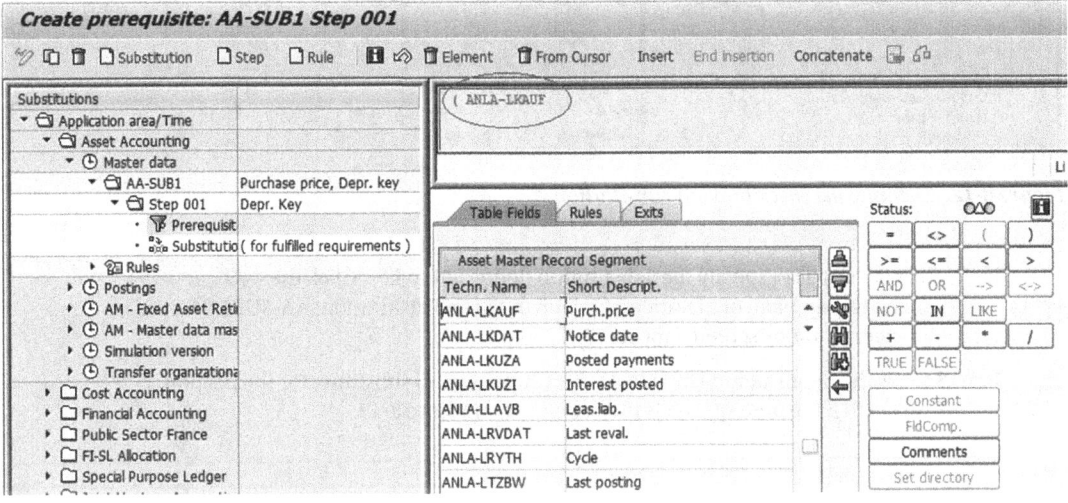

Figure 8-11. Defining the prerequisite for your substitution

199

    b.   Click the greater or equal to ⌐>=⌐ button on the right pane of the screen, then click the ⌐ Constant ⌐ button on the right pane of the screen. The Enter Constants screen pops up.

    c.   Enter the asset purchase price 80000 in the Purch.price field and click the Continue ☑ button on the bottom-right side of the screen.

    d.   Click the close bracket ⌐) ⌐ button on the right pane of the screen.

14.   Second, let's define Condition 2 for your substitution:

    a.   Click the operator ⌐AND⌐ button on the right pane of the screen to link Condition and Condition 2.

    b.   To define the prerequisite for Condition 2, click the open bracket ⌐ (⌐ button, and then search for the technical name ANLB-AFASL (Dep. Key) and double-click on it. The technical name ANLB-AFASL is copied into the upper section of the screen.

    c.   Click the equals ⌐ = ⌐ button and then click the ⌐ Constant ⌐ button. The Enter Constants dialog box pops up.

    d.   Enter the depreciation key (LINS) you want to substitute in the Dep. Key field. You can access a list of depreciation key using the matchcode by the Dep.Key field.

    e.   Click the close bracket ⌐) ⌐ button. Your Boolean statement will look as shown in Figure 8-12.

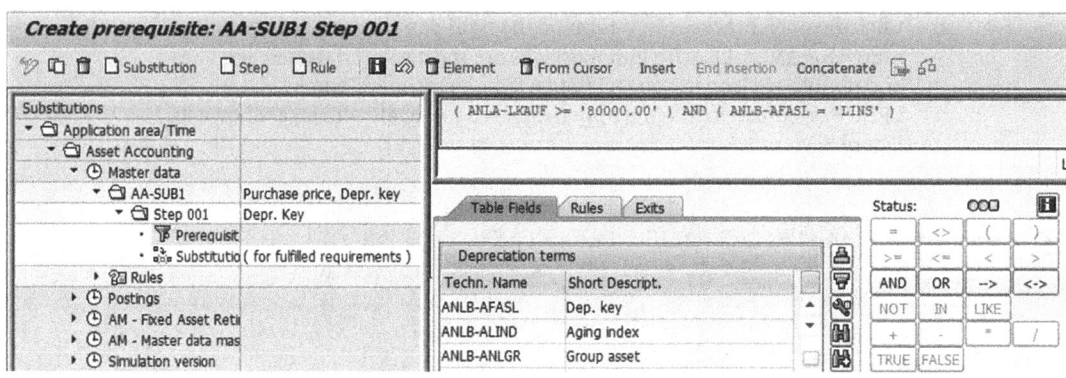

Figure 8-12. *Defining the check for your substitution*

15.   The next step is to specify the substitution depreciation key. Click the ⌐Substitutions⌐ icon on the left pane of the screen for Step 001. The Substitution: AA-SUB1 – Step 001 – Substitutions screen appears.

16.   Specify the depreciation key (LINA) you want to use to substitute for the posting key (LINS) if the prerequisite is met, as shown in Figure 8-13.

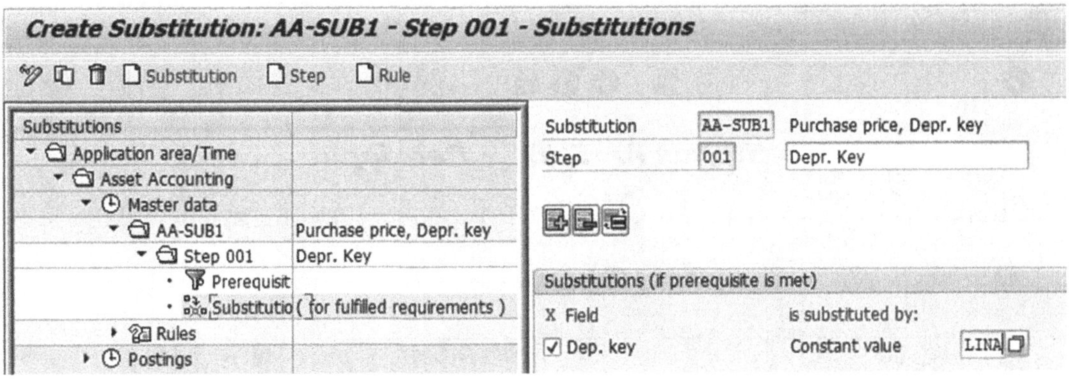

Figure 8-13. *Specifying the substituted value for your substitution*

17. Click the Enter ✅ button at the top-left side of the screen and save 💾 your work.

■ **Note** When you execute a depreciation run, the system substitution manager will automatically substitute the depreciation key LINS with LINA and perform the depreciation calculation using the depreciation key LINA. You will learn how to perform a depreciation run in Chapter 12 in the periodic processing section.

Now let's test your substitution you have defined and activate it.

Testing Your Subsitution

It is important to simulate your substitution, in order to check if your values are correct.

1. Click the Back 🔙 button at top of the screen to return to the Change Substitution: AA-SUB1 (Header data) screen.

2. Click the ⎡Substitution⎤ button on the menu bar at the top-left side of the screen.

3. Click Simulate on the drop-down menu. The Simulation: Substitution AA-SUB1 – Data input screen is displayed.

4. Enter the values for purchase price (80000) in the Purch.price Value field and the Depreciation Key (LINS) in the Dep.key Value field, as shown in Figure 8-14. You can access each value using the matchcode next to each field.

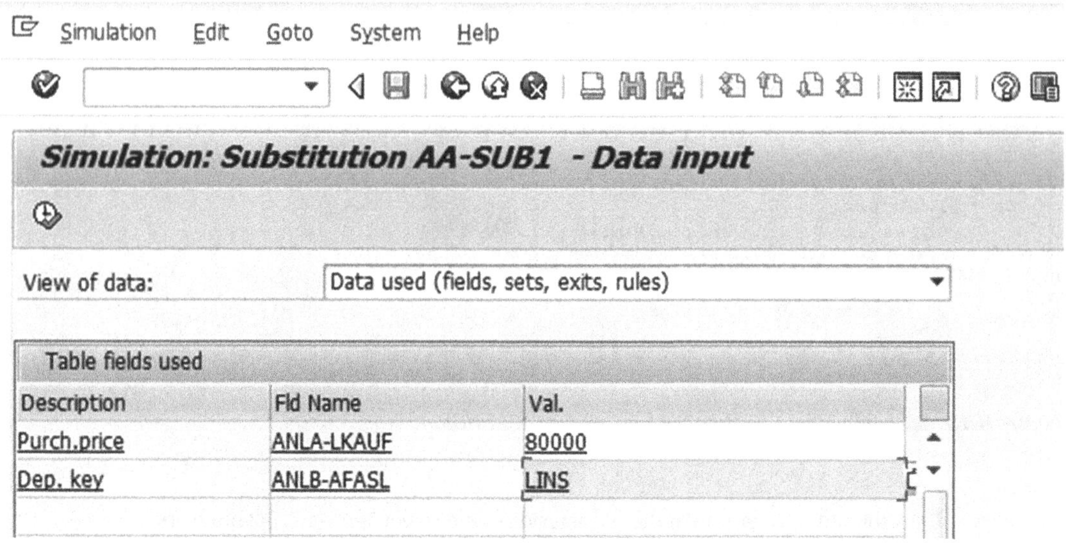

Figure 8-14. *Substitution simulation to check if your values specifications are correct*

5. Click the Enter ✅ button and then click the ⊕ Execute button at the top-left side of the screen. The Simulation: Substitution AA-SUB1 screen appears with your Boolean statement set to True.

6. Click the Back ⟲ button twice. The Simulation screen pops up with the question, "Do you want to exit the simulation of Substitution?"

7. Click the ⎡___Yes___⎤ button at the bottom of the screen. This brings you back to the Change Substitution: AA-SUB1 (Header data) screen.

8. Save 🖫 your substitution.

Finally, you need to activate the substitution you defined for your company code in order to be able to use it.

Activating Substitution

Like validation, you have to activate your substitution in the application you are using it in.

1. To activate the substitution, you can use this transaction code: GGB4. Enter the transaction code in the command field at the top-left side of the screen (the command field is a special input field in SAP screen that users can use to access a screen quicker, instead of using the standard menu path). Click the Enter ✅ button. The Select Action: Valid./Subst. Menu screen appears.

2. Click the ⎡___Activate valdatn/substn___⎤ button. The Activation of Validation/Substitution screen appears.

3. Select Asset Accounting from the list of application areas and then click the ⎡___Substitution___⎤ button at the bottom of the screen in the Activation Objection section of the screen. The Change View "Master Data Substitution (Asset Accounting)": Overview screen appears.

4. To specify the settings for the substitution activation, click the ⌞New Entries⌟ button at the top-left side of the screen. The New Entries: Overview of Added Entries screen appears. Update the following fields:

- **Company Code:** Enter the company code (7200) you are applying to this substitution.

- **FGTab:** Enter the field groups table (A – Asset master data (Table ANLA). You can access a list of standard field groups using the matchcode.

- **Log.fld.gr:** Enter the logical field group (001 – General Data). SAP comes with a list of standard logical field groups that you can choose from. You can display the list of the logical group fields using the matchcode.

- **Subst:** Enter the substitution you defined (AA-SUB – Purchase price, Depr.key). You can also display a list of substitutions using the matchcode by the Subst. field.

- **Active:** Normally, the system will default to the Inactive option. To display the list of options available with this step, use the drop-down arrow by the Active field and select the Active option. Your specification should look like the one shown in Figure 8-15.

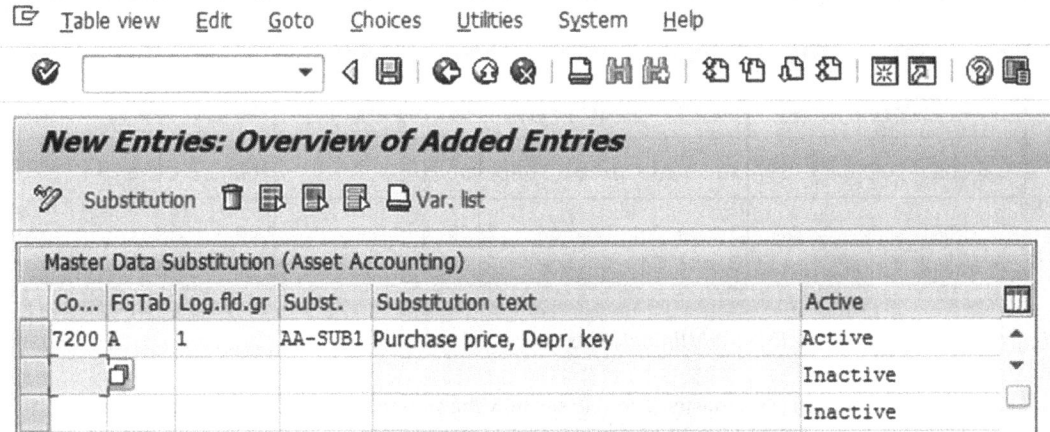

Figure 8-15. *The screen showing the result of the substitution condition you defined*

5. Click the Enter ✓ button at the top-left side of the screen and save ⊟ your work.

Displaying Substituted Fields

You may want to display the substituted fields. To do this, click the ⌞ Substituted fields ⌟ button on the Select Action: Valid./Subst. Menu screen. The Enter Table and Field pops up. Enter the substitution field table key (ANLB) in the Substitution Table field and the Substitution Field key (AFASL) in the Substitution field. Click the Continue ☑ button at the bottom-right side of the screen. The Valid./Subst.: List for Substituted Fields screen appears displaying the substituted field, as shown in Figure 8-16.

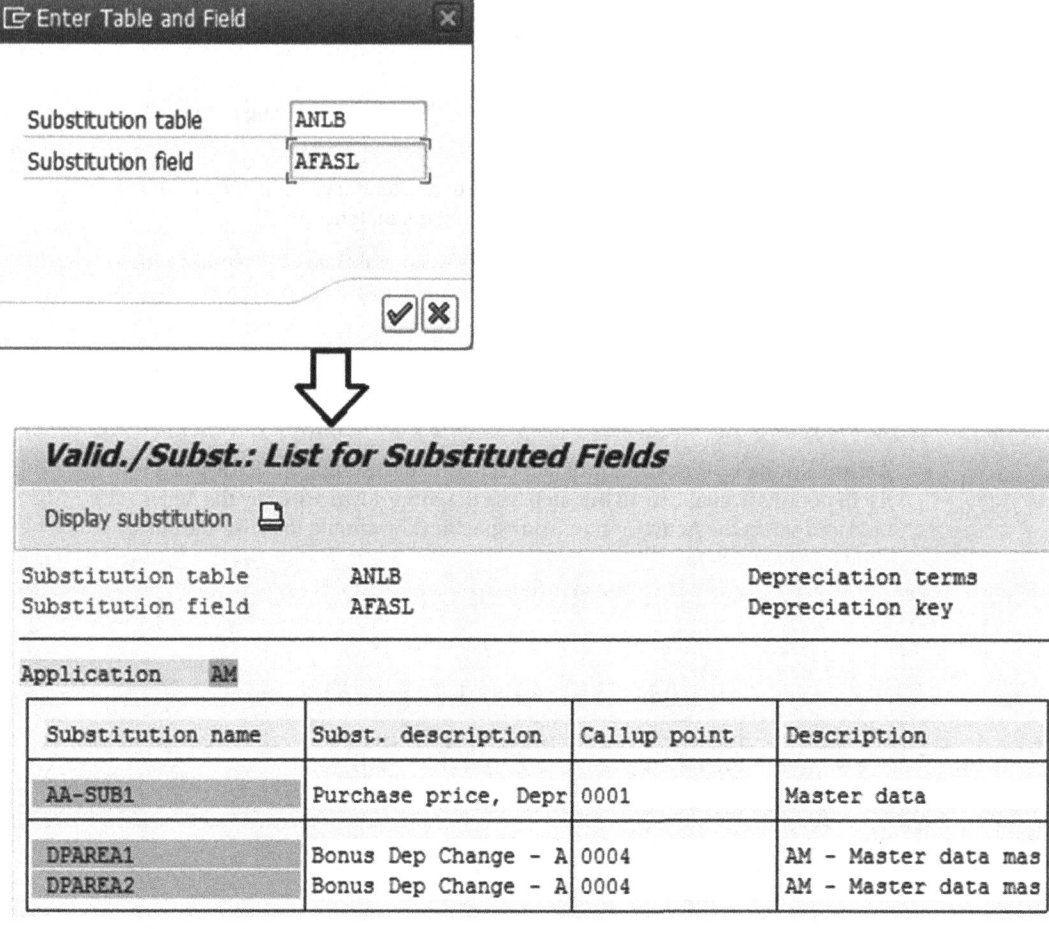

Figure 8-16. *Displaying the list of substituted fields*

Finally, you'll create an asset master record to see how the system will execute the substitution you created in this chapter.

Creating Asset Master Data

To create asset master data for a newly acquired asset, complete these steps:

1. Use transaction code: AS01 by entering it in the command field at the top-left side of the screen. The Create Asset: Initial screen appears.

2. Using the data in Table 8-1, update the fields.

Table 8-1. *The Data to Update the Create Asset Master Data Screen*

Field	Value	Descriptions
Asset Class	AS3000	This is the asset class you used for your substitution.
Company Code	7200	This is the company code you are using for your substitution.
Number of Similar Assets	1	This is defaulted by the system.

3. Click the ⌞Master data⌟ button at the top-right side of the screen. The Create Asset: Master data screen appears.

4. Enter a short description of the acquired asset (Machine Z) in the Description field.

5. Click the Time-dependent tab at the top of the screen to proceed to the time-dependent page of the screen.

6. Enter your cost center (1100) in the Cost Center field.

7. The next step is to assign a business partner (vendor) to the asset. To proceed to the area of the screen where you will perform this assignment, click the Origin tab to move to the origin area of the screen. Enter the vendor's account (100544) in the Vendor field.

8. It is purported that the asset was acquired from an external vendor. It is also assumed that the asset is a newly acquired asset. So activate the Asset purch. New check box and enter the acquisition year (2015) in the Orig.Acqis.Year field.

9. Finally, click the Deprec. Areas tab to move to the depreciation area of the screen. The depreciation key (LINS) and the asset useful life (10) are defaulted by the system for each depreciation area from your previous settings. Otherwise, you can enter them yourself. Enter the ordinary depreciation start date (01.01.2015) in the ODep Start field. This may be defaulted by the system. Otherwise, enter them yourself. This is the date you want the system to start calculating depreciation for your asset.

10. Click the Enter ✓ button and 💾 save your master data.

Posting Asset Transactions

Using your discretion, post some transactions with values over 150000 for external acquisition with vendor using the asset number 3003 (Machine Z), which you created in the asset master data in asset class (AS3000) you used for your substitution.

▦ **Note**   Fixed asset posting was covered in Chapter 7. You can use it as a reference if you are not sure how to post assets.

Summary

This chapter explained what validation is and covered the various Boolean statements that can be used in validation. For example, prerequisite statements, check statements, etc. You learned how to define validation for asset master data. As part of validation configuration, you looked how to test the validation defined using validation simulation. Finally, you learned how to activate validation.

Secondly, you looked at what substitution is. In the process, you looked at the procedure involved in defining substitution. You then went on to look at statements involved in substitution, such as the prerequisite statement and substitution value(s). You then learned how to define substitution for asset master data using Boolean logic/statements and operators like AND and OR. To simplify the complications involved in customizing substitution, you saw a flowchart diagram that illustrated how substitution is performed. After defining substitution, you performed a substitution simulation to validate if values are true or false. You finally looked at how to activate substitution and display substituted fields.

The next chapter looks at information systems by looking at the customizing steps involved in defining history sheet versions and history sheet groups. You will be looking at other aspects of information systems, like individual assets using asset explorer, and asset balances by performing depreciation comparison and manual depreciation. Finally, you will look at the day-to-day activity reports for asset transaction, asset acquisitions, and asset retirements.

■ ■ ■

CHAPTER 9

Reporting with Asset Accounting

This chapter looked at how to customize information systems and generate day-to-day activities reports. In this chapter, you learn:

- What an information system is
- How to define asset history sheet
- How to use asset explorer
- How to display asset balances reports
- How to create depreciation reports in explanations for profit and loss account statement
- How to generate day-to-day activities report

Information Systems in Asset Accounting

In order for management at varied levels to be able to make decisions concerning the utilization of assets, they need to be equipped with some important information in the form of a report. An information system provides these needs—such as asset monitoring, controlling, and planning—to meet specific requirements. Therefore, an information system is a flexible tool for collecting, analyzing, and evaluating data in FI-AA. In SAP, the information system component contains a variety of standard reports that are modifiable to meet your reporting needs.

The entire fixed asset portfolio in an organization can be massive. Therefore, when report generation can impair the performance of the system, it is recommended that reports be generated using background processing. This can be carried out in the selection screen of the report program.

As part of customizing the information system, you will define:

- Sort versions for asset reports
- Asset history sheets for asset history sheet versions and asset history sheet groups

Sort Versions for Asset Reports

Sort versions are used to determining sorting keys and totaling data records for asset reports. SAP comes with standard sort versions that you can use when you run the report. We recommend that you stick to the standard sort versions supplied by SAP, instead of creating your own sort version. However, to define information systems in asset accounting, you can use this menu path: Financial Accounting (New) ➤ Asset Accounting ➤ Information System ➤ Define Sort Versions for Asset Reports.

The Asset History Sheet

Asset history sheet has a vital role as a substitute to the balance sheet from the asset accounting viewpoint. Changes in the asset portfolio can be displayed in a history sheet in a given fiscal year. You can define any number of history versions in FI-AA. In the asset history sheet configuration, you define the following:

- Asset history sheet versions

- History sheet groups

SAP comes with standard asset history sheet versions you can use as is or adapt to meet your requirements.

Defining Asset History Sheet Versions

The asset history sheet version defines the format and content of the report. In this step, you define the individual asset history sheet versions for your asset history sheet reporting. The asset history sheet is made up of up to 99 columns, and from column 00 to column 99, you can enter values for your report. Asset history sheet versions are used in report RAGITT01 (the technical name for ABAP report for asset history sheet). The report GAGITT01 is for defining asset history sheets according to country-specific requirements and other reports relating to asset transactions.

SAP comes with standard history sheet versions such as total depreciation, acquisition values, asset history sheet in compliance with EC directive 4, transferred reserves, asset history sheet for Denmark, etc.

The asset history sheet versions supplied by SAP are typically sufficient for this requirement and we advise that you stick with them, as they are industry-specific.

To define asset history sheet versions, you can use the following procedure:

1. Use this menu path: Financial Accounting (New) ➤ Asset Accounting ➤ Information System ➤ Asset History Sheet ➤ Define History Sheet Versions. The Choose Asset History Sheet Version screen appears. It contains the list of asset history sheet versions, as shown in Figure 9-1.

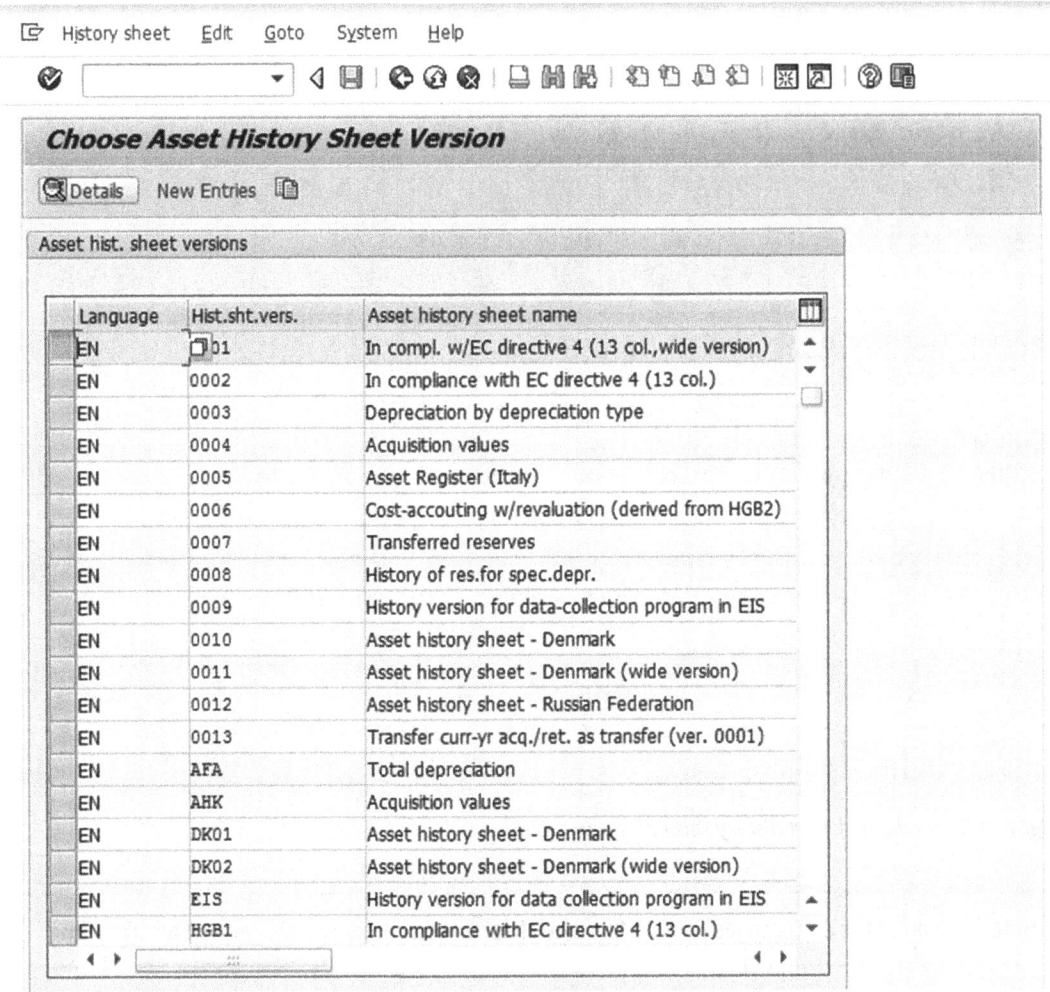

Figure 9-1. *The List of asset history sheet versions supplied by SAP*

2. To look at the settings for individual asset history sheet versions, select the asset history sheet version you want and click the [Details] button at the top-left side of the screen. The Information screen pops up with the information "Do not change objects in the SAP name range".

3. Click the Continue ✔ button at the bottom-right side of the screen. The Maintain Asset History Sheet Version: EN 0001 screen appears. It displays the predefined settings by SAP, as shown in Figure 9-2.

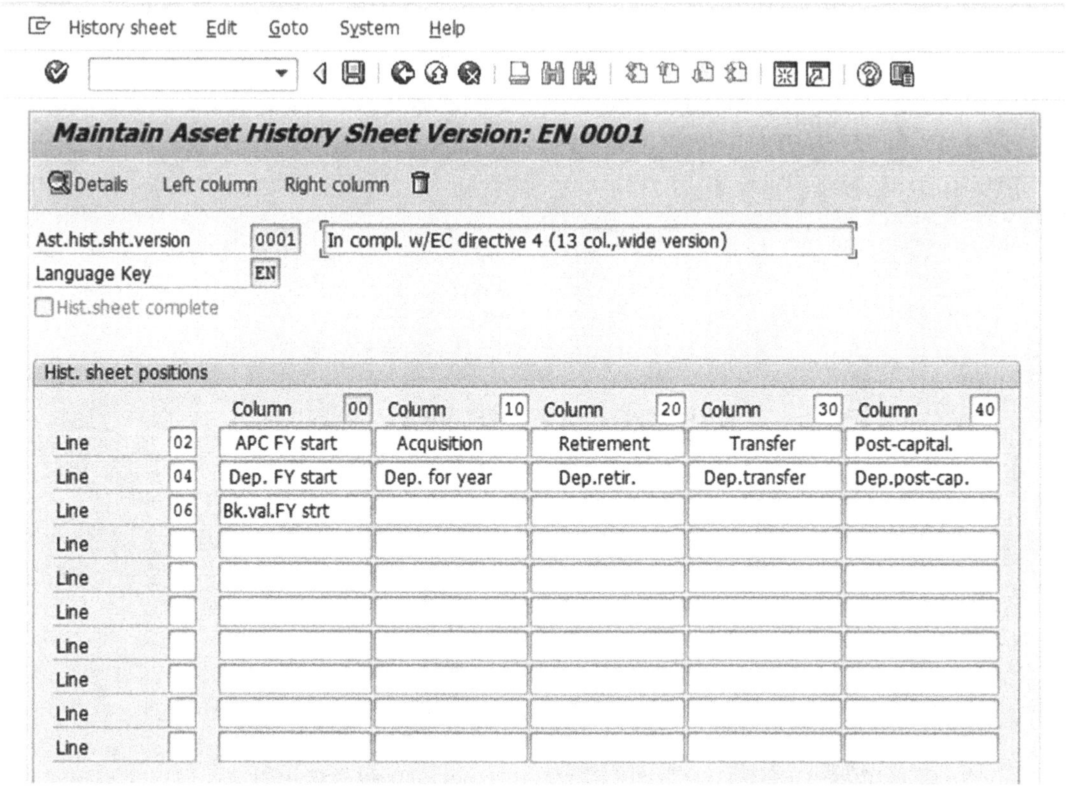

| History sheet | Edit | Goto | System | Help |

Maintain Asset History Sheet Version: EN 0001

🔍 Details   Left column   Right column   🗑

| Ast.hist.sht.version | 0001 | In compl. w/EC directive 4 (13 col.,wide version) |
| Language Key | EN | |

☐ Hist.sheet complete

Hist. sheet positions

		Column	00	Column	10	Column	20	Column	30	Column	40
Line	02	APC FY start		Acquisition		Retirement		Transfer		Post-capital.	
Line	04	Dep. FY start		Dep. for year		Dep.retir.		Dep.transfer		Dep.post-cap.	
Line	06	Bk.val.FY strt									
Line											
Line											
Line											
Line											
Line											
Line											
Line											
Line											

Figure 9-2. Predefined asset history sheet version settings

▪ **Note**   Do not make any changes here, as this may affect the asset history sheet version functionality.

Defining History Sheet Groups

The classification of transaction types for the definition of history sheet groups are carried out by assigning them to a history sheet group. SAP delivers the standard transaction type groups relevant for the asset history sheet. It is therefore, recommended that you use the standard history sheet groups supplied by SAP instead of creating your own. You can define a history sheet group using this menu path: Financial Accounting (New) ➤ Asset Accounting ➤ Information System ➤ Asset History Sheet ➤ Define History Sheet Groups. The Change View "Asset History Sheet Group and Name" Overview screen appears. It lists the list of defined asset history sheet group numbers and names predefined by SAP, as shown in Figure 9-3.

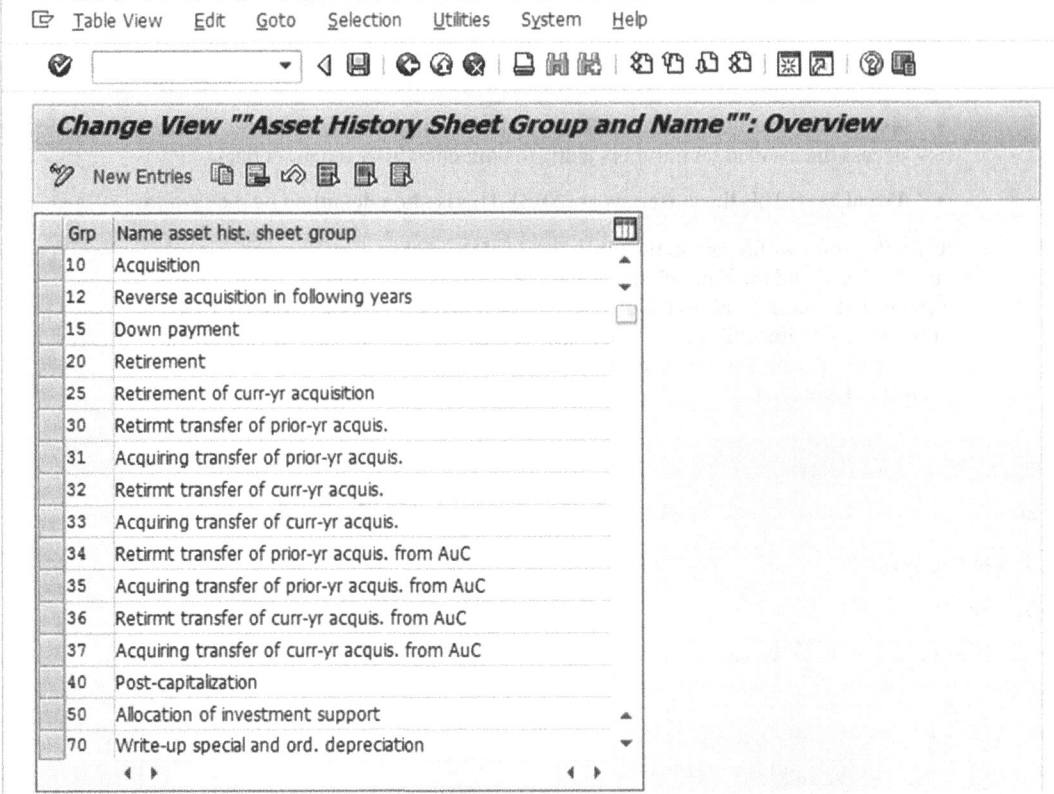

Figure 9-3. The list of defined asset history sheet group numbers and names predefined by SAP

Creating Reports in Asset Accounting

In this activity, you will be looking at how to execute reports for individual assets, asset balances, and day-to-day activities.

Using Asset Explorer

In individual assets you can use the Asset Explorer for each asset in the system. Asset Explorer shows an overview of an asset transactions and comparison values for a number of years, which include APC transactions, acquisition value, and planned ordinary depreciation for each depreciation area represented in your company code.

You can access the Asset Explorer screen and its information using the following steps:

1. Use this menu path: Accounting ➤ Financial Accounting ➤ Fixed Assets ➤ Information System ➤ Reports on Asset Accounting ➤ Individual Assets ➤ Asset Explorer. The Asset Explorer screen appears.

2.   Enter the display criteria in the following fields in the header section of the screen:

   • **Company Code:** Enter your company code (7200) in the Company Code field.

   • **Asset:** Enter the asset number (3002) you are using for Asset Explorer. You can access the list of asset numbers using the matchcode by the Asset field.

   • **Fiscal Year**: This the current year (2015). This is often defaulted by the system.

3.   Click the Enter ✅ button on the top-left side of the screen. The Planned values are displayed and the depreciation areas list is displayed on the left pane of the screen. The Planned values tab displays the planned value book depreciation for the selected depreciation area. The planned values screen also displays values relating to APC transaction, acquisition value, and ordinary depreciation, as shown in Figure 9-4.

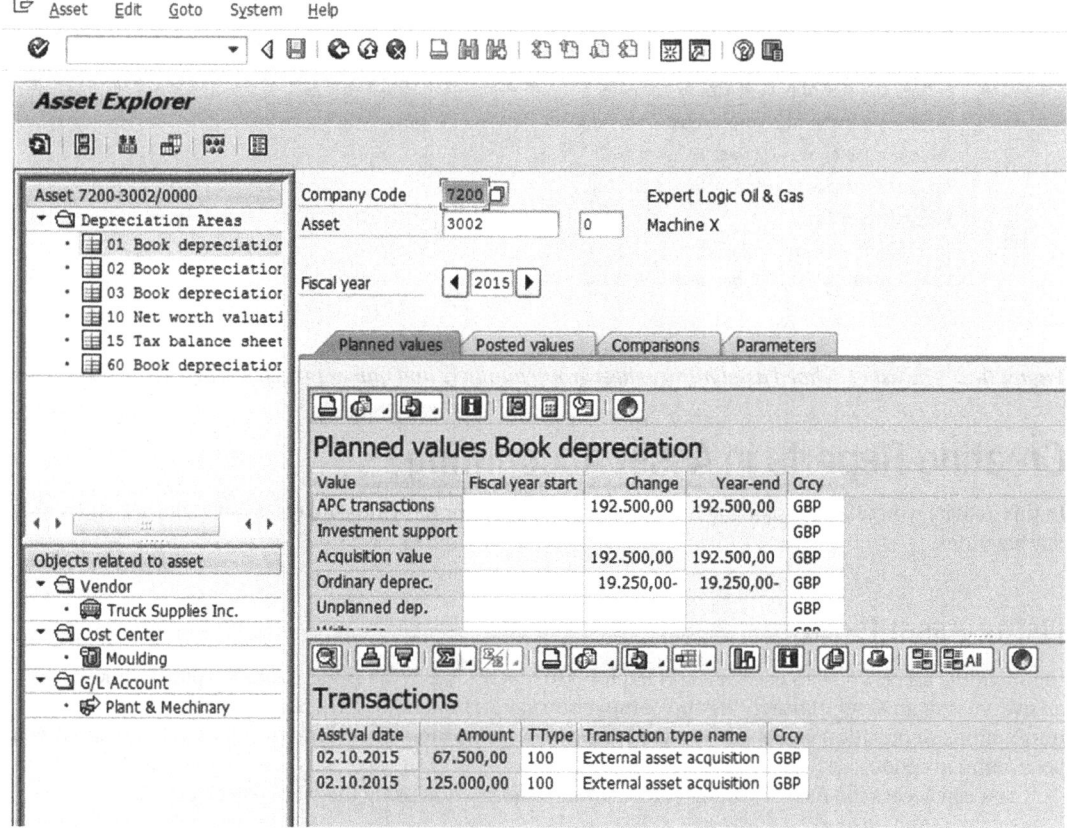

Figure 9-4. *The Asset Explorer screen displaying the activities related to an asset, such as APC value, acquisition value, and ordinary depreciation*

4. To proceed to the next page, click on the Posted Values tab. This screen displays the acquisition values of the asset and the depreciation values posted in depreciation run.

5. The next step in this activity is to click the Comparisons tab. This will take you to the comparison page of the screen. This screen shows the APC transactions, acquisition value, ordinary depreciation, and the net book value for multiple years.

6. Finally you can click on the Parameters tab to go to the parameter page. This screen displays the settings for the parameters used in the calculation of depreciation. This includes the depreciation key, the asset life, etc.

Displaying Asset Balance Reports

You can display asset balance reports by

- Asset number
- Asset class
- Business area
- Cost center

Displaying Asset Balances by Asset Number

To display asset balances report by asset number and then run a report, follow these steps:

1. Use this menu path: Accounting ➤ Financial Accounting ➤ Fixed Assets ➤ Information System ➤ Report on Asset Accounting ➤ Asset Balances ➤ Balance Lists ➤ Asset Balances ➤ by Asset Number. The Asset Balances screen appears.

2. Enter the company code (7200) you are using for your asset balances asset in the Company Code field and the asset number (3002) in the Asset Number field. The other settings are defaulted by the system.

3. You have three radio button options you can choose from on the asset balances screen in terms of how you want your report to be displayed:

- List assets
- Main number only
- Group totals only

4. Click the Execute ⊕ button on the top-left side of the screen to generate your report. The Asset Balances – 01 Book Deprec. screen displays your asset balances report for the specified depreciation area by asset number, as shown in Figure 9-5.

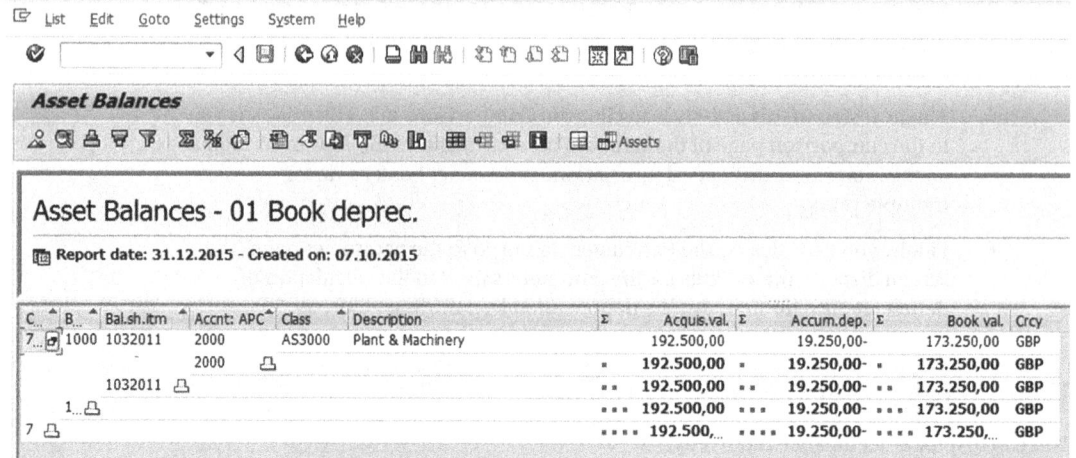

Figure 9-5. *Asset balances report by asset number*

Displaying Asset Balances by Asset Class

The Asset Class function will allow you to display asset balances report by asset class. To execute the report for asset balances by asset class, do the following:

1. Use this menu path: Accounting ➤ Financial Accounting ➤ Fixed Assets ➤ Information System ➤ Report on Asset Accounting ➤ Asset Balances ➤ Balance Lists ➤ Asset Balances ➤ by Asset Class. The Asset Balances screen appears.

2. Update the screen using the data shown in Table 9-1.

Table 9-1. *The Data to Update the Asset Class Asset Balances Screen*

Field	Value	Description
Company Code	7200	This is the company code you are generating your report from.
Asset Class	3000 -8000	Enter the asset class range that you want to include in your report. You can display a list of the asset classes in the system using the matchcode by the Asset Class field.
Report Date	31.01.2015	This is defaulted by the system as the last day of the current fiscal year.
Depreciation Area	01	Enter the depreciation area you want to generate your report from in this field. For example, 01-Book Depreciation.
Sort variant	0001	Sort variant is defaulted by the system, but you can choose a sort variant from the list of variants, by using the matchcode function.
List assets	Select	This will give you detailed display. You also can select Group Totals to display only total figures.
Use ALV grid	Select	ALV grid is a display option. This is also defaulted by the system.

3. Click the Execute ⊕ button on the top-left side of the screen to generate your
    report. The Asset Balances – 01 Book Deprec. screen displays your asset balances
    report for the specified depreciation area by asset class, as shown in Figure 9-6.

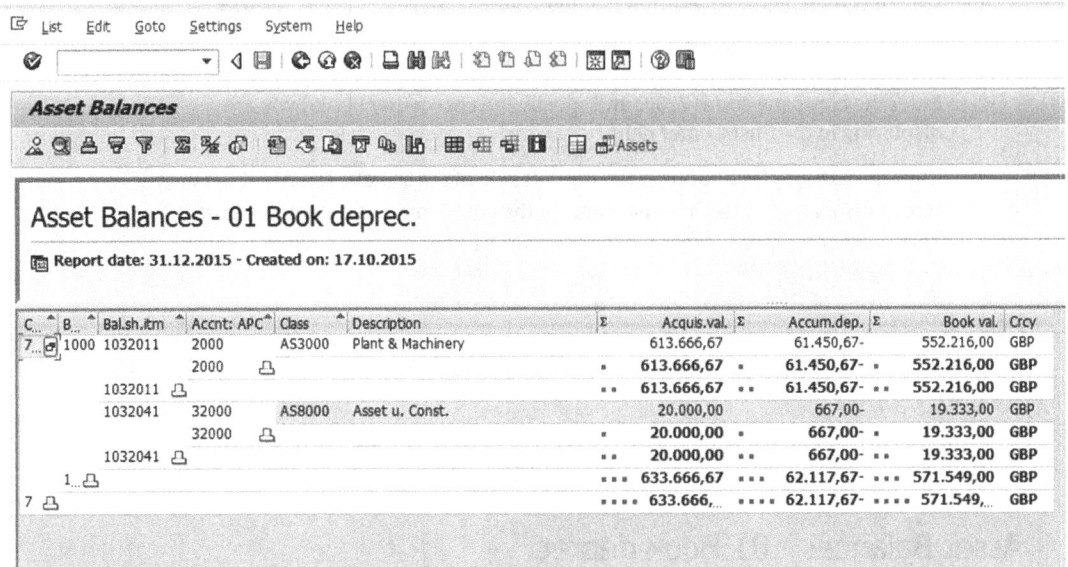

Figure 9-6. *Asset balances report by asset class*

Displaying Asset Balances by Business Area

This step will allow you to display asset balances reports by business area. Perform the following steps to
generate the report for asset balances using the business area:

1. Use this menu path: Accounting ➤ Financial Accounting ➤ Fixed Assets ➤
    Information System ➤ Report on Asset Accounting ➤ Asset Balances ➤ Balance
    Lists ➤ Asset Balances ➤ by Business Area. The Asset Balances screen appears.

2. Enter the company code (7200) in the Company Code field and specify the
    business area (1000) you are using for your report in the Business Area field.
    You can access a list of the asset classes using the matchcode by the Business
    Area field.

3. Click the Execute ⊕ button on the top-left side of the screen to generate your
    report. The Asset Balances – 01 Book Deprec. screen appears displaying your
    asset balances report for the specified depreciation area by business area.

Displaying Asset Balances by Cost Center Report

You can also display the report for asset balances by using the cost center. Perform the following steps to display cost center reports in asset accounting:

1. Use this menu path: Accounting ➤ Financial Accounting ➤ Fixed Assets ➤ Information System ➤ Report on Asset Accounting ➤ Asset Balances ➤ Balance Lists ➤ Asset Balances ➤ by Cost Center. The Asset Balances screen is displayed.

2. Enter the company code (7200) and specify the cost center (1100) you are displaying in the Cost Center field.

3. Click the Execute ⊕ button on the top-left side of the screen. The Asset Balances screen displays the asset's transactions in the cost center, as shown in Figure 9-7.

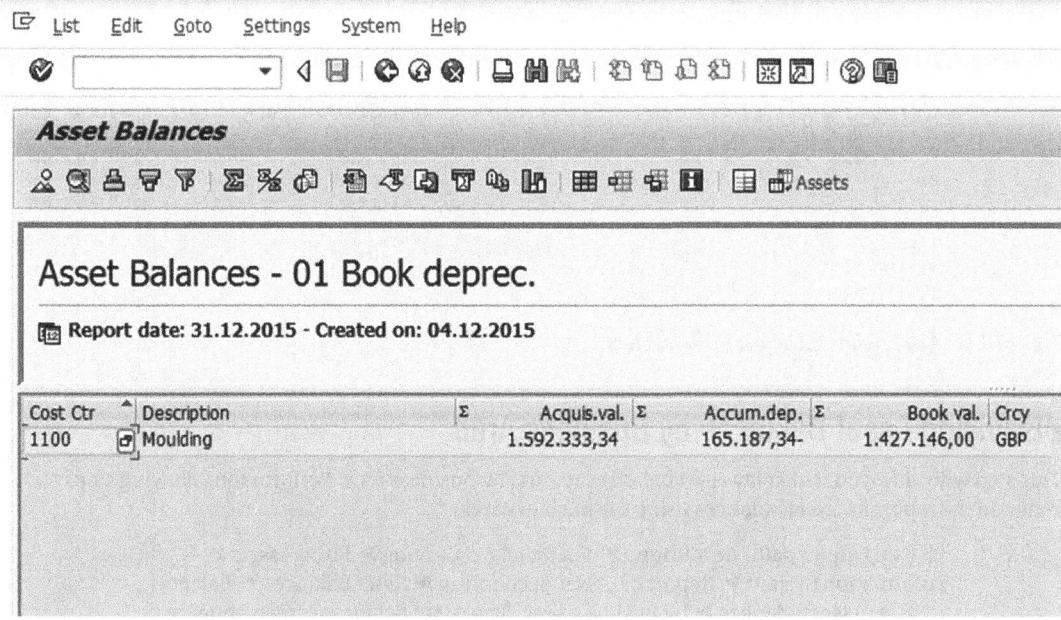

Figure 9-7. Displaying asset balances reports by cost center

Creating an Asset History Report

The asset history sheet has an important reporting function in SAP. From an asset accounting point of view, asset history is often seen as an important addenda to the balance sheet in the sense that it shows changes in the asset portfolio arising from transactions during the fiscal year. SAP provides standard asset history sheets in the system that you can use for your report. You can display asset history sheets using subnumber, asset class, or business area. Asset history sheets can be called up as list assets, main number only, or group totals only.

Follow these steps to create an asset history report:asset history

1. To call up the screen for creating an asset history report, you can use this menu path: Accounting ➤ Financial Accounting ➤ Fixed Assets ➤ Information System ➤ Report on Asset Accounting ➤ Notes to Financial Statements ➤ International ➤ Asset History Sheet. The Asset History Sheet screen appears, as shown in Figure 9-8.

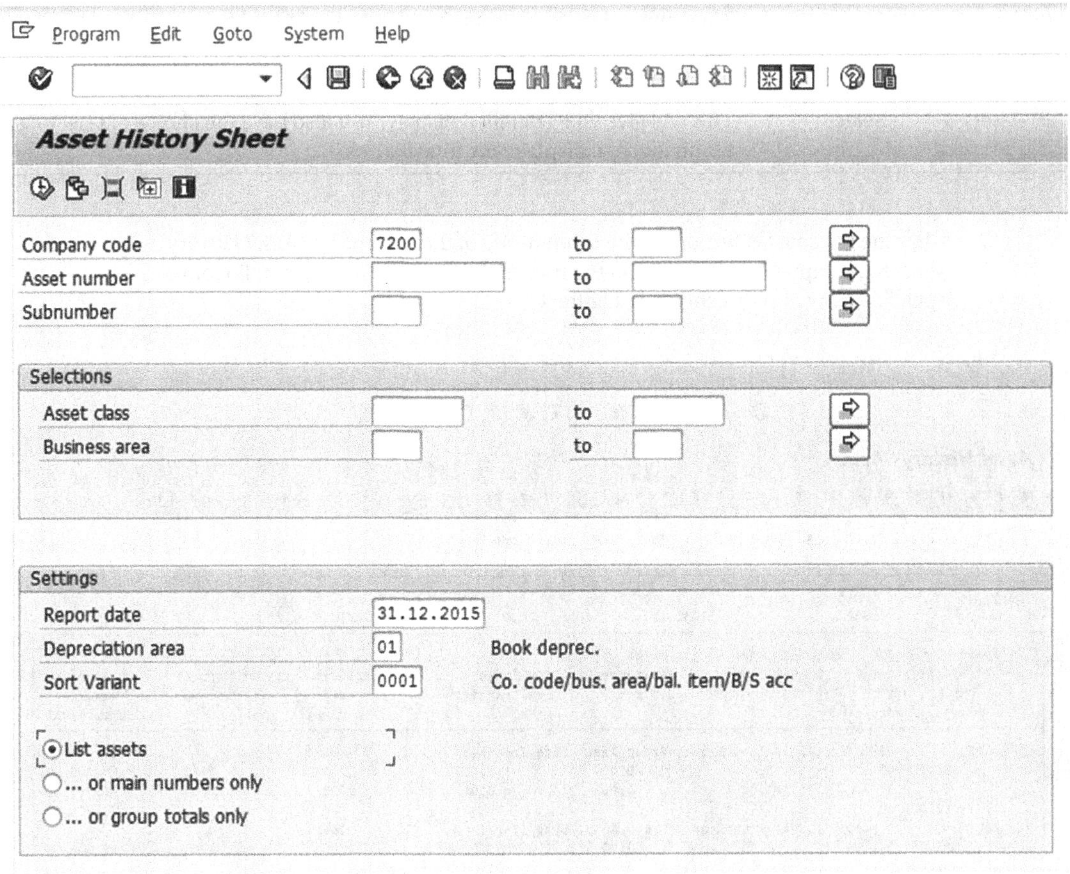

Figure 9-8. *The initial screen for asset history sheet specification*

2. Update the fields using the data in Table 9-2.

Table 9-2. *The Data to Update Asset History Sheet Screen*

Field	Value	Description
Company Code	7200	Enter the company code you want to generate your report from.
Report Date	31.12.2015	This is defaulted by the system as the last day of the current fiscal year.
Sort Variant	001	The appropriate sort variant is defaulted by the system, but you can choose a sort variant from the list of variants using the matchcode function.
List Assets	Select	This will give you a detailed display. You also have the choice of selecting group totals to display only total figures.

3. Click the Execute ⊕ button on the top-left side of the screen. The Asset History sheet report appears displaying all the transactions in your asset portfolio for the specified asset class, as shown in Figure 9-9.

Figure 9-9. *The Asset History sheet report displaying all the transactions in your asset portfolio for the specified asset class*

Creating Depreciation Reports in Explanations for Profit and Loss Statement

Explanations for profit and loss statements contain a list of individual depreciation types that can be used to create reports that serve as supplements to the profit and loss statements. The depreciation types you can use in this activity include total depreciation, ordinary depreciation, special depreciation, unplanned depreciation, and transfer reserves. In this step, we are going to cover the two common report types—total depreciation reports and ordinary depreciation reports.

Total Depreciation Reports

Total depreciation reports display the asset APC, the accumulated depreciation/planned depreciation, and the net book value of the asset in the specified fiscal year.

To execute a total depreciation report, you can use this menu path: Accounting ➤ Financial Accounting ➤ Fixed Assets ➤ Information System ➤ Report on Asset Accounting ➤ Explanation for P&L ➤ International ➤ Depreciation ➤ Total Depreciation. The Depreciation screen is displayed. Enter the company code (7200) you are using for the total depreciation report in the Company Code field and the corresponding asset class (AS3000) in the Asset Class field. Click the Execute ⊕ button on the top-left side of the screen. The Depreciation report screen displays the asset value, the accumulated depreciation, and the net book value of the asset(s) in question, as shown in Figure 9-10.

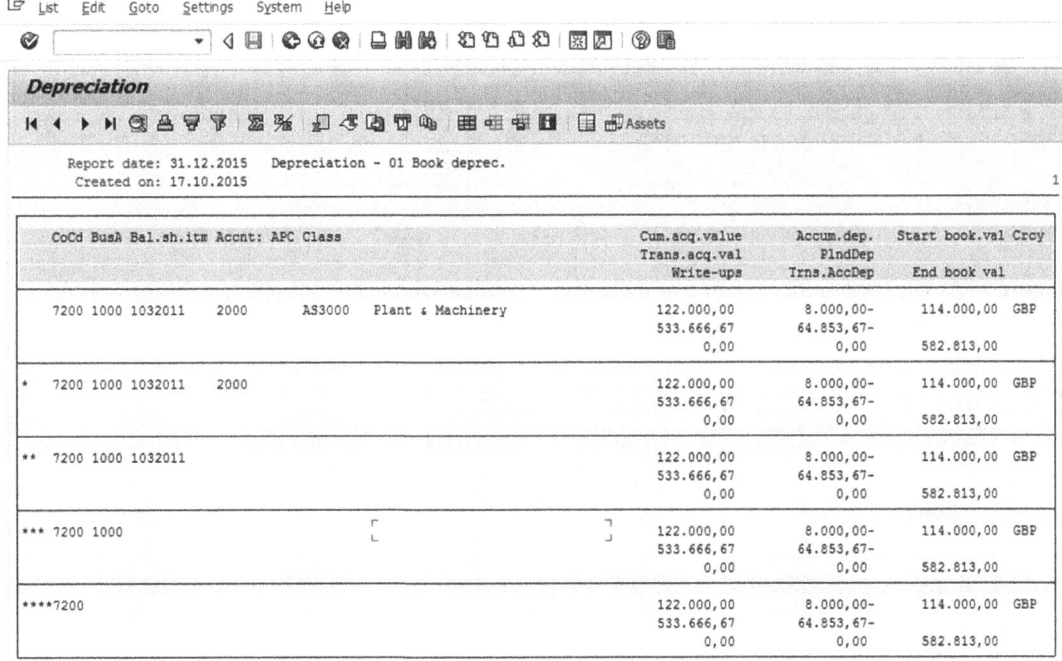

Figure 9-10. *The Depreciation report screen containing the asset value, the accumulated depreciation, and the net book value of the asset*

Ordinary Depreciation Reports

This function will allow you to generate the report for ordinary depreciation for the specified fiscal years.

To execute an ordinary depreciation report, you can use this menu path: Accounting ➤ Financial Accounting ➤ Fixed Assets ➤ Information System ➤ Report on Asset Accounting ➤ Explanation for P&L ➤ International ➤ Depreciation ➤ Ordinary Depreciation. The Depreciation screen is displayed. Enter the company code (7200) you are using for the total depreciation report in the Company Code field and click the Execute button on the top-left side of the screen. The Depreciation report screen appears displaying the depreciation for each asset for the current and previous fiscal years, as shown in Figure 9-11.

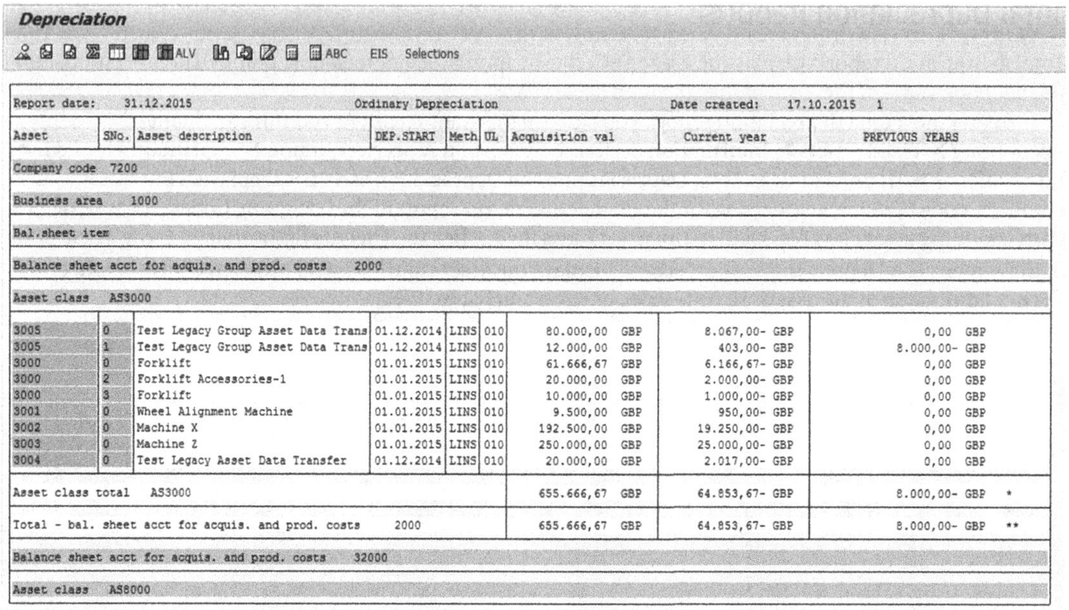

Depreciation

ALV ABC EIS Selections

Report date: 31.12.2015 Ordinary Depreciation Date created: 17.10.2015 1

Asset	SNo.	Asset description	DEP.START	Meth	UL	Acquisition val	Current year	PREVIOUS YEARS
Company code 7200								
Business area 1000								
Bal.sheet item								
Balance sheet acct for acquis. and prod. costs 2000								
Asset class AS3000								
3005	0	Test Legacy Group Asset Data Trans	01.12.2014	LINS	010	80.000,00 GBP	8.067,00- GBP	0,00 GBP
3005	1	Test Legacy Group Asset Data Trans	01.12.2014	LINS	010	12.000,00 GBP	403,00- GBP	8.000,00- GBP
3000	0	Forklift	01.01.2015	LINS	010	61.666,67 GBP	6.166,67- GBP	0,00 GBP
3000	2	Forklift Accessories-1	01.01.2015	LINS	010	20.000,00 GBP	2.000,00- GBP	0,00 GBP
3000	3	Forklift	01.01.2015	LINS	010	10.000,00 GBP	1.000,00- GBP	0,00 GBP
3001	0	Wheel Alignment Machine	01.01.2015	LINS	010	9.500,00 GBP	950,00- GBP	0,00 GBP
3002	0	Machine X	01.01.2015	LINS	010	192.500,00 GBP	19.250,00- GBP	0,00 GBP
3003	0	Machine Z	01.01.2015	LINS	010	250.000,00 GBP	25.000,00- GBP	0,00 GBP
3004	0	Test Legacy Asset Data Transfer	01.12.2014	LINS	010	20.000,00 GBP	2.017,00- GBP	0,00 GBP
Asset class total AS3000						655.666,67 GBP	64.853,67- GBP	8.000,00- GBP *
Total - bal. sheet acct for acquis. and prod. costs 2000						655.666,67 GBP	64.853,67- GBP	8.000,00- GBP **
Balance sheet acct for acquis. and prod. costs 32000								
Asset class AS8000								

Figure 9-11. *The Depreciation report screen displaying the depreciation for each asset for the current and previous fiscal years*

Creating Day-to-Day Activities Reports

A day-to-day activities report consists of the daily transactions relating to assets in asset accounting. You can display daily operations of asset accounting for individual assets or a group of assets using the following report functions:

- Asset transactions
- Asset acquisitions
- Asset retirements

Asset Transactions Reports

To execute the report for asset transactions, you can use this menu path: Accounting ➤ Financial Accounting ➤ Fixed Assets ➤ Information System ➤ Report on Asset Accounting ➤ Day-to-Day Activities ➤ International ➤ Asset Transactions. The Asset Transactions screen appears. Enter the company code (7200) in the Company Code field and the asset class (3002) you are using in your report in the Asset Class field. Then click the Execute ⊕ button on the top-left side of the screen. The Asset Transaction screen appears, displaying the report containing your company code, asset class, and asset balance, as shown in Figure 9-12.

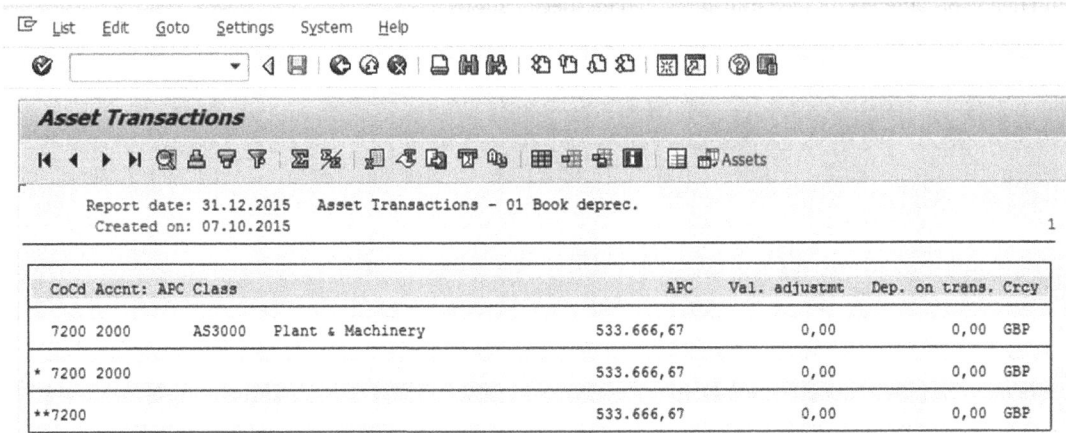

Figure 9-12. *The Asset Transactions report screen displaying your company code, asset class, and asset transaction balance*

Asset Acquisitions Reports

To execute the report for acquired assets, use this menu path: Accounting ➤ Financial Accounting ➤ Fixed Assets ➤ Information System ➤ Report on Asset Accounting ➤ Day-to-Day Activities ➤ International ➤ Asset Acquisitions. The Asset Acquisitions screen appears. Enter your company code (7200) in the Company Code field and the asset class in the Asset Class field. Then click the Execute ⊕ button on the top-left side of the screen. The Asset Acquisitions screen appears, displaying your company code, asset class, and the total value of asset acquisitions.

Asset Retirement Reports

To display the report for the retired assets, you can use this menu path: Accounting ➤ Financial Accounting ➤ Fixed Assets ➤ Information System ➤ Report on Asset Accounting ➤ Day-to-Day Activities ➤ International ➤ Asset Retirements. The Asset Retirements screen appears. Enter your company code (7200) in the Company Code field and the asset class in the Asset Class field. Click the Execute ⊕ button on the top-left side of the screen. The Asset Retirements screen appears, displaying your company code, asset class, and the total value of retired assets.

Summary

This chapter looked at what information system means in asset accounting. You learned about the steps involved in customizing information systems, saw sort versions for asset reporting, and learned how to define asset history sheet versions.

Finally, you looked at how to use asset explorer in asset accounting and explored various ways of generating reports in asset accounting, such as asset balances and day-today activities reports.

In the next chapter, you will be looking at asset data transfers. As part of asset data transfer customization, you will look at how to set company code status, specify a sequence of depreciation areas, and define parameters for data transfer with date specifications.

CHAPTER 10

■ ■ ■

Transferring Asset Data

This chapter introduces you to the basic aspects of asset data transfer and explains how they are configured in SAP ERP. You will learn how to:

- Set company code status
- Specify sequence of depreciation areas
- Set parameters for data transfer

Customizing Legacy Data Transfer

When the configuration of Asset Accounting component and the classification of your assets are complete, the next step is to carry out legacy data transfer. Legacy data transfer is the transfer of the old asset data from the previous system to the SAP system. The asset master records and asset transactions are transferred from the fiscal year up to go-live. The transfer of assets transactions does not update the corresponding reconciliation accounts in Financial Accounting (balance sheet) automatically. A manual reconciliation is carried out later in another step in the balance sheet.

The following options are available in Asset Accounting for transferring legacy data to SAP system:

- Automatic data transfer
- Manual online transfer
- Legacy data transfer using Microsoft Excel

We will only be looking at manual data transfer in this chapter.
The following steps are required as part of the customizing of legacy data transfer:

- Setting company code status
- Specifying the sequence of depreciation areas
- Setting the parameters for data transfer

In this section, we cover each of these steps.

Set Company Code Status

In this customizing step, you will specify the status of asset data transfer in the company code for old asset data transfer from the previous system to Sap system. SAP provides four options of status you can choose from:

> 0 - Asset data transfer completed (the specification of this status is important after go-live. This allow posting only and no transfer will be carried out).

> 1 - Asset data transfer not yet completed (this is a transfer status; asset values can be changed during transfer, but posting is not possible).

> 2 - Test company code with data transfer always allowed (this status is a test mode; in this company code you carry out data transfer and carry out posting).

> 3 - Company code deactivated – later reporting allowed (this status when specified, you will not be able to perform transfer and posting in this company code; only reporting is possible)

In our example, we'll use 2:

1. To set company code status. You can use this menu path: Financial Accounting (New) ➤ Asset Accounting ➤ Asset Data Transfer ➤ Set Company Code. The Change View "FI-AA: Set status of the company code": Overview screen appears as shown in Figure 10-1.

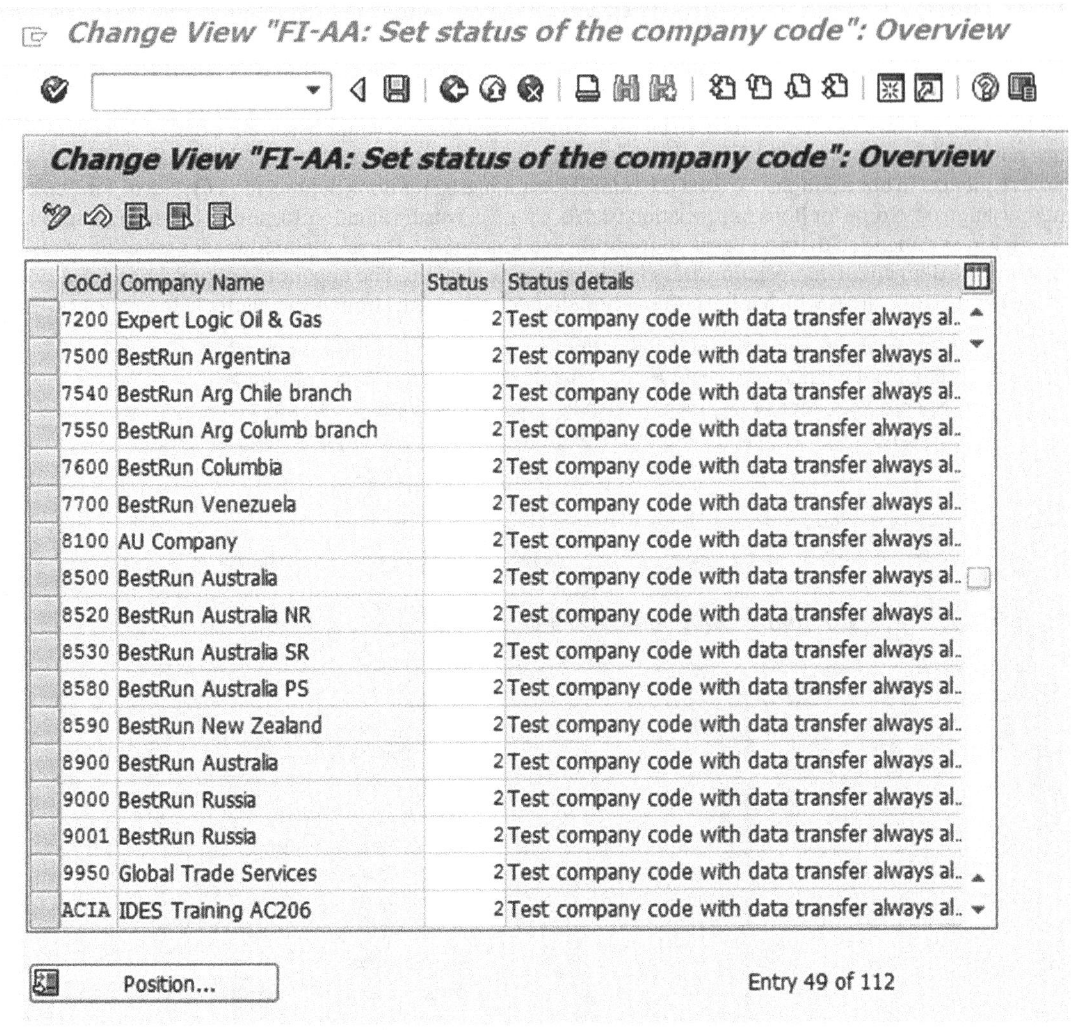

Change View "FI-AA: Set status of the company code": Overview

Change View "FI-AA: Set status of the company code": Overview

CoCd	Company Name	Status	Status details
7200	Expert Logic Oil & Gas	2	Test company code with data transfer always al..
7500	BestRun Argentina	2	Test company code with data transfer always al..
7540	BestRun Arg Chile branch	2	Test company code with data transfer always al..
7550	BestRun Arg Columb branch	2	Test company code with data transfer always al..
7600	BestRun Columbia	2	Test company code with data transfer always al..
7700	BestRun Venezuela	2	Test company code with data transfer always al..
8100	AU Company	2	Test company code with data transfer always al..
8500	BestRun Australia	2	Test company code with data transfer always al..
8520	BestRun Australia NR	2	Test company code with data transfer always al..
8530	BestRun Australia SR	2	Test company code with data transfer always al..
8580	BestRun Australia PS	2	Test company code with data transfer always al..
8590	BestRun New Zealand	2	Test company code with data transfer always al..
8900	BestRun Australia	2	Test company code with data transfer always al..
9000	BestRun Russia	2	Test company code with data transfer always al..
9001	BestRun Russia	2	Test company code with data transfer always al..
9950	Global Trade Services	2	Test company code with data transfer always al..
ACIA	IDES Training AC206	2	Test company code with data transfer always al..

Position...   Entry 49 of 112

Figure 10-1. The specification of asset data transfer status for the company code

2. Search for your company code (7200) using the [Position...] button at the bottom left of the screen and specify the status (2 – Test company code with data transfer always allowed) of asset data transfer for your company code. You can access the list of status of asset data transfer in the company code using the matchcode function.

3. Click the Enter ✔ button at the top left of the screen and save 💾 your settings.

Specifying the Sequence of Depreciation Areas

In this activity, you will define the number sequence for each depreciation area in your company code. This specification will determine how the asset data transfer transaction are presented in the system. There is no hard rule to how this is done. You can use any number sequence of your choice. For example, you can use number sequence 1, 2, 3, 4, and so on, or number sequence 2, 4, 6, 8, and so on, for your depreciation area sequence. In our example, we used the number sequence 02 for Book depreciation 01, No. 04 for Book depreciation 02, No. 06 for Book depreciation 03, No. 8 for Net worth valuation 10, and so on (see Figure 10-3).

It is recommended that you begin your number sequence with the nondependent depreciation areas first and the dependent depreciation areas last in your specification. The dependent depreciation areas are those depreciation areas which inherit values and depreciation terms from other depreciation areas:

1. To specify the sequence of depreciation areas, you can use this menu path: Financial Accounting (New) ➤ Asset Accounting ➤ Asset Data Transfer ➤ Specify Sequence of Depreciation Areas. The Change View "Company code selection: Overview screen appears, displaying the list of company codes in the system, as shown in Figure 10-2.

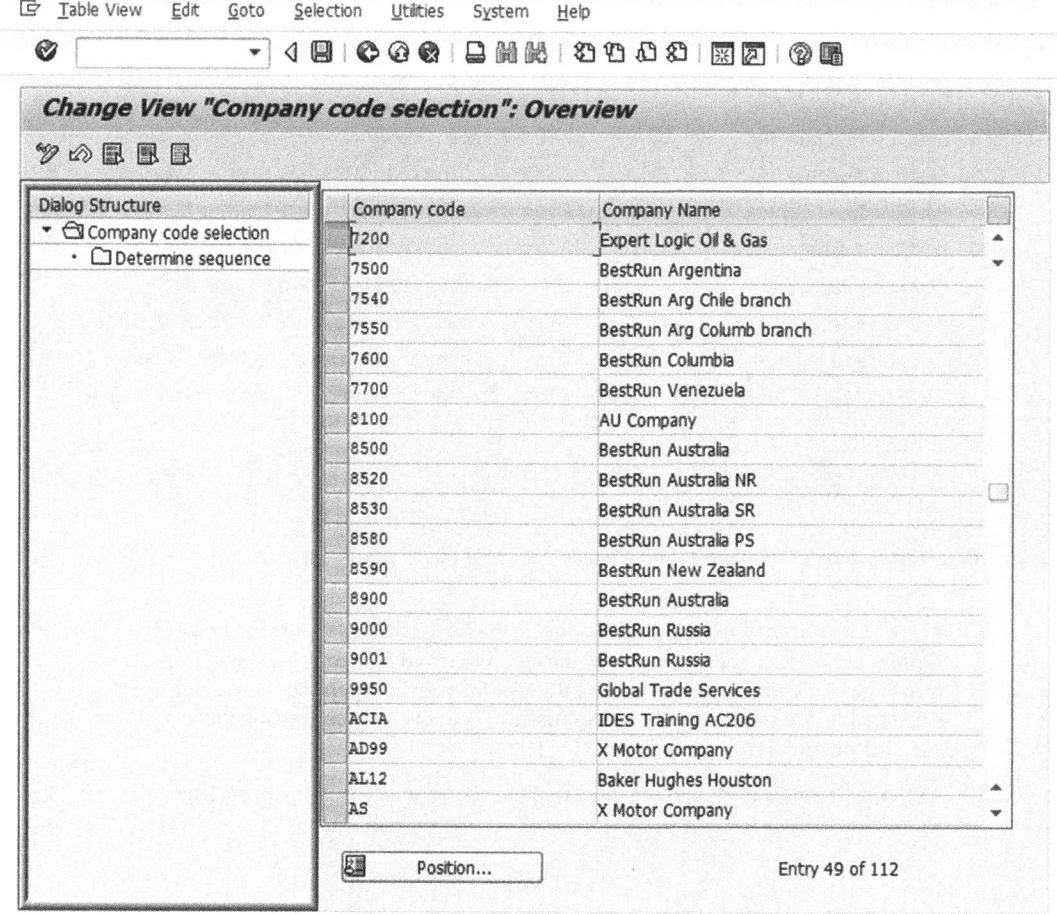

Figure 10-2. *The list of company codes in the system from which you can choose to determine the sequence by which the system presents the depreciation areas for asset data transfer*

2. Search for your company code using the ▩ [Position...] button at the bottom left of the screen. Your company code will be displayed at the top of the displayed company codes list.

3. Select your company code by clicking on it and double click the Determine sequence folder in the Company code selection folder on the left pane of the screen. The Change View "Determine sequence": Overview screen appears. This is the initial screen where you define sequence presents the depreciation areas for asset data transfer.

4. Click the [New Entries] button at the top left of the screen. The New Entries: Overview of Added Entries screen appears. Update the screen using the data in Figure 10-3.

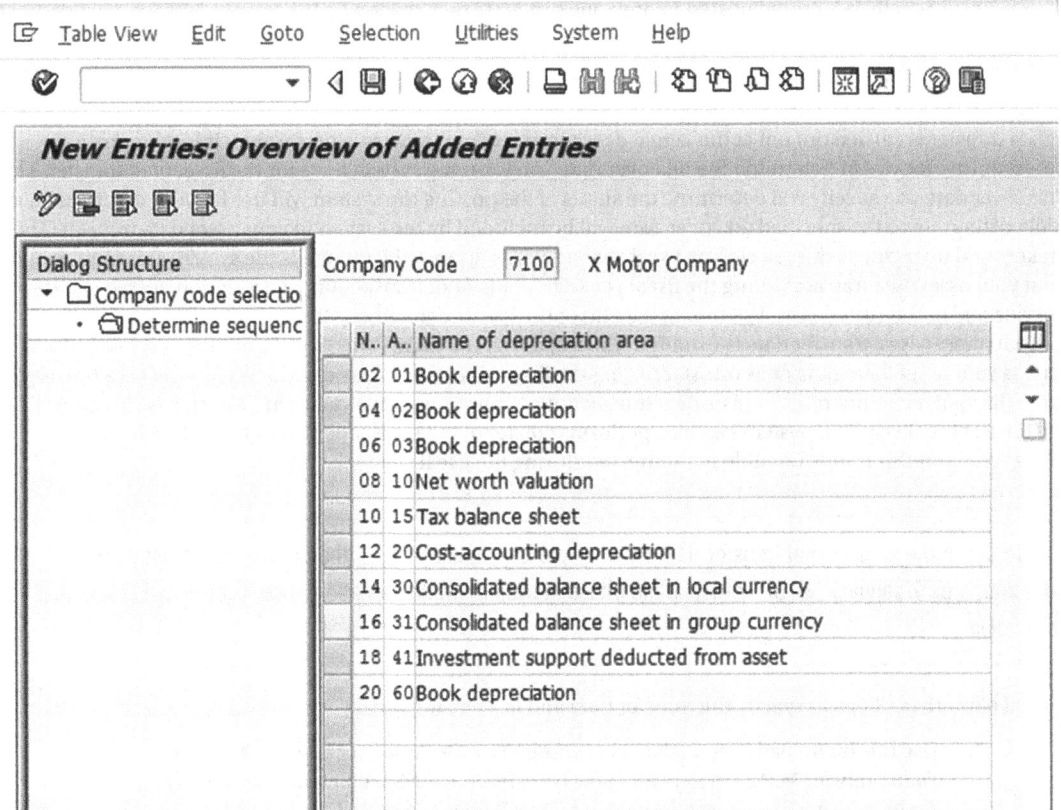

Figure 10-3. *The screen where you determine the sequence that the system presents for the depreciation areas for asset data transfer*

5. Click the Enter ✅ button at the top left of the screen to confirm if the system accepted your entries and save 🖫 your specification.

Setting the Parameters for Data Transfer

You will specify the parameters for data for the asset data transfer in this step. The transfer date is simply the cut-of date of legacy data. As part of the customizing of parameters for data transfer you perform data specifications which includes the transfer date/last closed fiscal year, last period posted in previous system (transfer during fiscal year) and other customizing options.

Date specification

Two date settings are specified in relation to time of the old data takeover from the previous system to the SAP system:

- Specify transfer date/last closed fiscal year
- Specify last period posted in previous system (Trans.during FY)

Specify Transfer Date/Last Closing Fiscal Year

Data transfer is carried out not at the actual date the asset data transfer is performed. It is therefore a prerequisite for you to determine the takeover date you want the system to us for the asset data transfer. The takeover date you specify will determine the status of the posting the system will use for your asset transfer. All postings up to the specified takeover date will be included by the system in your asset data transfer. The takeover date includes the last closing fiscal year as well. This specification tells the system you want to carry out your asset data transfer during the fiscal year. The transfer of transaction/depreciation posted can be performed in the current fiscal year or at the end of the fiscal year without transactions.

In most cases, transfer date is usually at the last day of the fiscal year. If this is not the case, the system treats your asset data transfer as transfer during the fiscal year. One of the drawbacks of asset data transfer is that the system cannot transfer historical transactions. Only cumulative values are transferred from the end of the last fiscal year. The system can also perform transfer of the transactions that took place in the current fiscal year, but this is only possible in for transfer during the fiscal year.

■ **Note**   If the actual asset transfer date for example is 1 January 2015, the go-live date must be one day later (i.e., 2 January 2015). Go-live is the phase in system implementation to cut over to live productive operation.

Follow these steps to specify the transfer date and last closing fiscal year:

1. Use this menu path: Financial Accounting (New) ➤ Asset Accounting ➤ Asset Data Transfer ➤ Parameters for Data Transfer ➤ Date Specifications ➤ Specify Transfer Date/Last Closed Fiscal Year. The Change View "FI-AA: Date of Legacy Data Transfer": Overview screen, containing the list of company codes in the system in Figure 10-4.

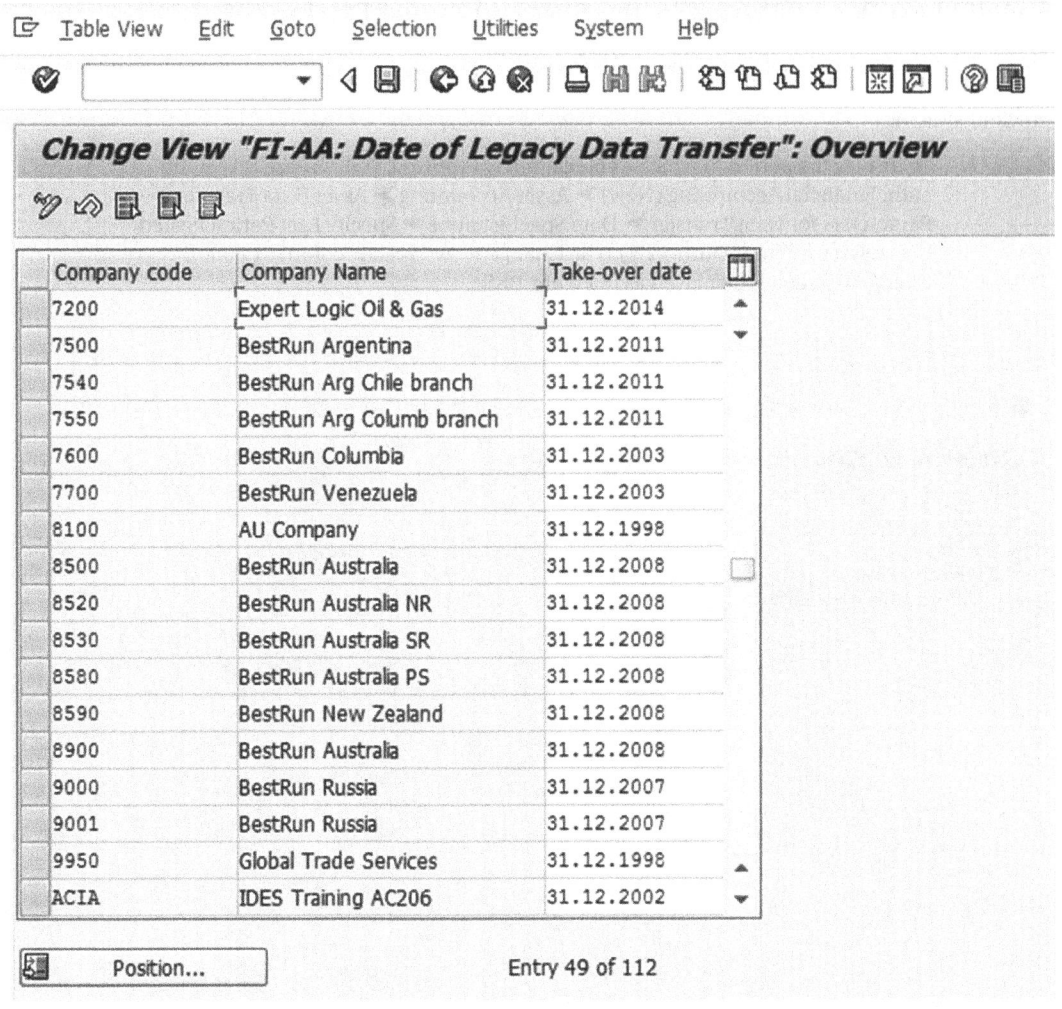

Figure 10-4. The screen where you specify the take-over date for asset data transfer

2. Enter the date for your asset transfer in the Take-over date field for your company code. You can use the data in Figure 10-4 as a reference for your specification.

3. Click the Enter ✅ button at the top left of the screen to confirm if the system accepted your entries and save 🖫 your specification.

Specify Last Period Posted in Prv.System (Transf.During FY)

This specification is rarely used in practice. It is only used when you want to carry out an old asset takeover during the fiscal year. In this step, you will specify the period in which depreciation was posted in the previous system.

1. To display the period in which depreciation was posted, you can use this menu path: Financial Accounting (New) ➤ Asset Accounting ➤ Asset Data Transfer ➤ Parameters for Data Transfer ➤ Date Specifications ➤ Specify Last Period Posted in Prv.System (Tranf.During FY). The Change View "Specify company code": Overview screen is displayed as in Figure 10-5.

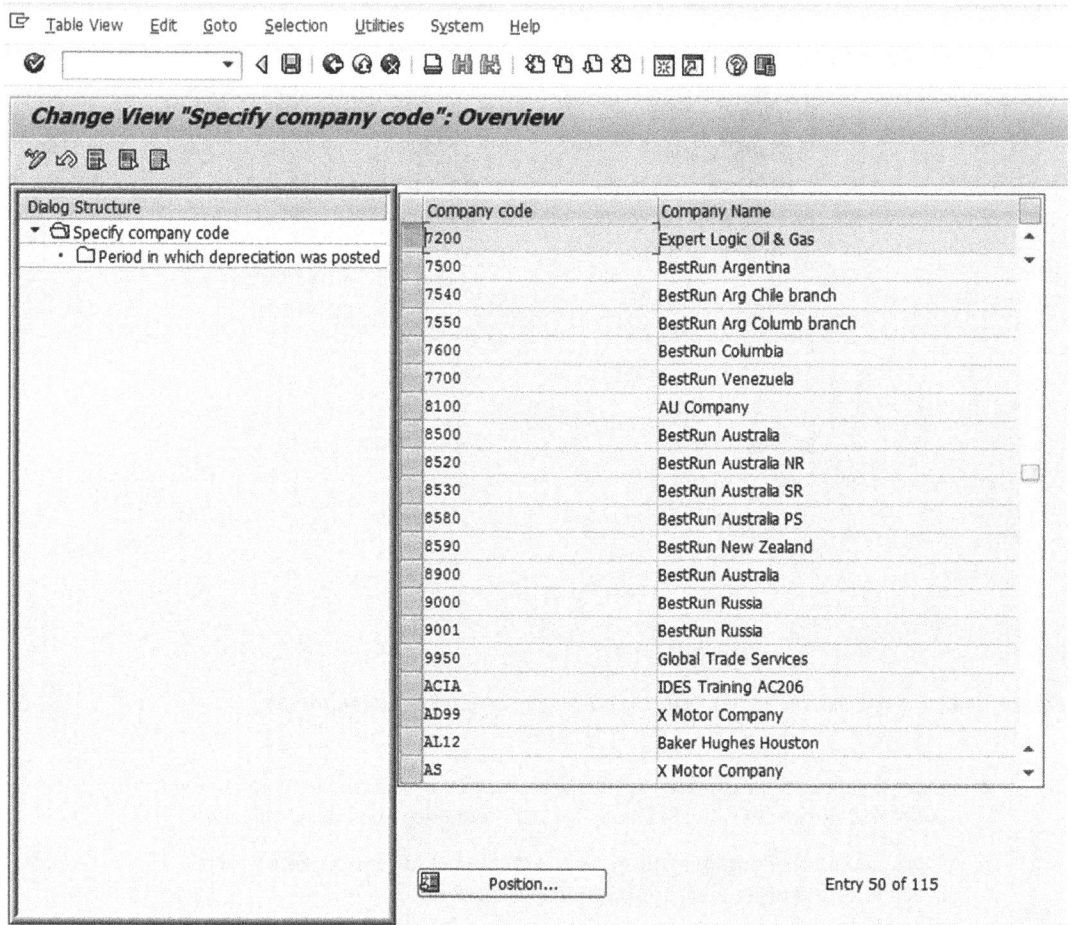

Figure 10-5. *The initial screen where period in which depreciation was posted*

2. Search for your company code using the [⊞ Position...] button at the bottom left of the screen. Your company code will be displayed at the top of the displayed company codes list.

3. Select your company code by clicking on it and double click the Period in which depreciation was posted folder in the Company code selection folder on the left pane of the screen. The Change View "Period in which depreciation was posted": Overview screen appears.

Options

Options customizing is part of parameter for data transfer specifications. The specification of options is an enhancement to the configuration of asset data transfer. You can specify the following options in SAP Asset Accounting:

- Specify Entry of Net Book Value without accumulated ordinary depreciation
- Recalculate depreciation for previous years
- Recalculate base insurable values
- Recalculate base replacement values
- Transfer foreign currency areas

Specify Entry of Net Book Value (No Accum. Ordinary Depre.)

You can carry out this specification if the net book values method of asset valuation is used in the previous system. Net book value is asset value less depreciation. Historical APC and accumulated depreciation method is quite different from net book value method. The transfer of net book value can only be performed manually, you will not be able to perform this function using the automatic data transfer (i.e., using batch input procedure). Batch input is one of the general methods you can use to transfer bulk data into SAP system.

You can perform the specification of entry of net book value, you can use this menu path: Financial Accounting (New) ➤ Asset Accounting ➤ Asset Data Transfer ➤ Parameters for Data Transfer ➤ Options ➤ Specify Entry of Net Book Value (No Accum. Ordinary Depre.). The Change View "FI-AA: Legacy data transfer, entry of net book value": Overview screen appears, displaying the list of possible company code you can specify entry of net book value. Using the [⊞ Position...] button at the bottom left of the screen, search for your company code and activate the Enter net book value checkbox. Click the Enter ✅ button at the top left of the screen and save 💾 your specification.

Recalculate Depreciation for Previous Years

This specification allow you to recalculate the accumulated depreciation from the previous years during the legacy asset data transfer, based on defined SAP depreciation rules. This is possible when a depreciation area is newly entered and the values for a depreciation area need to be recalculated in the system.

You can carry out recalculation based on the condition that the APC was acquired at the time of the asset capitalization, whereas the recalculation is only possible for the book depreciation area in the company codes that are still in test mode:

1. To carry out the recalculation of depreciation for past years, you can use this menu path: Financial Accounting (New) ➤ Asset Accounting ➤ Asset Data Transfer ➤ Parameters for Data Transfer ➤ Options ➤ Recalculate Depreciation for Previous Years. The Change View "Company code selection": Overview screen appears showing the list of existing company codes in the system.

2. Using the [🔲 Position...] button at the bottom left of the screen. Select your company code (7200) and double click the Calculate accumulated depreciation folder in the Company code selection on the left pane of the screen. The Change View "Calculate accumulated depreciation": Overview screen appears, containing the list of depreciation areas in your company code, as shown in Figure 10-6.

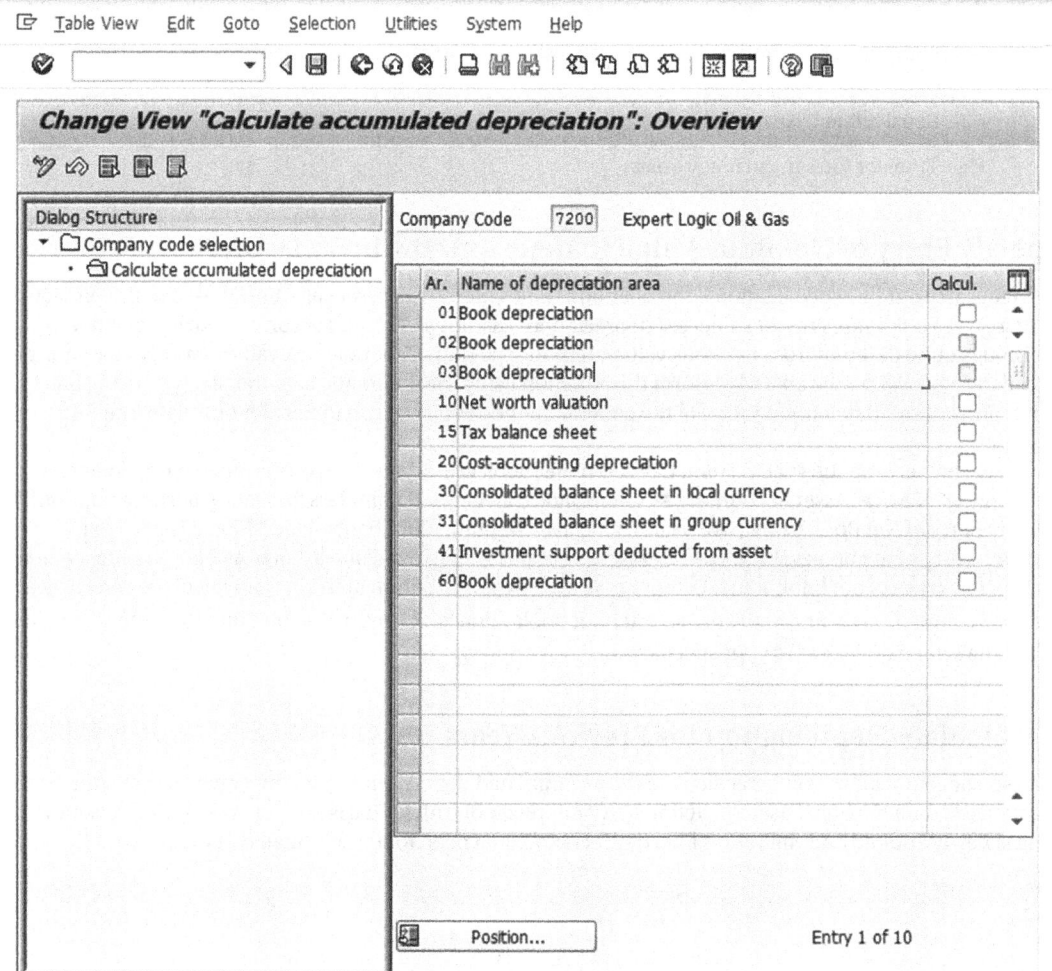

Figure 10-6. The screen where you activate the calculation of accumulated depreciation for the previous years

3. Activate each of the depreciation areas you want the system to recalculation depreciation from the previous year. You do this by checking the Calculation checkbox on the right side of the screen for the appropriate depreciation areas.

4. Click the Enter 🗸 button at the top left of the screen and save 🖫 your specification.

▪ **Note** You only perform this specification when you want to recalculate depreciation for the previous years during old asset data takeover.

Recalculate Base Insurable Values

This customizing step is necessary only when you want to recalculate base insurable values. The specification you carry out will determine if the system should recalculate the base insurable value during old asset data takeover.

To carry out base insurable values recalculation, you can use this menu path: Financial Accounting (New) ➤ Asset Accounting ➤ Asset Data Transfer ➤ Parameters for Data Transfer ➤ Options ➤ Recalculate Base Insurance Values. The change View "FI-AA: Legacy data transf., recalculate base insurance value overview screen comes up. This is the screen where you will specify if you want the system to recalculate base insurable values during old asset takeover by simply enabling the CumIn.val checkbox on the screen for your company code.

Recalculate Replacement Values

This customizing step is necessary if you want the system to calculate new replacement values using the index series stored in the system when performing legacy data transfer.

Follow these steps to perform the depreciation area/company code specification which you would want the replacement values to be calculated during the legacy asset data transfer:

1. Use this menu path: Financial Accounting (New) ➤ Asset Accounting ➤ Asset Data Transfer ➤ Parameters for Data Transfer ➤ Options ➤ Recalculate Replacement Values. The Change View "Company code selection": Overview screen appears, containing the list of existing company code in the system.

2. Search for your Company code using the ▦ Position... button. Select your company code from the list of displayed company code and double click the Calculate replacement folder in the Company code selection on the left pane of the screen. The Change View "Calculate replacement value": Overview screen appears, displaying all the depreciation areas in your company code, as shown in Figure 10-7.

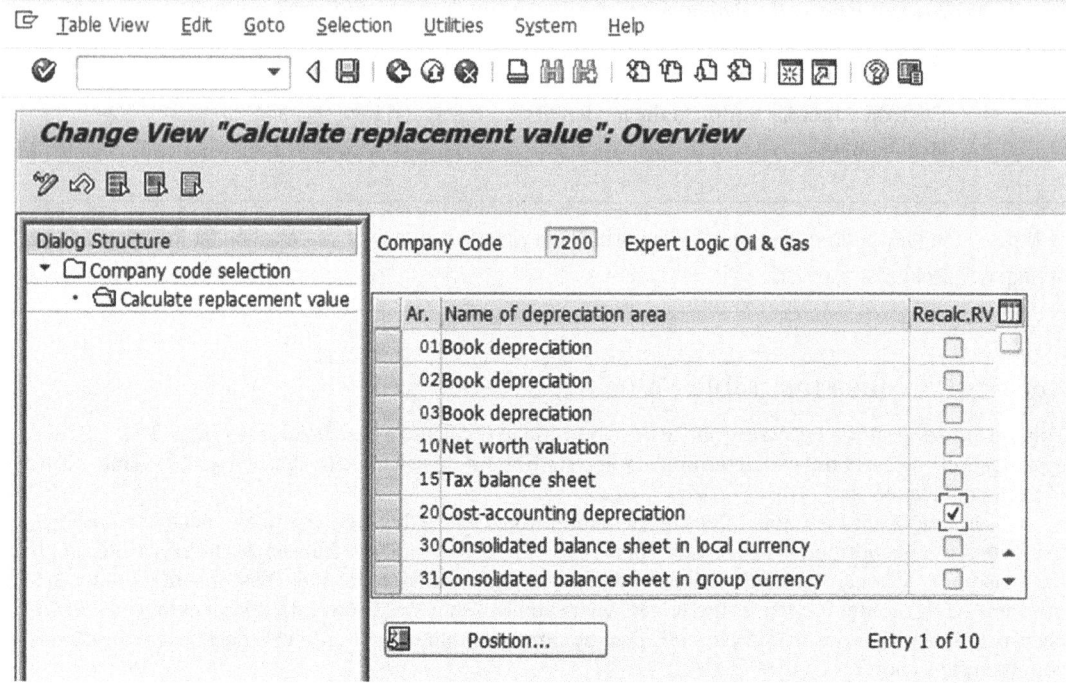

Figure 10-7. *The screen where you specify that the system should calculate replacement value during legacy asset data takeover*

3. Check ReCalc.RV checkbox of the appropriate recalculate replacement value to activate this function.

4. Click the enter 🗹 button at the top left of the screen and save 🖫 your specification.

Transfer Foreign Currency Areas

This customizing step is necessary only if you want to manage depreciation areas in foreign currency. This specification allows you specify that foreign currency areas can receive values when performing old asset data takeover. This specification is only applicable to areas that are managed in foreign currency.

To carry out the specification of transfer foreign currency area function, complete these steps:

1. Use this menu path: Financial Accounting (New) ➤ Asset Accounting ➤ Asset Data Transfer ➤ Parameters for Data Transfer ➤ Options ➤ Transfer Foreign Currency Areas. The Change View "Company code selection": Overview screen appears. This screen will allow you to select the company code from the list of existing company code you want to use for the transfer of foreign currency.

2. Select your company code (7200) from the list of displayed company codes in the system, as shown in Figure 10-8.

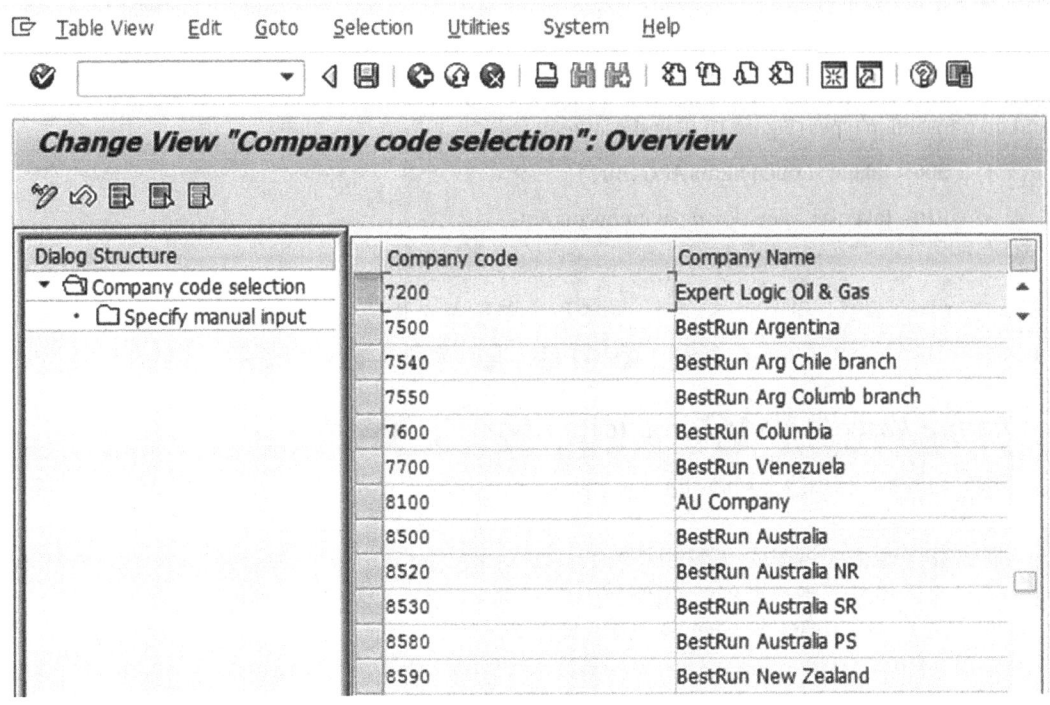

Figure 10-8. *The existing company code in the system from which you can select company code you are using for the transfer of foreign currency*

3. To proceed to the actual screen where you will carry out the specification of transfer foreign currency areas in your company code, double click the Specify Manual input folder in the Company code selection folder in the Dialog Structure. The View "Specify manual input": Overview screen appears, displaying the list of depreciation areas in your company code.

4. Specify the depreciation areas you want to perform foreign currency transfer during old asset data transfer. You can do this by checking the Manually checkbox for the appropriate depreciation areas on the right side of the screen.

5. Click the Enter 🗸 button at the top left of the screen and save 🖫 your specification.

Define Transaction Types for Transfer of Open Items

In this customizing step, you will define transactions types you want to use for assets under construction with line item management. Line items from the view point of Asset Accounting are the display of asset values for each transaction. Line item contains items such as the transaction type, asset value date, posted amount, depreciation, proportional value adjustments, and so on. The specification of transaction types for transfer of open items is not necessary if you do not have any asset under construction during old asset data transfer.

To define transaction types for transfer of open items, you can use this menu path: Financial Accounting (New) ➤ Asset Accounting ➤ Asset Data Transfer ➤ Parameters for Data Transfer ➤ Define Transaction Types for Transfer of Open Items. The Change View "FI-AA: Transaction types": Overview screen appears. This is the initial screen where you define transaction types for transfer of open items. SAP comes with standard transaction types (Figure 10-9) in the system:

- 900 – Takeover open items APC (AuC)

- 910 - Takeover open down payments on AuC

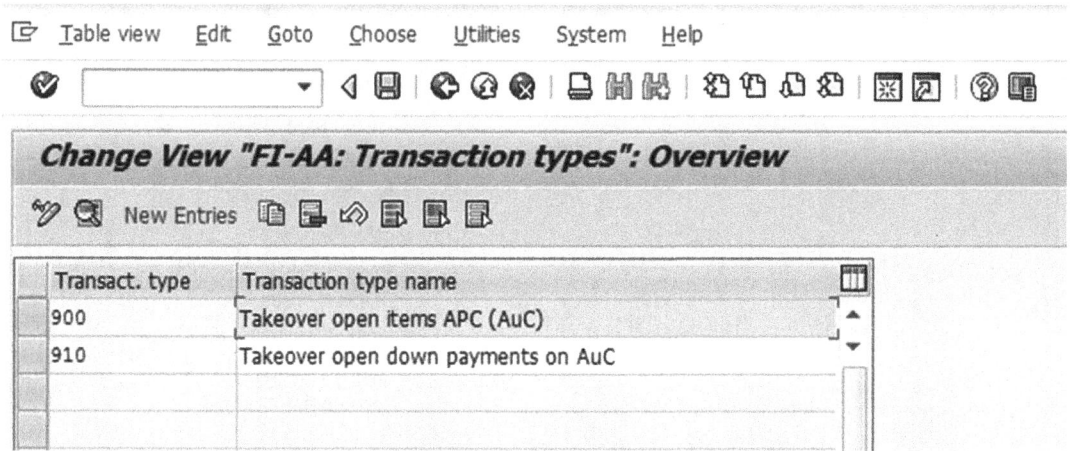

Figure 10-9. *The standard transaction types supplied by SAP that you can use for transfer of open items*

To display the settings for each transaction type settings for the takeover of open items from a previous system, you can double click on any of the transaction type on the screen. The Change View "FI-AA: Transport types": Details screen appears (Figure 10-10), showing the settings for the transaction type in question.

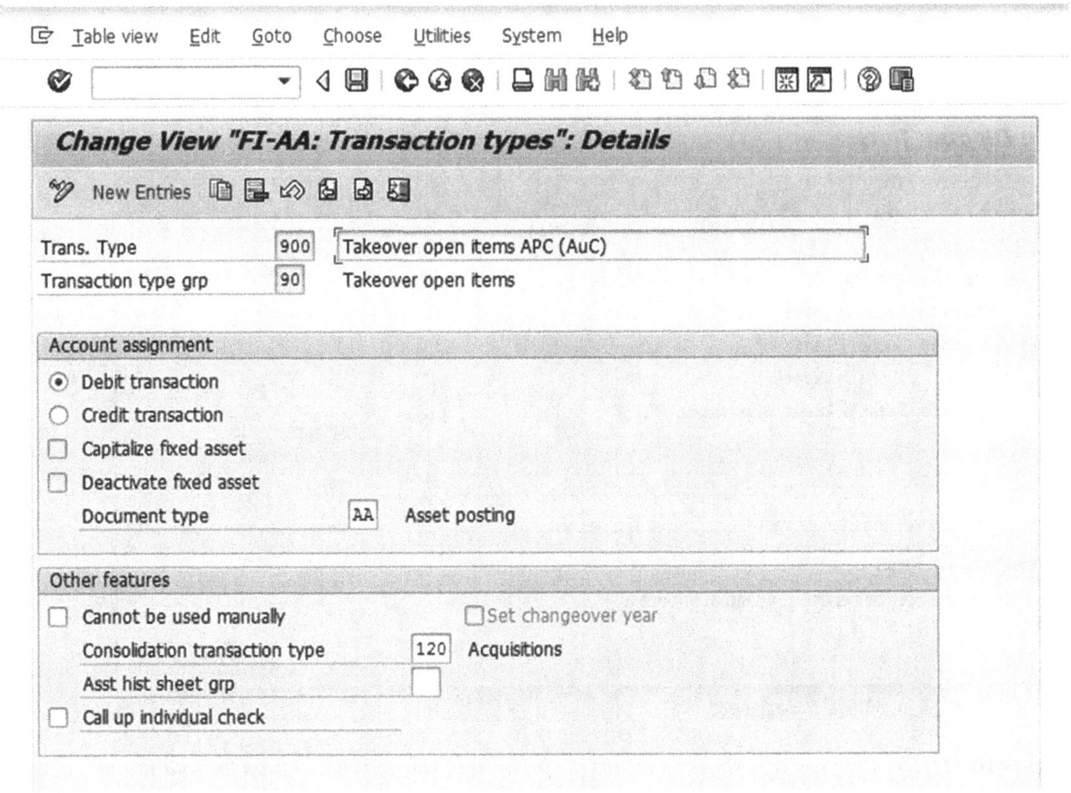

Figure 10-10. *The settings for transaction type for takeover open items APC (AuC)*

Manual Legacy Asset Data Transfer

The next step in the customizing you enter old asset data from the previous system in the SAP system using manual online legacy asset data transfer. You have two options you can choose from:

- Create/Change/Display Legacy Asset
- Create/Change/Display Legacy Group Asset

Create/Change/Display Legacy Asset

In this activity you can create/change/display legacy asset for each asset. To access the screen where you can carry out this function, you can use this menu path: Financial Accounting (New) ➤ Asset Accounting ➤ Asset Data Transfer ➤ Manual Online Transfer ➤ Create/Change/Display Legacy Asset. The Choose Activity screen appears, as shown in Figure 10-11, displaying activities that you can choose from.

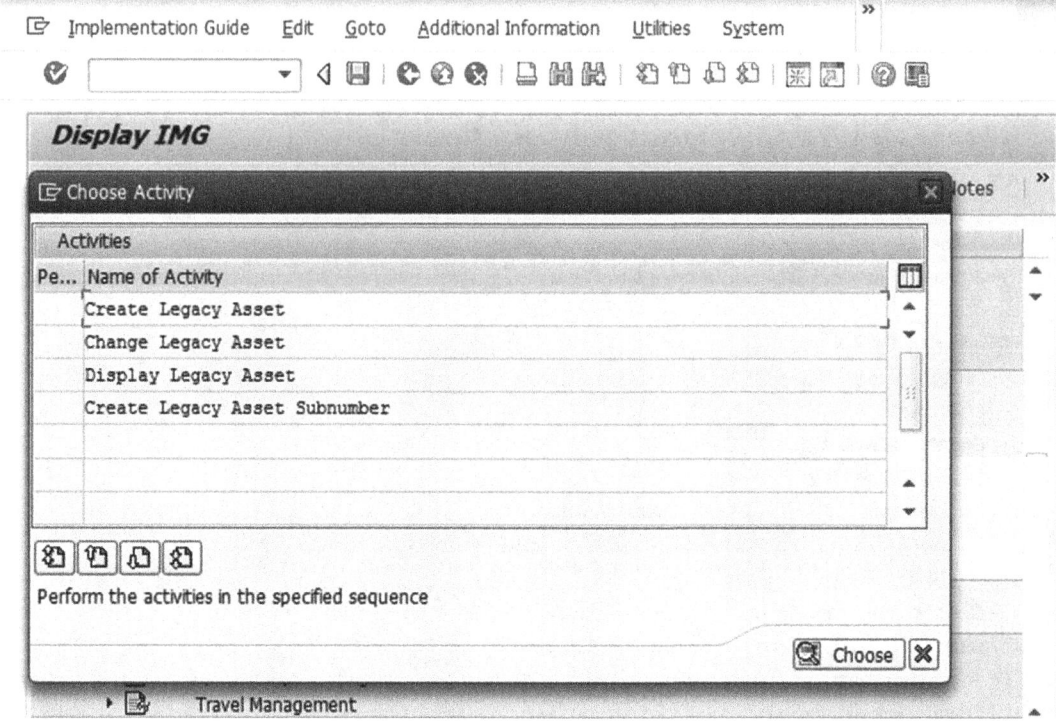

Figure 10-11. *The activity screen showing the list of options that you can choose from for your manual asset data transfer*

Create Legacy Asset

First, you need to create asset master data for the asset you want to take over:

1. To create legacy asset master data, select the Create Legacy Asset from the displayed list of option (Figure 10-10) and click the [🔍 Choose] button at the bottom right of the screen. The Create Legacy Data: Initial screen appears.

2. Enter data in the following fields:

    - **Asset Class**: Enter the asset class (AS3000) you want to use for your asset legacy asset master data in this field.

    - **Company code**: Enter the company code (7200) that the legacy asset data is applicable to in this field. This is the company code you making the transfer from.

3. Click the [Master data] button at the top left of the screen. The Create Legacy Data: Master Data screen appears (Figure 10-12). This the screen where you will create the master data for your legacy asset.

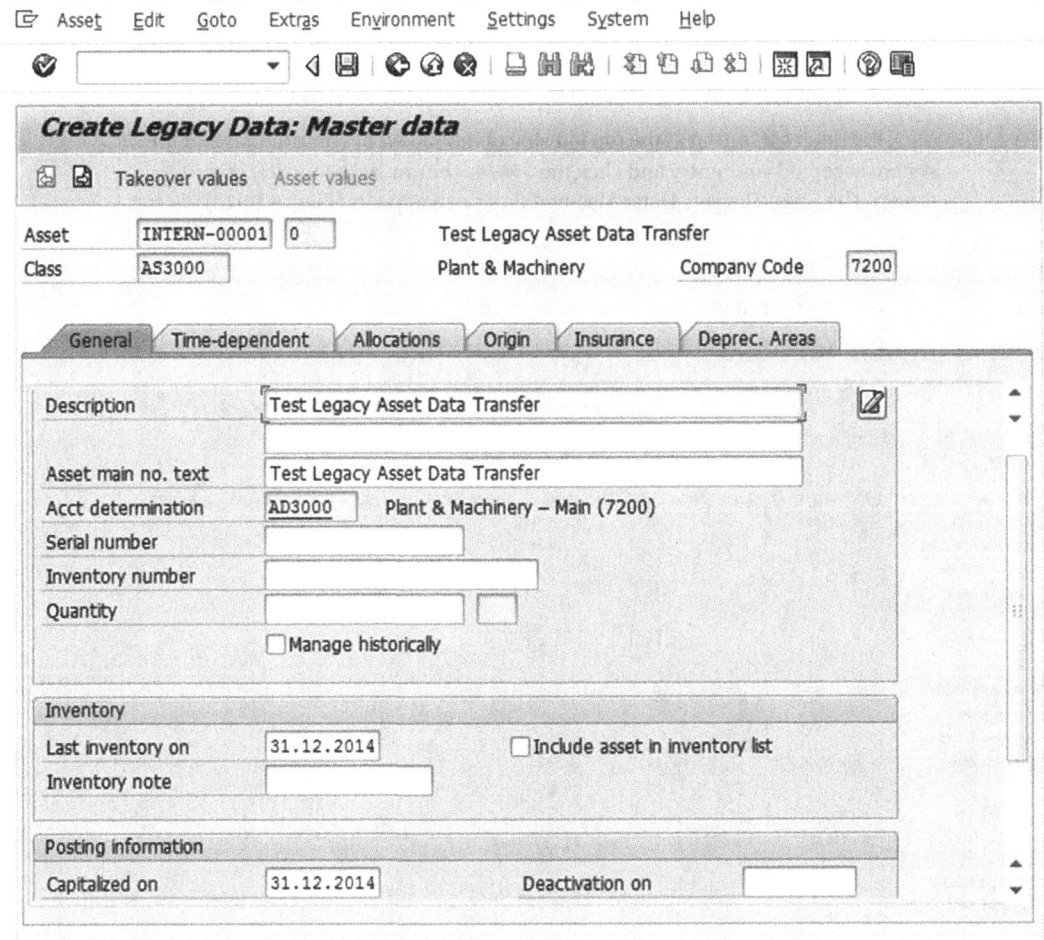

Figure 10-12. *The screen where you create the master data for your legacy asset data*

4. Update the following fields:

- **Description**: Enter a description for your asset legacy in this field.

- **Last Inventory on**: Enter the transfer date in this field (i.e. the last closed fiscal year). This data determines the status to be used for the transfer. If you assume that you want to transfer the asset in fiscal year 2015, the transfer date should be 31/12/2014.

5. Click the Enter 🕑 button at the top left of the screen. The Posting information section of the screen is expanded.

6. Enter the capitalization date in the Capitalized on field. This is the date that you want the system to commence capitalization of the asset in question.

■ **Note** The capitalization data is a required entry when creating master data for a legacy asset. The depreciation start date and the expired useful life are determined by the system based on the period control in the depreciation key.

---

7. As part of the master data creation for your legacy asset, you also have to enter the appropriate cost center for the asset in the master date. Click the Time-dependent tab at the top of the screen to go to the time-dependent page of the screen. Enter the cost center (1100) in the Cost Center field for the asset in question.

8. Click the Enter ✅ button at the top left side of the screen to confirm that that the system accepted your entry and click the ⌴Takeover values⌴ button at the top left of the screen. The Create Legacy Data: Master data screen appears (Figure 10-13).

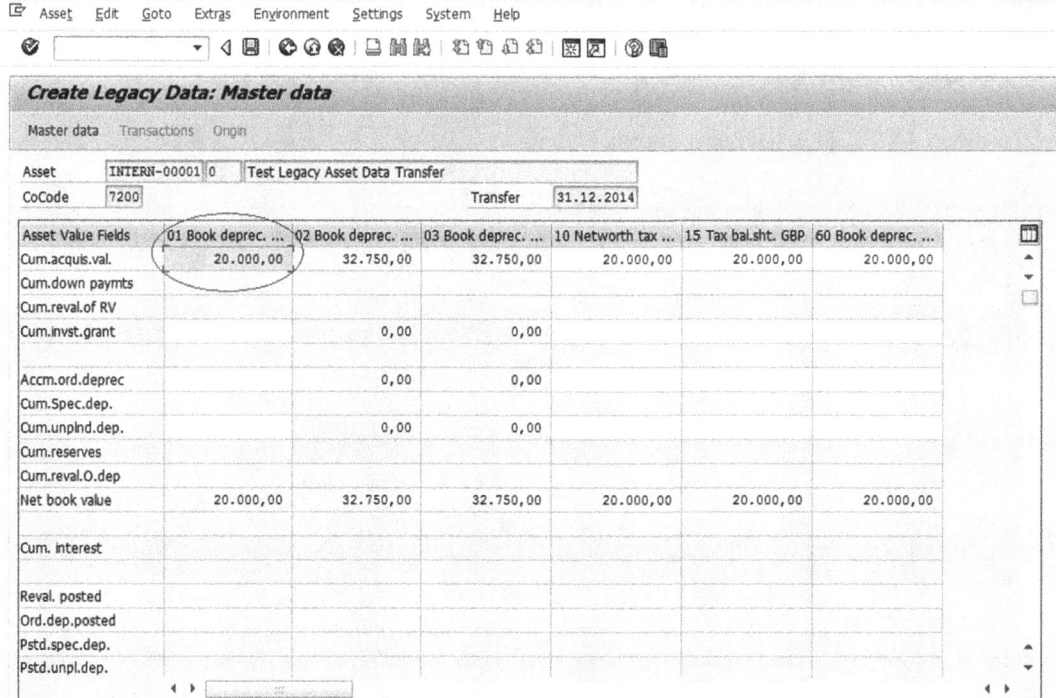

Figure 10-13. *The screen where you maintain the acquisition value and accumulated depreciation value*

9. Enter the legacy asset value in the cumulative acquisition value (for example, 20,000) in the Cum.acquis.val field circled in Figure 10-13.

Change Legacy Asset

In this step, you can carry out some changes in the master data for the asset legacy data you have created:

1. To perform this function, select the Change Legacy Asset from the displayed list of option (refer to Figure 10-10) and click the ⌴Q Choose⌴ button at the bottom right of the screen. The Change Legacy Data: Initial screen appears.

2. Update the following fields:

- **Asset**: Enter the asset number (3004 – Test Legacy Asset Data Transfer) of the legacy asset you want to change in this field.

- **Company Code**: Enter the company code (7200) that you are making legacy asset data transfer from in this field.

3. Click the Master data button at the top left of the screen to proceed to the next screen, the Change Legacy Data: Master data screen shown in Figure 10-14.

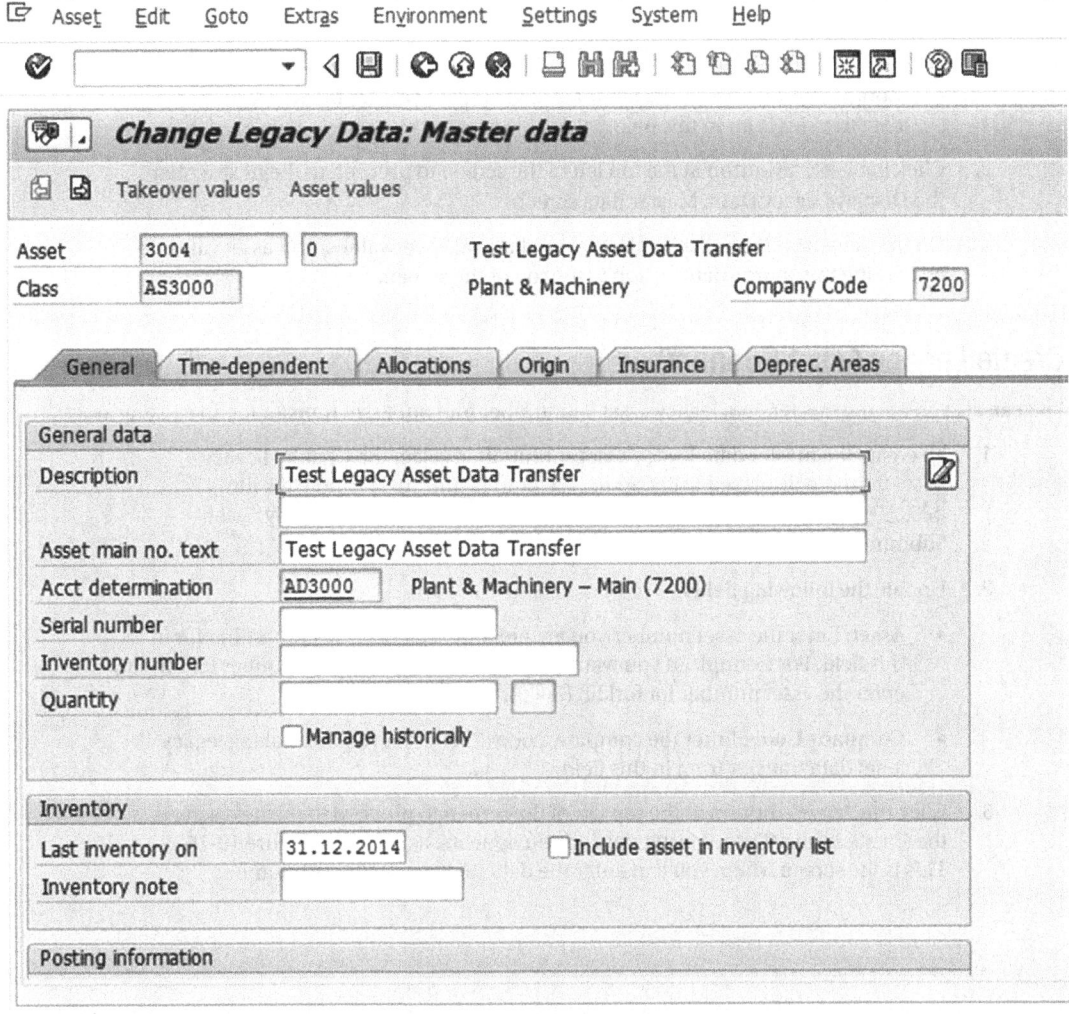

Figure 10-14. *The screen where you make changes to the master data for your legacy asset*

4. On this screen, carry out appropriate changes to your master data legacy asset. Click the Enter ✅ button at the top left side of the screen to confirm that that the system accepted your entry and save 🖫 your changes.

Display Legacy Asset

You can display the master data of the legacy asset you have created, but you will not be able to make any changes in this step:

1. To display the master data for legacy asset, select the display Legacy Asset from the displayed list of option on the Choose Activity screen (refer to Figure 10-11) and click the `Q Choose` button at the bottom right of the screen. The Display Legacy Data: Initial screen appears.

2. Update the following fields:

   - **Asset**: Enter the asset number (3004 – Test Legacy Asset Data Transfer) of the legacy asset you want to display in this field.

   - **Company Code**: Enter the company code (7200) you are making legacy asset data transfer from in this field.

3. Click the `Master data` button at the top left of the screen to proceed to the next screen the Display Legacy Data: Master data screen.

4. On this screen you can display the master data, takeover values, and asset values by clicking the appropriate button at the top of the screen.

Create Legacy Asset Subnumber

You can also create the master data legacy asset subnumber for your asset transfer for an existing asset:

1. To create the master data legacy asset subnumber, select the Change Legacy Asset from the displayed list of option (refer to Figure 10-11) and click the `Q Choose` button at the bottom right of the screen. The Create Legacy Asset Subnumber: Initial screen appears.

2. Update the following fields:

   - **Asset**: Enter the asset number you are creating legacy asset subnumber for in this field. For example, if you want to create a legacy asset subnumber for forklift, enter the asset number for forklift (3000).

   - **Company Code**: Enter the company code (7200) that you are making legacy asset data transfer from in this field.

3. Click the `Master data` button at the top left of the screen to proceed to the next screen the Create Legacy Data: Master data screen appears, as shown in Figure 10-15. This is the screen where you can enter the data for legacy asset subnumber.

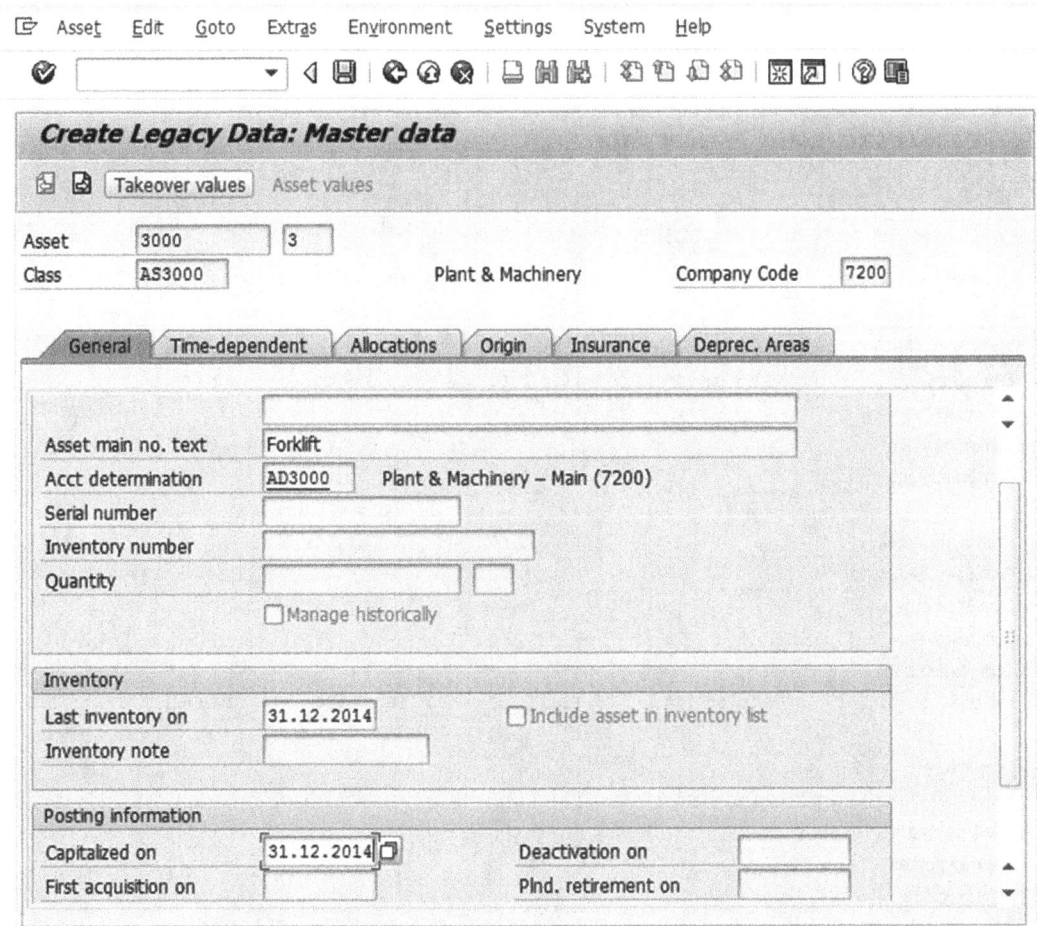

Figure 10-15. *The screen where you create the master data for your legacy asset subnumber*

4. The Asset main no. text field is defaulted by the system. However, you can update the following field:

   • **Last Inventory on**: Enter the transfer date in this field (i.e. the last closed fiscal year). This data determines the status to be used for the transfer.

5. Click the Enter 🗸 button at the top left of the screen. The Posting information section of the screen is expanded.

6. Enter the capitalization date in the Capitalized on field. This is the date that you want the system to commence capitalization of the asset in question.

7. Click the ⌷Takeover values⌷ button at the top left of the screen. The Create Legacy Data: Master data screen appears (Figure 10-16).

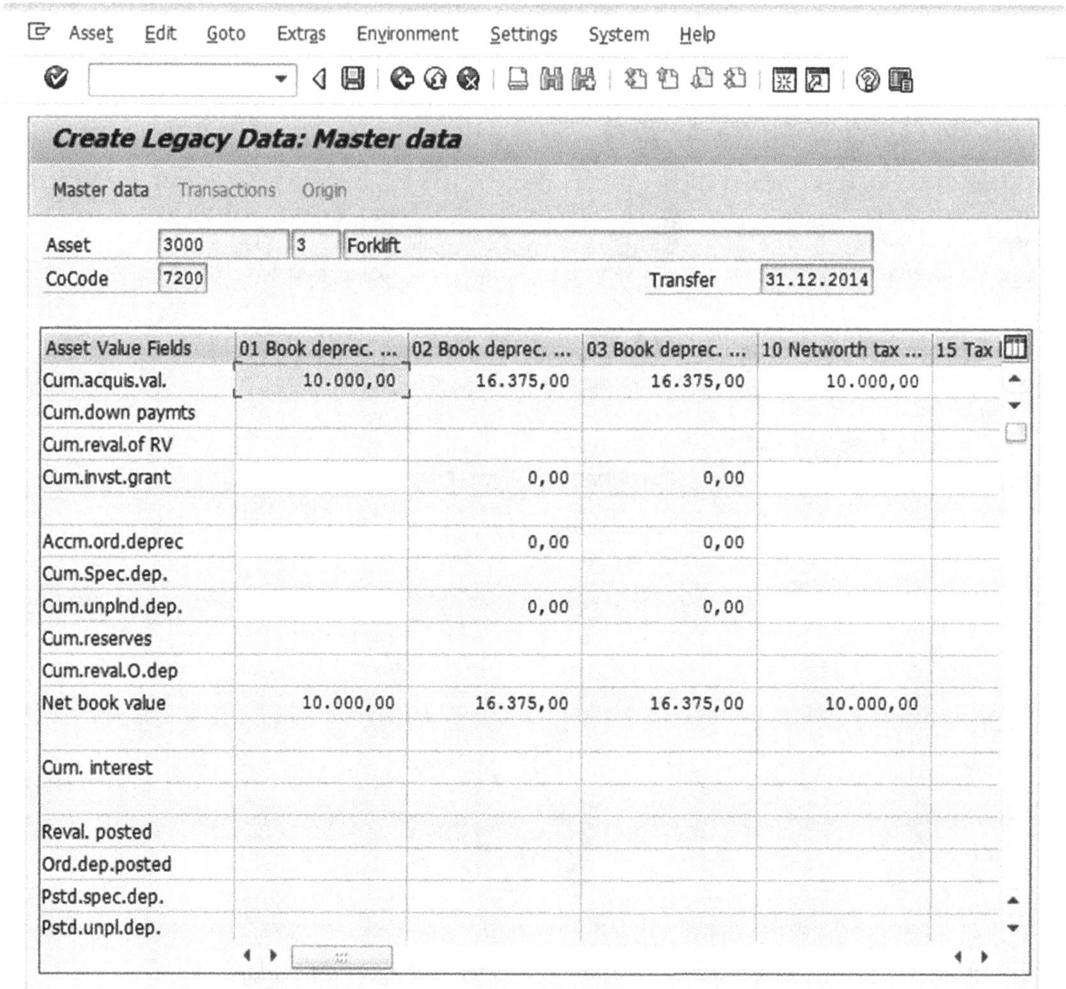

Figure 10-16. *The screen where you maintain the acquisition value and accumulated depreciation value for the legacy asset subnumber*

8. Enter the legacy asset value in the cumulative acquisition value (for example, 10,000) in the Cum.acquis.val field and click the Enter ✅ button at the top left of the screen and save 💾 your specification.

Create/Change/Display Legacy Group Asset

In this activity you can create/change/display legacy asset for the old asset group. To access the screen where you can carry out this function, you will use this menu path: Financial Accounting (New) ➤ Asset Accounting ➤ Asset Data Transfer ➤ Manual Online Transfer ➤ Create/Change/Display Legacy Group Asset. The Choose Activity screen appears, displaying activities you can choose from:

- Create old asset (group asset)
- Change old asset (group asset)
- Display old asset (group asset)
- Create subnumber for old asset (group asset)

Create Old Asset (Group Asset)

You can create an old group asset in this step using an online transaction:

1. To call up the screen where you can create old group asset, select the Create old asset (group) from the list of displayed activities on the Choose Activity screen and click the [🔍 Choose] button at the bottom right of the screen. The Create Legacy Group Asset: initial screen appears.

2. Enter the asset class number (AS3000) you are using for your legacy group asset in the Asset Class field and enter the related company code (7200) in the Company code field.

3. Click the Enter 🗸 button at the top left of the screen. The Create Legacy Data: Master data screen appears.

4. Update the following field:

   - **Description**: Enter a short description that best describes your asset legacy in this field.

   - **Last inventory on**: Enter the transfer date in this field (i.e., the last closed fiscal year date).

5. Click the Enter 🗸 button at the top left of the screen. The Posting information section of the screen is expanded.

6. Enter the capitalization date in the Capitalized on field.

7. Click the Time-dependent tab at the top of the screen to go to the time-dependent page of the screen, and enter the cost center (1100) in the Cost Center field for the group asset.

8. Click the Enter 🗸 button at the top left side of the screen to confirm that that the system accepted your entry and click the [Takeover values] button at the top left of the screen. The Create Legacy Data: Master data screen appears (Figure 10-17).

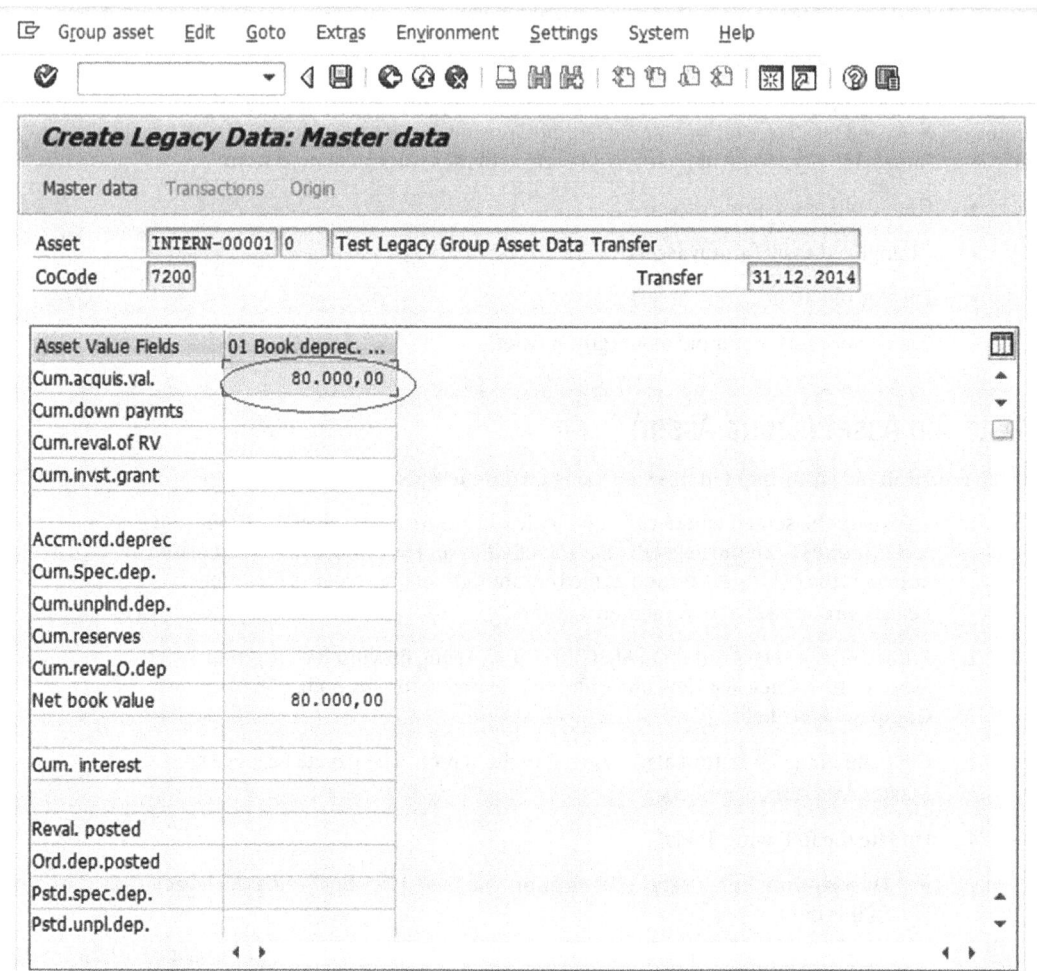

Figure 10-17. *The screen where you maintain the acquisition value and accumulated depreciation value for the group asset*

9. Enter the legacy asset value in the cumulative acquisition value (for example, in this activity, we used 80,000 as the asset value, circled in Figure 10-15).

10. Click the Enter ✅ button at the top left of the screen and save 💾 your specification.

Change Old Asset (Group Asset)

In this step, you can make some changes to the old asset group you have created:

1. To do this, select the Change old asset (group asset) form the displayed activities options on the Choose Activity screen and click the [Choose] button at the bottom right of the screen. The Change Legacy Group Asset: Initial screen appears.

2. Update the following fields:

    • **Group asset**: Enter the group asset number you created above in this field. You can access the group field numbers in the system using the matchcode by the Group asset field.

    • **Company Code**: Enter the corresponding company code (7200) in this field.

3. When you click the Enter ✓ button at the top left of the screen, the Change Legacy Data: Master data screen appears.

4. On this screen you can make the following changes in the master data of the group asset data:

    • The description

    • Last inventory on

    • Business area

    • Cost center

    • Depreciation key

    • The asset useful life

    • Ordinary depreciation start date

5. When you have made your changes, Click the Enter ✓ button at the top left of the screen and save 💾.

Display Old Asset (Group Asset)

In this step, you can disclose the old asset group master data you have created:

1. To do this, select the Display old asset (group asset) from the list of displayed activities on the Choose Activity screen and click the [Choose] button at the bottom right of the screen. The Display Legacy Group Asset: Initial screen appears.

2. Enter the group asset number of the Group asset you want to display in the Group asset field (you can access the list of group asset using the matchcode) and the corresponding company code in the company code field.

3. On this screen, you can display the depreciation areas, the takeover values or the asset values by clicking on appropriate button at the top of the screen.

■ **Note**   In this activity you will not be able to carry out any changes in the master data, because this is only a display function.

Create Subnumber for Old Asset (Group Asset)

You can also create a subnumber for the old asset group that you have created in this step:

1. To display the screen where you can perform this function, select the Create subnumber for old asset (group asset) from the list of activities options displayed on the Choose Activity screen and click the [Choose] button at the bottom right of the screen. The Create Legacy Group Asset Subnumber: Initial screen appears.

2. Enter the group asset number (3005) of the group asset you created in the Group asset field, enter the corresponding company code (7200) in the Company code field, and click the Enter ✔ button at the top left of the screen. The Create Legacy Data: master data screen appears.

3. After you click the Enter ✔ button, the posting information section of the screen expands. Enter the Capitalization date in the Capitalized on field as shown in Figure 10-18.

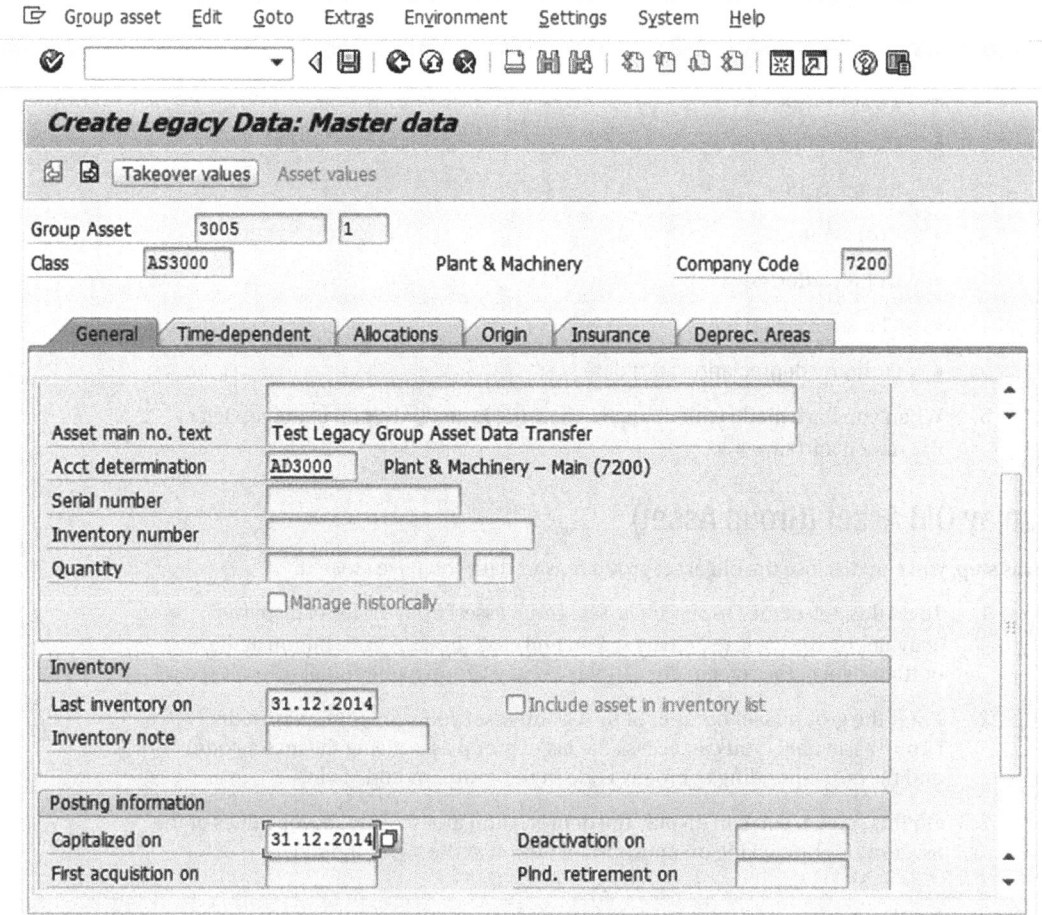

Figure 10-18. *The screen where you create the master data for your legacy asset subnumber for the old asset group*

4. To proceed to the screen where you will specify the Asset Value and the accumulated depreciation for your legacy asset subnumber, click the Takeover values button at the top left of the screen. The Create Legacy Data: Master data screen, as shown in Figure 10-19.

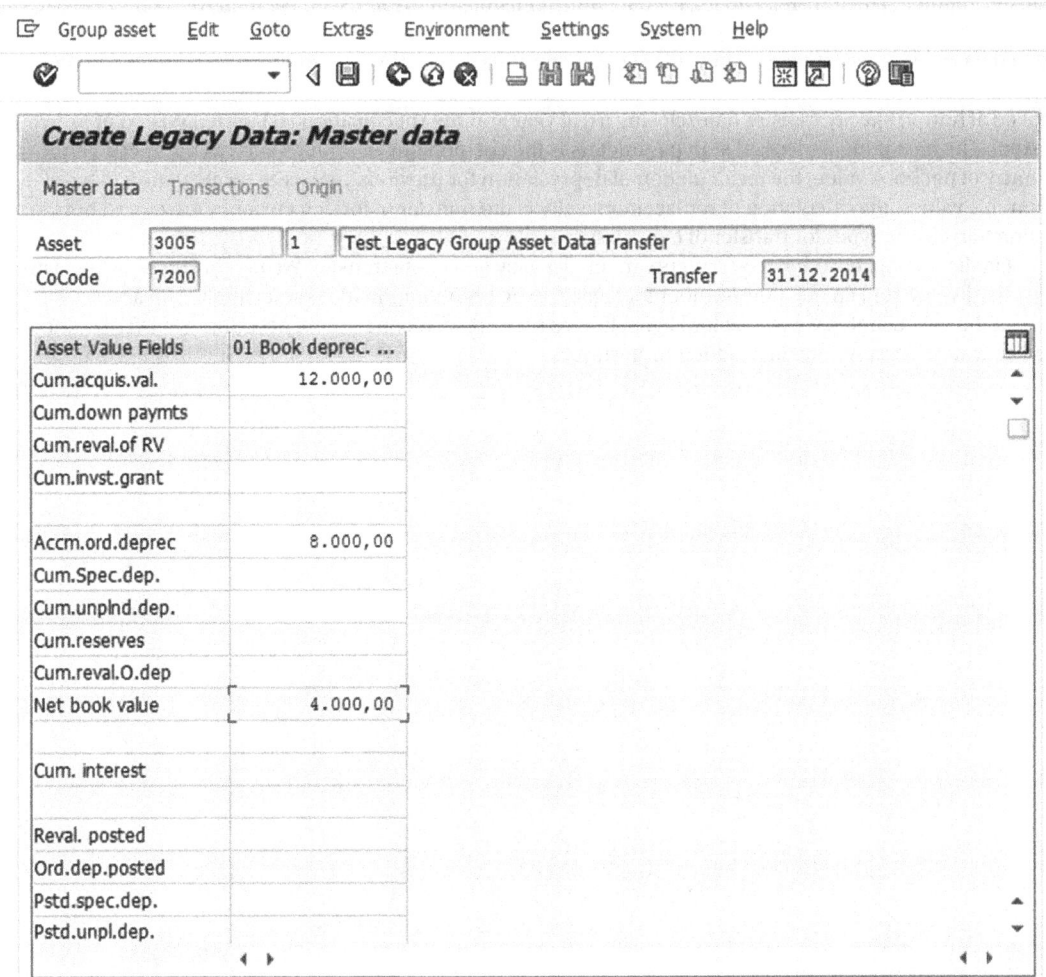

Figure 10-19. *The screen where you maintain the acquisition value and accumulated depreciation value for the old asset group*

5. Enter the asset value in the Cum.acquis.val. field and the corresponding accumulated ordinary depreciation in the Acc.ord.deprec. field, respectively.

6. When you click the Enter 🗸 button at the top left of the screen the system will default the net book value. Save 🖫 your entries.

Summary

In this chapter, we introduced you to the basic concepts of asset data transfer and looked at the configuration steps involved in asset data transfer. We started by explaining what legacy data transfer is and outlined various options available to you when performing Asset legacy data transfer—for example, automatic data transfer, manual data transfer, and legacy data transfer using Microsoft Excel. We then went on to look at various steps involved in the customizing of legacy data transfer. As part of the customizing process of legacy asset data transfer, we taught you how to set company code status, specify sequence of depreciation areas. We then looked at the settings involved in the customizing of parameters for data transfer. In so doing, we looked at how to specify transfer date/closing fiscal year and the specification last period posted in previous system. The next thing we looked at in parameters is the customizing of options such as the specification of entry of net book value, the recalculation of depreciation for previous years, the recalculation of base insurable values, the calculation of replacement values, the transfer of foreign currency areas, and how to define transaction types for transfer of open items.

Finally, we looked at how to configure manual legacy asset data transfer. We taught you how to create, change, display, and create a subnumber for legacy asset, both for individual asset and group asset.

In the next chapter, we will be looking at how to set or reset reconciliation accounts, transfer balances, and activate company code in production startup.

■ ■ ■

CHAPTER 11

Preparing for Production Startup

This chapter looks at the basic steps involved in preparing for production startup that are necessary for your SAP system before going live after you have completed your functional requirements and the corresponding customizing. In this chapter you will learn how to:

- Perform consistency checks

- Set or reset reconciliation accounts

- Activate company codes

- Perform an expert overview

Checking Consistency

Once you have completed the technical aspects of your functional configuration and the corresponding customization, it is important that you perform check on their consistency. It is recommended that you carry out a complete check on your settings by working through all of the previous steps and that you print out the settings before production startup. In this step you will carry out consistency overview reports on:

- Asset classes

- Charts of depreciation

- Company codes

- Depreciation areas

- Asset G/L accounts

- FI-AA customizing

In practice, it is necessary to print out all the reports.

To check the plausibility of your system settings, you can use this menu path: Financial Accounting (New) ➤ Asset Accounting ➤ Preparing for Production Startup ➤ Check Consistency. The Choose Activity screen appears, displaying possible activities that you can carry out, as shown in Figure 11-1.

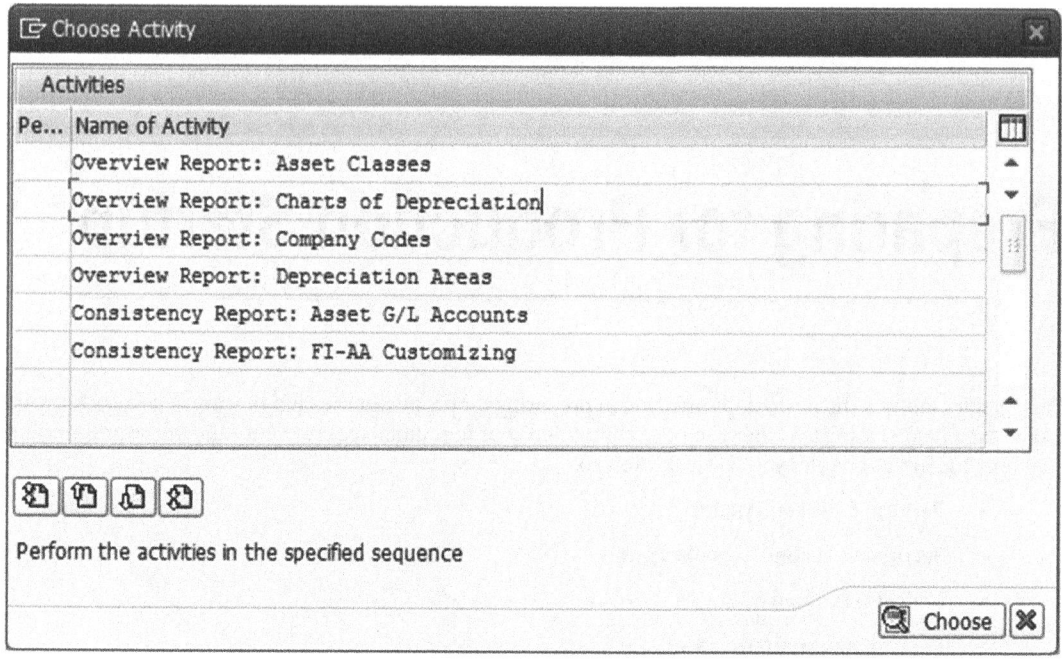

Figure 11-1. *The list of activities on which you can carry out a consistency test*

It is recommended that you perform these activities in order of sequence from the top down in order to avoid missing any steps. We will go through each of the activities in order.

Overview Report: Asset Classes

To execute the overview report for asset classes per chart of depreciation, perform the following steps:

1. Select Overview Report: Asset Classes from the list of the displayed activities options and click the ⊞ Choose button at the bottom right of the screen. The Display Asset Classes per Chart of Depreciation screen appears (see Figure 11-2).

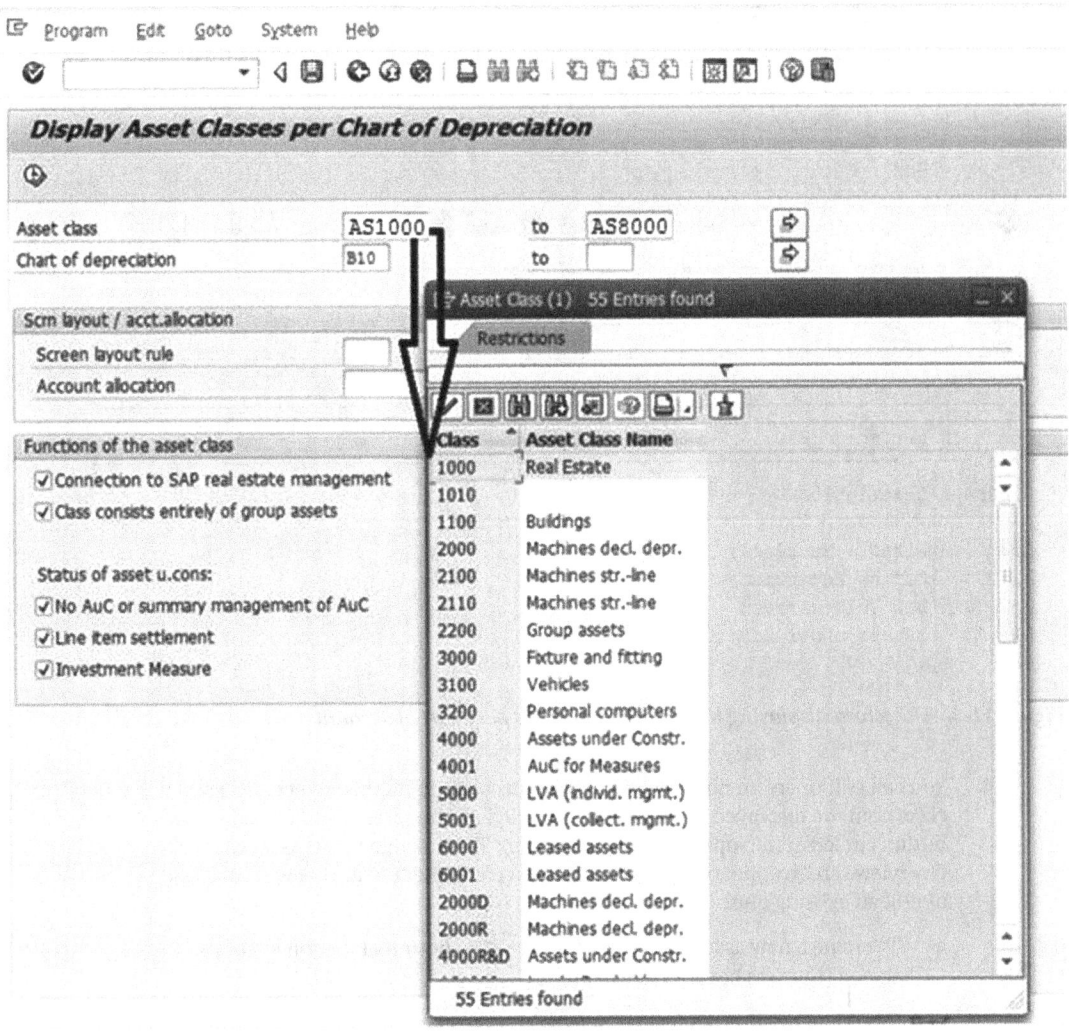

Figure 11-2. *The specification of the range of asset class you are including in your report and a list of asset class in your chart of depreciation*

2. Enter data in the following fields:

    - **Asset class**: Enter the range of your asset class (1000-UT200) in the Asset class fields, respectively. You should enter the first asset class number on the asset class list in the first field and the last asset class number in the second asset class field. You can display the asset class list using the matchcode by each asset class field, as shown in Figure 11-2.

    - **Chart of depreciation**: Enter the chart of depreciation code or key (B10) that you want to include in your report in this field. You can enter an individual chart of depreciation in the chart of depreciation field or a range of chart of depreciation in the chart of depreciation fields, respectively.

3. Click the Execute ⊕ button at the top left side of the screen. The List Asset Classes per Chart of Account screen in Figure 11-3 appears, showing the list of the asset classes in your chart of account.

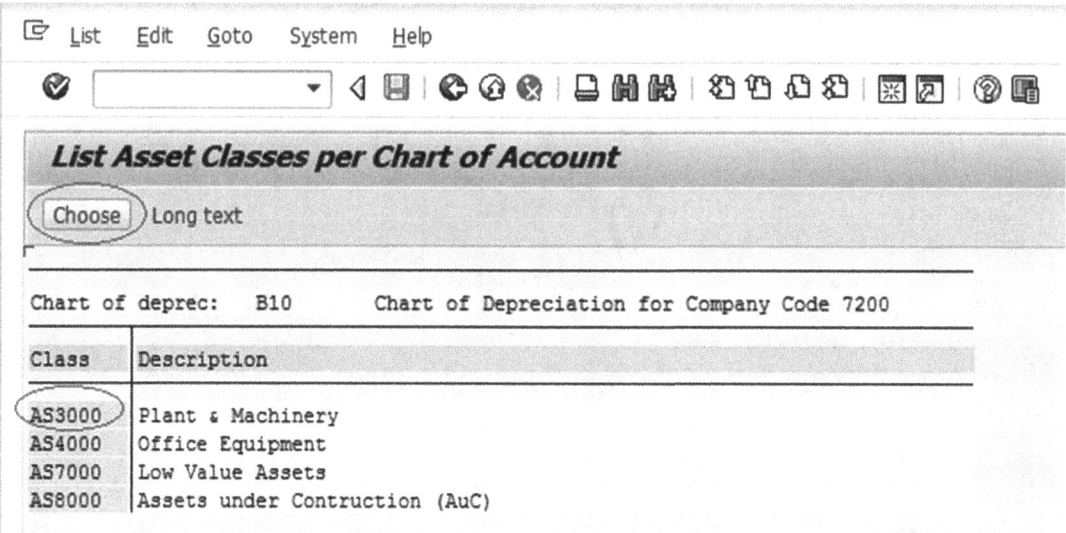

Figure 11-3. *The screen displaying the list of asset classes per chart of account*

4. You can edit or create new asset classes in this step. To do this, select any asset class from the displayed asset classes as circled on the screen, and click the [Choose] button circled at the top left side of the screen. The Change View "Asset classes": Overview screen appears. On this screen you can either create a new asset class or edit an existing one:

    a. To create a new asset class, click the [New Entries] button at the top left of the screen (this was covered in Chapter 1).

    b. To edit an existing asset class, select the asset class that you want to edit from the list of displayed asset classes on the Change View "Asset classes": Overview screen and click the Details ⊠ button at the top left of the screen. The Change View "Asset classes": Details screen appears. On this screen you will carry out any modifications on an existing asset class.

5. When you have edited or created your asset class, click the Enter ⊘ button and save ⊟.

The next step is to return to the choose activity screen to execute the next report.

Overview Report: Charts of Depreciation

In this step, you will display the charts of depreciation and depreciation keys in the system:

1. To display charts of depreciation and depreciation keys in the system, select the overview report: Charts of Depreciation from the list of the displayed activities options and click the ⬚ Choose button at the bottom right of the screen. The chart of depreciation and depreciation keys screen appears, displaying the charts of depreciation and depreciation keys in the system as shown in Figure 11-4.

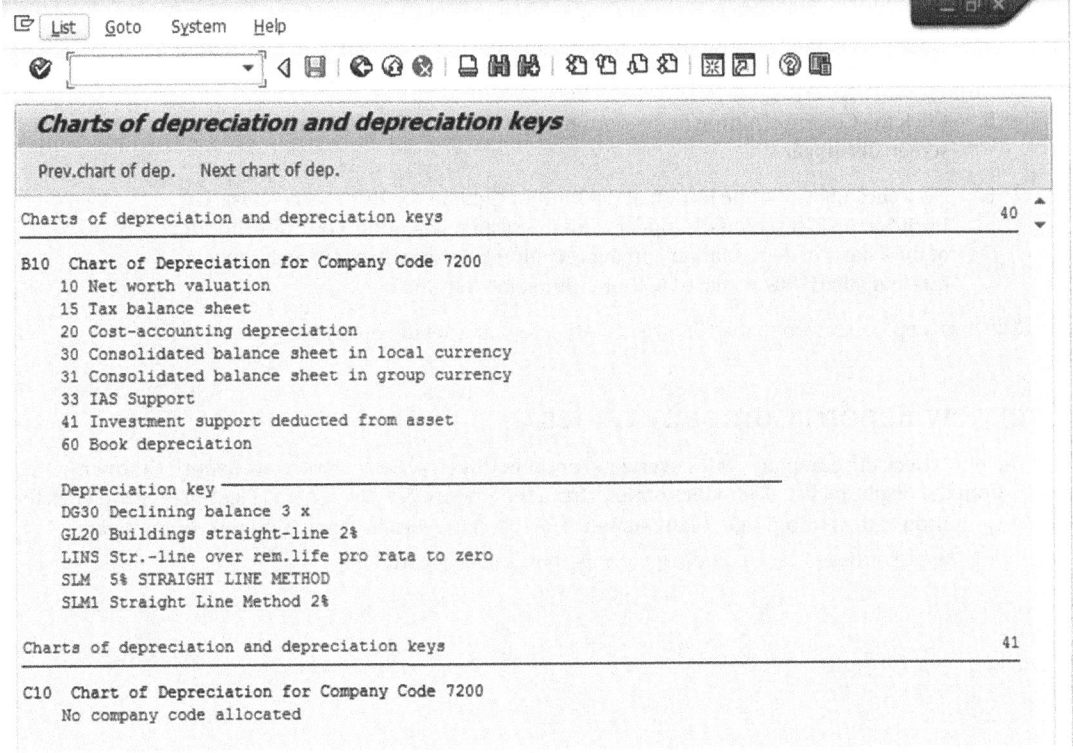

Figure 11-4. List of the charts of depreciation and depreciation keys in the system

---

■ **Note** Using the scroll arrows on the right side of the screen, you can search for the charts of depreciation for your company code.

---

2. You can print this report by clicking the ⌷List button on the menu bar at the top left of the screen and selecting Print form the pull-down menu. The Print List screen pops up.

3. Specify the output device (LP01) that you are using for printing your report and the number of copies.

4. Click the Continue ✅ button at the bottom right of the screen. The Information screen pops up with the information that "Formatting set to 'X_65-200."

5. Click the Continue button at the bottom right of the screen. The Information screen disappears.

6. Now click the Continue button at the bottom right on the Print Screen List. The Print Screen List screen disappears and the system will notify you at the bottom of the Charts of depreciation and depreciation keys screen that "Spool request number 0000198044 created without immediate output."

The next step is to return to the Choose activity screen to execute the next report.

Overview Report: Company Codes

You can only check the company codes overview report in this step. Select Overview Report: Company Codes from the displayed list of activities options from the Choose Activity screen (Figure 11-1) and click the ⌷ Choose button at the bottom right of the screen. The Checking the Company Codes screen appears, displaying the properties of each company code as shown in in Figure 11-5.

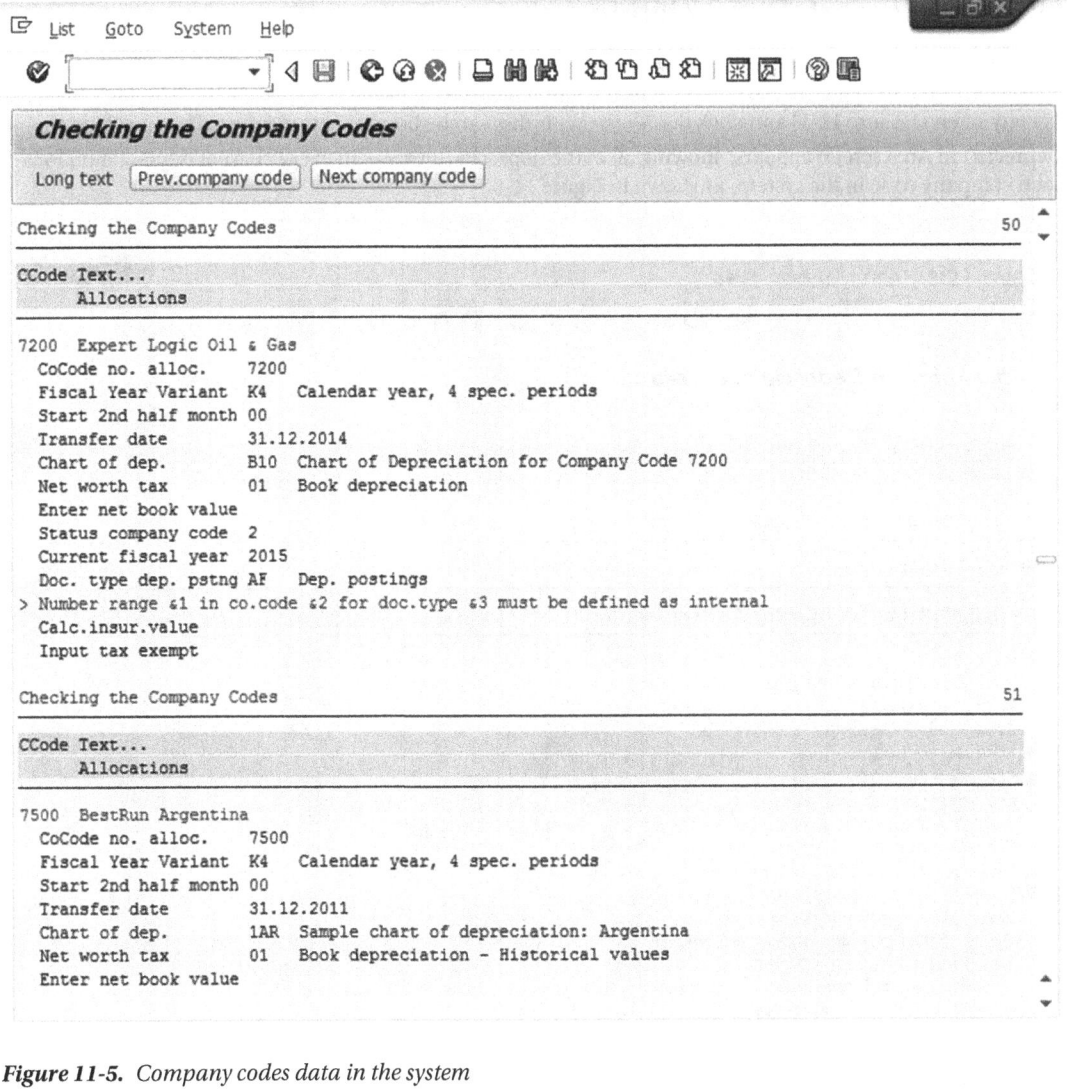

Figure 11-5. Company codes data in the system

■ **Note** You can access any company code in the system using the Prev.company code and Next company code buttons at the top of the screen.

The next step is to return to the Choose activity screen to execute the next report.

Overview Report: Depreciation Area

In this step you will only check the company code that you created in Chapter 1. To check the depreciation areas in the system, select the Overview Report: Depreciation Area from the list of activities on the Choose Activity screen (Figure 11-1) and click the ![Choose] button at the bottom of the screen. The Checking the Depreciation Area screen appears, showing all of the depreciation areas in every chart of depreciation for each company code in the system, as shown in Figure 11-6.

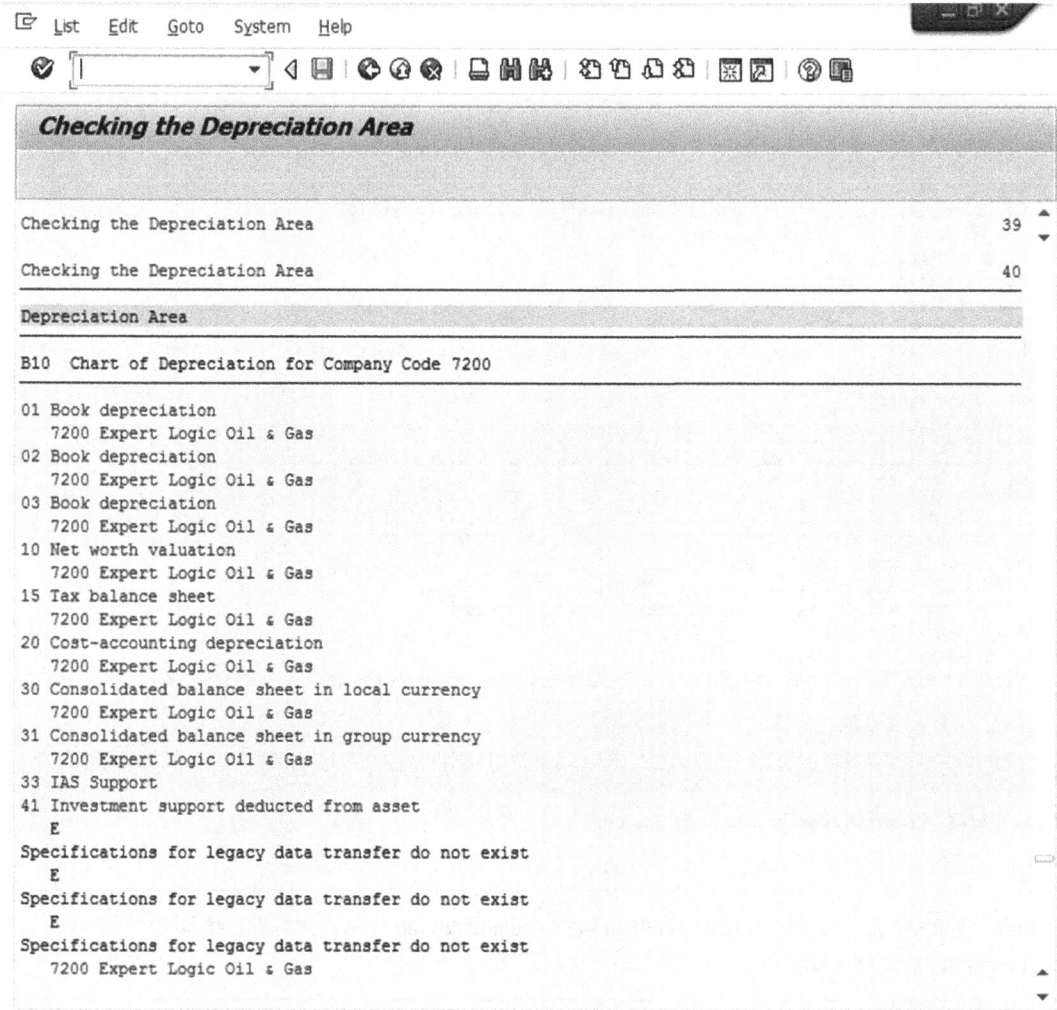

Figure 11-6. *The list of depreciation areas in each chart of depreciation for each company code in the system*

The next step is to return to the Choose activity screen to execute the next report.

Consistency Report: Asset G/L Accounts

The next step in this activity is to check the G/L accounts for asset. You can do this by generating a consistency report for asset G/L accounts. To execute a consistency report for asset G/L accounts, select the Consistency Report: Asset G/L Accounts from the displayed list of activities (Figure 11-1) and click the `Q Choose` button at the bottom right of the screen. The FI-AA: Customizing consistency check for G/L accounts screen appears. Enter the company code (7200) for which you are generating the consistency report in the Company code field and click the Execute ⊕ button at the top left of the screen. The Document lines: Display messages screen pops up, displaying the chart of accounts existing in the specified company code and the accounts not existing in the company code in question, as shown in Figure 11-7.

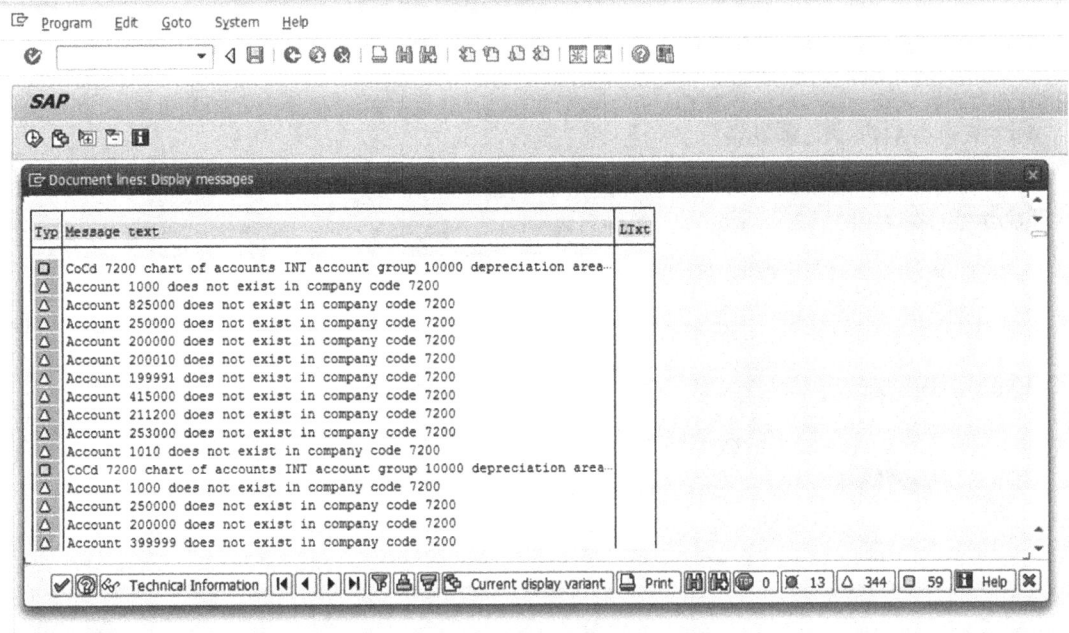

Figure 11-7. *The chart of accounts existing in the your company code and the accounts not existing in the same company code*

The final step is to return to the Choose activity screen to execute the next report

Consistency Report: FI-AA Customizing

The final step in the Check Consistency test is to perform a consistency report for the customizing activities in FI-AA.

To carry out a consistency report for FI-AA customizing, select the Consistency Report: FI-AA from the displayed list of activities (Figure 11-1) and click the `Q Choose` button at the bottom right side of the screen. The Consistency Check Report FI-AA Customizing screen appears with a list of the consistency check report, showing the status of each step. The consistency check status report shows whether errors occurred or no errors occurred in each step, as shown in Figure 11-8.

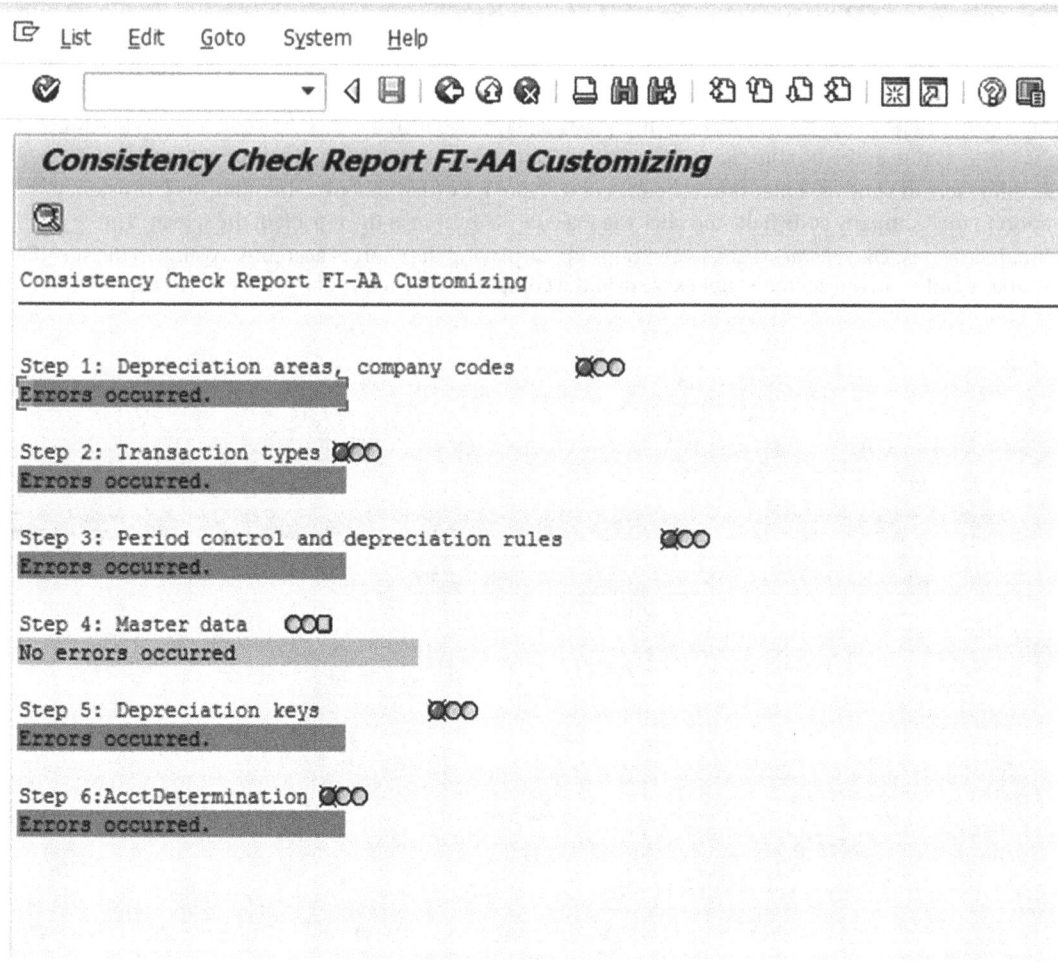

Figure 11-8. *A consistency check status report for each customizing step in FI-AA*

You can investigate the errors that occurred in each step by displaying error messages in another screen. To do this, select Errors occurred for the step that you want to investigate. You will investigate all steps that show that error occurred, beginning with the first one. Select the error (Step 1) and click the Details 🔍 button at the top left of the screen. The Step 001: Display messages screen pops up, displaying the list of errors that occurred in Step 1: Depreciation Area, company codes, as shown in Figure 11-9.

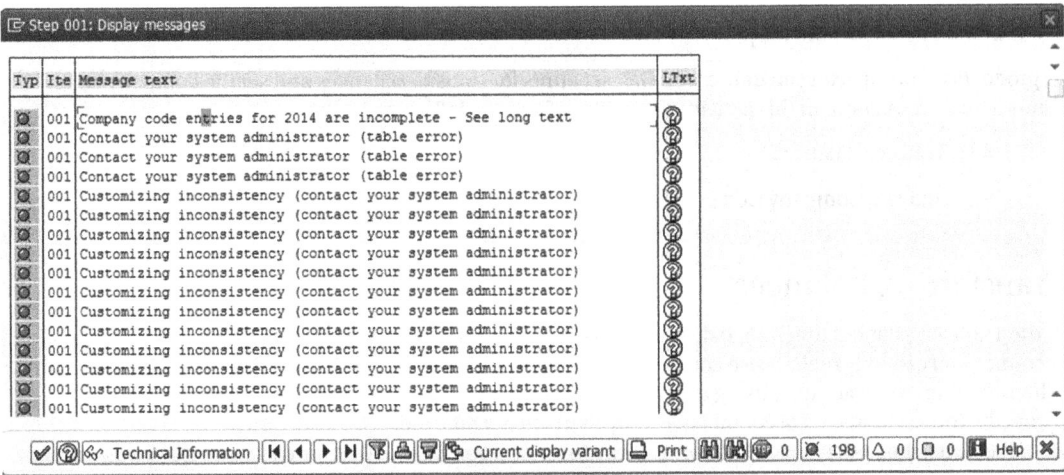

Figure 11-9. *The list of errors that occurred in Step 1: Depreciation Area, Company codes*

If you are not sure of the steps to take to resolve the errors that occurred in the customizing steps displayed, click each of the Long text ⑨ icons to the right of the errors to display the Performance Assistant. For example, when you click the Long text ⑨ icon to the "Company code entries for 2014 are incomplete – See long text" error displayed on the screen, the Performance Assistant screen appears as shown in Figure 11-10, giving you instructions on how to resolve the error.

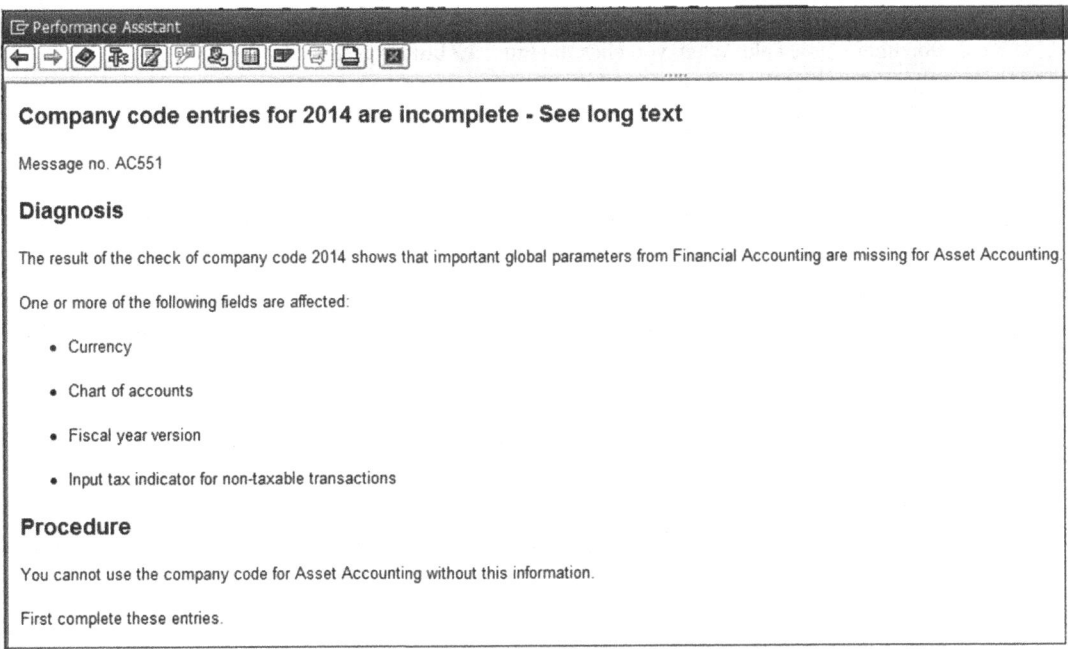

Figure 11-10. *The Performance Assistant specifying the error message number, diagnosis, and procedure that you can take to resolve the error that occurred*

Production Startup

In production startup, you can determine G/L accounts for transfer balances and set the company code status to live production. In this activity, you will perform the following steps:

- Transfer Balances
- Activate Company Code

Transferring Balances

In the Transfer balances function, balances can be posted to G/L accounts that are defined as reconciliation accounts. You can only make these corrections as long as the company code is not live for Asset Accounting. When you transfer legacy data using a legacy asset transaction, the corresponding balances of the reconciliation accounts in FI (Financial Accounting) are not affected.

The transfer of asset data to the component Asset Accounting (FI-AA) from a legacy system using the legacy data transfer transaction has no influence on the corresponding reconciliation accounts in SAP Financial Accounting. This means that there is no automatic creation and reconciliation of balances. The system does not automatically perform account reconciliation balances. Instead, reconciliation of balances is conducted manually:

1. To proceed to the initial screen where you can perform transfer balance, use this men path: Financial Accounting (New) ➤ Asset Accounting ➤ Preparing for Production Startup ➤ Transfer Balances. The Enter Transfer Posting: Initial Screen appears. The system automatically updates the document date and the posting date using the current date, and the period using the accounting period.

2. Enter the company code (7200) you use to make your transfer balances in the Company Code field and enter the document type (AA – Asset Posting) in the Document Type field. When you click the Enter ✅ button at the top left of the screen, the Enter Transfer Posting: Transfer Data screen appears. This is the screen where you will assign the G/L accounts for the transfer of balances.

3. Specify the G/L account that you want to transfer balances.

4. Click the Enter ✅ button at the top left of the screen and save 💾 your settings.

▓ **Note**   You can copy balances from any suspense accounts to the FI-AA reconciliation accounts.

Activating Company Code

In this customizing step, you will activate the company code by setting the status to the live indicator (0) for the company code from the test phase (2) when you have completed all your legacy data transfer. The importance of setting your company code to live indicator is to ensure that the program that deletes test data did not delete data from live company codes.

▓ **Note**   Reconciliation accounts for FI are not affected by transfer of legacy data, it is therefore important to perform account balances reconciliation before you set your company code to live status after legacy data transfer.

To set company code status to live (production status), complete the following steps:

1. Use this menu path: Financial Accounting (New) ➤ Asset Accounting ➤ Preparing for Production Startup ➤ Activate Company Code. The Change View "FI-AA: Set status of the company code": Overview screen appears as shown in Figure 11-11.

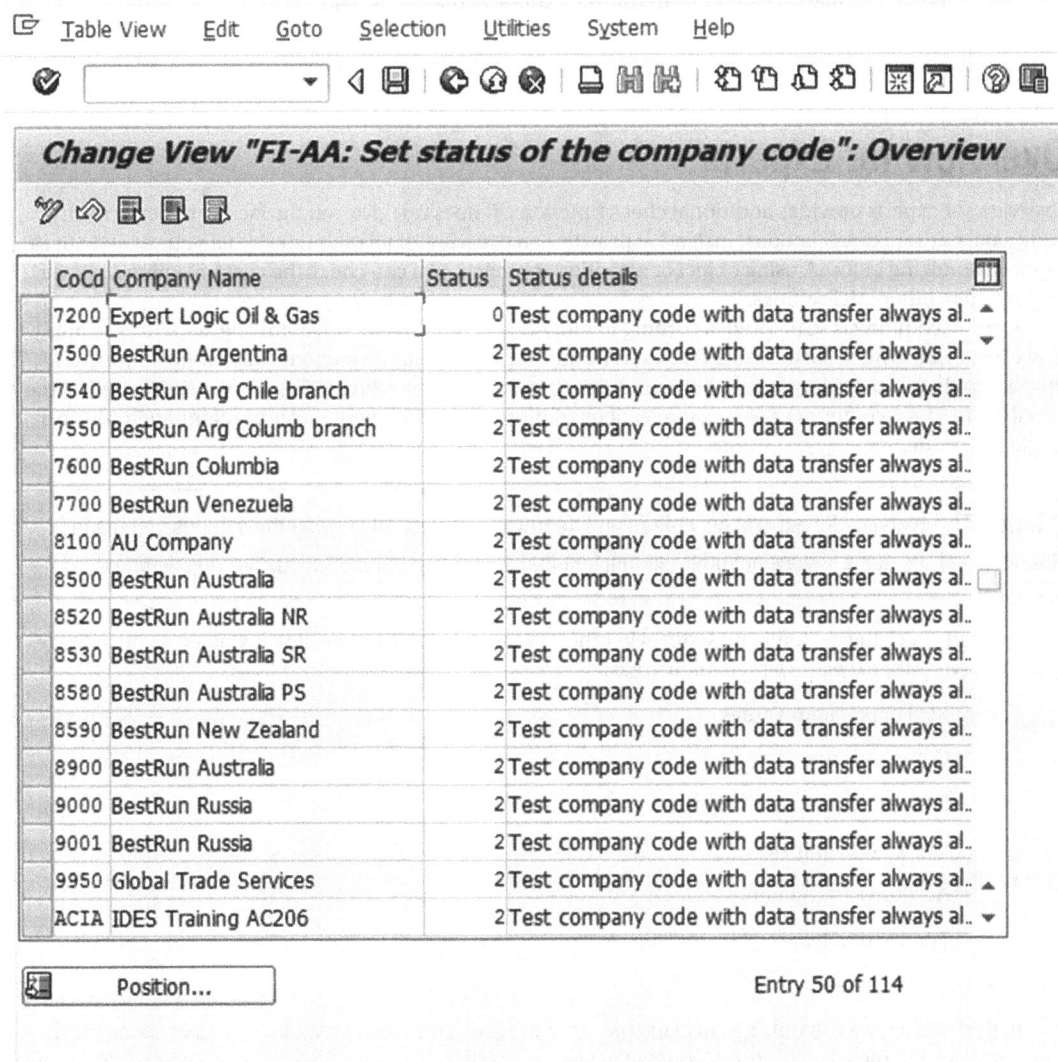

Figure 11-11. Setting the specification of the company code status to live (production status)

2.   Search for your company code (7200) using the [🔲 Position...] button at the bottom left of the screen.

3.   Specify the status for your company code by entering the status (0 – Asset data transfer completed) in the Status field. By setting the status to the live indicator (0), your company code is activated. You can access the list of standard status supplied by SAP in the system using the matchcode function.

4.   When you have entered the appropriate status in the status field for your company code, click the Enter ✅ button at the top left of the screen and save 💾 your settings.

Overview for Experts

Overview for experts provides additional check functions. It does not give you the facility to perform any additional customizing functions. Instead, it provides an overview of all of the steps that you carried out in when customizing in FI-AA using object or activities approach. You can check the customization that you performed in other IMG settings.

Asset Accounting is structured according to functions in SAP to make customizing steps easy to apply. However, because most customizing for Asset Accounting is structured systematically based on functions, this means that your organization's requirements are structured according to functions as portrayed by the functions in FI-AA component. For example, depreciation areas as a function can be maintained within a single IMG node.

▪ **Note**   The overview for experts only offers an integrated approach of viewing the settings you made in other customizing steps. It does not offer the function that allows you to perform customizing settings.

You can check the customizing settings in other places in FI-AA for the following objects and activities in the Overview for experts: Depreciation areas:

- Real depreciation areas
- Company code
- Depreciation areas of company codes
- Legacy data transfer
- Account assignments
- Transaction types
- Asset classes

In this activity, we will only be checking the settings for depreciation areas and company code settings. You can check the remaining settings yourself in your spare time. The steps for checking customizing activity is the same.

Checking Depreciation Areas Settings

Perform the following steps to check depreciation areas settings using the expert overview approach:

1. Use this menu path: Financial Accounting (New) ➤ Asset Accounting ➤ Overview for Experts ➤ Check Depreciation Areas. The Display View "Chart of depreciation": Overview screen appears as shown in Figure 11-12.

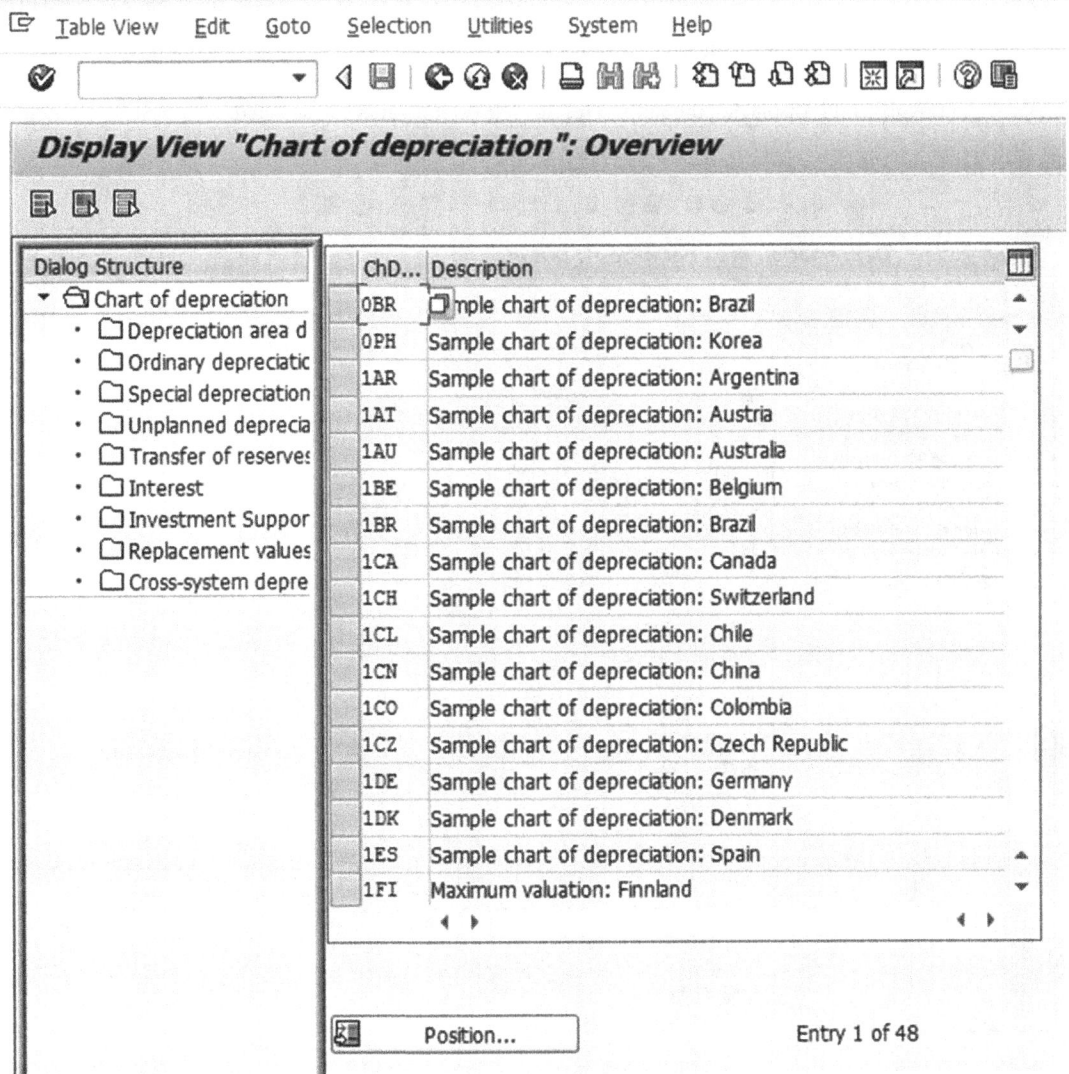

Figure 11-12. The list of chart of depreciation that you can check

2. You will notice that the list of objects that you can check in the chart of depreciation are displayed in the Dialog Structure on the left pane of the screen. Search for your chart of depreciation (B10) using the [⊞ Position...] button at the bottom left of the screen. Select your chart of depreciation (B10) from the displayed list of chart of depreciation and double click the Depreciation area definition folder on the left pane of the screen. The Display View "Depreciation area definition": Overview screen appears, displaying the list of depreciation areas in your chart of depreciation on the right side of the screen.

3. To display the settings for each depreciation, Select the depreciation area you are displaying from the displayed list and click the Details 🔍 button at the top left of the screen. The Display View "Depreciation area definition": Details screen appears (Figure 11-13) displaying the settings for the depreciation area you selected.

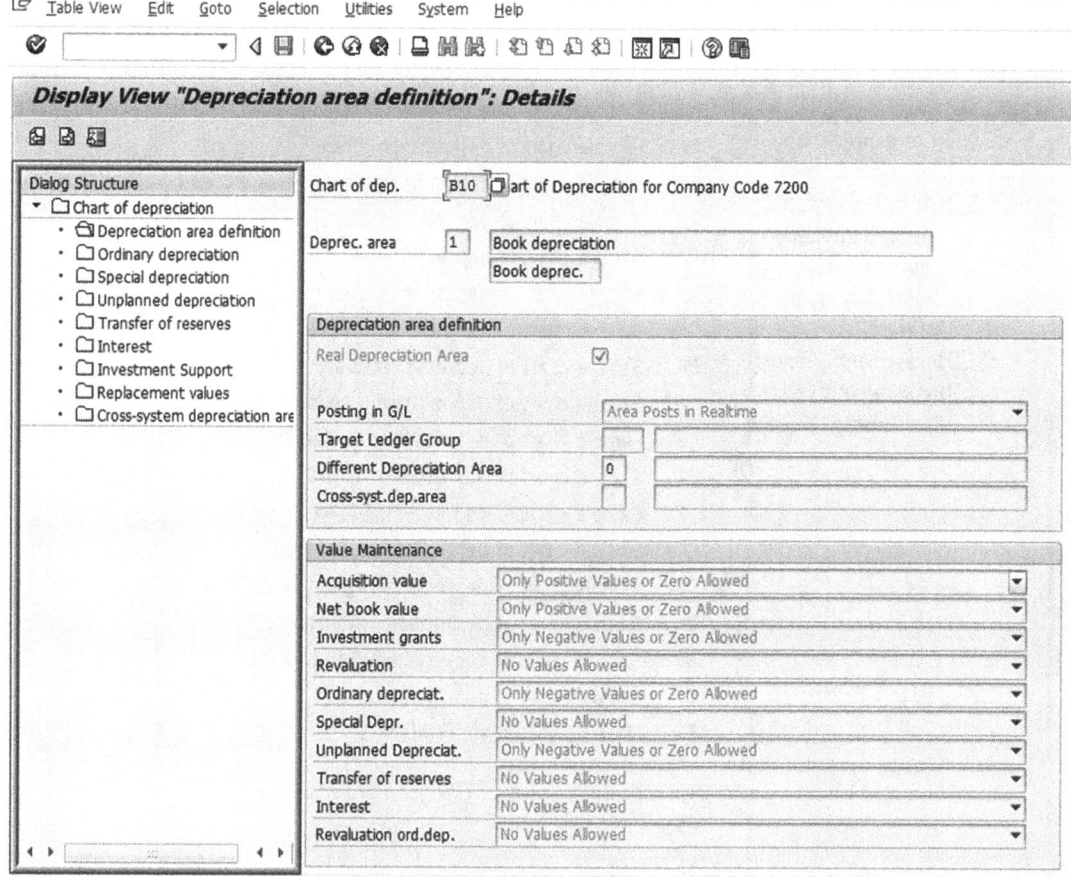

Figure 11-13. *The screen displaying the selected depreciation area*

You can repeat this process for the remaining objects on the Dialog Structure (such as Special depreciation, Unplanned depreciation, Transfer of reserves, Interest, Investment Support, Replacement Values, and Cross-system depreciation area).

Checking Company Code Settings

To check the customizing settings for company codes, you can follow these steps:

1. Use this menu path: Financial Accounting (New) ➤ Asset Accounting ➤
    Preparing for Production Startup ➤ Activate Company Code. The Display View
    "Company codes": Overview screen appears as shown in Figure 11-14.

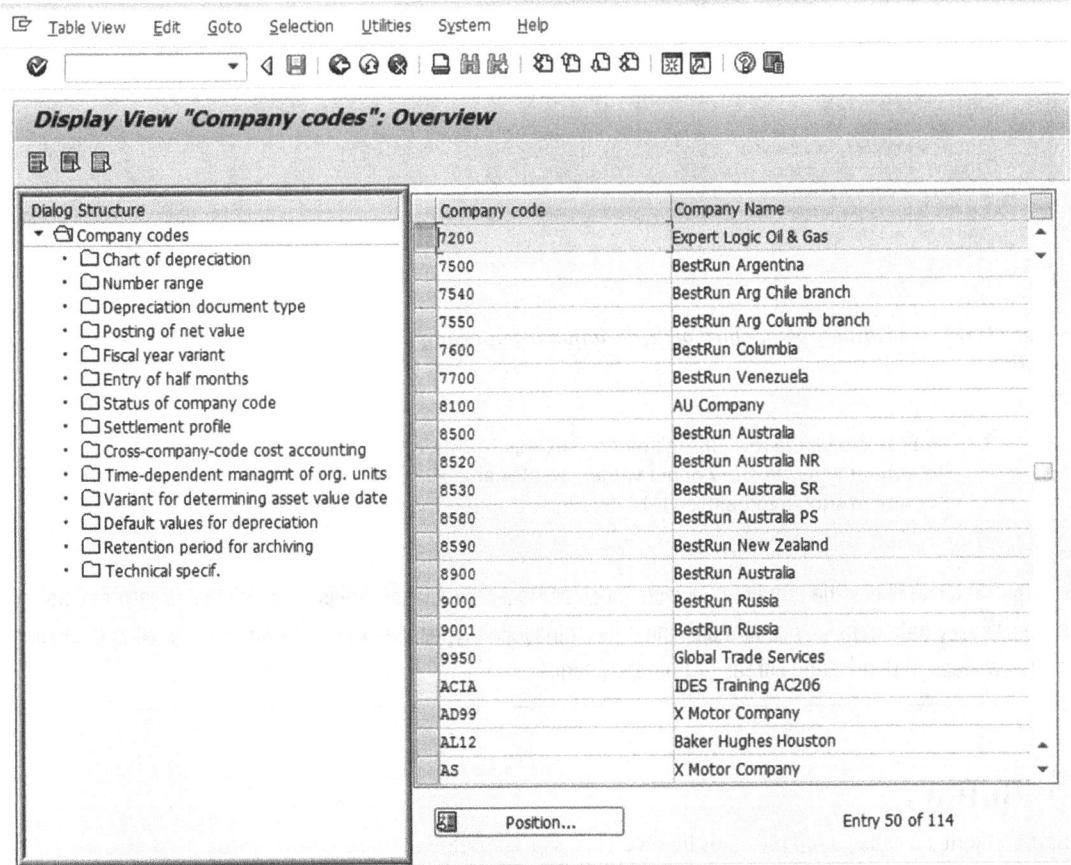

Figure 11-14. *The list of company codes in the Expert overview*

2. Select your company code from the list of the displayed company codes on the
    left pane of the screen and double click the item for which you want to check the
    settings. The Display View "Chart of depreciation": Overview screen appears as
    shown in Figure 11-15, displaying your company code chart of depreciation.

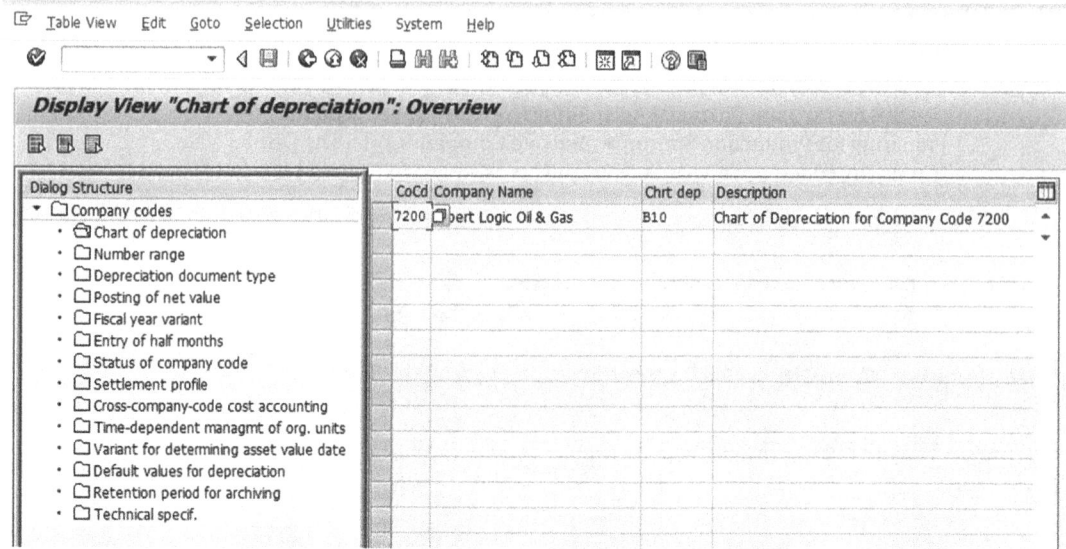

Figure 11-15. *The display of the chart of depreciation in your company code using the Expert overview function*

3. You can check the remaining objects (such as Number range, Depreciation document types, Posting of net value, Fiscal year variant, etc.) on the left pane of the screen shown in Figure 11-14, by repeating step 2 for each one.

■ **Tip**   You can check the remaining objects (such as Real depreciation areas, Depreciation areas of company codes, Legacy data transfer, Account assignments, Transaction types, and Asset classes) by following the Expert overview steps in Depreciation areas or Company codes.

Summary

In this chapter, we discussed the steps involved in the preparation of production startup. We performed consistency checks of technical aspects of functional and corresponding customization. We carried out carried out consistency overview reports on asset classes, charts of depreciation, company codes, depreciation areas, asset G/L accounts, and FI-AA customizing.

We also looked at the steps involved in production startup. You learned how to transfer balances and activate company codes in the production status.

Finally, we looked at the Expert overview to see how to display and check other customizing activities in FI-AA.

In the next chapter, we will be looking at how to execute a depreciation run, perform the revaluation of a balance sheet for asset fiscal year change and year end closing.

■ ■ ■

CHAPTER 12

Processing Periodic Programs

This chapter introduces you to the basic settings or the special programs you need to run in a number of applications within SAP ERP at the end of each fiscal year in order to ensure that adequate settings and processes relating to the appropriate applications for the following fiscal year is ready for you to work in. You will learn how to perform:

- Depreciation Runs
- Log for Posting Runs
- APC Values Posting
- Asset Fiscal Year Changes
- Year End Closing

Depreciation Run

Depreciation is part of periodic processing and it is executed at the company code level. Data relating to depreciation, such as capitalisation date, useful life, scrap value, value date, and so on are defined in each asset master record. Depreciation is run periodically to take care of the calculation of assets depreciation. Once a depreciation run is carried out, the system automatically post planned depreciation to the corresponding general ledger control accounts. To see how this works, we will post some external asset acquisitions.

Posting External Asset Acquisitions

In this section we will post some external asset acquisitions that you will be applying to you're the depreciation run in the next section. To post external asset acquisitions, complete the following steps:

1. Using Transaction Code F-90, post some backdated external asset acquisitions. The Acquisition from purchase w. vendor: Header Data screen is displayed.

2. Enter the information in Table 12-1 in the screen:

Table 12-1. *Data to post backdated external asset acquisitions*

Fields	Values	Descriptions
Document date	01.01.2015	Enter a backdated document (at least three months back) in this field.
Type	KR	The document type is defaulted by the system.
Company Code	7200	Enter your Company code here.
Posting date	01.01.2015	Use the same date as your document date.
Currency/Rate	GBP	This is defaulted by the system using the company code local currency. You can change this by using overwriting the field content.
PstKy	31	Posting key for Credit Vendor—this will allow the system to post values to the appropriate GL accounts.
Account	100544	Because this transaction is an external acquisition, using the matchcode enter a vendor's account in this field.

3. Click the Enter ✅ button at the top left of the screen. Then Enter Vendor invoice: Add Vendor item screen appears.

4. Using information in Table 12-2, enter data in this screen.

Table 12-2. *Data to post backdated external asset acquisitions -2*

Fields	Values	Descriptions
Amount	200000	Enter asset acquisition amount in this field.
Calculate tax	Select	When you activate the Calculate tax checkbox, the system will carry out tax calculation from the Amount posted using the specified tax code.
Text	Machine-Y	Enter a short text describing your asset.
Bline Date	01.01.2015	The baseline date is defaulted by the system as the posting date.
PstKy	70	Debit Asset—this will allow the system to post values to the appropriate GL accounts.
Account	3000-0	Enter the Asset class that this asset belongs to in this field. This will enable the system to place your asset in the appropriate asset class group.
TType	100	Transaction Type—external asset acquisition

5. Click the Enter ✅ button at the top left of the screen. This will take you to the next screen.

6. Using the data in Table 12-3, update this screen.

Table 12-3. *Data to post backdated external asset acquisitions*

Fields	Value	Description
Amount	*	By entering this sign in this field, the system will copy the amount from the previous screen into this field. It is also possible to enter the amount in this field.
Tax Code	B1	This is the tax code for input tax. The system will apply this tax code in the calculation of the tax on the asset acquisition amount.

7. Click the Enter ✅ button at the top left of the screen. You will notice that the asset amount you entered in the previous screen is copied into the amount field.

8. On the menu bar, select Document at the top left of the screen, and select Simulation from the list of the dropdown menu. The Enter Vendor invoice: Display Overview screen is displayed showing the line items of your entries.

9. Click the Post 🖫 button at the top left of the screen to post your entries.

■ **Tip** Using your discretion, post more APC (Acquisition and Production Costs).

The next step in this activity is to perform a depreciation run.

Depreciation Posting Run

By executing a depreciation run, the system will post the different depreciations calculated and relayed interests to the appropriate G/L accounts in FI or cost accounting. It is recommended that you first perform a test run before carrying out an actual run.

1. You can perform a depreciation posting run, using this menu path: Accounting ➤ Financial Accounting ➤ Fixed Assets ➤ Periodic Processing ➤ Depreciation run ➤ Execute. The Depreciation Posting Run screen appears. This is the screen where you perform depreciation posting run.

2. Update the Depreciation Posting Run screen using the data in Table 12-4.

Table 12-4. *The data to update the Depreciation Posting Run screen*

Fields	Values	Descriptions
Company Code	7200	Enter the Company Code from which you want to generate your report.
Fiscal Year	2015	Our company code accounting year. This is usually 12 months.
Posting period	01	Posting period is normally 1–12 months when posting transaction to G/L. The system will execute depreciation posting run for the period you specify here.
Planned posting run	Select	The system automatically defaults the radio button. This function allows planned depreciation to be posted.
List assets	Select	In order for the system to display assets list, select this checkbox.
Test Run	Select	The system normally selects Test Run checkbox as a default. When executing Depreciation Posting Run, it is advisable to firm perform a test run before performing a productive run. This will enable you to spot any error before actually performing a productive run that will post depreciation to the G/L accounts.

■ **Note**   The current posting period for the company you are using for this exercise is 01 (January). The fiscal year is 1st January 2015 to 31st December 2015.

3. Click the Execute ⊕ button at the top left of the screen in order to perform the Depreciation Posting Run. The Limitation online screen pops up with the message "Online processing is limited to approx. 1000 assets." relating to the Depreciation Posting Run.

4. Choose the ⌐ Yes ⌐ button at the bottom left of the screen. The Depreciation Posting Run for Company Code 7200 screen appears as shown in Figure 12-1.

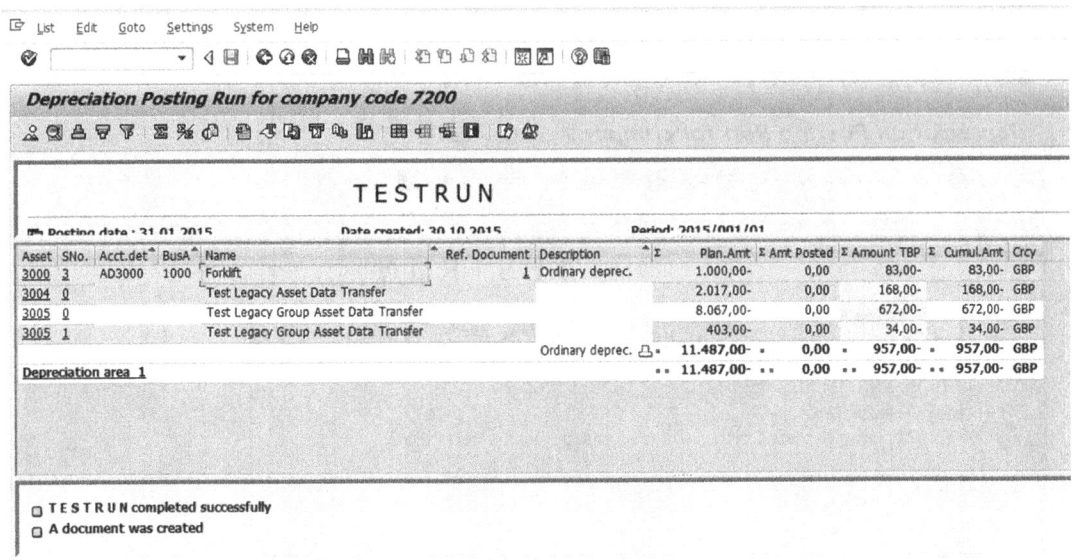

Figure 12-1. *Depreciation Posting Run in Test mode*

■ **Note**   This message is only displayed in the test run and not in the productive run, because the productive run is executed in the background session.

You may encounter problems when executing a depreciation posting run if you skip a period in a posting circle during a depreciation posting test run. The system will issue an error message at the bottom of the screen that "TESTRUN was terminated. Refer to the error log." and a warning message that No documents were created in this run". If this is the case, you will need to investigate the reason why the error occurred. You can do this by clicking the Error List (F7) ⚙ Button at the top right of the screen to trace the error. Document lines: Display Messages screen pops up with a list of the likely reasons why the error(s) occurred as shown in Figure 12-2.

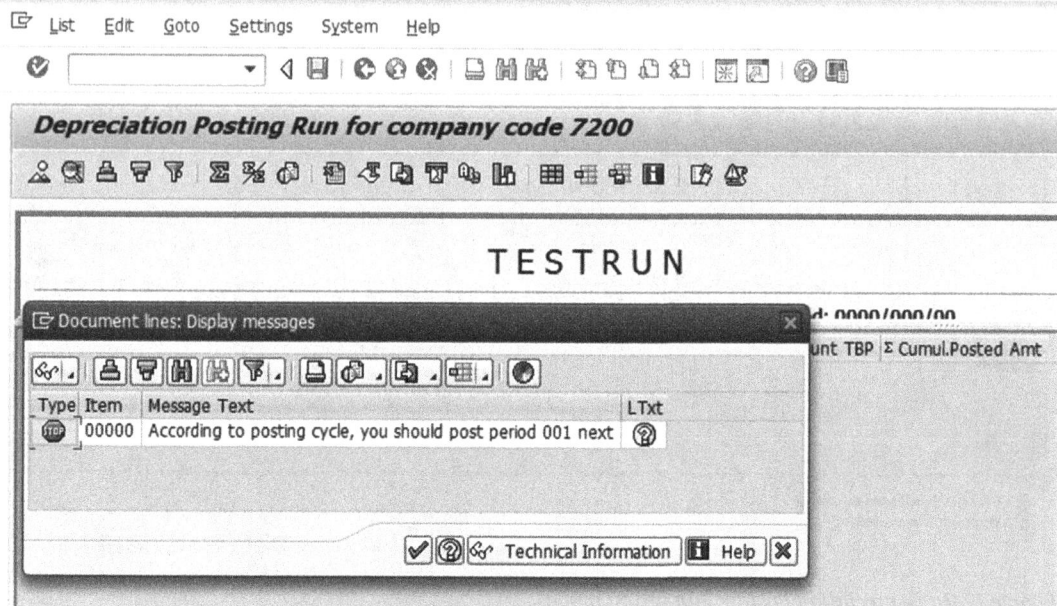

Figure 12-2. *Document line displaying the error that has occurred in your depreciation posting run*

5. From the displayed message, it is obvious that a posting period is skipped. Click the Enter ☑ button at the bottom of the screen and click the Back 🔙 button at the top of the screen to return to the Depreciation Posting Run screen.

6. On the Depreciation Posting Run screen, enter the skipped posting period – 001 in the Posting Period field and execute your depreciation post run by clicking the Execute ⊕ button at the top left of the screen.

7. As your test run has completed successfully, click the Back 🔙 button to return to the Depreciation Posting Run screen in order to execute a Depreciation Posting Run in productive mode.

8. On the Depreciation Posting Run screen, deactivate the Test Run checkbox on the Parameter for the test run section of the screen in order to run your depreciation in the productive mode. The next step is to execute in background processing.

9. On the menu bar, click Program at the top left of the screen and then click Execute in Background from the drop down menu. The Background Print Parameters screen is displayed.

> ▪ **Note** Depreciation posting runs often involve huge data processing, which may slow down the system response time. Hence, it is advisable to execute a Depreciation Posting Run while other processes are going on. Background processing allows you to automate routine tasks and at the same time optimize the use of computer resources.

10. Specify the Output device that you want to use for printing your work by updating the following field using the data in Table 12-5.

Table 12-5. *The data to update the Background Print Parameter screen*

Fields	Value	Description
Output Device	LP01	Enter the printer that you want to use for printing depreciation report.
Number of copies	1	This defaulted by the system. You can change the number of copies you want print.
Print all	Select	The Print All radio button is defaulted by the system. If you don't want to print all of the document, you can specify the exact page(s) you want to print using the Print from page.

11. Choose the Continue ☑ button to the right of the screen. The Information screen pops up specifying your print formatting setting as Formatting set to "X_65_132".

12. Click the Continue ☑ button at the bottom right of the screen. The Start Time screen pops up, as shown in Figure 12-3. On this screen you have several options to choose from based on how you want to print your work.

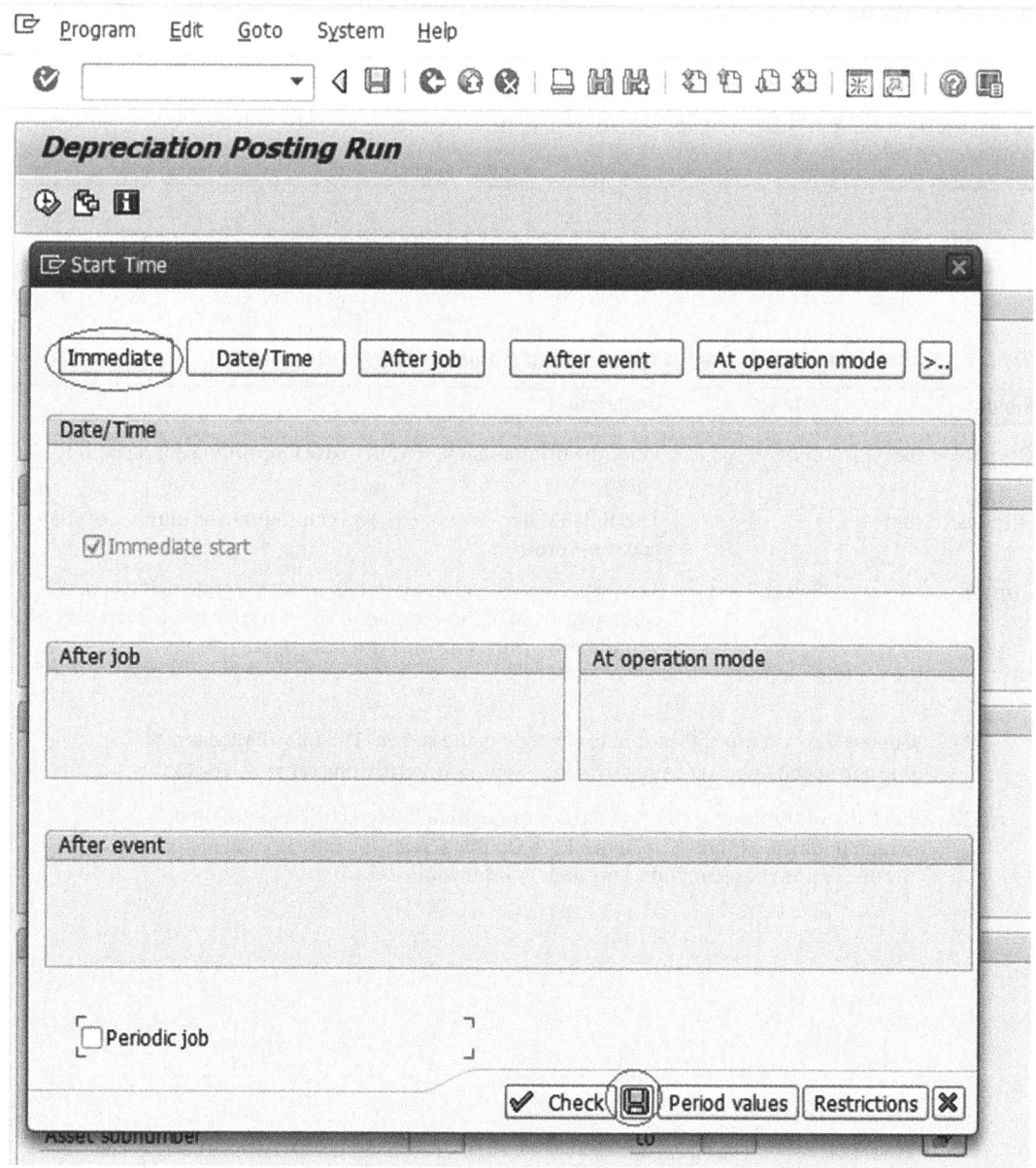

Figure 12-3. The screen where you specify the time that you want your print program to start

■ **Note**   The Date/Time button will allow you to run job at a later date/time; the After job button will allow to run a job after a specific job, and so on.

13. Click the [Immediate] button from the available options on the top of the screen for print to start immediately and click the Save 🖫 button at the bottom right of the screen. The system will notify you at the status bar at the bottom of the screen that "Background job was scheduled for program RAPOST2000."

14. Repeat the steps for the remaining periods

Job Overview

Let's view the status of the depreciation run.

1. On the depreciation Run screen go to the menu bar and follow the menu path: System ➤ Services ➤ Jobs ➤ Job overview or use transaction code (TC): SM37. The Simple Job Selection screen appears.

■ **Note**   System automatically defaults the Job name and user name.

---

2. Click the [⊕ Execute] button at the top left of the screen. The Job Overview screen appears displaying the list of print job in your print spooling as shown in Figure 12-4.

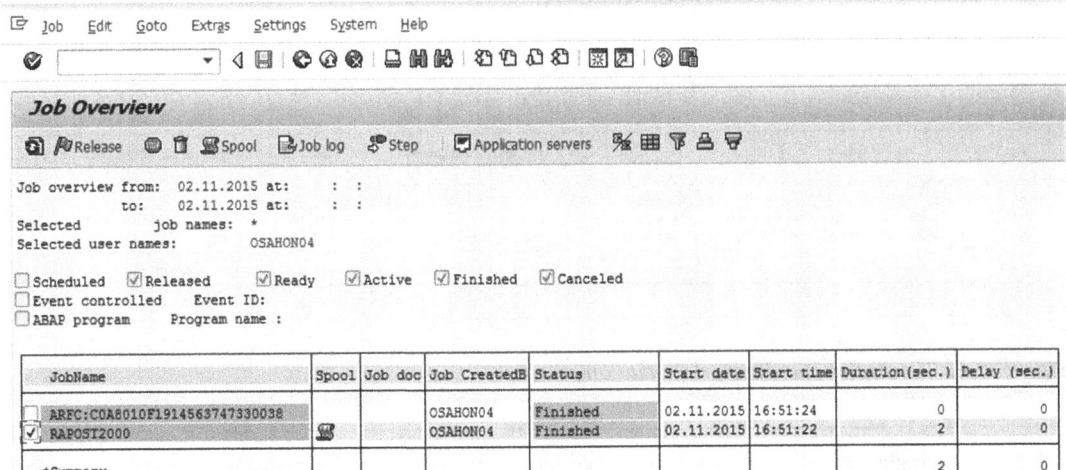

Figure 12-4. *The list of print jobs in the spool request*

3. Select the last item on the joblist (RAPOST2000) by selecting its checkbox and choose [🖫 Spool] button at the top left of the screen to send spool request to output controller. The Output Controller: List of Spool Requests screen appears.

4. Select the appropriate spool number from the list of spool requests displayed using the most recent data the spool request was generated, as shown in Figure 12-5.

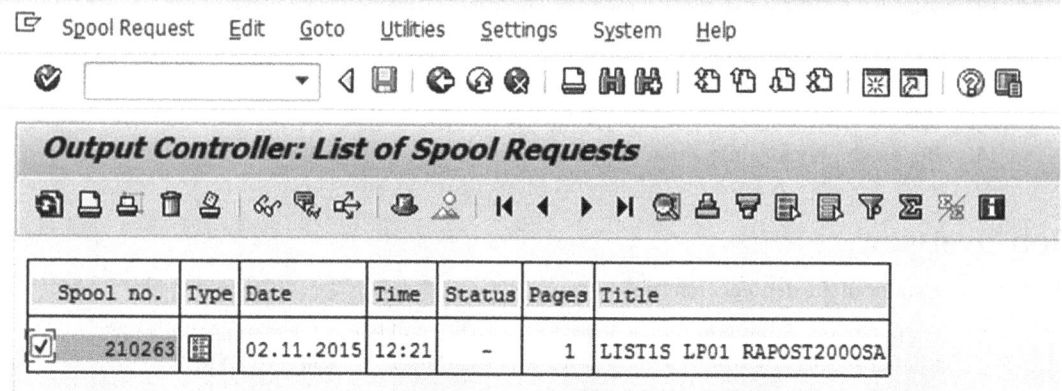

Figure 12-5. *The list of items in the spool request*

5. To display the posting period in question and the list of depreciation per asset for the period, click the Display content (F6) 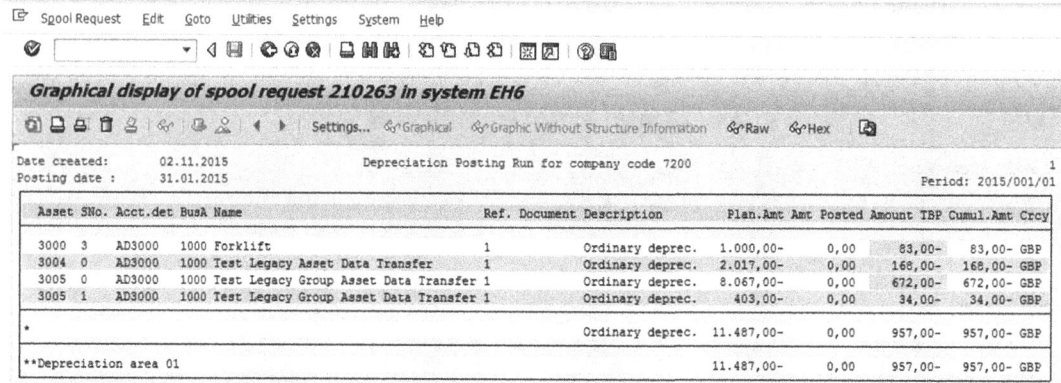 button at the top left of the screen. The Graphical display of spool request 210263 in system EH6 screen is displayed (Figure 12-6).

Figure 12-6. *The display of ordinary depreciation per asset*

■ **Note**   The system automatically displays the posting period and list of depreciation per asset as shown in Figure 12-6 above.

Log for Posting Run

The importance of executing a display log for the posting run for depreciation is that it allows you to display depreciation posted for a given period using the report RAPOST2000. The RAPOST2000 is a standard executable ABAP (Advanced Business Application Programming) report program supplied by SAP in SAP ERP.

This report allows you to further analyze details of depreciation and account assignment for each asset by accessing the ABLP log table created by the system during the depreciation run.

This report allows the system to access the ANLP log table that was created when you performed the depreciation posting run. ANLP is a standard table used for storing Asset Periodic Values data.

To perform a depreciation posting run, follow these steps:

1. Use this menu path: Accounting ➤ Financial Accounting ➤ Fixed Assets ➤ Periodic Processing ➤ Depreciation run ➤ Display Log. The Log of Posting Run screen appears.

2. Enter the data from Table 12-6.

***Table 12-6.** Data to update the log posting run screen*

Fields	Value	Description
Company Code	7200	Enter the company code in which you are performing the Log of Posting Run in this field.
Fiscal Year	2015	This is the fiscal year you want to display Log for depreciation.
Posting Period	001	The period to display log for depreciation for within a given fiscal year.
List assets	Select	By selecting this option, this allows you to display a list of assets as part of the display log for depreciation.

3. Click the Execute ⊕ button at the top left of the screen. The Log of Posting Run for company code 7200 appears showing the list of log for posting run depreciation for your company code as shown in Figure 12-7.

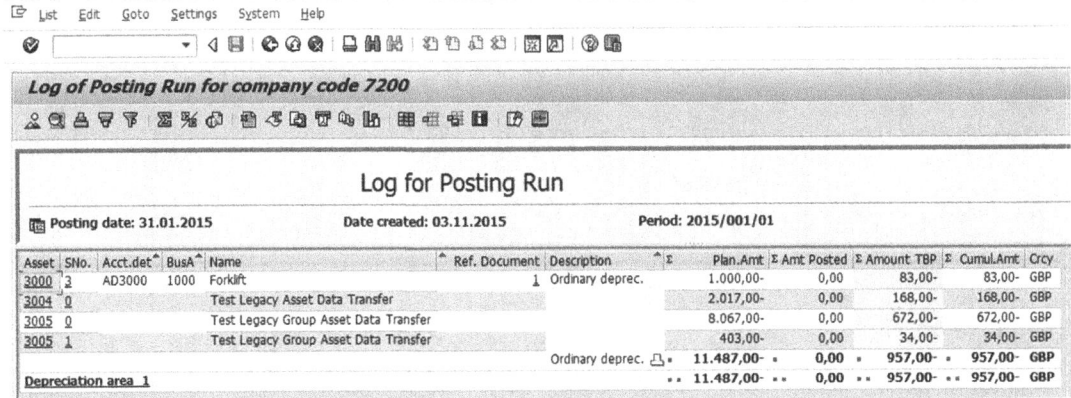

***Figure 12-7.** The screen displaying log of posting run for depreciation*

4. To go to the Asset Explorer containing the entire accounting document generated, you can double click on the Asset number on displayed on the screen.

APC Values Posting

Periodic asset posting program allows you to post APC values of depreciation areas that you assigned to the chart of depreciation periodically. The benefit of this program is that it allows the system to post the values of depreciation areas directly to the general ledger in FI, thereby avoiding the use of batch-input session which is now discontinued. During transaction posting, it is possible to update the values of depreciation areas to a ledger. The system can update values directly from other depreciation areas including APC values in the depreciation areas according to the specifications you made in your customizing definition.

■ **Note**   Before performing APC Values Posting make sure that:

- The depreciation area is set to post APC and depreciation periodically to the general ledger in the chart of depreciation.

- Account assignments are maintained for each depreciation area.

- A document type is specified for the periodic posting run.

You can perform APC value posting, using these steps:

1. Use this menu path: Accounting ➤ Financial Accounting ➤ Fixed Assets ➤ Periodic Processing ➤ APC Values Posting. The Periodic Asset Posting screen appears (Figure 12-8).

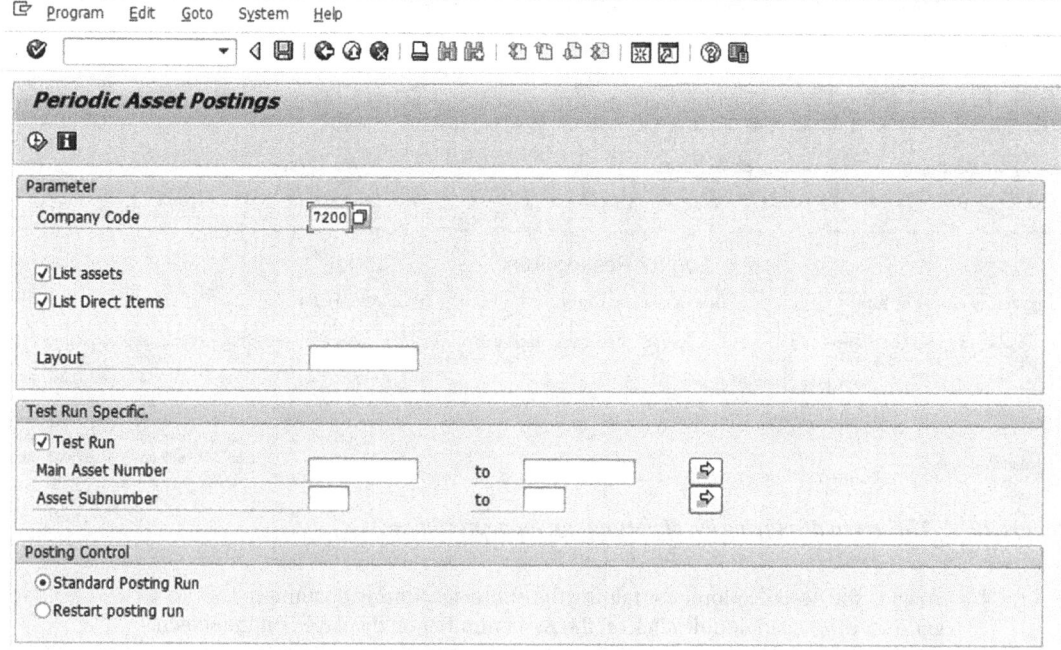

Figure 12-8.   *The screen where APC Values Posting is carried out*

2. Enter your company code (7200) in the Company Code field. This is the code that you will use for your APC values posting.

■ **Note**   You will notice that the following items are defaulted automatically by the system:

- List Assets

- List Direct Items

- Test Run

- Standard Posting Run

---

3. Click the Execute ⊕ button at the top left of the screen. The Limitation online screen appears, specifying the maximum asset you can process using test-run mode is limited to 1000 assets approximately.

4. Click the ⎣ Yes ⎦ button at the bottom right of the screen. This will take you to the list of APC Values in test-run mode.

5. The next step now is to carry out a productive APC Values Posting in the background mode. To do this you have to return to the Periodic Asset Postings screen by clicking the Back ↺ button at the top left of the screen. The Periodic Asset Postings screen appears.

6. Deactivate the Test run checkbox by removing the tick.

7. Select the ⎣ Program ⎦ button on the menu tab at the top left of the screen and then Execute in Background on the pull-down menu. The Background Print Parameters screen appears.

8. Enter the printer device in the Output Device field – LP01. The system will automatically defaults Number of Pages as 1.

9. Click the Continue ☑ button at the bottom right of the screen. The Information screen pops up showing the formatting set for your background print parameters.

10. Click the Continue ☑ button at the bottom right of the screen. The Start Time screen appears with various options you can apply to your background processing.

11. Click the ⎣Immediate⎦ button at the top left of the screen to schedule background job to start immediately.

12. Click the Save 💾 at the bottom right of the screen. The system will notify you on the status bar at the bottom of the screen that "Background job was scheduled for program RAPERB2000."

Asset Fiscal Year Change

Fiscal Year Change is nothing other than merely changing from the previous calendar year to the current calendar year. It is the opening of a new fiscal year in Asset Accounting for a given company code. When you perform a fiscal year change, the asset values balance from the old fiscal year are carried forward to the new fiscal year. Upon the completion of fiscal year change, you can post asset values both the new and the old fiscal year at the same time.

■ **Note**   The following are some things worth knowing about fiscal year change:

- When fiscal year changed is carried out, the cumulative asset values from the old fiscal year are carried forward to the new fiscal year.

- As long as the year-end closing has not been conducted, you can still make postings to the old fiscal year.

- When you start a report in the update mode assets values are carried forward from the old fiscal year to the new fiscal year. At this junction you can make postings to the new fiscal year.

- A fiscal year change is only carried out for the new fiscal year.

- You will not be able to post business transactions in the new fiscal year, not until you have performed fiscal year change.

- In SAP R/3 you have the option of opening up to a maximum of two fiscal years at any given point in time.

- You can only carry out fiscal year change in the last month of the old fiscal year.

- The asset values carried forward in the fiscal year affected by postings arising from the old fiscal year are automatically corrected by the system.

- The system performance can be enhanced by first performing fiscal year change in test run mode with assets not exceeding 1000 in the foreground, while productive fiscal year change is carried out in background processing.

- You may not necessarily need to carry out year-end closing in order to be able to carry out fiscal year change.

You can carry out fiscal year change, using this menu path: Accounting ➤ Financial Accounting ➤ Fixed Assets ➤ Periodic Processing ➤ Fiscal Year Change. The Asset fiscal year change screen appears (Figure 12-9).

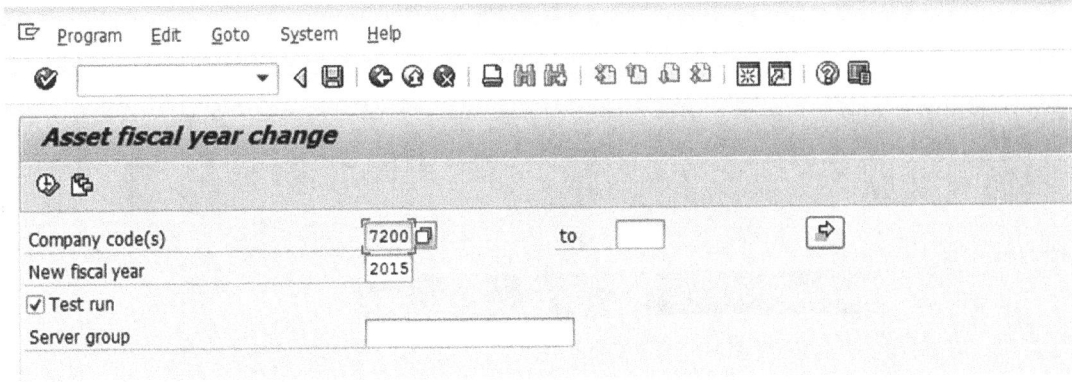

Figure 12-9. *Asset fiscal year change in test run mode*

We will go through a test run first and then make a productive fiscal year change.

Test Run

To complete a test run fiscal year change, complete the following steps:

1. On the Asset fiscal year change screen, update the following fields:

    - **Company code(s):** Enter your company code (7200) in this field. This is the company code you carry out fiscal year change.

    - **New fiscal year:** Enter the new fiscal year (2015) in this field. This is the year after the old (current) year.

    - **Test run:** Because it is recommended that you first carry out a test run fiscal year change, and then activate the test run checkbox. By activating this checkbox, this allows you to perform test run. Because the test run is activated, the system updates data in the database. This process can be run in the forefront or in background.

2. Click the Execute ⊕ button at the top left of the screen. The Limitation online screen pops up in Figure 12-10.

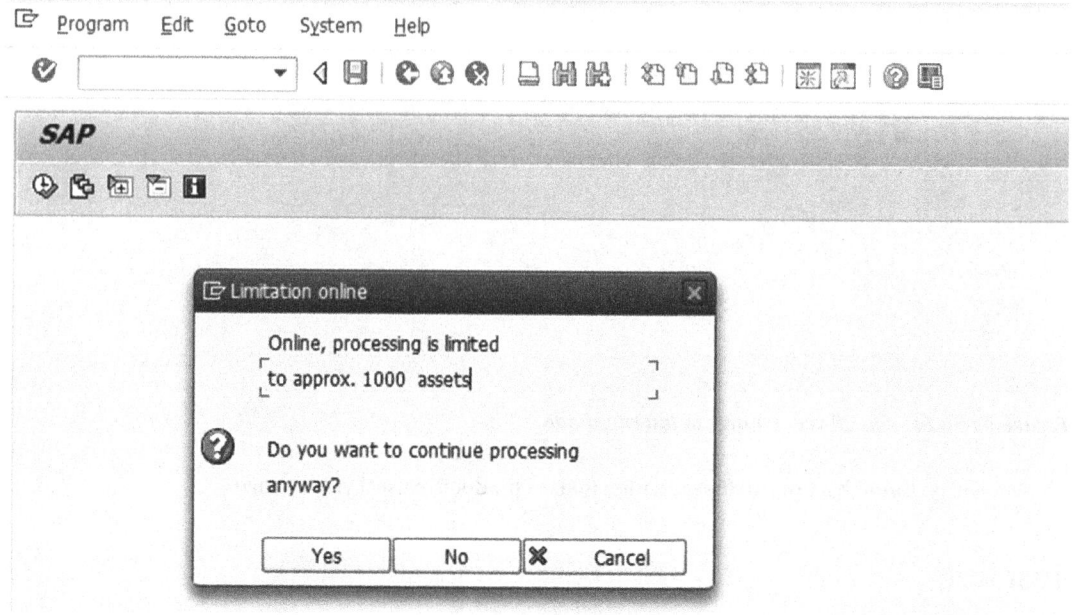

Figure 12-10. The limitation online screen specify the maximum assets you can process online simultaneously

3. Click the [Yes] button at the bottom left of the screen. The Asset fiscal year change screen appears displaying fiscal year change statistics in test version as shown in Figure 12-11.

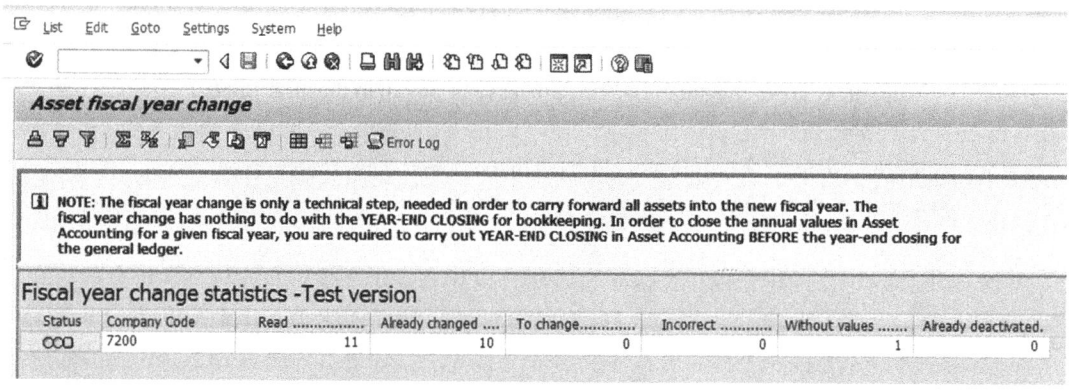

Figure 12-11. The fiscal year change statistical test version status

Productive Run

The next step is to carry out a productive fiscal year change in the background mode. You can use the following steps:

1. Return to the Asset fiscal year change screen by clicking the Back ↩ button at the top left of the screen. The Asset fiscal year screen appears.

2. Deactivate the Test run checkbox by removing the tick.

3. Complete the appropriate fields using the data in Table 12-7.

Table 12-7. *The data to update the Asset fiscal year change screen*

Fields	Value	Description
Company code(s0	7200	This is the code you want to change its fiscal year.
New fiscal year	2015	This is the year after current year.
Test run	blank	When deselect this checkbox, this allows you to perform productive run. This can be done in background processing.

4. On the menu bar at the top of the screen, click Program and select the Execute in Background on the pull down menu as depicted in Figure 12-12.

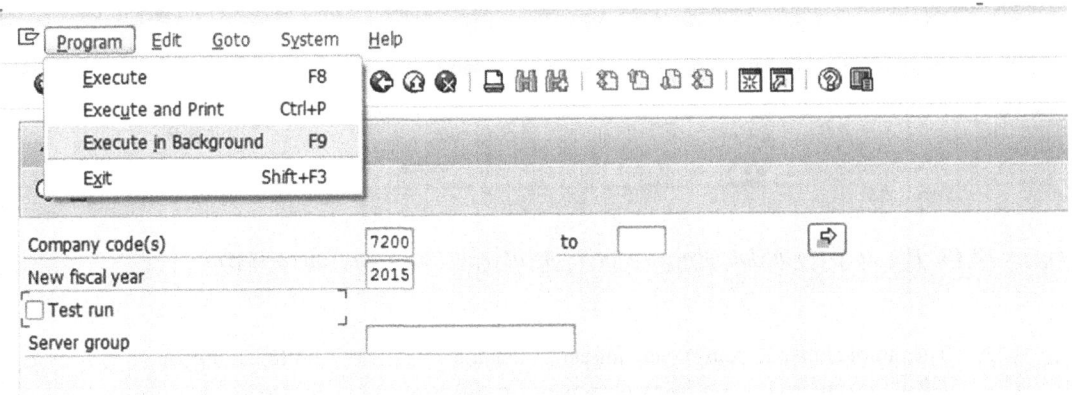

Figure 12-12. *Performing fiscal year change in backgrounding processing*

5. The Background Print Parameters screen appears. Enter the printer device in the Output Device field – LP01. The system will automatically default to the Number of Pages as 1.

6. Click the Continue ☑ button at the bottom right of the screen. The Information screen pops up showing the formatting set for your background print parameters.

7. Click the Continue ✅ button at the bottom right of the screen. The Start Time screen appears with various options that you can apply to your background processing.

8. Click the ⌷Immediate⌷ button at the top left of the screen to schedule background job to start immediately.

9. Click the Save 💾 button at the bottom right of the screen. The system will notify you on the status bar at the bottom of the screen that "Background job was scheduled for program RAJAWE00.

10. You can view the back ground job you have created for the fiscal year change you have carried out. You can do this using this menu path System ➤ Services ➤ Jobs ➤ Job overview as shown in Figure 12-13.

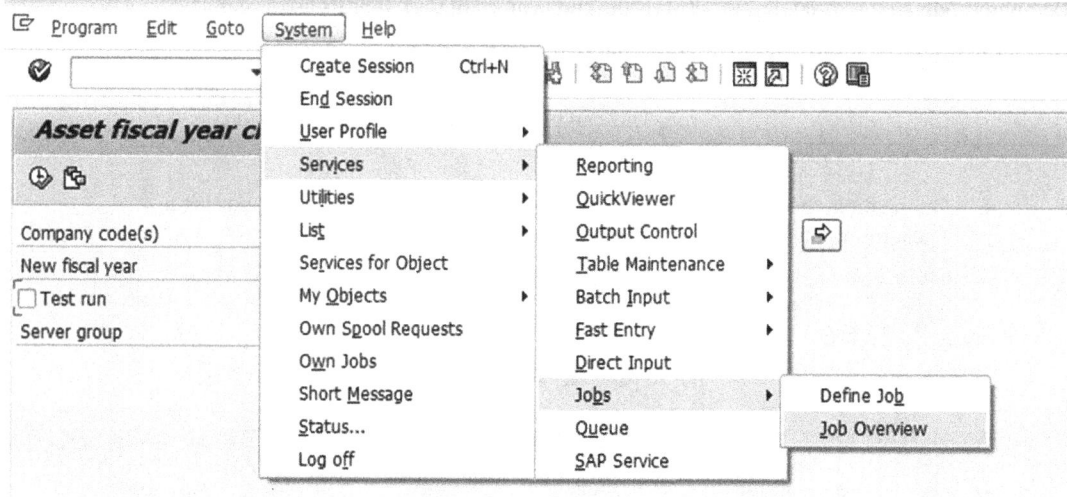

Figure 12-13. *How to get to the Job Overview for the fiscal year change that you carried out*

11. The Simple Job Selection screen appears. Click the ⌷⊕ Execute⌷ button at the top left of the screen. The Job Overview screen appears as shown in Figure 12-14.

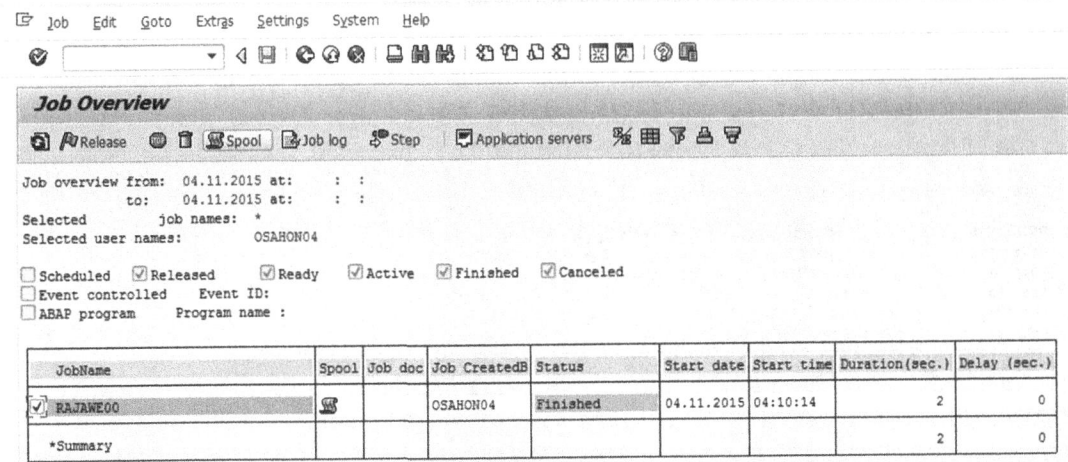

Figure 12-14. *The Job Overview screen showing the jobs in background processing*

12. Activate the job you want to send to spool request by making sure that the JobName checkbox is ticked. Click the 📇 Spool button at the top of the screen. The Output Controller: List of Spool Requests screen appears (Figure 12-15), showing the list of the spool request in the system.

Figure 12-15. *The list of spool request generated from the fiscal year change*

13. To identify the job you sent to the spool request, look for the most resent date and time from the displayed jobs, Activate Spool no. 211419 and click the 🔍 Display Contents (F6) button at the top of the screen to display print preview as shown in Figure 12-16.

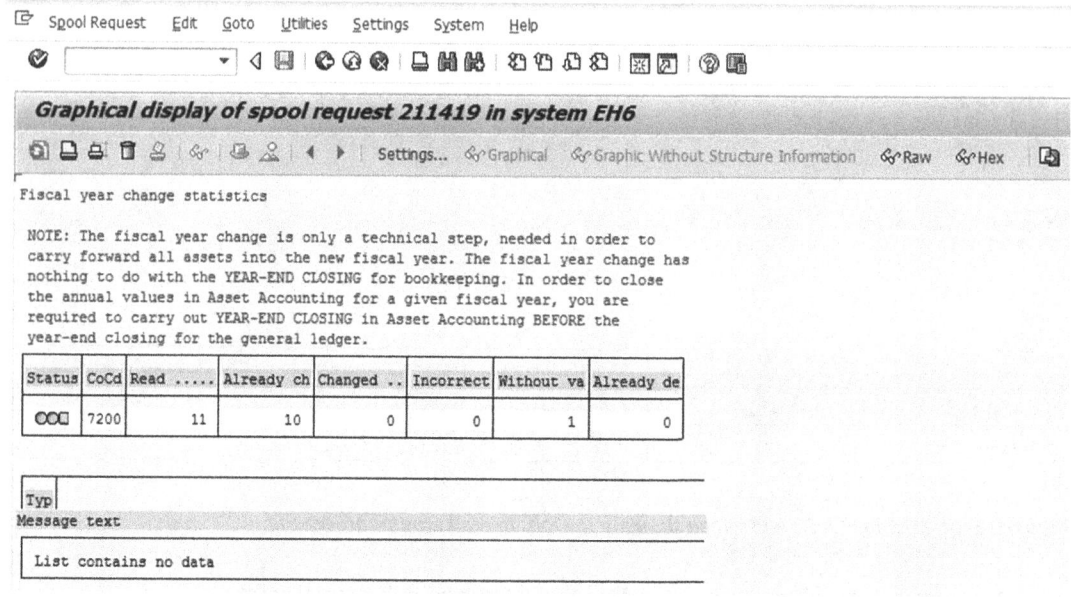

Figure 12-16. *The status of the fiscal year change carried out*

14. To print click the Print 🖨 button.

Year-End Closing

Asset Year End Closing is part of periodic processing in the SAP R/3 system for closing the fiscal year for at one or more company codes. In order to ensure that asset values included in the balance are accurate and not subsequently charged, it is absolutely imperative to perform a year-end closing. The main function of year-end closing is to block prior year values from be included in further depreciation calculations.

Generally, at the end of each fiscal year, it is compulsory that an enterprise produce a report of their performance in the form of a balance sheet, Profit and loss statement which is in line with the legal requirements of the country in which it operates. To generate an annual financial report including balance sheet, profit and loss statement, and notes to the accounts (the additional information relating to the financial statement) in the SAP R/3 system, you must first perform a year-end closing procedure.

▓ **Note**   Before executing a year-end closing, you must have completed the following:

- When a fiscal year is closed, it will no longer be possible to carryout modifications or post asset values in Asset Accounting for the closed fiscal year.

- It is recommended first of all to perform a year-end closing in Asset Accounting before you carry out the year-end closing in FI (General Ledger Accounting).

- You must carry out fiscal year change first before performing a year-end closing

- Before carry out a year-end closing, you must make sure that depreciations have been completely posted to the appropriate General Ledger in FI and that no error occurred during the depreciation calculation.

- You must make sure that all adjustments made to asset values have been completed and posted.

- You can only close the previous fiscal year. The current fiscal year must stay open.

Prior to year-end closing, the system carries out some checks make sure that:

- adjustments to asset value in the asset master record and depreciation calculations completed and accurate during posting.

- planned depreciation from automatic posting areas are posted accurately to the appropriate general ledger.

- depreciation balances that form part of period postings are posted completely and accurately to the appropriate general ledger.

- asset acquired during the period in question are fully capitalized. This check does not include assets under construction. It is therefore advisable in the asset class that you prevent this check being carried out on asset under construction.

In the event of any error, the system will display an error list and the reasons for those errors in the year-end closing log.

Performing Account Reconciliation

The account reconciliation function will allow the system to carry out the reconciliation of asset accounting balances with the corresponding GL accounts in FI.

▪ **Note**   Here are a few things you need to know before performing account reconciliation:

- Make sure that before performing this function, the last depreciation for the year has been completed and posted

- The report must be performed in background processing only

- Make sure that no asset posting is made while the report is running

- Make sure that the report is run before performing the year-end closing.

To carry out a year-end closing account reconciliation, complete these steps:

1. Use this menu path: Accounting ➤ Financial Accounting ➤ Fixed Assets ➤ Periodic Processing ➤ Year End Closing ➤ Account Reconciliation. The Reconcil. Program FI-AA <-> G/L: List of accounts showing differences screen appears. (Figure 12-17).

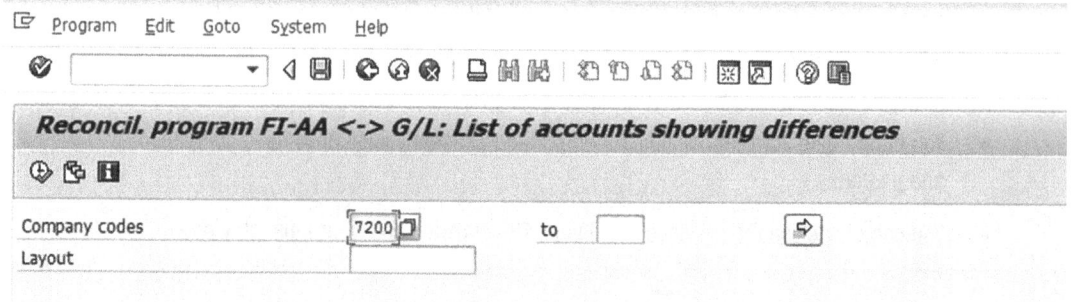

Figure 12-17. The screen where you execute the accounting reconciliation for year-end closing

2. Enter your company code (7200) in the company code field.

3. Select Program on the menu bar at the top left of the screen and then select Execute in Background on the pull-down menu. The Background Print Parameters screen appears.

4. Enter the printer device in the Output Device field – LP01. The system will automatically default to Number of Pages as 1.

5. Click the Continue ☑ button at the bottom right of the screen. The Information screen pops up, showing the formatting set for your background print parameters.

6. Click the Continue ☑ button at the bottom right of the screen. The Start Time screen appears with various options you can apply to your background processing.

7. Click the [Immediate] button at the top left of the screen to schedule background job to start immediately.

8. Click the Save ▦ at the bottom right of the screen. The system will notify you on the status bar at the bottom of the screen that "Background job was scheduled for program RAABST02".

9. To view the job created as a result of fiscal year change you have executed, on use the following menu path: System ➤ Services ➤ Jobs ➤ Job overview.

Executing a Year-End Closing

For the benefit of the financial statement, the execution of a year-end closing is important. A year-end closing allows the system to block the recalculation of depreciation values of the previous year fiscal and thus avoid the balanced values of fixed assets from the previous year fiscal year being changed.

Once you have executed a year-end closing in the SAP R/3 system, it will no longer be possible to post changed values within asset accounting as this function will block the closed year against a depreciation recalculation.

■ **Note** It is advisable that you first perform a test run once you are satisfied with your year-end closing before actually carrying out a productive year-end closing run. To carry out an actual productive year-end execution, repeat the process and deactivate the test run by removing the check in the test run checkbox.

Complete the following steps to execute a year-end closing:

1. Use this menu path: Accounting ➤ Financial Accounting ➤ Fixed Assets ➤ Periodic Processing ➤ Year End Closing ➤ Execute. The Year-end closing Asset Accounting screen appears (Figure 12-18).

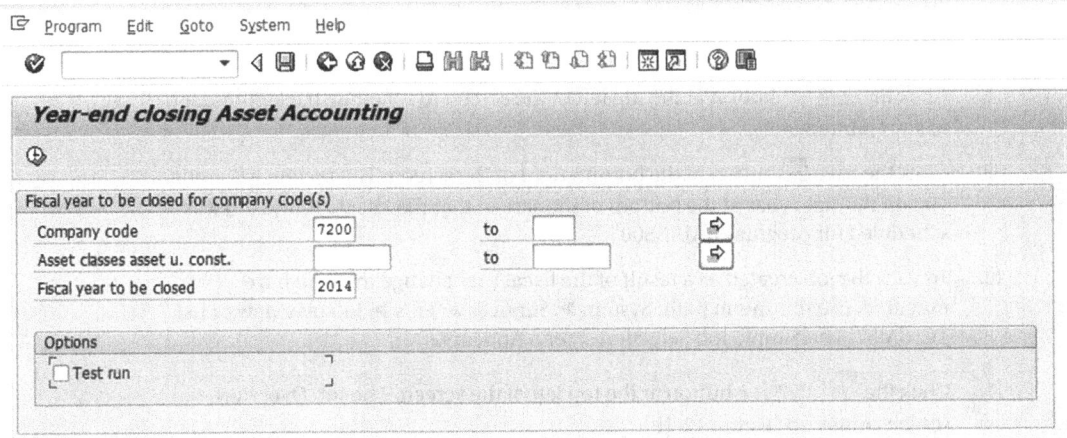

Figure 12-18. The screen where you execute a year-end closing

2. Using the data in Table 12-8, update your screen.

Table 12-8. The data to update the year-end closing screen

Fields	Value	Description
Company code(s0	C900	This is the code you want to execute the year-end closing.
Fiscal year to be changed	2014	The year that you are closing.
Test run	Blank	When you deactivate this checkbox, this allows you to perform a productive year-end closing run.

■ **Note** Make sure that you execute the year-end closing in a background processing for efficient system performance.

3. Click the Enter ✅ button at the top left of the screen to confirm if your entries were accepted by the system.

4. On the menu bar, choose Program ➤ Execute in Background. The Background Print Parameters screen appears.

5. Enter the printer device in the Output Device field – LP01. The system will automatically default to the Number of Pages as 1.

6. Click the Continue ☑ button at the bottom right of the screen. The Information screen pops up showing the formatting set for your background print parameters.

7. Click the Continue ☑ button at the bottom right of the screen. The Start Time screen appears with various options that you can apply to your background processing.

8. Click the Immediate button at the top left of the screen to schedule background job to start immediately.

9. Click the Save 💾 button at the bottom right of the screen. The system will notify you on the status bar at the bottom of the screen that the "Background job was scheduled for program RAJABS00".

10. To view the job created as a result of the fiscal year change that you have executed, use this menu path: System ➤ Services ➤ Jobs ➤ Job overview or use TC: SM37. The Simple Job Selection screen Appears.

11. Click the ⊕ Execute button at the top left of the screen. The Job Overview screen comes up (Figure 12-19).

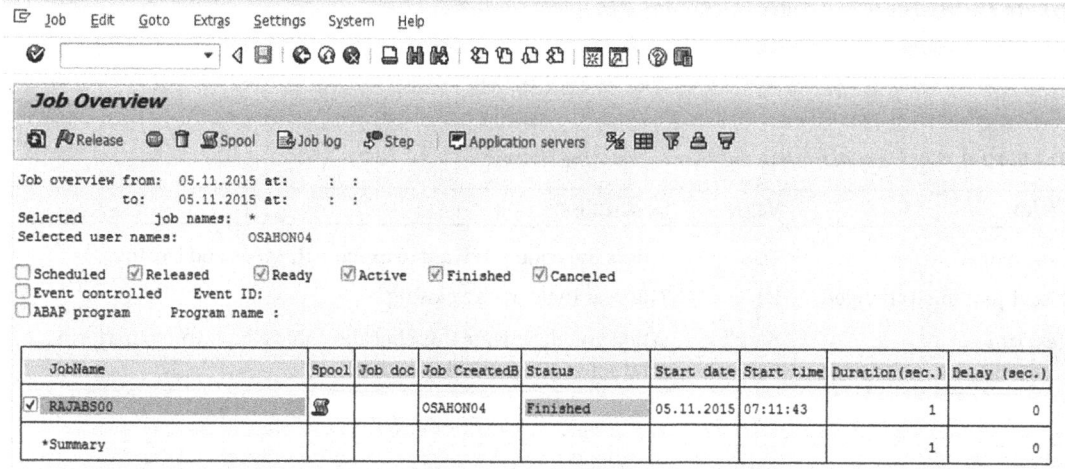

Figure 12-19. The Job Overview screen showing the jobs in background processing

12. Activate the job that you want to send to the spool request from the list of displayed job by making sure that the appropriate JobName checkbox is checked, as shown in Figure 12-19.

13. After you activate the RAJABS00 job, click on the ⬛ Spool button to spool job for printing. The Output Controller: List of Spool Requests screen appears (Figure 12-20).

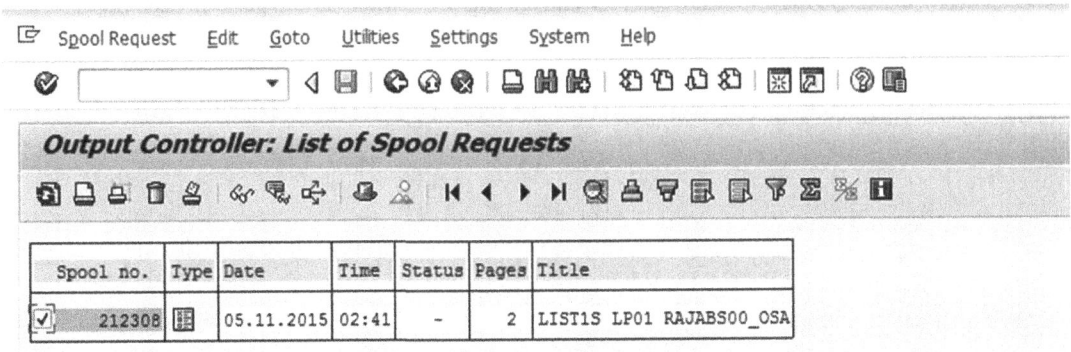

Figure 12-20. *The spool request generated from the year-end closing*

14. Activate the Spool no. and click the Display Contents (F6) 🔍 button.

15. To print, click the Print 🖨 button at the top left of the screen.

▪ **Note**   In the event of any error, the system will display error lists and reason for errors in the year-end closing log stating the assets that do not meet the system requirements for year-end closing.

Do not worry if your year-end closing is not posted complete. Remember that you may not have completed a 12-month period in this exercise. In practice at the end of 12-month period which is a full year, hopefully the system should close your year-end successfully.

Summary

In this chapter we looked at how to perform periodic programs and other special programs needed for year-end closing activities. First, we looked at how to execute a depreciation run for each period and how depreciations are posted to the appropriate G/L accounts in FI. We looked at how to perform depreciation run both in test-run mode and in productive mode respectively. We then looked at how to view the status of the depreciation you performed in Job Overview.

Second, we looked at the importance of a log for post run for posting depreciation and how the log for posting run is carried out. We also briefly talked about APC Values Posting and the checks that you need to carry out before performing APC values posting. We then went on to look at the processes involved in executing APC values posting.

Third, we explained briefly that we explained what asset fiscal year change is and what happens when you carry out fiscal year change. We then took you through the steps involved in executing fiscal year change in both test run mode and productive run. We went on to look at how to execute a fiscal year change in background processing and how to view the fiscal year change that you have executed.

Finally, we discussed the importance of year-end closing. We learned how to perform account reconciliation which is part of year-end closing and how to execute a year-end closing.

Useful General Ledger Accounts

This appendix includes some of the important general ledger accounts and their settings that you may find useful when customizing account determinations.

Table A-1. *Real estate and similar rights*

Fields	Values
Type/Description	
G/L Account	1000
Company Code	7200
Control in chart of accounts	
Account Group	Fixed assets accounts
Balance sheet account	Select
Short Text	Land and similar rights.
G/L ACCT Long Text	Real estate and similar rights.
Control Data	
Account Currency	GBP
Tax category	*(Only input tax allowed)*
Recon. Account for acct type	Assets
Line item display	Select
Sort key	018 (Asset number)
Create/bank/interest	
Field status group	G007

Table A-2. *Accum. Depn – real estate and similar rights*

Fields	Values
Type/Description	
G/L Account	1010
Company Code	7200
Control in chart of accounts	
Account Group	Fixed assets accounts
Balance sheet account	Select
Short Text	ADP – real estate
G/L ACCT Long Text	Accum. Depn – real estate and similar rights
Control Data	
Account Currency	GBP
Tax category	*(Only input tax allowed)*
Recon. Account for acct type	Assets
Line item display	Select
Sort key	018 (Asset number)
Create/bank/interest	
Field status group	G007

Table A-3. *Plant & Machinery*

Fields	Values
Type/Description	
G/L Account	2000
Company Code	7200
Control in chart of accounts	
Account Group	General G/L accounts
Balance sheet account	Select
Short Text	Plant & Mach.
G/L ACCT Long Text	Plant & Machinery
Control Data	
Account Currency	GBP
Tax category	*(Only input tax allowed)*
Recon. Account for acct type	Assets
Create/bank/interest	
Field status group	G007 (Acct accts (w/o accumulated depreciatn)

Table A-4. *Accumulated depreciation-plant*

Fields	Values
Type/Description	
G/L Account	2010
Company Code	7200
Control in chart of accounts	
Account Group	Fixed assets accounts
Balance sheet account	Select
Short Text	ADP-P&M
G/L ACCT Long Text	Accumulated depreciation-plant
Control Data	
Account Currency	GBP
Tax category	Leave blank
Recon. Account for acct type	Assets
Create/bank/interest	
Field status group	G001 General(with text, allocation)

Table A-5. *Machinery and equipment*

Fields	Values
Type/Description	
G/L Account	11000
Company Code	7200
Control in chart of accounts	
Account Group	Fixed assets accounts
Balance sheet account	Select
Short Text	Machinery and equip
G/L ACCT Long Text	Machinery and equipment
Control Data	
Account Currency	GBP
Tax category	*(Only input tax allowed)*
Recon. Account for acct type	Assets
Create/bank/interest	
Field status group	G007 (Acct accts (w/o accumulated depreciatn)

Table A-6. *Accumulated depreciation – machinery and equipment*

Fields	Values
Type/Description	
G/L Account	11010
Company Code	7200
Control in chart of accounts	
Account Group	Fixed assets accounts
Balance sheet account	Select
Short Text	ADP-mach./equipment
G/L ACCT Long Text	Accumulated depreciation-machinery and equipment
Control Data	
Account Currency	GBP
Tax category	Leave blank
Recon. Account for acct type	Assets
Create/bank/interest	
Field status group	G001 General(with text, allocation)

Table A-7. *Low value assets*

Fields	Values
Type/Description	
G/L Account	12000
Company Code	7200
Control in chart of accounts	
Account Group	Fixed assets accounts
Balance sheet account	Select
Short Text	Low value assets
G/L ACCT Long Text	Low value assets
Control Data	
Account Currency	GBP
Tax category	*(Only input tax allowed)*
Recon. Account for acct type	Assets
Create/bank/interest	
Field status group	G007 (Acct accts (w/o accumulated depreciatn)

Table A-8. *Depreciation – Low value assets*

Fields	Values
Type/Description	
G/L Account	12010
Company Code	7200
Control in chart of accounts	
Account Group	Fixed assets accounts
Balance sheet account	Select
Short Text	Depr. LVA
G/L ACCT Long Text	Depreciation-Low value assets
Control Data	
Account Currency	GBP
Tax category	Leave blank
Recon. Account for acct type	Assets
Create/bank/interest	
Field status group	G001 General(with text, allocation)

Table A-9. *Fixtures and fittings*

Fields	Values
Type/Description	
G/L Account	21000
Company Code	7200
Control in chart of accounts	
Account Group	Fixed assets accounts
Balance sheet account	Select
Short Text	Office equipment
G/L ACCT Long Text	Fixture and fittings
Control Data	
Account Currency	GBP
Tax category	*(Only input tax allowed)*
Recon. Account for acct type	Assets
Create/bank/interest	
Field status group	G007 (Acct accts (w/o accumulated depreciatn)

Table A-10. *Accumulated depreciation – fixtures and fittings*

Fields	Values
Type/Description	
G/L Account	21010
Company Code	7200
Control in chart of accounts	
Account Group	Fixed assets accounts
Balance sheet account	Select
Short Text	ADP – fixts/fittgs
G/L ACCT Long Text	Accumulated depreciation – Fixtures and fittings
Control Data	
Account Currency	GBP
Tax category	Leave blank
Recon. Account for acct type	Assets
Create/bank/interest	
Field status group	G001 General(with text, allocation)

Table A-11. *Low value assets (fixtures and fittings)*

Fields	Values
Type/Description	
G/L Account	22000
Company Code	7200
Control in chart of accounts	
Account Group	Fixed assets accounts
Balance sheet account	Select
Short Text	LVA (fixts/fittgs)
G/L ACCT Long Text	Low value assets (fixtures and fittings)
Control Data	
Account Currency	GBP
Tax category	*(Only input tax allowed)*
Recon. Account for acct type	Assets
Create/bank/interest	
Field status group	G007 (Acct accts (w/o accumulated depreciatn)

Table A-12. *Depreciation – LVA office equipment*

Fields	Values
Type/Description	
G/L Account	22010
Company Code	7200
Control in chart of accounts	
Account Group	Fixed assets accounts
Balance sheet account	Select
Short Text	ADP – LVA (fixts/fittgs)
G/L ACCT Long Text	Depreciation – LVA office equipment
Control Data	
Account Currency	GBP
Tax category	Leave blank
Recon. Account for acct type	Assets
Create/bank/interest	
Field status group	G001 General(with text, allocation)

Table A-13. *Asset under construction*

Fields	Values
Type/Description	
G/L Account	32000
Company Code	7200
Control in chart of accounts	
Account Group	Fixed assets accounts
Balance sheet account	Select
Short Text	Assets und.constrctn
G/L ACCT Long Text	Asset under construction
Control Data	
Account Currency	GBP
Tax category	*Only input tax allowed*
Recon. Account for acct type	Assets
Line item display	Select
Sort key	018 (Asset under construction)
Create/bank/interest	
Field status group	G007 Asset accts (w/o accumulated depreciatn)

Table A-14. *Depreciation – assets under construction*

Fields	Values
Type/Description	
G/L Account	32010
Company Code	7200
Control in chart of accounts	
Account Group	Fixed assets accounts
Balance sheet account	Select
Short Text	Depreciation - asset
G/L ACCT Long Text	Depreciation – assets under construction
Control Data	
Account Currency	GBP
Tax category	Leave blank
Recon. Account for acct type	Assets
Create/bank/interest	
Field status group	G001 General(with text, allocation)

Table A-15. *Depreciation – Plant & Mech*

Fields	Values
Type/Description	
G/L Account	34020
Company Code	7200
Control in chart of accounts	
Account Group	Fixed assets accounts
Balance sheet account	Select
Short Text	Depreciation – P&M
G/L ACCT Long Text	Depreciation – Plant & Mech.
Control Data	
Account Currency	GBP
Tax category	Leave blank
Recon. Account for acct type	Assets
Create/bank/interest	
Field status group	G001 General(with text, allocation)

Table A-16. *Capitalized formation expenses*

Fields	Values
Type/Description	
G/L Account	55000
Company Code	7200
Control in chart of accounts	
Account Group	General G/L accounts
Balance sheet account	Select
Short Text	Capitalized formation
G/L ACCT Long Text	Capitalized formation expenses
Control Data	
Account Currency	GBP
Tax category	*(Only input tax allowed)*
Sort key	018 (Asset number)
Create/bank/interest	
Field status group	G007 Asset accts (w/o accumulated depreciatn)

Table A-17. *Trade Payable - domestic*

Fields	Values
Type/Description	
G/L Account	140000
Company Code	7200
Control in chart of accounts	
Account Group	General G/L accounts
Balance sheet account	Select
Short Text	AP-domestic
G/L ACCT Long Text	Trade Payables – domestic
Control Data	
Account Currency	GBP
Tax category	- (Only input tax allowed)
Recon. Account for acct type	Customers
Sort key	001 (Posting date)
Create/bank/interest	
Field status group	G067 (Reconciliation accounts)

Table A-18. *Trade Receivable – domestic one-time*

Fields	Values
Type/Description	
G/L Account	140010
Company Code	7200
Control in chart of accounts	
Account Group	General G/L accounts
Balance sheet account	Select
Short Text	Trade Receivables
G/L ACCT Long Text	Trade receivables – domestic one-time
Control Data	
Account Currency	GBP
Tax category	+ (Only output tax allowed)
Recon. Account for acct type	Customers
Create/bank/interest	
Field status group	G067 (Reconciliation accounts)

Table A-19. *Input tax*

Fields	Values
Type/Description	
G/L Account	154000
Company Code	7200
Control in chart of accounts	
Account Group	General G/L accounts
Balance sheet account	Select
Short Text	Input tax
G/L ACCT Long Text	Input tax
Control Data	
Account Currency	GBP
Tax category	< (Input Tax Account)
Create/bank/interest	
Field status group	G001 General (with text, allocation)

Table A-20. *Output tax*

Fields	Values
Type/Description	
G/L Account	175000
Company Code	7200
Control in chart of accounts	
Account Group	General G/L accounts
Balance sheet account	Select
Short Text	Output tax
G/L ACCT Long Text	Output tax
Control Data	
Account Currency	GBP
Tax category	> (Output Tax Account)
Create/bank/interest	
Field status group	G001 General (with text, allocation)

Table A-21. *Asset acquisition clearing not integrated*

Fields	Values
Type/Description	
G/L Account	199990
Company Code	7200
Control in chart of accounts	
Account Group	General G/L accounts
Balance sheet account	Select
Short Text	Clear asset acquis.
G/L ACCT Long Text	Asset acquisition clearing not integrated
Control Data	
Account Currency	GBP
Tax category	- (Only input tax allowed)
Open item management	Select
Line item display	Select
Sort key	001 (Posting date)
Create/bank/interest	
Field status group	G008 (Assets area clearing accounts)

Table A-22. *Income – price variances*

Fields	Values
Type/Description	
G/L Account	281000
Company Code	7200
Control in chart of accounts	
Account Group	General G/L accounts
P&L statement acct	Select
P&L statmt acct type	X (Unappropriated retained earnings from previous yr)
Short Text	Income – price varia.
G/L ACCT Long Text	Income – price variances
Control Data	
Account Currency	GBP
Tax category	- (Only input tax allowed)
Line item display	Select
Sort key	001 (Posting date)
Create/bank/interest	
Field status group	G014 (MM adjustment accounts)

Table A-23. *Cost-accounting depreciation*

Fields	Values
Type/Description	
G/L Account	481000
Company Code	7200
Control in chart of accounts	
Account Group	General G/L accounts
P&L statement acct	Select
P&L statmt acct type	X (Unappropriated retained earnings from previous yr)
Short Text	Cost-acctg deprec.
G/L ACCT Long Text	Cost-accounting depreciation
Control Data	
Account Currency	GBP
Tax category	- (Only input tax allowed)
Create/bank/interest	
Field status group	G001 General (with text, allocation)

Table A-24. *Loss made on asset retirement w/o revenue*

Fields	Values
Type/Description	
G/L Account	482000
Company Code	7200
Control in chart of accounts	
Account Group	General G/L accounts
P&L statement acct	Select
P&L statmt acct type	X (Unappropriated retained earnings from previous yr)
Short Text	Loss On Asset
G/L ACCT Long Text	Loss made on asset retirement w/o reven.
Control Data	
Account Currency	GBP
Line item display	Select
Sort key	001 (Post date)
Create/bank/interest	
Field status group	G008 (Assets area clearing accounts)

Table A-25. *Proceed from disposal/sale fixed assets*

Fields	Values
Type/Description	
G/L Account	820000
Company Code	7200
Control in chart of accounts	
Account Group	General G/L accounts
P&L statement acct	Select
P&L statmt acct type	X (Unappropriated retained earnings from previous yr)
Short Text	Proceeds from dispos
G/L ACCT Long Text	Proceeds from disposal/sale fixed assets
Control Data	
Account Currency	GBP
Tax category	+ (Only output tax allowed)
Line item display	Select
Sort key	001 (Post date)
Create/bank/interest	
Field status group	G052 (Accounts for fixed asset retirement))

APPENDIX B

Useful Transaction Codes

This appendix includes some of the important transaction codes you can use as a reference in getting to a task within the system. Each screen within SAP system is assigned a unique transaction code which you can use to navigate a system task within SAP quicker instead of following the conventional navigation menu path that uses a tree structure that may be time consuming. You can access a task in the system by entering a transaction code into the command field at the top left of the screen.

Table B-1. *Organizational Structure*

Description	Transaction code
Check Country – Specific Settings	OA08
Copy reference Chart of Depreciation	EC08
Copy/Delete Depreciation Areas	OADB
Assign Chart of Depreciation to Company code	OAOB
Specify Number Assignment Across Company Codes	AO11
Specify Account Determination in Asset Classes	**S_ALR_87009195**
Create Screen Layout Rules in Asset Classes	S_ALR_87009209
Defining the Number Range Interval for Asset Classes	AS08
Defining Asset Classes	OAOA

Table B-2. *Integration of Asset Accounting with General Ledger*

Description	Transaction code
Defining how Depreciation Areas Post to General Ledger in FI	OADX
Assigning G/L Accounts	AO90
Specifying the Posting Key for Asset Posting	OBYD
Defining Field Status Variants	OBC4
Change Field Status for Posting Keys	OB41
Check Assignment of Company Code to Field Status Variant	OBC5
Assigning Company code to Field Status Variant	OBC5
Assigning Input Tax Indicator for Non-Taxable Acquisitions	OBCL
Specifying Financial Statement Version for Asset Reports	OAYN
Define Document Types	OBA7
Specifying the Document type for Posting Depreciation	AO71
Specify Intervals and Posting Rules	OAYR

Table B-3. *Valuation of Fixed Assets*

Description	Transaction code
Set Chart of Depreciation	OAPL
Specify Transfer of APC Values	OABC
Specify Transfer of Depreciation Terms	OABD
Set-Up Areas for Parallel Valuation	OABD_WZ
Determine Depreciation Area in the Asset Class	OAYZ
Deactivate Asset Class for Chart of Depreciation	AM05
Specify LVA asset classes	OAY2
Specify amount for low value assets	OAYK
Specify Rounding of Net Book Value and/ or Depreciation	OAYO
Specify Changeover Amount	OAYJ
Specify Memo Value for Depreciation Areas	OAYI
Specify Asset Classes without Memo Value	OAAW
Shortened Fiscal Years – Define Reduction Rules for Shortened Fiscal Year	OAYP
Shortened Fiscal Years – Maintain Depreciation Key	AFAMA
Specify areas for individual period weighting	OAYL
Weight period in fiscal year version	OA85
Define Depreciation Area for Foreign Currencies	OAYH
Specify Depreciation Areas for group Assets	OAYM
Specify Asset Classes for Group Assets	OAAX

Table B-4. *Depreciation in Asset Accounting*

Description	Transaction code
Determine Depreciation Areas for Ordinary Depreciation	OABN
Assign Accounts for Ordinary Depreciation	AO93
Define Unit-of-Production Depreciation	AO25
Determine Depreciation Areas for Special Depreciation	AOBSS
Calculate Ordinary Depreciation before Special Depreciation	AOBK
Assign Accounts for Special Depreciation	AO94
Determine Depreciation Areas for Unplanned Depreciation	OABU
Assign Accounts for Unplanned Depreciation	AO95
Define Transaction types for Unplanned Depreciation	AO78
Limit Transaction Types to Depreciation Areas	AOXE
Defining Depreciation Key for Calculation Methods using Declining-Balance Methods	AFAMD
Defining Depreciation Key for Calculation Methods using Multi-Level Methods	AFAMS
Defining Depreciation Key for Calculation Methods using Maintain Period Control Methods	AFAMP
Default Values – Propose Values for Depreciation Areas and Company Codes	AFAM_093B
Default Values – Proposed Acquisition Only in Capitalization Year for Company Codes	AFAM_093C
Assignment of Calculation Method to Depreciation Key	AFAMA
Maintain Period Control	AOVS
Define Calendar Assignments	OAVH
Generate Period Control	OA84
Define the Cutoff Value Key	ANHAL
Define Maximum Base Value	OAW2
Develop Enhancement for Determining Base Value	CMOD
Develop Enhancement for Depreciation Method	CMOD
Develop Enhancement for Changeover Method	CMOD

Table B-5. *Special Valuation in Asset Accounting*

Description	Transaction code
Specify Gross or Net Procedure for Reserves for Special Depreciation	AOYQ
Assign Accounts for Reserves for Special Depreciation	AO99
Determine Depreciation Areas for Transferred Reserves (Differed Gain)	OABM
Assign Accounts for Reserves for Transferred Reserves (Differed Gain)	AO96
Define Transaction Types for Transfer Reserves	AO80
Limit Transaction Types to Depreciation Areas	OAXH
Determine Depreciation Areas for Investment Support	OABX
Define Investment Support Measures	ANVEST
Assign Accounts for Investment Support	AO88
Limit transaction type to depreciation areas	OAXI
Check Transaction Types for Investment Support Measure	AO83
Determine Depreciation Areas for Index Replacement values	OABW
Define Index Series for Index Replacement values	OAV5
Enter Index Series in the Asset Classes	OAYZ
Determine depreciation areas for Revaluation for the Balance Sheet	OABW
Define Revaluation Measures for Revaluation for the Balance Sheet	AUFW
Develop Enhancement for Revaluation	CMOD
Define Transaction Types for Revaluation	AO84
Limit Transaction Types to Depreciation Areas for Revaluation	OAXJ

Table B-6. *Master Data in Asset Accounting*

Description	Transaction code
Define Screen Layout for Asset Depreciation Areas	AO21
Define Tab Layout for Asset Master Data	AOLA
Assign Tab Layouts to Asset Classes	AOLK
Create Asset Master Record	AS01
Create the Master Record in fixed asset for Group Assets	AS021
Create Sub-Number for Asset	AS11
Create Sub-Number for Asset	AS24
Change Asset Master Record	AS02
Change Asset Master Record in Group Asset	AS22
Display Asset Master Record	AS03
Display Group Asset Master Record	AS23
Asset Explorer	AW01N
Lock Asset Master Record	AS05
Lock Group Asset Master Record	AS25
Delete Asset Master Record	AS06
Delete Group Asset Master Record	AS26

Table B-7. *Transactions in Asset Accounting*

Description	Transaction code
Define Transaction Types for Acquisitions	AO73
Limit Transaction types to Depreciation Areas for Transaction	OAYA
Define Account Assignment Category for Asset Purchase Orders	OME9
Specify Asset Class for Creating Asset from Purchase Order	OMQX
Assign Accounts to Transaction	AO85
Allow Down Payment Transaction Types in Asset Classes	OAYB
Define Transaction Types for Retirements	AO74
Limit Transaction Types to Depreciation Areas	OAXB
Define Transaction Types for Subsequent Costs/Revenues	AO81
Determine Posting Variants for Gain / Loss Posting	OAYS
Define Transaction Types for Write-Up Due to Gain/Loss	AO82
Determine Asset for Gain/Loss Posting Per Class	OAKB
Determine Asset for Gain/Loss Individually (Substitution)	OA01
Post Net Book Value Instead of Gain/Loss	AO72

(continued)

Table B-7. (*continued*)

Description	Transaction code
Define Transaction Types for Retirement Transfers	AO76
Define Transaction Types for Acquisition Transfers	AO75
Specify Posting Variant for Retirement Transfers	OAY1
Define Transaction Types for the Capitalization of Assets under Construction	OAXG
Allow Transfer Transaction types for Asset Classes for the Capitalization of Assets under Construction	OAYB
Determine Cost Element for Settlement to CO Receiver for the Capitalization of Assets under Construction	AO89
Define/Assign Settlement Profiles for the Capitalization of Assets under Construction	OAAZ
External Acquisition Posting with Vendor	F-90
Acquisitions with Automatic Offsetting Entry	ABZON
Posting Credit Memo in Invoice year	ABGL
Posting Credit Memo in in Next Year	ABGF
In-House Production	ABZE
Capitalize Assets under Construction - Distribute	AIAB
Capitalize Assets under Construction - Settlement	AIBU
Reverse Settlement of AuC	AIST
Asset Transfer within Company Code	ABUMN
Intercompany Asset Transfer	ABT1N
Asset Sale with Customer	F-92
Asset Sale without Customer	ABAON
Asset retirement by Scrapping	ABAVN

Table B-8. *Validation and Substitution in Asset Accounting*

Description	Transaction code
Define Validation for Asset Master Data	OACV
Define substitution for creating assets	OACS
Define substitution for mass changes	OA02

Table B-9. *Information System and Day-to-Day Activities Report*

Description	Transaction code
Define Sort Version for Asset Accounting	OAVI
Define History Sheet Versions	OA79
Define History Sheet Groups	OAV9
Asset Explorer	AW01N
Ordinary Depreciation for Explanation for P&L	S_ALR_87012006
Asset transactions for Day-to-Day Activities Reporting	S_ALR_87012048
Asset Acquisitions for Day-to-Day Activities Reporting	S_ALR_87012050
Asset Retirements for Day-to-Day Activities Reporting	S_ALR_87012052

Table B-10. *Transferring Asset Data in Asset Accounting*

Description	Transaction code
Specify Sequence of Depreciation Areas	OAYE
Specify Last Period Posted in Prv.System (Transf.During FY)	OAYC
Recalculate Depreciation for Previous Years	OAYF
Recalculate Replacement Values	OAYG
Transfer Foreign Currency Areas	OAYD
Define Transaction Types for Transfer of Open Items	AO79

Table B-11. *Preparation for Production Startup in Asset Accounting*

Description	Transaction code
Check Consistency: Overview Report: Asset Classes	ANKA
Check Consistency: Overview Report: Charts of Depreciation	OAK1
Check Consistency: Overview Report: Company Codes	OAK2
Check Consistency Overview Report: Depreciation Area	OAK3
Consistency Report: Asset G/L Accounts	OAK4
Consistency Report: FI-AA Customizing	OAK6
Preparing for Production Startup - Transfer Balances	OASV

Table B-12. *Executing Periodic Program in Asset Accounting*

Description	Transaction code
Execute Depreciation run.	AFAB
Job overview	SM37
Display Log	AFBP
Fiscal Year Change	AJRW
Year End Closing - Account Reconciliation	ABST2
Execute -Year End Closing	AJAB

Index

A

G, H

I, J, K

L

M

Get the eBook for only $5!

Why limit yourself?

Now you can take the weightless companion with you wherever you go and access your content on your PC, phone, tablet, or reader.

Since you've purchased this print book, we're happy to offer you the eBook in all 3 formats for just $5.

Convenient and fully searchable, the PDF version enables you to easily find and copy code—or perform examples by quickly toggling between instructions and applications. The MOBI format is ideal for your Kindle, while the ePUB can be utilized on a variety of mobile devices.

To learn more, go to www.apress.com/companion or contact support@apress.com.